Museums, Libraries and Urban Vitality

ALSO BY ROGER L. KEMP
AND FROM McFARLAND

Strategic Planning for Local Government:
A Handbook for Officials and Citizens (2008)

Cities and Growth: A Policy Handbook (2008)

Museums, Libraries and Urban Vitality: A Handbook (2008)

Homeland Security for the Private Sector: A Handbook (2007)

Cities and Cars: A Handbook of Best Practices (2007)

Homeland Security Handbook for Citizens and Public Officials (2006)

Cities and Nature: A Handbook for Renewal (2006)

Cities and the Arts: A Handbook for Renewal (2004)

Community Renewal through Municipal Investment:
A Handbook for Citizens and Public Officials (2003; paperback 2007)

Model Government Charters: A City, County, Regional, State, and
Federal Handbook (2003; paperback 2007)

Regional Government Innovations:
A Handbook for Citizens and Public Officials (2003; paperback 2007)

How American Governments Work: A Handbook of City, County, Regional,
State, and Federal Operations (2002; paperback 2007)

The Inner City: A Handbook for Renewal (2001; paperback 2007)

Main Street Renewal: A Handbook for Citizens
and Public Officials (2000; paperback 2006)

Local Government Election Practices: A Handbook for Public Officials
and Citizens (1999; paperback 2006)

Forms of Local Government:
A Handbook on City, County and Regional Options
(1999; paperback 2007)

Managing America's Cities:
A Handbook for Local Goverment Productivity
(1998; paperback 2007)

Economic Development in Local Government:
A Handbook for Public Officials and Citizens (1995; paperback 2007)

Privatization: The Provision of Public Services
by the Private Sector (1991; paperback 2007)

Museums, Libraries and Urban Vitality

A Handbook

Edited by ROGER L. KEMP
and MARCIA TROTTA

McFarland & Company, Inc., Publishers
Jefferson, North Carolina, and London

LIBRARY OF CONGRESS CATALOGUING-IN-PUBLICATION DATA

Museums, libraries and urban vitality : a handbook /
edited by Roger L. Kemp and Marcia Trotta.
p.   cm.
Includes bibliographical references and index.

ISBN-13: 978-0-7864-3468-8
softcover : 50# alkaline paper ∞

1. Museums — Social aspects — United States — Handbooks, manuals, etc.
2. Libraries — Social aspects — United States — Handbooks, manuals, etc.
3. Museums — Economic aspects — United States — Handbooks, manuals, etc.
4. Libraries — Economic aspects — United States — Handbooks, manuals, etc.
5. City planning — United States — Case studies.   6. Cities and towns —
United States — Case studies.   7. Community life — United States — Case studies.
8. United States — Social conditions —1980- .   9. United States — Economic
conditions — 2001- .   10. United States — History, Local.
I. Kemp, Roger L.   II. Trotta, Marcia.
AM11.M74   2008   027.073 — dc22   2008016018

British Library cataloguing data are available

Cover photographs ©2008 Shutterstock

Manufactured in the United States of America

*McFarland & Company, Inc., Publishers
Box 611, Jefferson, North Carolina 28640
www.mcfarlandpub.com*

This book is dedicated to
Francesca and *Anika*
the next generation of
library and museum users

Acknowledgments

Grateful acknowledgment is made to the following organizations and publishers for granting permission to reprint the material contained in this volume

American Association of Museums
American Library Association
American Planning Association
Congressional Quarterly Inc.
Illinois State Library
International City/County Management Association
League of California Cities
Real Estate Communications Group
Rice University
Southern Interior Forest Extension & Research Project
State of Florida
The Getty Conservation Institute
The H.W. Wilson Company
Urban Land Institute
Urban Libraries Council
Virginia Commonwealth University
Western Illinois University
World Future Society

Table of Contents

Part III: The Future

Preface

Museums and libraries are important aspects of the cultural fabric of communities throughout America. According to the American Library Association, there are more than 16,500 public libraries in our cities and towns. The American Associations of Museums records more than 17,000 museum sites in municipalities throughout the country. These figures reveal that there are more than 33,500 museums and libraries throughout our nation or, on average, about 520 of these cultural institutions in each state.

For the purpose of this book, a library is defined as a place where books and related sources of information are kept for use by the public, but are not for sale. A museum is an institution that is devoted to the procurement, care, and display of objects of lasting interest in a particular subject area. Although the following list is not definitive, it illustrates the breadth of our country's cultural repository organizations:

City and town museums, libraries, and archival services.
County or state museums, libraries, and archival services.
Business and company museums, libraries, and archives.
Museum and gallery libraries and archives.
Library archives and special collections.
Moving image collections.
Historic house museums and libraries.
Charity and charitable archives.
Digital museums, libraries, and archives.

Special interest museums, libraries, archives, and collections.
University museums, libraries, and archives.
Tribal museums, libraries, and archives.

Both museums and libraries, public as well as private, provide an extraordinary range of services to all segments of our diverse population. In addition to being centers of information, and providing support for both formal and informal learning, these institutions preserve and celebrate our culture, as well as our heritage.

Our research has confirmed our personal observations that museums and libraries are also playing a significant role in many aspects of community economic development. Cultural attractions are at the forefront of those programs designed to stimulate private investment, create jobs, and promote tourism. Both museums and libraries are becoming the anchors in many downtown development and redevelopment projects. The reasons for this, as demonstrated in this volume, are quite clear: libraries and museums hold a significant level of trust, esteem, and user satisfaction among their respective client bases, those citizens that live in those cities and towns where these cultural amenities and attractions are available. Those public officials who lead our community museums and libraries are innovators, and have found ways to collaborate with businesses, educational institutions, as well as government agencies, to provide these worthwhile programs throughout the country.

1

Surveys have proven beyond any doubt that libraries, museums, and other cultural attractions not only improve the quality of life, but also attract a diverse patronage, as well as nurture those citizens who live within those communities having these cultural attractions. Most importantly, museums and libraries serve as people connectors — just what our cities and towns need for their rebirth and revitalization.

The case studies, or best practices, that are presented in this volume will give the reader an overview of these important and significant national trends. The editors hope that municipal policy-makers, as well as the citizens they serve, will see that they have the tools available to begin the rebirth process for their respective communities. Let libraries and museums serve as the gateway, and substantial anchors, of your community's revitalization efforts, as well as its successful economic future.

This reference work assembles, for the first time, material based on a national literature search, and makes this information available to citizens and public officials throughout the United States in a single volume. The goal of this work is to help educate citizens and public officials on how best to use these state-of-the-art practices to improve the quality-of-life in their own cities, towns, and neighborhoods.

This new field has slowly evolved over the past decade in cities throughout the nation. Every effort has been made to include the very best case studies that have been published during this period.

This volume proves that, beyond a doubt, museums and libraries, and other cultural attractions, are now serving as the cornerstone of economic development and redevelopment programs and projects in communities of all size throughout the nation.

Also assembled for the first time are valuable informational resources, which are the various appendices. Evolving definitions and acronyms, as well as important state and national directories, are provided. Special mention must be made of the Regional Resource Directory, which allows the reader to contact public officials in those communities featured in the "best practices" section of this volume. In this regard, additional information may easily be obtained from public officials in cities and towns throughout America about the details of those best practices presented in this volume. Also important is the National Resource Directory, which brings together nationwide professional and research organizations that focus on the subject of this volume — cities and culture. It is hoped that the resources available from these organizations and institutions will be used by citizens and public officials to facilitate the development of cultural attractions in their respective communities, regardless of their size or geographic location.

The editors of this volume were recently informed that the International City/County Management Association (ICMA) has received a grant from the Bill & Melinda Gates foundation to fund a new program titled : *Local Government and Public Library Partnership Initiative.* This new program has an advisory board consisting of city managers and library directors. No doubt the synergy created by this group working together during the coming years will lead to a discussion of the best practices, and how libraries can improve the quality of life and sustainability of cities throughout the nation. This volume represents the first codification of knowledge in this, hopefully. rapidly evolving field.

Lastly, we would like to personally thank representatives from numerous organizations for granting us permission to reprint the chapters contained in this volume. These organizations include professional associations, universities, research organizations, institutes, other nonprofit organizations, as well as commercial publishers. All of these organizations, institutions, and companies, provided valuable materials that contribute to the significance of this volume.

Marcia Trotta
Roger L. Kemp
Spring 2008

Introduction

Marcia Trotta *and* Roger L. Kemp

In cities and towns throughout the country, there is significant evidence that community development and renovation is being centered around libraries and museums. Libraries and museums have been the traditional cultural foundations of communities throughout history. These two organizations appear to be the spark that is revitalizing many older neighborhoods in large urban cities and small rural towns. Libraries and museums create a perception in our minds as being committed to traditions and, simultaneously, are the organizations that demonstrate a forward-looking attitude by their adaptation and utilization of new technologies over the years.

Today's libraries and museums are not only often located at community centers, but also serve as the cornerstone of the center of these municipalities. They have become a much-needed anchor and focal point for our neighborhoods. In a society that is continually challenged to meet the needs of diverse citizens, and as well as provide equity and equality of access, libraries and museums also step up to the plate as the providers of life-long learning. Many individuals and families use the services of libraries and museums, since these services are typically free or provided at a minimal charge to citizens.

Culture in and of itself is a valuable resource. By investing public funds in cultural improvements in a comprehensive manner, the resulting developments benefit the entire community, as well as improve the quality of life. From our research, we have found a growing number of policymakers who are beginning to understand that policies that are friendly to libraries, the arts, and museums — or culture in general — can be instruments in furthering more general public policy goals. Businesses and individuals very often consider their city's or town's overall cultural offerings when making a decision to move to a community, or to relocate from one to another. They recognize that the value of these organizations surpasses the potential tourism that they attract. Cultural organizations are appreciated for their resources. That is, the services of the staff, and of the programs, that are considered an integral part of a community's workforce development program.

If we compare modern day American communities to most European cities and towns we find a striking absence of "public space." In Europe, the medieval marketplace is still the center of economic, civic, and social life. It provides a backdrop where people can talk together, work together, coordinate activities, and prepare for community festivals of all types. In other words, it has the means of bringing together diverse members of the community in a single place. This has been the tradition in Europe, and other countries, for centuries.

Here in the United States, our "town greens" were means to perform a similar function. The "Main Street" where civic buildings, museums, and libraries sprung up lost their original meaning and central function when the movement to the suburbs began. Although there are still some traditional town centers with public space in existence, many have lost their traditional function. Still many other town centers in suburbia have public spaces, but frequently they are decentralized and lack a cultural focus point, one traditionally provided by libraries and museums. Creating public spaces by encouraging libraries and museums parallels urban European city centers that have performed so well over the centuries. These spaces not only benefit the individuals in the cities in which they are located, they clearly benefit the community's cultural, economic, and social well-being.

The research conducted for this volume led to the above insights about the revitalization of America's cities and towns, the need for a town center and, to bring people back downtown, cultural attractions such as museums and libraries.

These chapters in this book reflect the various initiatives and best practices that have evolved so far in our nation in this rapidly evolving and dynamic field. Modern planning, economic development, and redevelopment practices that achieve the goal of restoring and promoting culture in our urban centers and their neighborhoods are featured.

The various case studies represent state-of-the-art examples on how local governments, nonprofit and profit organizations, and public officials are using new planning, development, and redevelopment practices to encourage cultural amenities in urban and suburban areas with the goal of revitalization.

The various case studies contained in the best practices section are typically applied in a piecemeal and incremental fashion in cities and towns. For the most part, citizens, nonprofit organizations, and public officials are preoccupied with projects within their communities. They do not have the time to find out what other neighboring cities and towns are doing in this area, let alone what other communities are doing throughout the nation. For this reason, the various case studies represent an important codification of knowledge.

This reference work assembles, for the first time, materials based on a national literature search, and makes this timely information available to citizens and public officials throughout the United States. The goal of this volume is to help educate citizens, as well as their public officials, on how to use these new planning, economic development, and redevelopment practices to improve their own communities.

For ease of reference, this volume is broken down into four sections. The first section introduces the reader to the rapidly evolving field of cities and culture. The second section and, by design, the longest, includes numerous case studies, or best practices, on how cities and towns are taking measures to create, preserve, restore, and expand their cultural attractions — primarily museums and libraries. The next section focuses on the future of creating cultural attractions to restore our nation's inner cities, its neighborhoods, as well as restore life to our suburbs. Several appendices are also included in the last section to promote a greater understanding of this new field. Based on this background information, and the conceptual schema developed to present this resources collected for this book, the four primary sections of this volume are set forth and explained in greater detail below.

Cities and Culture: Chapters in this section describe the relationship of cities to their centers, what citizens expect in their downtowns. The first chapter focuses on evolving planning practices being used to develop cultural attractions in city centers. The following two chapters examine the critical role of museums and libraries in the revitalization of our cities and towns and how they contribute to the local economy in a positive manner, as well as how they serve to attract other types of development, and hence people to our inner cities and main streets. The last chapter in this section discusses rural areas and community development, and the critical role of libraries in providing the essential information and programs to facilitate this process.

The Best Practices: The boroughs, cities, communities, and towns examined in this volume, including the states/provinces and countries in which they are located, are shown below. A brief description of the best practices being used to promote cities and culture are also set forth in alphabetical order. These case studies represent an important and significant effort to obtain a body of knowledge on the best practices available in the dynamic and evolving field of bringing a sense of place to America's communities, as well as to renew and enhance them for future generations. This codification of knowledge is the essence of this volume.

Cities:
Baltimore
Boston
Brooklyn
Charleston
Christchurch
Cincinnati
Denver
Des Moines
Hartford
Germantown
Indianapolis
Kansas City
Lanark
Little Rock
Los Angeles
Memphis
Minneapolis
Miramar
Pekin
Philadelphia
Phoenix
Portland
Price Rupert
St. Louis
St. Paul
San Jose

Santa Clarita
Seattle
Tacoma
Tallahassee
Toronto
Valencia
Wakefield

States:
Arizona
Arkansas
California
Colorado
Connecticut
Florida
Illinois
Indiana
Iowa
Maryland
Massachusetts
Minnesota
Missouri
New York
Ohio
Oregon
Pennsylvania
South Carolina

Tennessee
Texas
Washington

Provinces:
British Columbia

Ontario

Countries:
Canada
New Zealand
United States

Selected Best Practices:

Attracting people through cultural amenities
Branch libraries and economic development
Citizen input stimulates cultural awareness
Creating a sense of place with cultural improvements
Cultural amenities and economic transformation
Demographics, museums, and libraries
Economic development for cultural amenities
Economic development incentives using culture attractions
Education and cultural attractions
City center renewal and culture
Creating public spaces and places
Green branch library exhibits smart growth practices
Joint cultural facilities (city and university library)
Libraries educate public on smart growth practices
Literacy and economic development
Main street renewal and public cultural facilities
Mixed-use development with cultural anchors
Neighborhood revitalization using libraries and museums
New economic development models focusing on culture
Planning practices stressing cultural improvements
Promotion and advertising using cultural attractions
Public capital expenses on cultural projects stimulates private investment
Public spaces and cultural amenities
Redevelopment focusing on museums and libraries

Restoration and preservation of cultural facil-
   ities
Revitalization with cultural developments
Rural revitalization using libraries
Selling culture and the arts
Value of cultural attractions
Urban cores and cultural amenities
Using culture to promote the arts

The Future: The third, and final section, of this volume examines national trends on emerging economic development and planning practices that focus on how to create public places and main streets using cultural amenities as the focal point. The first chapter in this section focuses on urban design and the public realm and how cultural attractions such as museums and libraries play an important part in inner-city and neighborhood renewal programs. The next chapter examines contemporary urban planning practices focusing on cultural amenities, which should be around for decades. These new urban design concepts rely on cultural attractions such as museums and libraries. The next chapter discusses how to build creative communities and the importance of cultural organizations in this process. Another chapter sets forth how to place a value on our cultural attractions and amenities, a new field of discipline in the public sector. The final chapter reviews the likely future that cultural amenities, such as museums and li-

braries, will remain the focal point of both urban and rural development and redevelopment strategies and plans in our cities and neighborhoods during the coming years.

Appendices. Appendices include a list of acronyms and definitions for libraries and museums, a cultural policy timeline for our nation, a bibliography for this new field, and two comprehensive reference directories. The first is a regional resource directory for those readers who wish to follow up on any of the best practices mentioned in this volume. All of the municipal governments included in the best practices section of this volume have been included in this directory. The second is a national resource directory that describes all of the major professional associations and research organizations serving local governments in those professional fields related to cities and culture. A listing of cultural organizations in the fields of libraries, museums, and the arts, is also included for reference purposes. Much of this information has been assembled for the first time in the relatively new, and rapidly evolving, field of cities and culture.

The use of cultural facilities and amenities to revitalize our urban centers and their neighborhoods is here to stay. As more citizens and public officials focus on the cultural renewal of America's cities this field should increase in importance during the coming years.

CHAPTER 1

New City Centers and Culture

Christopher Duerksen *and* C. Gregory Dale

The traditional city center is where the action is. We show it off to visitors. It sets one community apart from another and makes each one special. Some people work in the center, many others live nearby, and nearly everyone goes there for government services, shops, musical concerts, or summer festivals.

The old, small city downtown is what often comes to mind when the concept of a city center is brought up: drug, sporting goods, and dry goods stores, and the best restaurants in town. City hall, the courthouse, post office, and city park were often nearby, with picnic tables and a bandshell. Downtown was the place to go; it defined the community and was the place to be for civic celebrations.

Many suburban communities have no old downtown. Or, to paraphrase Gertrude Stein, there is no "there" there. To critics, increasingly suburban communities look bland and homogenous. Little distinguishes one place from another. They criticize suburban development as continuous and repetitive — a series of isolated land uses separated by parking lots, roads, and landscaped buffers.

More importantly, an increasing number of citizens are voicing these same concerns in local community planning meetings. Citizens express concern over a "lack of a sense of place," lack of "community character," and

the need for creating a "community focal point." Their voices are heard at the grassroots level in suburbs across the country.

Many suburban communities have responded by trying to create new city centers, hoping to inject a liveliness and sense of place into their communities. Industry publications such as *Urban Land, Shopping Centers, Stores,* as well as planning publications, document the growing desire for a new kind of public life — one that is walkable, compact, full of diversity and vitality, one that contains shopping, civic life, and leisure. There is a need for a location that provides an experience of uniqueness, a sense of place, connected not by parking lots, but by people.

What is a "city center" in today's suburban context? Based on the diverse nature of new city centers being developed around the country, this is a difficult question to answer. Some new city centers are dense and urban in character, while others emphasize a park-like setting. What they all share, however, is an underlying motivation to create a community focal point that emphasizes human scale.

Our study began as part of a planning effort for the City of Lenexa, Kansas. Six city center initiatives were initially evaluated based on a case study survey of people involved in those projects. We focus here on a series of is-

Originally published as "Creating City Centers," *The Commissioner*, Summer 1999, by the American Planning Association, Chicago, IL. Reprinted with permission of the publisher.

sues related to variables affecting the success of city centers.

As a general theme, we urge communities who are considering city centers to analyze carefully the economics of local real estate development. While there are many exciting physical design issues involved in creating a "sense of place," ultimately the success of a new city center rests heavily on solid economic foundations. Consider these issues early in the planning process.

Achieving the Right Mix of Uses and Density

A judicious mix of uses and density is one of the most critical components. Single land uses alone cannot support a city center. A center that caters strictly to daytime office uses, for example, will not generate the required number of people for retail uses to survive. A combination of uses and activities are needed to attract sufficient numbers and varieties of people. A diverse mix of uses and people makes the space active, exciting, and commercially viable.

Commercial Uses. Like the traditional marketplace, commercial uses are usually a critical part of the city center's success; they anchor the center. Retail uses can complement daytime office uses well.

Civic and Institutional Uses. Traditionally, the marketplace may have been a gathering place; today civic and cultural institutions add identity and focus and as well the critical mass needed for success. Libraries and museums add to the center and help create the community's sense of itself. Government offices promote stability and daytime traffic.

In addition, planners should include public spaces such as plazas, squares, and parks. Impromptu and holiday celebrations reinforce a sense of community identity and every community should have the space to hold them.

Residential Uses. Every city center we studied has a strong residential component, either within the center or located nearby. Therefore, consider providing different types of housing for different market segments either in the city center or within walking distance. On-site or adjacent condominiums, townhouses, or second- and third-story flats, combine to provide the high densities needed for successful pedestrian-oriented city centers. Critical mass is needed to make the commercial sites viable for investors. Abundant and varied housing is one way to achieve the necessary critical mass.

Financing

Communities have used a variety of financing mechanisms and have exhibited great creativity in developing the financing. Often public and private mechanisms are involved. Generally, most development costs were assumed by the developer. Public funds, when used, finance the infrastructure, streets, street furniture, landscaping, lighting, and sometimes land acquisition.

Financing mechanisms for city center development or redevelopment vary widely. Some centers are built entirely with private funds. Other communities utilized tax increment financing, constructed publicly owned facilities such as parking structures, created business improvement districts, levied special taxes, and awarded tax credits, grants, or even funding. The latter was provided through the federal Intermodal Surface Transportation Efficiency Act program.

Planning and Management

Involving local citizens in the planning process helps ensure awareness of, and support for the city center. The results? A better project. Public meetings, focus groups, neighborhood meetings, and other methods have been incorporated into the planning process.

Many of the city centers were initially conceived of in broader-based, comprehensive planning efforts that the community was undertaking.

As indicated above, understanding the market is essential. A solid market analysis helps the community and the developer position the city center so it will be viable in the local and regional market. A market study must be conducted for both regional and local markets. We live in the age of specialty marketing, so it is important to understand the area's demographics and the market that is currently being served. A benefit of this assessment is that you can identify what might be missing in the market and define an appropriate niche for your community's city center.

The local jurisdiction must also have a strong working relationship with the developers. Because city centers are a unique land use, their development requires a high degree of communication regarding issues such as access, street standards, or design standards. Both the local government and the developers need to work cooperatively on details such as siting, infrastructure, signage, parking, etc.

A city center also requires top quality management once the project is in place. Commonly, the site is managed by an association of business owners, but might also be a public/private cooperative venture.

Creating a "Sense of Place"

A successful city center can be the focus of commerce, local government, or cultural activity — or all three. It must be more than just a mix of unconnected uses. It should be a place to gather. One way to create a lively city center is to tie our important civic institutions — the community library, courthouse, etc. — to modern commercial activities. Successful city centers have pulled these elements back together, combining government, civic, and non-government activities. To help create a sense of place through the city center, consider the following:

- Identify the community's distinguishing features, its history, and its values.
- Create gateways to the city center that symbolize the character and quality of the community.
- Celebrate civic involvement and public accomplishments.
- Choose a conspicuous site that can serve the whole community. This is particularly true when community buildings will be located in the city center.
- Include artistic elements that can be changed or that will provide interest, for example, interactive sculpture or fountains.
- Schedule special events, celebrations, ceremonies, and activities in the city center.
- Encourage people to care about the place. Let them become involved in its creation or care.
- Try to balance aesthetics with function.
- Encourage outdoor vendors and entertainers.
- Be aware of sensory impressions. Memorable places provide memorable experiences.

Access, Traffic and Parking

High density land use can lessen the need for automobile transportation if most goods and services are located conveniently for public transportation and pedestrians. Although promoting pedestrian use and scale is an important goal, there will continue to be a need for roadways, traffic management and parking requirements.

A lesson we learned from the communities we studied is that there are a number of ways for dealing with access, traffic, and parking. These include:

- Plan the city center as a multi-use destination served by multimodal transportation.

- Consider the transportation system(s) as interdependent elements that serve the city center, the surrounding community, and the region.
- Design with the convenience and pleasure of the visitor in mind.
- Provide easy to understand directional signs; access to the city center should be uncomplicated.
- Use uneven paving surfaces, such as brick, to slow down traffic.
- Narrow the street at pedestrian crossings.
- Permit on-street parking. Keep parking lots to the rear of buildings as much as possible, even if it means the merchant must have a rear entrance.
- Break up large parking lots into small individual landscaped lots scattered throughout the city center.
- Use the street level of a parking garage for retail shops and services.
- Add facades to parking structures that will make them architecturally compatible with surrounding structures.
- Provide landscape buffers between streets and parking lots; use abundant landscaping within parking lots.

Designing Spaces for People

Whether the community's objective is to foster civic pride, create a "sense of place," or promote economic development, people are the critical factor. This obvious observation is often overlooked in the rush for monumental and cutting-edge design in the building of a new city center. An abundant supply of pedestrians is critical for commercial success. Cater to the pedestrian through:

- Providing narrower streets.
- Providing ample sidewalks.
- Using weather sheltering devices — awnings or covered walkways.
- Developing of a pedestrian scale and keeping building heights to a modest level.
- Designing simple, logical, understandable circulation systems for pedestrians and motorists.
- Eliminating "dead spaces." Pedestrians should experience a continuous street wall of shops and services. Empty lots, blank facades, etc., can be a detriment to pedestrian traffic.
- Creating wider sidewalks near traffic intersections which are easier for pedestrians to cross and will also slow down traffic.
- Limiting the size of blocks to 200 to 300 feet, whenever possible.
- Requiring connections to the surrounding neighborhood.
- Providing consistent, easy to read, identifiable directional signs. Including signs that indicate routes to special events and important places.
- Encouraging use by different groups and subgroups of people, and discouraging one group's domination.
- Providing food services, such as takeout food and outdoor cafes; including outdoor tables.
- Providing appropriate furnishings for the intended activities.

In addition, in successful city center designs, plazas, parks, and pedestrian and bike trails link the center to the rest of the community. These areas also serve as places for festivals and celebrations.

Transit

Planners and urban designers often advocate mass transit as a cornerstone for city center success. However, this is not always borne out by the communities studied. Nonetheless, the relationship between land use and transportation is important. Dense land uses are efficient and are the underpinning of successful public transportation — particularly rail. Transit stops at a city center increase the potential customer/user base for the transit line. Transit riders provide additional pedestrian traffic and therefore provide a larger market base. At the very least, communities should preserve public transit opportunities for future development.

Conclusion

City centers are likely to continue to emerge as an alternative to conventional suburban development. They offer the opportunity to create a focal point for the community that is often lacking in growing suburban areas. The long range viability of the city center concept rests on the ability of communities and developers to work together to create a center that meets the physical design needs of the community and addresses the economic realities faced by the private sector.

CHAPTER 2

Planning for Cultural Attractions

Nancy Moses

Twenty years ago, urban economic development was aimed at preserving and attracting manufacturing industries. Today, the tables have turned. Local governments are finding that commerce and tourism drive their local economies. And in this new economic climate, arts and culture are making an important difference. Cultural attractions — art museums, historic sites, cultural districts, theaters, performing arts centers, galleries, cinemas, and zoos — always have been important quality-of-life amenities. Today, these have become much more. In the hands of farsighted local government managers, cultural organizations can become cultural assets useful in spurring downtown development, attracting new residents and businesses, and transforming a community into a thriving tourist destination.

Cultural Attractions Can Drive Urban Growth

In Europe, arts and culture have been central to urban revitalization for decades. Now, in the United States, smaller cities and towns are beginning to use their cultural assets to drive a range of growth strategies. Arts and culture are playing a pivotal role in neighborhood revitalization, as artists transform derelict neighborhoods into vibrant cultural districts. Performing arts centers are serving as anchors for downtown commercial and residential development. These new attractions are luring suburban residents in for evenings of fun and entertainment.

In one of the most exciting developments of the past decade, localities are finding that their cultural assets can help expand the population of their downtowns. Two analyses of the 2000 U.S. Census, one by the University of Pennsylvania's department of city and regional planning and one produced jointly by the Brookings Institution and the Fannie Mae Foundation, have documented dramatic increases in the numbers of downtown residents.

From census to census, San Diego's downtown population grew by 16 percent; Norfolk, Virginia, saw a rise of 21 percent; and the number of Pittsburgh's downtown residents increased by 67 percent. "Downtown growth is from young professionals and older 'empty nesters' who want to be near entertainment, restaurants, and cultural amenities," reports an article in the May 7 edition of *USA Today*. And this trend is not simply a turn-of-the-millennium phenomenon. As the nation's

Originally published as "Have a Plan and Make the Most of Arts and Culture," *Public Management*, Vol. 83, No. 11, December 2001, by the International City/County Management Association, Washington, D.C. Reprinted with permission of the publisher.

79 million baby boomers reach retirement age, experts predict that more will be trading in their suburban homes for downtown condos near restaurants and theaters.

And localities are finding that cultural attractions spur new business development. Urban planners have long recognized that corporations base their decisions on where to relocate on local quality-of-life, including the availability of cultural resources. Now, they realize that the arts play an important role in fostering emerging businesses.

"In the 1990s, cities were actively recruiting dot-com companies, but the crash of this industry ended this trend," says Barry Seymour, assistant director of the Delaware Valley Regional Planning Commission. "The newest urban development strategy is to attract the smart entrepreneurs and let them figure out the next growth industry. This means that local governments now are looking to develop the quality-of-life amenities and cultural attractions that appeal to these young people."

Finally, many communities are using their cultural industries to tap into the growing market of cultural tourists, those with the largest disposable incomes. Cultural tourists not only buy tickets to blockbuster art exhibits and performance festivals, but also eat in local restaurants, shop in local stores, and book rooms in local hotels, inns, and bed-and-breakfast establishments.

Building Cultural Organizations into Economic Assets

Localities large and small can use four basic strategies to build local cultural organizations into cultural assets. First, they can create new homes for local organizations. Doylestown, Pennsylvania, for example, transformed an abandoned prison into the Mitchner Museum, which is now a centerpiece of its cultural district. Chula Vista, California, is exploring transforming an old theater into a visual and performing arts center.

Second, cities can found new cultural entities. Cleveland built the new Rock & Roll Hall of Fame and Museum and used it to anchor a residential development.

Third, communities can invite major institutions to set up satellite operations in their locales. Camden, New Jersey, is looking into establishing a branch of the Philadelphia Zoo. This approach takes its cue from health care and higher education, sectors that have long realized the benefit of building cities and campuses close to where their customers live.

And finally, communities can hold signature events that promote their identity and give visitors a reason to go there. The nation's calendar is filled with thousands of events: the Annual Indian Fair and Market in Phoenix, Arizona; the Brazo River Festival in Waco, Texas; Elvis Week in Memphis, Tennessee; and the Bavarian Maifest in Leavenworth, Washington.

Basic Economics of the Cultural Industry

Whether they expand existing cultural organizations, build new ones, bring in branches of big-city attractions, or create signature festivals, communities seeking to make the most of their arts and cultural resources must first understand the basic economics of the cultural industry. The most important fact is that art and cultural organizations are extremely market-sensitive, with ticket sales accounting for about 50 percent of their operating revenues. When arts organizations expand, the new programs and staff they add dramatically increase their costs, thus raising the bar on the dollars they must earn.

Many cultural organizations are adept at raising dollars to build a new home, but few possess the expertise needed to plan for their expanded operations. Arts managers tend to underestimate their new operating costs and overestimate their projected attendance revenues. When the audiences fail to reach the numbers predicted, organizations may find themselves facing shocking operating deficits. A National Cultural Facilities Study by the Nonprofit Finance Fund "found countless cases where improperly planned, financed, and managed facilities harmed the program, as well as a few examples of the inverse."

Most important from government's point of view, cultural managers and their boards often miss the chance to maximize the benefits that their new facility can bring to the local economy. While arts organizations realize how an exciting new facility can enhance their activities, many fail to recognize that these capital investments can also help to transform the communities outside their doors.

Places that want to maximize the economic benefits of cultural development need to partner with their cultural industries. Local government managers and their economic planners know the processes and pitfalls of facilities financing and construction. They see the bigger picture of urban revitalization, and they are adept at capitalizing on opportunities. When governments take the lead in cultural development planning, new museums, theaters, and festivals can become important additions to their economic development toolkits.

Key Issues in Cultural Development Planning

A cultural development plan uses a community's cultural assets — its history, architecture, museums, performing arts, and more — to spur economic growth and tourism development. Plans are best devised and carried out as part of an overall urban revitalization program. They should explore these issues: the unique identity of the community; its cultural assets; its regional and tourist markets; the prime location(s) for new cultural facilities; strategic alliances that could be made with national entities; buy-in needed from key interest groups; optimal scale and sequencing of the cultural plan; and costs and revenue sources.

Vision and Identity

Every community has a unique identity, a story rooted in its past and its place on the national scene. Cultural development plans begin by diagnosing a community's identity, then use this identity to create a sense of place and a position in the marketplace.

A community's identity is best used to shape its long-term vision and the developmental path needed to achieve it. It becomes the benchmark against which all new initiatives are measured. The identity of a community also becomes its "brand," the centerpiece of the marketing strategy it uses to draw new residents, businesses, and visitors.

Cultural Assets

Development plans feature inventories of communities' cultural assets: their strengths, needs, and opportunities. This kind of inventory analyzes the capstone experiences that make the community an appealing place to live and visit. It targets organizations with the greatest potential for growth, while identifying the mix of new elements and experiences needed to underscore the community's identity and to enliven the experience.

Inventories of cultural assets view a city or county from a visitor's perspective. Coordinated signage and streetscaping are especially important for tourists and others familiar with the lay of the land. Standardization of the operating hours of historic homes and museums makes them easier to promote as a package.

Markets

Communities and their cultural organizations serve a number of markets: local residents, regional residents, and, in some cases, national and international visitors. Analyzing these markets' demographic and psychographic characteristics is key to cultural development planning.

Market data are available from a variety of sources: downtown and business associations, local and regional planning agencies, convention and visitor bureaus, and cultural alliances. Individual cultural attractions also collect information on their audiences and memberships.

Market analyses are essential in guiding strategic cultural investments. Communities located in regions with high populations of school-age children, for example, might gain the most from new family attractions like zoos and children's museums. As people age, their interest in history increases, so communities with aging populations might consider investments in history museums and historic sites. Young singles seek spectacles and diversity; they are drawn to places with a rich mix of cutting-edge art, music, cinema, and opera. As city and county populations become more ethnically diverse, the offerings of their arts organizations should reflect this diversity.

Cultural markets are as segmented as the markets for other optional consumer purchases. Analyzing a community's current market and prospective market is essential in shaping the menu of cultural assets needed to attract and serve them.

Location

Museums and performing arts centers are as site-sensitive as department stores: the right location can anchor a retail district, while the wrong site can kill the project. An elegant historic building might at first appear to be a perfect place for a new museum, but if the location is wrong, the new museum can rapidly "morph into" a white elephant.

The best sites for cultural attractions are accessible by public transit and by car and are near shopping, restaurants, and parking facilities. The right location can drive a remarkable transformation of a downtown. Baltimore's National Aquarium, for instance, was placed in its Inner Harbor, where it helped to attract other museums, as well as restaurants and hotels.

Strategic Alliances

A community's background and its cultural assets offer opportunities for links with other locales and facilities that can help advance its potential. High-profile national organizations like the Smithsonian Institution are developing affiliate museums across the nation. Heritage trails link rural towns, parks, and historic sites and turn the whole into a visitor-friendly experience. The National Trust for Historic Preservation's Main Street Program works to foster streetscape improvements and to revitalize downtowns. In fact, strategic alliances with other destinations in the region, state, and nation can propel a local cultural attraction into a national draw.

Buy-in

In order to succeed, government, business, and civic leadership must embrace cultural development plans. So, cultural planners should reach out to a broad range of interests: cultural boards and cultural alliances; arts, humanities, and historical commissions; tourism and economic development entities; and downtown and business associations. Political leaders and government officials should be brought on board, as well as the print and electronic media.

The optimal development plan advances the agendas of diverse organizations and encourages each to bring its resources to the table. The objective is to assure early buy-in, so that all leadership interests share a sense of ownership. Most important, the plan ought to become the responsibility of local government — the entity with the clout, connections, and commitment to assure its realization. Placing cultural development in the hands of the local government's economic development agency assures the greatest prospect for long-term success.

Scale and Sequencing

The scale and sequencing of a plan must be carefully designed to reflect the realities of the local arts and cultural industry. The best plans are based on a clear understanding of the time and investment needed to achieve results. For example, new arts festivals can take three to five years to build an audience. Good plans include multiyear schedules that support overall revitalization programs.

Expense and Income

Finally, plans should include estimates of associated costs for their own launching, implementing, and monitoring. Effective plans set feasible financial goals. They identity resources from a diverse pool of funders and supporters; philanthropic organizations; local, county, state, and national government; civic organizations; volunteer groups; preservation and historical societies; cultural and educational organizations; and private businesses.

When a cultural development plan becomes part of an overall development agenda, it becomes possible to tap into urban revitalization funding streams. Economic development agencies can creatively combine the sources they tap for downtown revitalization with the sources that cultural organizations can use to build and operate. Today, farsighted managers have an opportunity to make the most of their local governments' arts and cultural resources. Comprehensive plans can bring localities new facilities to anchor their commercial districts, new offerings to keep their downtowns lively day and night, and new attractions to strengthen their positions in the marketplace of destinations. As more people seek to live in downtowns and to visit them, the timing is right for local governments to take their cue from the arts and get the show up and running.

CHAPTER 3

The Role of Museums

Kathleen Sylvester

Is Art Necessary?

A lot of politicians think not. Not when governments face huge deficits. Not when social programs are being slashed. In hard times, in many places, art begins to look like a frill. Its budget tends to be small; its constituency is perceived as narrow. It is an obvious target for budget cutters.

And it is being cut. State support for the arts is down 22 percent from last year. The reductions have ranged from less than 1 percent in some places to 70 percent in New York State. The governors of Michigan and Virginia initially proposed abolishing their state arts agencies altogether. "Even though the funding for a state arts council is usually less than one one-thousandth of the state budget," says Kimber Craine of the National Assembly of State Arts Agencies, state officials will cut the program in the interest of "meeting the deficit."

That is the stated reason. Most often, there are unstated ones as well: Complaints about elitism. Images of ugly sculpture — incomprehensible to the average taxpayer but commissioned at public expense. Pornography. It has been four years since the National Endowment for the Arts got into trouble for its funding of the works of Robert Map-

plethorpe and Andres Serrano, but those controversies continue to echo through all levels of government. "The pornography issue is not [directly] part of the discussion about arts funding in Michigan," says Richard Dunlap of that state's art council, "but it's always part of the background."

The truth is, politicians who want to crusade against subsidized art have a wide variety of ammunition to use against it. They can cite not only the suspicions of taxpayers but a phalanx of conservative scholars who have been making the same arguments in more erudite fashion. "Government support of art," Harvard government professor Edward C. Banfield wrote a few years ago, "involves a transfer of income in the wrong direction.... Museum-goers and concert-goers are mostly relatively prosperous as compared with the average taxpayer. Why should the 'poor' subsidize the 'non-poor'?"

For those who run arts programs, none of this has been easy to take. But after a couple of years of battering, arts supporters have begun to regroup. They are developing a simple strategy: Combat the notion of art as a frill. Sell the arts a different way — as a tool for economic development, and as a tool for ameliorating social problems. And they are having some success.

Originally published as "How to Sell the Arts," *Governing*, Vol. 5, No. 7, April 1992, by Congressional Quarterly Inc., Washington, D.C. Reprinted with permission of the publisher.

Public funding of the arts is not a revered American tradition. At the federal level, it began only in 1965, with the creation of the National Endowment for the Arts. When the NEA was established, it has a built-in mechanism to funnel 25 percent of its funding to the states, so state arts councils were created to receive those funds. Within a few years, public funding of the arts had gained acceptance, and local arts councils began to proliferate. There are now more than 3,800 such local organizations, and one-third of them receive public funding.

In recent years, local public funding of the arts has eclipsed both state and federal arts spending. This fiscal year, the federal government will spend about $176 million on the arts, and states will spend about $215 million. Local governments are expected to spend about $500 million. In fact, while state funding is declining sharply and federal spending remains flat, local public support for the arts has grown by more than 5 percent from fiscal 1991—a respectable increase in a recession.

Why? Robert Lynch of the National Assembly of Local Arts Agencies says there is one overarching reason: "People are more attached to art in their own backyard." At the local level, decision-makers find it hard to cut funding for the symphony or the museum down the street. They respond to evidence that arts programs attract spending and create jobs. And when the arts expand beyond the boundaries of art galleries and museums and symphony halls, they respond to the notion that the arts are a positive social force in their communities.

Joseph Riley, the longtime mayor of Charleston, South Carolina, has used those arguments to build his arts program into a popular and politically impregnable institution. The centerpiece of that program is Piccolo Spoleto, the city-run companion to the world famous Spoleto Festival U.S.A., held in Charleston every year. "People would rather cut garbage collection service," Riley says,

"than to say we're not going to have the Piccolo Spoleto festival."

What Riley and his administration have done is develop Piccolo Spoleto as a sort of populist companion to the better known festival. While Spoleto patrons in black tie attend ticket-only events in the city's elegant symphony halls and theaters, as many as 120,000 people wander through the city enjoying Piccolo Spoleto events in 50 or 60 "nontraditional" sites. There are performances in parking lots and garages, in storefronts and churches. They range from the folk music of South Carolina's Low Country to the Great Piccolo Spoleto Kite Flying Contest. Most of the events are free.

The two festivals, according to Riley, have a $50 million-a-year economic impact on the Charleston area. "You can always argue for the arts on an economic development basis," he says. "The statistics are there, and it's an easy case to make." But he is equally adept at using the second approach: arts programs as builders of community. "I remind people what the symphony does for the school system; what it does with its free concerts," Riley says. Charleston has never reduced its funding for the arts in all the years since the programs got underway.

Reaching out to the community is not new for arts programs. "It's a movement," says Riley, "that started about 20 years ago in the large cities and has been happening ever since." But in the current climate of recession and tight budgets, it is no longer just a clever innovation. It is, for many arts programs, a recipe for survival.

Across the country from Charleston, in San Diego, a similar strategy is working. Arts advocates are selling their program as a way to enhance the city's public reputation and improve life in its high-crime neighborhoods at the same time.

Victoria Hamilton, director of the San Diego Commission on Arts and Culture, makes the case that the town known best for the Navy, the Zoo, and Sea World stands to gain by developing a new image as an "arts destination." In one of the first joint ventures with another city department, Hamilton's commission will spend the next three years working with the San Diego convention and visitors' bureau to try to make that happen.

At the same time, the commission is trying to become an agent for social change. Working as part of the city's steering committee for neighborhood pride and protection, the arts community is putting on programs with the parks and recreation department and the city libraries. An African dance and drumming troupe gives performances and lessons in local recreation centers. A replica of a Hmong village was built in the courtyard of the Laguna Vista library; its completion was celebrated by the local Asian community with authentic food and music.

Atlanta and surrounding Fulton County, Georgia, provide still another example of the change in approach. There, arts advocates are quick to concede that, over the years, some charges of elitism have been true.

"We have not been very responsive to citizens," says Harriet Sanford, director of the Fulton County Arts Council. "We have been funding what the arts community says it needs, not what the citizens say they need." Some museum programs were driven by the interests of their curators; some symphony offerings were dictated solely by the tastes of artistic directors. Often, Sanford says, "we built our institutions from the inside out and forgot to invite people in."

But now, Fulton County's arts programs are looking for ways to join in the social welfare functions of government. What about the problems of senior citizens? asks Sanford. "Is there a role for the arts there? What about human services?" The answer in both cases has been yes.

Because senior citizens in public housing are relatively immobile, the commission has started going to them — offering classes in the housing projects or taking them on cultural outings. And neighborhood recreation centers, which were once viewed narrowly as sports facilities, now are being used to present dance and visual arts programs in the community.

Art or drama lessons might seem an unlikely strategy for keeping a teenage girl from dropping out of school or becoming pregnant, but Sanford insists it makes sense: "If a young woman has to show up every day at a certain time, wearing certain clothes, she has learned discipline. And if she is able to complete a project that she chose for herself, she has gained self-esteem."

And while developing the arts as a social program, the commission is trying to do one other thing: build a stronger political constituency by changing its reputation among other public employees. "They don't know who we are and what we do," says Sanford, and when it comes to budget time, people who are worried about the future of their own jobs resent money spent on the arts. In Fulton County this year, pains have been taken to explain the economic development of art and culture to county workers. In case the arguments alone don't sway them, discount tickets are made available.

One way or another, it seems to be helping. The county arts budget is down slightly this year, from $3.4 million in 1990 to $3.1 million in 1992, but it has maintained itself remarkably well. In fact, Fulton County spends more than 30 times as much on the arts as it did just a dozen years ago.

While arts advocates work to build their political support, they also are searching for new mechanisms of funding. There are a remarkable number of creative ones out there, especially at the local level. Aspen, Colorado, pays for art with a portion of its estate transfer tax; Miami and Houston designate part of their hotel/motel taxes. Denver earmarks a portion of its sales tax. There also are an estimated 187 "one percent for the arts" programs which require that a percentage of the construction cost of any public building be designated for art in or near that building. This kind of funding provides some insulation from the uncertainties of the budgeting process.

State arts programs are now beginning to look for the same sort of insulation. In Montana, for instance, arts council director David Nelson calls his state's $6.2 million cultural trust fund "a gem." It's there, Nelson says, "during the tough times when you need it the most."

The trust was established in the late 1970s, when Montana was flush with coal revenues. Aware that this money would dwindle as coal reserves diminished, state officials decided to put some of it in a cultural trust. Its first use was the restoration of the murals in the state capitol building; the rest was designated for "other cultural activities."

Now, when the Montana legislature meets every other year, its long-range planning committee spends two weeks considering the recommendations of an arts review panel; the legislature then appropriates money from the trust for projects it approves. "For two weeks," says Nelson, "our programs get wonderful exposure." While there is always some resistance to the idea of using state funds for the arts — the legislators who tell Nelson, "I don't ask anyone to pay for my fun"— the program is gaining political support.

And it is leveraging money in communities across the state. One of the first things Nelson did was to create challenge grants, giving communities an opportunity to build their own endowments by raising a combination of private and local government funds to match state funding. With a 3–1 matching requirement, the state money has leveraged $2 million with grants to 20 organizations over the years. That may not seem to be a lot of money, but Nelson suggests it may be the future of arts funding. "The arts world," he says, "is just learning the value of stability and slow growth."

Other states, including Connecticut, Nebraska and North Dakota, now have similar trusts. Alabama, Rhode Island and Oregon use income-tax checkoffs. Maryland is considering a tax checkoff plan, while Missouri is debating a tax on cable television. In Iowa and Arizona, a portion of state lottery funds go to the arts, while Tennessee uses money earned from the sale of vanity license plates. In most cases, these revenues are nowhere near sufficient to fund an entire arts budget. Tennessee's vanity plate revenues, for instance, bring in only about $175,000 a year. But that money provides a minimum amount of funding arts agencies can count on in good years and bad.

Whatever stability creative financing may offer, however, the fact remains that when an arts program is under fire, grassroots political support matters most. That has proven true lately in state after state.

Until this year, for example, the budget of the Ohio Arts Council had grown steadily for a decade. But in the middle of a major budget crisis, Governor George V. Voinovich proposed cutting it in half. "A lot of people felt that we had increased our growth too quickly," says director Wayne Lawson, "and there was also an expectation that we could make up the funding loss with corporate and foundation support."

But that help didn't materialize. Corporations and foundations in Ohio directed their philanthropic attention to helping out threatened social programs. Arts funding appeared to be in serious trouble — until letters started pouring in to the legislature. The Ohio Arts Council funds programs in every county in the state, and although the legislature had rarely heard praise for them, it heard plenty of complaints when the programs were in jeopardy.

It changed the popular perception that state arts funding went only to large cultural institutions in big cities. In the end, a 10 percent cut was agreed upon; it was expanded to 16 percent when all state agencies took an additional 6 percent cut. "The way things turned out, we were not singled out," says Lawson.

In Michigan, Governor John Engler took office in 1991 vowing to abolish the state's arts program altogether. All state funding of the arts was frozen, and many small arts projects simply went out of business. "It was a wrenching time," recalls Richard Dunlap of the Michigan Council for Arts and Cultural Affairs. But the governor's decision sparked a measurable response from businesses — from the people who make money from the restaurants and parking lots adjacent to the theaters and art galleries.

A summit meeting that included the governor, the arts activists and the business community resulted in a compromise. Arts funding has been cut from $13 million to $5 million, and the arts commission has been moved into the state's commerce department. The new council also will assume responsibility for distributing Michigan's equity funding — money to reimburse urban areas for amenities they provide to non-residents. The state will provide much less ongoing support for arts, concentrating instead on limited projects or capital expenditures. It will be required to try to bring in more private support, increase its matching requirements and try to foster more collaborations.

It does not exactly represent a triumph for the arts community in Michigan, but compared to the extinction that appeared to lie ahead, it strikes advocates as a relief. "We have a new life," says Dunlap, "and a new mission." He hopes the new council can make the case that state arts funding is seed money for new art and new commerce. "It is research and development money," he says, "just like the R&D money in the business world."

In Massachusetts, it was exactly that kind of argument that gave arts programs a reprieve from the governor. Four years ago, the Massachusetts Cultural Council had a generous budget of $27 million. Its fortunes fell as the state's economy was crushed, and by this year its budget had been whittled to $3.6 million.

Director Rose Austin says the council had been ineffective in making its case. But this year, the council went to Governor William Weld with a detailed analysis of how its program help the schools and how they boost tourism, the state's second-largest industry. The analysis was framed in terms of "return on investment," with evidence that the $27 million arts budget in 1988, for example, had an impact of $1.2 billion on the state economy.

Austin says the council went through an elaborate soul-searching process, and even revised its mission statement. A rather vague statement that called for "stimulating appreciation of the arts" was revised to one that calls for "contributing to the economic vitality of our communities." Weld was convinced, and is supporting an arts budget request for $6.1 million. Now the council must make its case to the legislature.

CHAPTER 4

The Role of Libraries

Urban Libraries Council

Local economies today are in rapid transition, moving from bases of manufacturing and service industries to information and idea industries. Accompanying this transformation are a number of radical changes in preferred work skills, business and service models, local-to-global networks, and definitions of what make places "attractive." Given these changes, communities are reassessing their assets and development strategies in light of what is needed to succeed in the new and next economies.

Strategies for building a strong economic base are being realigned. Human resource strategies are coming to the fore, as jobs created in the new economy require highly educated and technologically-skilled workers. Strategies to keep a vibrant base of small business, traditionally a major source of local job creation, intact and competitive in a very mobile and global entrepreneurial environment are also emerging. Increasingly, physical development strategies are moving away from enticing outside firms with tax abatements and other incentives, to building on local strengths, mixing-up residential, commercial and cultural activities to create vibrant, high quality-of-life cities.

Public libraries are logical partners for local economic development initiatives that focus on people and quality of life. Libraries are widely available, highly regarded public institutions that provide a broad range of information services and support for diverse constituencies. In this era of economic transformation, the business of public libraries is being recast. Public access to digital information and technology is a draw for libraries. Their open structure, combined with the power of new digital collections, technology, and training, position them to help communities make the transition from manufacturing and service economies to high tech and information economies.

Public libraries build a community's capacity for economic activity and resiliency. Many families and caregivers rely on the library to provide important preschool reading and learning. Many people entering the workforce rely on libraries to get them online. Local businesses are increasingly tapping into the library's online databases to keep themselves competitive and to find synergistic new business opportunities. Library facilities often anchor downtown and commercial developments, and are attractive neighborhood amenities.

These are the essential findings uncov-

Originally published as "Executive Summary" in *Making Cities Stronger: Public Library Contributions to Local Economic Development*, January 2007, by the Urban Institute, Washington, D.C. Reprinted with permission of the publisher.

ered by researchers from the Urban Institute, as they teamed up with the Urban Libraries Council, an association of large metropolitan public libraries, to investigate the impact of public libraries on local economic conditions. *Making Cities Stronger: Public Library Contributions to Local Economic Development* adds to a growing body of research that notes a shift in the role of public libraries — from passive, recreational reading and research institutions to active economic development agents. The study was commissioned by the Urban Libraries Council (ULC) and funded by the Bill & Melinda Gates Foundation and Geraldine R. Dodge Foundation.

This report highlights the specific ways local governments, agencies, and libraries are working together to achieve benefits for individuals, agencies, and the community at large in four areas:

Early literacy services are contributing to long-term economic success. As the strong correlation between investments in early literacy and long-term economic success is documented, public libraries are expanding beyond their traditional story time services, engaging in high-impact strategies with community partners. Many libraries across the country are leading public awareness campaigns, reaching new mothers with materials and resources that promote reading early and often. Extensive community-wide training on early literacy with home and professional child care givers is increasing the quality of child care, and levels of school readiness and success. From Providence (RI) to San Luis Obispo (CA), public libraries are reaching young children and families in diverse neighborhoods. These services are the first link in a chain of investments needed to build the educated workforce that ensures local competitiveness in the knowledge economy.

Library employment and career resources are preparing workers with new technologies. With an array of public computers, Internet access, and media products, public libraries are a first point of entry for many new technology users. A 2006 survey by Hart Research found that 70 percent of people on the computers in libraries only have access through that source. Now that job readiness, search and application information are all online, libraries are expanding training opportunities, often in collaboration with local workforce agencies, which focus on using and building technology skills. Ninety-two percent (92%) of public libraries surveyed for this report provide computer instruction on a monthly basis. Library workforce service models are also as mobile as the shifting economy, as illustrated in Memphis (TN), where the JobLINC mobile center that started as an initiative for a single high-need neighborhood has now expanded services to cover the entire county, with high levels of use not only by job-seekers but by employers as well. With an increasing number of local training partnerships, library resources and facilities are reducing the operation costs and broadening the outreach of other local workforce development agencies, contributing to a stronger community network for job readiness and worker "retooling."

Small business resources and programs are lowering barriers to market entry. One of the biggest traditional barriers to small business has been access to current and comprehensive business product, supplier, and financing data. Libraries are the source for new online business databases that reach entrepreneurs around the clock. Researchers find that when libraries work with local and state agencies to provide business development data, workshops and research, market entry costs to prospective small businesses are reduced, existing businesses are strengthened, and new enterprises are created. Libraries are also in the vanguard, trying new strategies. The Columbus Public Library (OH) is working with a regional agency to provide business plan development seminars. In Brooklyn, the library hosts a business plan competition with a seed money prize. In Phoenix (AZ), the public library is part of a statewide network of business, economic development and library professionals who are seeking to expand and diversify the economic base by promoting more synergy among clusters of enterprises. Again, in this arena library resources and training facilities are reducing operations costs for other local agencies, and broadening those agencies' access to more people needing small business assistance. Overall, the community has more resources to support a strong small business sector.

Public library buildings are catalysts for physical development. Libraries are frequented local destinations. Urban Institute researchers repeatedly found that public libraries are highly regarded, and seen as contributing to stability, safety and quality of life in neighborhoods. They are bolstering downtown and suburban cultural and commercial activity. Among private sector developers of malls, commercial corridors, mixed-use developments and joint-use facilities, libraries are gaining recognition for other qualities — their ability to attract tremendous foot traffic, provide long-term tenancy, and complement neighboring retail and cultural destinations. Library buildings are versatile. They fit in a wide mix of public and private sector developments.

The study provides not only a snapshot of ways public libraries are successfully integrating resources and services with local economic development initiatives in cities coast-to-coast, it also provides some thought-starter ideas for broadening those strategies further, urging greater investment in data gathering, focused partnerships, and impact measures.

The study concludes that public libraries are positioned to fuel not only new, but next economies because of their roles in building technology skills, entrepreneurial activity, and vibrant, livable places. The combination of stronger role sin economic development strategies and their prevalence — 16,000 branches in more than 9,000 systems — make public libraries stable and powerful tools for cities seeking to build strong and resilient economies.

Note: To purchase copies of the research publication *Making Cities Stronger*, please contact the Urban Libraries Council at (312) 676-0999 or via e-mail at info@urbanlibraries.org.

CHAPTER 5

Rural Areas and Community Development

Bernard Vavrek

As America once had to adjust to the change from an agricultural to an industrial infrastructure, it is now confronted with a new challenge — dealing with a society predicated on information access and use. The singularly important question for us is, how does the library fit in, if at all? What difference does it make to the future of rural America, where daily information needs exist and must be met?

Kenneth Wilkinson[1] believes that the manifestations of technology have the potential to either rescue geographically remote areas from economic and social problems or add the proverbial final straw that will break the backs of communities struggling to exist. His major concern is that there is a crisis of *community*. Rural towns may cease being communities, with the capacity for development and growth, and become places — faceless nodes on a network.

The State of Rural Libraries

To discuss public librarianship in the United States it is necessary to keep in mind the fact that the majority of public libraries are located in small and rural areas. According to the National Center for Education Statistics' *Public Libraries in the United States: 1991*, 80 percent (7,210) of public libraries are located in population centers of fewer than 25,000 people. Of this 80 percent, three out of ten libraries (2,695) provide services in places of fewer than 2,500 individuals. The average library in these smallest areas is staffed by one full-time person, houses a collection of fewer than 10,000 books and serial volumes, and has a total operating budget of $18,892. In areas with populations up to 25,000, the average public library has three full-time staff persons, the book and serial volume collection size is 23,423, and the total operating budget is $110,000.

Planning Considerations

Library decision makers contemplating the roles of technology and interoperability at the community level may wish to consider the following comments.

Conservative Environment

Rural and small towns are traditionally conservative. They can be unfriendly to out-

Originally published as "Rural Libraries and Community Development," *Wilson Library Bulletin*, Vol. 69, No. 1, January 1995, by The H.W. Wilson Company, Bronx, NY. Reprinted with permission of the author.

siders and to new ideas. "We never did it that way before" is not the response of all community leaders in rural and small towns, but it is important to recognize that this attitude may exist. Unfortunately, the conservative approach may also be shared by the library personnel and trustees/board members, who see no reason to change the routines of life in their favorite place. Sometimes this flexibility exists because of lack of experience and education, an issue discussed below. Planning for the implementation of technology will continue to be a challenge in places where people have really not thought much about the library and its community role.

Professional Training

The most important factor limiting the present and future development of rural and small town information services is the lack of academically trained staff. Only about 21 percent of the full-time librarians in areas of fewer than 25,000 people have master's degree or equivalent, and in communities of fewer than 2,500 people, only 4 percent.

The reasons for this include: local satisfaction with the level of service, unwillingness to pay professional salaries, the relatively few schools of library and information science serving a geographically dispersed population, the inability of individuals to leave their positions to participate in structured training, and the attitude of some staff persons who don't recognize that they have a need to pursue formal education. Some of these problems are being assuaged by enterprising institutions that are aggressively offering long-distance educational opportunities to students either in person or via satellite/cable.

There is also a crucial need for continuing education. In addition to the schools of library and information science, library cooperatives and systems, regional libraries, and state library agencies have been attempting to provide consumers with what they want and need. Unfortunately, there are many library staff and trustees in need of CE, particularly pertaining to technology, that aren't being reached. And frequently there is little that is systematic about what is offered. Teleconferencing, for example, is an important and cost-effective way of providing new information; however, when the program fades, the questions start ("now where does that printer driver get installed?"). There may not be anyone available to provide the hand-holding that is needed.

Trustee Involvement

Trustee development is key to planning of any type, not just for technology. State library agencies deserve considerable credit for their efforts in attempting to provide workshops and other training modules for trustees. States such as Nebraska have gone further than most in establishing certification requirements for trustees to remain active. At the same time, anecdotal information from trustees and librarians around the country suggests that quite often the "us versus them" mentality prevails. If libraries in rural communities are to prosper, it cannot be done by rolling over trustees, who after all not only hire and fire the librarian but are responsible for the overall financial condition of the library. The trustees cannot proceed without the librarian, either. Clearly, the form of community development that is needed to insure that the library plans for the future, uses its resources wisely in consort with other community agencies, and becomes a true community information center begins with a mutual working trust between library staff and trustees/directors.

Surveys

Planners must be aware that the typical rural public library has probably never conducted any form of community or user survey. In the absence of statistical data describing the library's use and the attitude of clients toward available services, planning is done in an ad hoc manner, at best. As a substitute for survey data, library personnel will use interpersonal methods of information gathering, believing that they are familiar with everyone in the community who uses the library. This approach ignores new people who have moved into the service area and certainly does not include those individuals who are not card-carrying members of the library.

Marketing and Public Relations

The typical rural library is perceived by its public as primarily a place of books. Despite the wide variety of resources available even in the smallest library, user studies suggest that requests for best-sellers and leisure reading materials outstrip the demand for informational services such as reference.

Usually, small libraries do not have the funds to support their own public relations efforts. As a consequence, American Library Association–generated propaganda abounds, emphasizing books and reading.

In research I undertook, half of the nonusers studied indicated that the only library service they were familiar with was the provision of books, magazines, and newspapers.[2] This is also related to the intriguing response of both users and nonusers that the library was not one of the methods used for meeting daily information needs. Perhaps it is not surprising that user studies[3,4] also indicate that half of the American public does not use the public library because of a perceived lack of time and need.

Gender Balance

I would like to offer a final, particularly significant item for community information planners to consider as they ponder the future. Seventy percent of the users of nonmetropolitan public libraries are women. While the percentage has not been as dramatic, female users have outnumbered male users in studies of public libraries in general. The interesting

thing, however, is that in most instances analysts have spent little time considering why this is so and what it means.

A few years ago I heard an intriguing explanation for this from the young daughter of one of our research associates. She thought that it was easy to understand why the public library appears to be a place for women. "Usually, the librarian is a woman; the story hour is run by a woman; there are mostly romance books in the library; and when the library has a fundraiser, the prize is usually a quilt or something else that might appeal to women — as opposed to a fishing rod, for example." Although this interpretation may not withstand the rigors of a research investigation, at the emotional level it is telling. My friend Carole Hole would agree with at least one point, that female librarians have feminized the public library by choosing materials in their own image and to their own liking.

Starting with a Blank Screen

Public librarianship, created from the dynamic pressure of the need to reach mass markets in the nineteenth century, no longer has a role in the cyberspace of the information highway.

What exists now is not only the semantic problem of an institution looking for a new name, but the more fundamental problem of competing for a societal role that no longer exists. The Internet is the new librarianship. Essentially, what confronts all of us is starting over. Key to this new existence is the recognition that markets for information must meet needs that are increasingly individualized and must deliver products efficiently and at a competitive price.

There is no clear evidence that the library community is interested in and/or willing to change, reinvent, rethink, what it is currently doing. I have frequently suggested to graduate library science students that it is necessary to take a giant eraser and undo our history and begin with a new blank sheet of paper (or the electronic equivalent). While this would be difficult to accomplish, an intellectual rebooting is just what is needed. No effective differences will be created unless there is first a perception that change is really needed.

Valuable time and resources are being invested in the hope that some form of national library movement will orchestrate leadership that has not y et occurred. Libraries, at the present time, do not occupy the attention of the American psyche as we think they should. In this regard, for example, the American Library Association has become a relatively powerless organization as an agent of change. To offset the lack of a national thrust, responsiveness and creativity must continue to be generated at the consortial, regional, system, and local levels.

Because of the lack of a national library movement, efforts aimed at generating national roles — particularly for public libraries — are at best a symbolic exercise.[5] This is not to suggest that there aren't similarities of services or that nothing is to be gained by studying national norms. But our attention must be directed to the development of the local community. Crucial to the future of small town America and its information services is the articulation of specific roles that are determined at the local level. Roles (objectives) that are specific and measurable and involve regular feedback from a broad spectrum of consumers must function as the basis for present and future services.

Community-Enhancing Technology

Librarians and those responsible for library governance and support cannot win the game of information technology (IT) if IT is pursued as an end in itself. The competition from institutions with deeper financial pockets is a reminder of our limitations.

I recently spoke to a friend who is the director of a large public library and asked, where is all of the investment and planning for technology taking us? He answered, "What is the alternative?" Technology may indeed be inevitable, but it is not neutral; it is demanding and creates an insatiable desire for more. The straight line of IT as it is ever stretched enables information transfer to occur but erases for the consumer the tangibility of the library as an entity — something of which one may be a part. The community information center will not occupy the critical epicenter of the town's support if data services appear to come from a hole in the sky.

There are enormous opportunities, but cautionary signs should be placed along the information highways of rural and small towns, reminding those who are involved that the dynamics of technology, which have the opportunity to reduce the cost of operating in rural space, must be organized to sustain community development. Otherwise, communities will continue to falter and give way to "galactic cities," as my colleague Peirce Lewis refers to them — households spread throughout the countryside. While IT may reach these galactic citizens, they exist without a sense of community or belonging.

The realities and myths of rural America provide us with complicated challenges. If small and rural towns are to prosper, it will be due to the ongoing cooperation of leaders who have enabled community development and growth to take place. "As communities grow, so do needs for new and expanded services.... Our response to meet these many demands is for municipalities to work together. Cooperation is in the future of local government...."[6]

Clearly, this interoperability must proceed with consensus building as its aim. Those responsible for information services must be active agents in this process. Who knows, perhaps for the first time through these collective efforts, the vast majority of people will understand what information services are available and how they benefit themselves and the community of which they are a part.

The human and physical capacity to change rural America's information infrastructure is unevenly distributed. Great strides are being made in some areas, but some are still hamstrung by problems as basic as a poor local telephone infrastructure. These differences will be more than just a casual test of rural America's mettle.

We are confronted with the survival of rural America as a community-based society in a global economy. The occasion demands that individual and collective action be taken to help orchestrate the integration of community resources — human and informational — into a new dynamic continuum of developmental services. They must be targeted to specific needs and constantly monitored for their effectiveness. In this endeavor there are few models and limited experience, but the opportunity is clear and there is no alternative.

Notes

1. Kenneth Wilkinson, "Social Forces Shaping the Future of rural America" (paper presented at the meeting of the Information Futures Institute, Clarion, Pennsylvania, 1992).

2. Bernard Vavrek, *Assessing the Role of the Rural Public Library* (Clarion, PA: Department of Library Science, Center for the Study of Rural Librarianship, Clarion University of Pennsylvania, 1993).

3. Leigh Estabrook, *National Opinion Poll on Library Issues* (Champaign-Urbana, IL: Graduate School of Library and Information Science, Library Research Center, University of Illinois, 1991).

4. Vavrek, *Assessing the Role of the Rural Public Library.*

5. George D'Elia and Eleanor Jo Rodger, "Public Opinion about the Roles of the Public Library in the Community: The Results of a Recent Gallup Poll," *Public Libraries* 33, no. 1 (January/February 1994): 23–28.

6. Thomas Kurtz, *Intergovernmental Cooperation Handbook* (Harrisburg, PA: Pennsylvania Department of Community Affairs, 1992), 5.

CHAPTER 6

Baltimore Uses Museums to Create Public Space

Guillermo Lopez

Before the 1980 grand opening of Harborplace at the Inner Harbor — the downtown seaport project that reinvented the city's waterfront as a landmark retail, dining, and entertainment hub — Baltimore was a gritty, working-class, port city with an eclectic blend of disconnected ethnic neighborhoods. Its small-town feel and forthright industrial character had earned it the nickname "Charm City," a wry and affectionate sobriquet that was as much a testament to the geniality of its residents as an oblique reference to the city's provincial scale.

However charming it may have been, Baltimore was definitely not an economic powerhouse or a vital urban center. Tourists were not flocking to the Mid-Atlantic city, the housing market was not booming, and crime was on the rise. The increasingly empty downtown heart of the city — suffering population losses as the result of a postwar shift of residents to surrounding counties — fueled the growing perception that Baltimore was an urban dead end.

Harborplace, almost single-handedly, changed all that. Shortly after Harborplace opened, the revitalized Inner Harbor added to its list of attractions the new National Aquar-ium and a renovated and expanded Maryland Science Center. In the 1990s, Oriole Park at Camden Yards and a new Baltimore Ravens football stadium opened just blocks from the harborfront. Today, the vibrant, thriving waterfront is packed with shops, restaurants, museums, and attractions, with tourists and residents mingling amid street performers, vendors, and tour guides. The resurgent Inner Harbor and its attendant economic boom have inspired substantial peripheral development, with hotels, businesses, and residences springing up downtown and connecting to adjacent neighborhoods — a feverish pace of development that is still accelerating today in places like the nearby Harbor East mixed-use waterfront neighborhood.

What are the cultural, economic, and architectural forces that make Baltimore's Inner Harbor such a powerful economic engine? How do they work? And how does design help create the kinds of public spaces that generate development and inspire economic revival in an underperforming economy? Can design alone make the kind of difference that affects a city and a region?

An optimum public space is vibrant, comfortable, and accessible. It provides natu-

Originally published as "Public Design Space," *Urban Land*, Vol. 65, No. 3, March 2006, by the Urban Land Institute, Washington, D.C. Reprinted with permission of the publisher.

ral landmarks and intuitive pathways and connectors to frame its activity in ways that invite discovery and exploration. Well-designed public spaces combine intimate nooks with spacious gathering areas; they both stimulate social interaction and allow for private moments and personal reflection.

The fundamental tenet of community design — that public spaces are for people — may seem obvious, but it is too often overlooked. Well-executed public spaces attract people, make them comfortable, and give them a reason to stay and return.

Design can contribute to the creation of public spaces in a variety of ways. Lincoln Road in Miami's South Beach offers an example of how design decisions can change the complexion of a space. For decades a draw for film stars and holiday visitors looking for a nightclub, a movie, or a shopping experience, Lincoln Road succumbed to familiar pressures. By the 1950s, changing demographics, as well as self-contained luxury hotels and resorts that sealed themselves off from the street, had turned the road — once referred to as the "Fifth Avenue of the South" — into a dilapidated shell of its former self.

When Miami Beach architect Morris Lapidus closed seven blocks of the ten-block street to vehicle traffic in 1960, however, the transformation of Lincoln Road began. Though it was not until the 1980s that the area would truly flourish, it was Lapidus's design — a pedestrian promenade lined with retail and entertainment venues — that reflected a true South Beach ethos and set the stage for the radical changes to come. Today, Lincoln Road is considered a Miami landmark once again. Cafés, boutiques, and art galleries line the street, and pedestrians walk amid fountains, sculptures, and bustling sidewalks as they shop and people-watch.

Lincoln Road offers an instructive and stark reminder that the great designs of today generally are echoes of the past. To create compelling public spaces, people need look no further than their own history, where the pub-

lic square and main street have served as hubs of social activity and community interaction, allowing residents and visitors to run errands, chat with friends, or grab a bite to eat and a cup of coffee. Such places naturally become hubs of economic activity — centers of attention where performers, merchants, politicians, shoppers, and diners congregate to engage in day-to-day life.

Figure 1
What Constitutes a
Successful Public Space?

The Project for Public Spaces, a New York City–based nonprofit organization dedicated to development and maintenance of public spaces, lists four essential elements critical to their success:

- activities and uses;
- comfort and image;
- access and linkage; and
- sociability.

The current global development trend favoring town centers and more integrated outdoor mixed-use projects is an acknowledgment of the important role these spaces play in collective community narratives and of their efficacy in sparking commerce and trade. The architectural design of these spaces should reflect the character and spirit of the local community and display an organic connection to the surrounding physical and cultural environment. The key to designing spaces that can seamlessly incorporate a wide range of commercial, dining, and entertainment elements is to recognize and adhere to certain fundamental design strategies — to apply universal rules appropriate for projects big and small and all over the globe.

Simplicity and clarity are two design elements critical for any public space. Because people do not like to be confused or uncertain, landmarks and waypoints need to be established to break up the space. Some urban projects use individual city blocks to break down a larger space into manageable and discrete components, while still maintaining the long sight lines that unify and define the space. Breaking a development into linked sections gives visitors a chance to approach the project at their own pace and not feel overwhelmed, and to experience a sense of revelation and exploration.

Green space should be used wherever possible. A small park or a row of trees not only softens the architectural landscape, but also provides natural gathering places and anchor points. The village green, a concept as old as villages themselves, evokes that ingrained sense of community that adds to the comforting perception of permanence and livability.

People like to walk, move, and circulate through a space. Street grids, wayfinding materials, and structural elements should be used to create broad frameworks that encourage movement and interaction. Clearly defined starting and ending points, be they traditional anchors or strategically positioned elements like a fountain or plaza, can provide needed structure and spatial context. A seemingly endless expanse of storefronts or entertainment options can actually be too much of a good thing, creating what can feel to the visitor like a daunting challenge and discouraging casual visits.

Elements should be mixed together. While it behooves architects and developers to be sensible in determining their merchandise mix and architectural style — for example, few would think a Dollar Store should be adjacent to a Tiffany's or that a thatched roof belongs on a contemporary frame — there is an inherent energy and excitement in the juxtaposition of differing styles and the availability of a wide range of products, services, and entertainment options.

Ultimately, great design in public areas is about understanding the goals and limitations — as well as the possibilities — inherent in the creation of engaging, occupied spaces. Use of art for art's sake is a noble pursuit, but a counterproductive one when designing public space that must not only accommodate a wide variety of uses, but also encourage them.

Public spaces are to be lived in; they cannot, and must not, become museum pieces.

That is not to say that they must be boring or utilitarian. Many of the world's greatest public spaces, from the piazzas of Italy and Las Ramblas in Barcelona to Grand Central Station and Times Square in New York City, are better known for their colorful spirit, artistic energy, and cultural relevance than for their economic power. The animation, color, scale, lighting, cohesion, and physical and natural landscape of a place should work to transform shopping from running an errand to having an experience. As the Walt Disney Company can attest, people will pay more — much more — for an experience.

The financial benefits of successful spaces can be profound, affecting the surrounding infrastructure and boosting a region's economic outlook in a variety of ways. In general, the mechanisms that translate spaces into dollar signs fall into three broad categories:

Direct. A new development can provide initial and clearly measurable benefits. These include revenue generated through the sale of goods and services, higher wages due to an increase in local hiring, and additional monies contributed by new visitors — especially tourists, who can boost local cash flow substantially.

Secondary. A landmark public project can function like a pebble dropped into a pond, sending ripples of complementary development in all directions. Adjacent developments and needed support structures might include additional residential, restaurant, and hospitality options, as well as the presence of vendors and service providers newly positioned to capitalize on the influx of a customer base and income.

Intangible. The intangible benefits of well-designed public spaces, in some ways providing the most important and dramatic influence, are easily underestimated and often underappreciated. The sense of civic pride, community identification, and improved public perception can be a profound force. This phenomenon can be seen at work in places like Baltimore and, more recently, Detroit, where dramatic downtown projects are encouraging a return to city living.

High-quality design can overcome a host of seemingly insurmountable obstacles. Even in some of the most downtrodden and economically disadvantaged parts of the world, a well-designed public space can be commercially viable and provide a major boost to struggling local and regional economies.

Plaza San Marino, a shopping and entertainment development that opened in 2003 in Guayaquil, Ecuador, illustrates this mechanism in action. The city's new commercial and social hub, San Marino includes upscale fashion franchises, home furnishings outlets, a bookstore/café, and a Tower Records store, as well as restaurants and upscale entertainment venues that include a state-of-the-art 12-screen Cineplex with stadium seating. The enclosed galleria surrounded by the outdoor elements of an open leisure center blends tenets of modern town- and lifestyle-center architecture with the handcrafted detail and stylistic influences of distinctive South American design.

Many of the materials used to build the center were locally crafted: artisans hand carved much of the center's concrete, and iron for the detailed handrails was cast on site. Details throughout the space represent reproductions of existing architectural elements in the city, such as cast-iron lamps, kiosks, wrought-iron railings, hand-painted mosaic tiles, and accurate reproductions of traditional marble and stone details. An iconic 110-foot bell and clock tower is the center's landmark feature, giving San Marino a distinctive and instantly recognizable public face. Towers and cupolas, clay roof tiles, and plaster-finished stucco walls lend regional flavor, and intricate Gustav Eiffel–inspired ironwork and bold lighting elements provide distinctive structural highlights.

Partly because it provides a feeling of permanence and belonging to the age-old community of Guayaquil, the center draws heavily from its local population of nearly 2 million residents. From roof tile details to the rough-iron railings and fences, San Marino is 100 percent Guayaquil. Even the roof metal structures and skyline call to mind the old town areas of the city, reflecting the history and tradition of the city's architecture.

San Marino provides far-reaching economic benefits to the surrounding Guayaquil community, increasing the revenue stream through tourist and visitor dollars. The project has fostered a sense of civic pride, local and regional identity, and national and international recognition; affirmed local history and culture; and promoted a sense of connection and identification with global development and the modern economy.

In a country where 70 percent of the population lives below the poverty level and the per-capita gross domestic product is $3,200, San Marino posts close to $300 in sales per square foot and is visited by about 800,000 people a month. Places like San Marino demonstrate how design, by creating spaces that promote connection, comfort, and community, can boost a community economically and transcend boundaries.

In Baltimore, the Inner Harbor is viewed as a national landmark — an enduring and instantly recognizable icon that defines both the city's skyline and its storyline. Not only does it capture the spirit of the city, but also it symbolizes the transformation that has led to a booming — and ongoing — economic expansion.

The city is breaking new boundaries — from Best Buy's first-ever downtown location, to new parks, museums, and explosive residential growth adjacent to the Inner Harbor. More than $1 billion of new development is currently planned for Baltimore, and over 11 million tourists and others visit the city annually, contributing nearly $3 billion to the local economy.

The future is bright for public spaces. As

more and more cities, towns, and developers begin to appreciate the impact that well-designed public spaces can have on their communities — and their wallets — the more this encouraging trend will become a self-propagating phenomenon. At the same time, as cities and developers move away from the mentality of trying to squeeze out every last square foot of available leasable space and in the direction where the economic benefits of good architectural design will be recognized and embraced, they will be improving the quality of life, as well as the quality of public spaces.

CHAPTER 7

Boston Uses Museums to Revitalize Inner-City Area

Robert A. Brown

Boston has long been one of the country's most appealing cities, with its variety of livable neighborhoods, prestigious colleges and universities, well-known sports venues, Frederick Law Olmsted–designed parks, plus its rich history. However, the city's quality of life paid dearly for what in the mid–1950s was deemed improved transportation when an elevated expressway was cut through the central core, severing the Financial District from the waterfront and isolating the North End. The roadway exacerbated a perceived sense of social separation among the distinct neighborhoods of the downtown area and made navigation through the city difficult.

Now, after 20 years of planning and billions of dollars of construction in a project called the "Big Dig," the Central Artery has been replaced by a tunnel, and in what was once its shadow a 30-acre stretch of parkland known as the Rose Kennedy Greenway is taking form. (See "Green Renewal of Urban Life in Boston," page 58, July 2004.) For the past few years, discussions of the best approach to take with the newly reclaimed swath of city have occupied many of the country's design professionals as they engaged or enraged politicians and citizens. The strong sentiments

that surfaced after the expressway finally came down may seem surprising to some, given that serious work had been underway for nearly two decades by organizations that included the Massachusetts Turnpike Authority, the Boston Redevelopment Authority (BRA), the Central Artery Environmental Oversight Committee, and the Artery Business Committee, to name a few.

"The project was a 15-year secret, with most of the actual work going on underground," notes Ted Oatis, principal of the Boston-based developer Chiofaro Company, whose International Place office tower abuts the greenway. "People couldn't begin to imagine what it would be like, when it was filled with infrastructure, backstreet printing operations, and third-tier office buildings," explains Barbara Faga, chair of EDAW's board of directors, who came to Boston from the planning and designing firm's Atlanta office to work on one of the new parks. "It is transforming the city in the same way that major waterfront projects have transformed other cities. Before it happens, people see only the blight, not the vision."

Those with a vision of an expanded public realm and its benefits persevered through

Originally published as "Filling the Cut," *Urban Land*, Vol. 65, No. 3, March 2006, by the Urban Land Institute, Washington, D.C. Reprinted with permission of the publisher.

years of tough decisions aimed to balance relatively short-term difficulty against long-term gains. "In the 1980s, the BRA began to anticipate the changes we see today by requiring the designs that were submitted for properties adjoining the future park to have active faces to what was then the expressway," says Richard Garver, deputy director of planning and zoning at the BRA. "It wasn't easy." Others grappled with how to translate the mandated allotments of 75 percent parkland and 25 percent buildings into an inviting mixed-use environment that would satisfy the needs of the city as a whole and the specialized desires of the diverse neighborhoods touching the greenway.

By late 2002, the debate about what should happen on the land moved into the public sphere through a design competition for the green spaces adjoining the neighborhoods. The exhibition and discussion of the short-listed designs, called "Realizing the Vision," drew more than 700 participants to the Boston Public Library. There were op-ed pieces in the Boston Globe, programs on local television stations, and public forums titled "Beyond the Big Dig" that looked at national and international thinking about public open space.

From these discussions, the design community, led by the Boston Society of Architects and the Boston Society of Landscape Architects, in collaboration with other public and private entities, defined five urban design principles that could be used to evaluate the success of the community efforts to create vital urban parks. Those principles are:

- Build parks that are a common ground for all.
- Build parks that are uniquely Boston.
- Design the parks for the future.
- Connect the greenway parks to the larger park system and open-space system.
- Construct parks as a sustainable environment.

These are lofty goals for a site that by big-city park standards is small. Of the 27 acres, considerable space is dedicated to sidewalks, curbs, and other necessities. Still, what is left, especially in a city as compact and dense as Boston, will have an enormous impact for decades to come. This may help explain the lively, extended discussions in 2003 over the design character of the parks near Chinatown, the North End, and the Wharf District.

"This is valuable open space," maintains John Copley, principal of Copley Wolff Design Group of Boston and a member of the design team for the Wharf District Park. "There are 10 million square feet of office space within 500 feet of the wharf; that's a lot of office workers with no place to go. They are hungry for outdoor space." Faga, part of the same team, adds, "The Wharf District became a neighborhood around the notion of a park. It brought people together, and their input created a better park. There were strong feelings about what a park should be, given the Bostonian experience of the Common and the Public Gardens." So strong were the feelings that the team participated in 150 meetings over two years.

The other major components of the greenway plan are the cultural institutions that will be built on the parcels covering the ramps of the new Central Artery tunnel. Competition for these high-profile sites, strategically located at the major turns along the new parkway, attracted a number of interesting proposals. The winners include plans for a new YMCA, the Boston History Museum, and the New Center for Arts and Culture. Now the projects, with the exception of the arts and culture center, are struggling with the cost of construction over an active roadway, in addition to the normal pressures of nonprofit fundraising. A three-block segment of the park that has been committed to the Massachusetts Horticultural Society for the city's first botanical garden has had trouble coming up with money as well. Boston insiders, however, are optimistic that the city's donors will rally for these important cultural additions to the new park and the city.

While there is not yet a single blade of

grass, the effects of the new Rose Kennedy Greenway can already be observed in the rise of real estate values near the park. The Boston Globe reported in 2004 that a review of Boston tax assessment records showed "in the 15 years since the Central Artery tunnel began, the value of commercial properties along the mile-long strip ... increased to $2.3 billion, up 79 percent. That's almost double the citywide 41 percent increase in assessed commercial property values in the same period."

In the 18 months since that report, the property market along and near the greenway has continued to boom, and what Garver calls a "20-year mental investment" has turned out to be good business for those owners who put money into their properties along the potential park. Oatis cites his firm's obligation to design an expressway ramp next to International Place, which has now been torn down to reveal, at last, first-floor space with greenway frontage and long views. "In the long run, a view of the greenway is in many ways more valuable than one of the harbor," he says.

The view of and access to the park are literally and metaphorically turning around the buildings that line the greenway, with reverberations reaching into the surrounding districts. The national trend that has residents returning to downtown in significant numbers is driving a number of new developments along and near the greenway, where 4,000 housing units reportedly are being planned. Condominium conversions are leading the way, including projects such as the Othello on Beach Street near South Station in the Leather District, where local developer Jim Robertson reports that all eight of the 2,700-square-foot units have been sold for $1.25 million to $1.625 million. The Cresset Group is developing Lincoln Plaza at Lincoln and Essex streets, with 80 percent of the 85 studio, one-bedroom, and two-bedroom units already sold at prices ranging from $260,000 to $720,000.

New construction includes the Folio at 80 Broad Street in the Financial District, where new architecture frames a historic brick warehouse designed by architect Charles Bulfinch. The project, being developed by a partnership between an affiliate of the Suffolk Companies of Boston and Recap Capital Partners of New York City, has sold two-thirds of the 96 condominiums, which include studio, one-bedroom, and two-bedroom units priced at $470,000 to $1.3 million. Rose Associates of New York City is developing the Leighton, 162 condominiums located at South and Essex streets on a site originally planned for offices. Many more projects are near completion, while others are still being planned.

With the diverse mix of construction activity — from major cultural institutions designed by internationally recognized architects, to small condominium conversions, to even smaller public projects like expansion of a parcel of park to connect the greenway to the New England Aquarium — the city is repairing the rift created by the expressway 60 years ago. "The wonderful legacy of the whole project is that it is changing the landscape of the city," says Robert L. Beal, president of the Beal Companies, a Boston-based developer.

No small part of the healing of the cityscape comes from the newfound visual connections between neighborhoods and Boston Harbor. Not only are the views to the waterfront restored, but also the harbor itself, which benefited from a major cleanup begun in the late 1980s. The revitalized waterfront, with its inviting public walkway HarborWalk, is now an attractive destination whose proximity to the greenway extends the public realm.

The fostering of a sense of connection among the distinct enclaves that form the city, as well as with the harbor, is seen as a critical next step in the redevelopment of Boston as the greenway becomes a reality. The Crossroads Initiative, sponsored by the city, focuses on renovating and enlivening 12 downtown streets to reconnect the neighborhoods long divided by the elevated freeway. The program also aims to establish new relationships among the downtown districts.

Ken Greenberg, principal of Toronto-based Greenberg Consultants, who played a leading role in development of the Crossroads Initiative, sees enormous civic power in the reweaving of the urban fabric. "It is very dramatic to walk out now and see how places touch each other — something you could never see before," he says. "Promoting connectivity among these places will release a new energy in the city. There is a positive multiplier that happens with the juxtaposition of people and in surprise encounters of city living. We want to encourage that with great streets." Construction over the next seven to ten years of the Crossroads streets, which will form ribs along the green spine of the greenway, is expected to result in improved pedestrian environments, enhanced elements for wayfinding, increased activity along sidewalks, better traffic flow, and new opportunities for performances and placement of public art.

As the enormous physical effort of the Big Dig ends, the new challenge for the city is to maximize its return on this outsized invest-ment. In the past few years, the Rose Kennedy Greenway Conservancy, a nonprofit organization, was formed to serve as the steward for the greenway, and last year, conservancy chair Peter Meade named Nancy Brennan executive director. The conservancy is not only to maintain the park — it has a fundraising goal of $20 million over the next three years — but also to program it.

While the debates about the design, the programs, and myriad other issues will undoubtedly continue, the arrival of the Rose Kennedy Greenway is, by any measure, a landmark event. The city is ready, observes Rob Tuchmann, a partner in the Boston office of Wilmer Hale and a veteran of the Central Artery battles, having served both as chair of the Central Artery Environmental Oversight Committee and cochair of the Mayor's Central Artery Completion Task Force. "We have a limited budget, good bones in the design, and 100 years to get it right. Let's start."

CHAPTER 8

Brooklyn Links Museums and Libraries to Improve Public Services

Cheryl Bartholow

Considering their shared desire to increase access to their abundant resources, raise visibility among their constituents, and take advantage of cutting-edge educational technology, perhaps a major collaboration between three premier Brooklyn institutions was inevitable. In 1997, under visionary new leadership and in response to suggestions by elected officials and funders that they work together, the Brooklyn Children's Museum (BCM), Brooklyn Museum of Art (BMA), and Brooklyn Public Library (BPL) began to collaborate on a technology initiative that would attract young audiences to their locations. Called "Brooklyn Expedition," it features a Web site for children that links the collections and resources of all three institutions.

At the time, BCM was in the midst of strategic planning that identified providing greater access to its collections as a goal for its 1999 centennial. BPL, the fifth-largest library system in the United States, was celebrating its centennial with new technological and visitor service initiatives. BMA, home to the second-largest collection of art in the country, was preparing for the opening of a major Monet exhibition that would double its annual attendance. The "Brooklyn Expedition" project offered the three institutions the opportunity to work together on a major audience development initiative utilizing new technologies.

Over the past two years, "Brooklyn Expedition" has grown from a modest proposal to an extensive and ambitious project: a pioneering Web site that makes the collections of the three institutions accessible to young, families, and educators, while fostering inquiry-based learning. Our three-year goal is to create a dynamic resource that will help young people acquire visual, research, and technology literacy skills, and to provide a proven framework that can be maintained and expanded by all three partners in the future. (Visit "Brooklyn Expedition" at *www.brooklynexpedition.org* to see our work in progress.)

"This is a long-term partnership among the three institutions to incorporate new strategies for collaborative programming, cross-promotion, and cross-utilization of services that can be expanded to include other community and cultural organizations," says

Originally published as "Linking Up Museums and Libraries," *Museum News*, March/April 1999, by the American Association of Museums, Washington, D.C. Reprinted with permission of the publisher.

Kevin Allard-Mendelson, BPL's director of technology. Allard-Mendelson, Deborah Schwartz, BMA's vice president for education and programs, and I (director of programs at the children's museum) comprised the lead development group. Schwartz recalls: "In the beginning there were meetings when we would lay out our vision for the site, and then we would gasp at our ambition. Of course, we didn't know how complex what we were envisioning really was." Allard-Mendelson "knew that we could really raise the bar on the types of technologies we used for the 'Expedition' project, [but] what we have developed has far exceeded the then-existing technologies."

Of the three partners, the library clearly had the edge in technology and the expertise to lead the other two institutions into the cyber age. The two museum partners were in their technological infancy. BCM had begun work with the Association of Science-Technology Centers, Washington, D.C., and the Exploratorium, San Francisco, to pilot a Web resource based on their national traveling exhibition "Wild About Plants." But those plans, as well as plans for a museum Web site, were still at the talk stage. The children's museum, in fact, had only recently completed the installation of a museum-wide e-mail system. The Brooklyn Museum of Art had a promotional Web site, which was maintained off site and was accessible to staff on a limited basis.

The high-speed lines needed to connect the partners together ended just a few blocks from the Brooklyn Bridge, miles away from the three sites. To ensure that its 58 branches could be wired for the Internet and linked to the museums, the library initiated Brooklyn-wide discussions on creating an advanced telecommunications infrastructure. Library staff worked hard to get technology into BCM and BMA. Even before the high-speed lines and servers needed to sustain the project were installed at the museums, plans for the development of the site moved forward.

The lead team established the goals, framework, schedule, and budget for the project, and assembled a joint project team made up of education and technology staff from all three institutions. The team met to create the funding proposals necessary to secure the financial resources needed for the project. "We used the development of these documents to help us crystallize our goals and deliverables for the 'Brooklyn Expedition,'" says Schwartz. "There was an incredible trust and sharing between the institutions, which allowed us to acknowledge honestly what our needs for the project were."

In keeping with the project's name, the team decided to utilize the icons of a journey — a journal, site map, and graphic elements — that would allow visitors to imagine themselves on an expedition as they explored the Web site. One of our main goals was to encourage these Web explorers to make actual expeditions to the three institutions.

During the planning stage, we learned from conversations with children that quick explorations of Internet sites were the norm, and return visits were only likely to happen if a site proved particularly useful or fun. Thus we envisioned an on-line journal that would allow the site's visitors to record their journeys, save information and text, and resume their explorations where they had left off, regardless of where the "traveling" had been done — at the museums, library, or even at home. The team searched for a model but could not find any tools on the Internet designed to encourage or assist children with on-line research. We wanted our journal to be able to capture text and images, allow explorers to add their own notes, store items by keywords, and retrieve them to create reports. We conceived of "Brooklyn Expedition" as a research literacy tool that could be useful in the classroom, as well as in library and home settings. Because of its technological complexity, the development of the journal required a full year of work. (It is scheduled to be on-line in early April.)

An early challenge was to find themes that would allow each of our institutions to showcase a particular area of strength, be of general interest to children and their families, and complement a school curriculum. "Structures" and "Latin America" were the first themes chosen. The team began with "Structures," a wide-ranging, in-depth exploration that links the structures created by animals (including human animals) to the structures of animals themselves. We developed conceptual connections between BCM's "Bones, Bugs, and Beasts" exhibition, live animal program, and collections, and BMA's building and the Schenck house, a Dutch colonial home that is on display in the museum. The library added a unit on the structure of information, an exploration of the intricacies of the Dewey Decimal system. Each institution brought its own text and images to the table, and a write gave it a single voice.

In spring 1997, when planning first began for "Brooklyn Expedition," most Web sites couldn't compete with the sophisticated look and interactivity of a CD-ROM. Our initial plan had been to take materials developed for a printed format and translate them to pages within the Web site. And, with few exceptions, that is how "Structures" was developed. The initial site included a lot of textual information and static images and the overall experience was not unlike turning the pages of a book. It came as no great shock to us to find out that our young test audiences were not impressed. They wanted surprises and fun activities, and they wanted to be able to do something with the information they found. They found the facts they were learning "cool" but told us they would rather search for answers than be given information. One educator asked, "Why isn't it more like going to a children's museum, where you are an active participant?"

That was a major breakthrough point for us. We carefully reconsidered what we had, and what we ultimately wanted to create. Acknowledging that working in a new medium requires learning new skills, we rethought our roles and expanded the team to include an interactive Web designer. New design and ex-

periential goals were set, and the team revisited a goal that had been articulated early in the project but not fully realized — to base the Web site's design on object-based learning, a particularly important component of BMA's teaching methodology. Finally, the three partners agreed to allot the time and money necessary to achieve the vision. "Once the content started flowing, we really had to push the envelope on exploiting technology to deliver the functionality needed," says Allard-Mendelson. "The result is a set of tools that exceeds most of what you will find on the Web today, especially museum and library Web sites."

Rather than immediately redoing the "Structures" site, we decided to shift our focus to the "Latin America" site. The team carefully considered what kids had been saying about the site — from comments about the amount of text to which things got and, more important, held their attention. With Web sites, as with museum exhibitions, you have a limited time to make your point with an audience.

This time, rather than starting with content and using objects to illustrate it, we emphasized the objects themselves. "Gateway" objects introduce sub-themes such as "Awesome Animals," "Living Off the Land," or "Converging Cultures." For each of these sub-themes, books are presented as visual images and not just as bibliographic listings. (Just as the objects connect users to new pages of information, the book covers serve as links to other Web sites.) Text is handled differently as well. Information is now broken down into "bite-sized" portions so visitors can get to the point quickly. To encourage visitors to examine objects closely, rollovers or "mouseovers" (which allow the viewer to drag the cursor over an object) reveal provocative questions or interesting facts. In at least one case, a rollover allows the viewer to "turn over" and inspect a 15-century jaguar sculpture from Mexico (an experience not likely to occur in many art museums).

Organizing information, creating new conventions for viewers to follow, utilizing every square inch of screen space — with these goal sin mind, the "Latin America" site became our new standard. After it was launched in summer 1998 we spent our time reorganizing the "Structures" theme into the new format. The team is now developing our next theme, one of great interest to all three institutions — Brooklyn itself!

"At every point we examined what we had learned, and we made adjustments along the way," says Jill Fruchter, project manager for "Brooklyn Expedition." "One of the big issues was how to establish a consistent flow of communication between all the people involved. E-mail turned out to be our connective tissue." A Web-based production site allowed the group to post new design prototypes, text, and images for feedback and review, as well as keep track of background research and meeting notes. "The Web became our virtual office," adds Fruchter.

Throughout this process, recognizing and respecting the unique culture and particular needs of each of the three institutions was important. Despite the many similarities in our mission, values, and audience, we learned that each institution had its own processes and internal language. In order to learn to work together effectively, we needed to learn to understand and respect those differences.

Each of our institutions has its own distinct approach to thinking and learning. At BCM, project teams discuss how to create concrete, hands-on, collection-based activities that work for children. BMA emphasizes visual literacy, bringing its artworks to life for young people; its staff saw the Web site as an opportunity to make information not usually available to the public more accessible. For BPL, it was important that its collections be given equal weight with those of the museums. While these needs were not mutually exclusive, agreements about underlying pedagogy, appropriate length of text, and the design of learning activities were essential to create a product that received all three partners' seal of approval. "The child-oriented approaches BCM brought to the process were liberating for us," says the BMA's Schwartz. "Our orientation towards art often keeps us on the more serious side of fun." The insistence by BMA staff to maintain an integrity in the presentation of objects — to not let the information become "lightweight" — and BPL's technology vision challenged the group to explore new territories. Working together allowed us to achieve results that we could not have achieved on our own.

Despite all the work we have done and all we've accomplished over the past two years, we realize that much of what we envision still lies ahead. The development of the "Brooklyn" theme will include opportunities for local teens to work on developing the site. "Our institutions are youth-oriented, and we want this project to provide opportunities for young people to get engaged at a number of levels, not just as users," says Allard-Mendelson. Teen "explainers" will be trained to help introduce the site to public audiences, and will also help create enhancements to the site. BCM will lend its expertise to the development of the Explainer Corps, which will recruit youth from area middle and high schools, the New York City Museum School, and BCM's own nationally recognized Museum Team, an educational and employment program for community youth ages 7 to 18.

Securing funding for the $1.2-million project continues. Several funders have indicated their interest in the collaborative nature of the project. The Institute of Museum and Library Services awarded the project nearly $300,000 through a 1998 National Leadership Grant. Bell Atlantic, a lead funder, the Nathan Cummings Foundation, and the National Endowment for the Arts, have also made major contributions to the project.

Over the next few months teachers will learn about the site and its value as a classroom resource tool through intensive professional development sessions. Educators will be introduced to the potential of the journal as an Internet research tool and will visit the institutions to design their curriculum. Planned for the future are the creation of areas on the site to publish children's work, and an "Expedition" story line with interface characters who will appear in their special roles as an archaeologist, zoologist, museum curator, or architect. In addition, creating new links to existing museum and library programs and developing such activities as computer kiosks and special events for families will keep the team busy well into the next millennium.

The main benefits of the "Brooklyn Expedition" project are the new relationships we are building between the public and our institutions; the exciting information it will bring to children, parents, and teachers; and mutually beneficial alliances among the sponsoring institutions. But these are not the only advantages. Through our collaboration in this project, we have come to appreciate each other as colleagues and have learned from each other's strengths. In fact, the positive experience of working together has led to other major collaborations among a larger group of Brooklyn institutions. Schwartz sums it up: "The opportunity to work with colleagues on a long-term project developing connections and a comfort level with each other — that knowledge and trust — will have a long-term impact on us. It has already changed how we think about each other, and the way we are planning to work together in the future."

CHAPTER 9

Charleston Library Anchors Downtown Redevelopment Project

William Fulton *and* Chris Jackson

The years had not been kind to Calhoun Street. Charleston's main thoroughfare cuts across the peninsula separating the Cooper and Ashley rivers, the focal point of this historic South Carolina port city. But by the 1980s, much of the street had lost its colonial charm. Long stretches were dotted by vacant lots and rundown buildings.

It was on just such a bedraggled stretch of Calhoun Street that Mayor Joseph Riley announced a decade ago that he wanted to build the new main branch of the Charleston County Public Library. Since 1931, the main branch had been located a few blocks away on Marion Square, a small park surrounded by a cluster of landmark churches and the original home of the Citadel military academy. But that building was too small to support a growing collection and newer services like Internet work stations. Despite pressure to move the library to the suburbs, Riley fought to keep it downtown as an anchor of the city's revitalization effort. "Libraries see the comings and goings of all people in the neighborhood, and because of that they nourish the street on which they are located more than any other public facility," Riley says. At his urging, the city bought the two-acre parcel and donated it to the county.

Give It Credit

It is now a year since the opening of the $11 million main branch, and Calhoun Street is on the mend, with residential and retail projects under way nearby. Suburbanites regularly visit the new library, lured by the expanded collection and state-of-the-art computer facilities. Local residents hold neighborhood association meetings there, and teens gather to plan school projects.

The new library can't take all the credit for turning Calhoun Street around. But in Charleston, as in cities across the nation, both librarians and urban planners are recognizing that a library can be a strong contributor to revitalization efforts, whether downtown or in the neighborhoods.

"Libraries are, in many ways, neighborhood living rooms," says Norman Holman, a senior vice-president of the New York Public Library. "Communities change, but the library stays there."

Ever since Andrew Carnegie's philanthropy made them a common feature of American community life a century ago, libraries have well understood their role as community centers. Some Carnegie libraries originally had boxing rings and lecture halls.

But in the last decade or so, American libraries have been rediscovered as place-based assets. Searching for strong anchors for downtowns and neighborhoods, urban revitalization experts have rediscovered libraries and other cultural institutions as "attractions."

At the same time, however, libraries are becoming more active as community centers, often including day care centers and homework centers. Internet access has become a draw for patrons without home computers. "The library as a place is as critically important as the resources in the library," says Susan Goldberg Kent, director of the Los Angeles Public Library.

"Libraries can do anything," says Robert McNulty, president of the Washington-based Partners for Livable Communities, one of those who supports this broadening of the library mission. Others are concerned that the new emphasis on aggressive programming goes too far. Libraries risk becoming "just another custodial facility," says Glen Holt, executive director of the St. Louis Public Library.

Whom Do They Serve?

Controversy over the mission of the public library is nothing new. According to historical Abigail Van Slyck, author of *Free to All*, the definitive history of Carnegie libraries, civic leaders often disagreed with Andrew Carnegie on just this point.

Carnegie, whose impoverished Scottish family came to the U.S. in the late 1840s and who made a fortune in the steel industry, viewed public libraries primarily as a bootstrap for immigrants and working-class families. His building program — which resulted in the construction of 1,679 public libraries between 1886 and 1917 — emphasized neighborhood libraries. Civic leaders, in contrast, envisioned monumental downtown libraries that would become "elite preserves."

As a compromise, Van Slyck writes, most big city library boards "embraced a two-tiered system of library facilities: a grand central library (built with or without Carnegie's financial help) in a City Beautiful setting, and more modest branches erected in working-class neighborhoods."

By the middle of this century, the urban public library had become a staple of upward mobility — well described by Philip Roth in his 1959 novel, *Goodbye Columbus*. In the 1960s and '70s, however, the flight of the middle class to the suburbs took its toll, and city libraries had to struggle to maintain patronage — and funding.

Ports of Entry

Quite apart from their place-based role, public libraries have changed dramatically in the past decade. In many cities, libraries have become ports of entry to new immigrants, providing them with a wide variety of services.

"We have partnered with Catholic Charities to help people in finding temporary housing," says Ramiro Salazar, director of the Dallas Public Library. "People use the library to teach English as a second language, literacy, and citizenship classes."

Many librarians are eagerly plunging into the social service arena, but Glen Holt, the director of the St. Louis Public Library and a former urban studies professor, is more cautious. "That's like a mouse getting into bed with an elephant," he says. "Libraries can't be everything." While acknowledging the library's role in the community, Holt adds, "I don't want the public library to become the public housing of the 2010s or the welfare system of the 2030s."

Partly as a result of such fears, some cities are focusing on the library buildings themselves, rather than on community service. The Seattle Public Library recently passed a multimillion-dollar bond measure to revamp its branches. At the same time, the system has reaffirmed traditional library pursuits by dubbing 1999 "The Year of the Collection."

To bolster their facilities, many financially pressed public libraries are learning the language of economic development. Holt's St. Louis system is an example. A recent survey of library users estimated that the library, which costs taxpayers $15 million a year to operate, provides the community with $67 million a year in benefits.

Crossroads

Today's libraries face two major challenges: the Internet and sophisticated retailing. On the one hand, the Internet has eliminated the reason for using the library — the need to find certain information. Meanwhile, the big retailers (especially bookstore chains) have used a casual atmosphere and comfortable seating to attract students and others who once hung out in the local library.

"Why this is coming to the forefront now is that libraries are at a crossroads," says Joseph Keenan, director of the public library system in Elizabeth, New Jersey. "People no longer need to go to the library to get a piece of information or research a paper." Nor do they need the library for intellectual stimulation or entertainment. "Barnes & Noble has lectures and readings. Even Burger King has story time," he says.

These challenges have forced libraries to reposition themselves as place-based assets in a way that dovetails nicely with urban revitalization efforts. The Internet, for example, has not eliminated the need for libraries, as many librarians feared it would. In many cases, it has reinforced the library's role as a place to go for information. Many public libraries now have large banks of Internet computers available to the public, thus increasing patronage and interest in the libraries.

"A lot of business people use the library for the Internet because they have access to human help, financial research, and genealogy," says Joseph Rizzo, an architect with the Hillier Group in Princeton, New Jersey, who has worked on many library projects.

Libraries have also begun to fight back by returning to their Carnegie roots as social centers — a trend that also reinforces their place-based role in the community. A decade ago, many libraries were converting their meeting rooms into storage areas to house expanding collections. Now they are reopening these meeting rooms — or as is the case of the new downtown Denver library, building so many new meeting rooms that they create a kind of mini-conference center.

Elsewhere, public libraries are promoting homework centers, bookshops, and other compatible retail uses, and they've made space for cultural activities such as art exhibits and museum shows. Chicago's Harold Washington Library, which opened in 1991 on a prime downtown block, has all these features and a white tablecloth restaurant to boot.

Librarians have changed, too. "My training in the 1980s focused only on the discipline," says Keenan. "It did not provide an understanding of how we made our libraries network with our community." Today, he notes, librarians have become entrepreneurs.

Bricks and Mortar

The effect of these changes on America's cities is striking. Downtown libraries rank with retail and entertainment complexes as redevelopment anchors in cities like San Francisco, Seattle, Nashville, and Memphis. Ironically, many — originally sited outside the commercial core — are today well positioned to anchor new development projects because the downtown has expanded around them in the intervening decades.

Nor is the library phenomenon limited to big cities or cities with established historic districts like Charleston. Muncie, Indiana, is about to begin a major expansion of its downtown library as part of a broader renewal effort. The city's original Carnegie library was built more than 90 years ago and is now far too small. A generation ago it might have been razed, but now it will be expanded to serve as a downtown anchor, along with a convention center and children's museum. "A lot of synergy can take place at the library if it works with the community that surrounds it," says library director Virginia Nilles.

Crucial though libraries may be downtown, they may be even more important in urban neighborhoods. Once overshadowed by their downtown counterparts, neighborhood branch libraries can now offer a much wider range of services because of the Internet, CD-ROMs, and other electronic forms of information. "What you can do now in a small branch library with limited space is unbelievable because of information technology," says Los Angeles librarian Susan Kent.

Nor are branches confined to library buildings. In Elizabeth, New Jersey, a new branch library shares space in a city-owned neighborhood center with a senior center, a clinic, and a preschool program. "The beauty of this arrangement is that I don't pay any overhead," says library director Keenan. "We just provide the collection and a small staff and the branch is used by most everyone who comes into the center."

In Ventura, California, a renewal program in a low-income neighborhood has combined a new library with affordable housing. Using federal community development block grant funds, the city last year renovated a 1920s retail and apartment building, putting affordable units on the upper floors and a branch library below. The new library has the highest walk-in traffic of any of Ventura County's 15 libraries, underscoring the synergy between library and neighborhood.

In Portland, Oregon, the smallest branch library is located in a mostly vacant strip mall. When the heath food chain Natures Fresh bought one of the vacant storefronts for a new store, the company was adamant about keeping the adjoining library in place.

There's no mystery about that, says Eleanor Jo Rodger, president of the Urban Library Council, a national association of large public libraries. When a library goes in, "foot traffic goes up," and the area "becomes livelier and a more interesting place to be."

In the end, there may be a disagreement about the exact role a library should play in the community, but there is little question that both downtown and neighborhood libraries are potential catalysts for urban revitalization. "Libraries have always known they are community assets," says Los Angeles's Susan Kent. And especially today, she adds, "there are very few public places that are welcoming to everybody."

CHAPTER 10

Christchurch Museums and Libraries Create Economic Development Model

Jonathan Walters

Set dramatically at the eastern edge of the sweeping Canterbury Plain, with the South Alps mountain range in the background, the city of Christchurch looks like a New Zealand version of Boulder or Berkeley. The scenery is gorgeous, the pace is relaxed, and the center of town is sprinkled with old-fashioned pubs, ethnic restaurants, local shops and international boutiques. The laid-back quality of life seems somehow to be symbolized by the shallow, meandering Avon River, which forms a serpentine park running through the heart of downtown.

But the easy informality of Christchurch belies something very interesting and important: It is the best-run city in the world.

Some of this is obvious even to the most casual observer. Buses and trolleys go everywhere and do it frequently. The streets are litter-free. Panhandling is virtually unheard of. The law enforcement presence is so subtle as to be almost subliminal, but the crime rate is ludicrously low. Amenities abound, from museums and community theater to indoor pools and vast stretches of rugby pitch. There is a public library within walking distance of al-

most every neighborhood in town, and where there isn't, there are plans to build one. "All children should have access to one," says the Christchurch policy director, Jonathan Fletcher, "without coming to the central city."

But if many of the successes and efficiencies of Christchurch are visible to the naked eye, others are not. There is, for example, the highly evolved management and financial accounting system. And there is a remarkable ethos of civic involvement.

All of this has direct roots in national politics, in the sweeping reforms passed by New Zealand's Parliament in the late 1980s. These measures wiped out traditional bureaucracy at the federal level, and swept in a whole new set of business-like procedures, ranging from the elimination of civil service restrictions to the establishment of full accrual accounting for government agencies. These changes rolled down to all three of the major cities, Auckland and Wellington as well as Christchurch. But it is Christchurch that took them the most seriously.

One way to appreciate that is to peruse the city's Strategic Statement, its annual blue-

Originally published as "Urban Role Model," *Governing*, Vol. 15, No. 13, October 2001, by Congressional Quarterly Inc., Washington, D.C. Reprinted with permission of the publisher.

print for management and operation. The Statement is a highly accessible state-of-the-city report, outlining current projects and future goals, all linked to basic economic and demographic projections. It reaches down to the specifics of sewers and street maintenance, as well as the operational philosophy of museums and libraries. But it also covers the broadest issues of housing, health and welfare, listing general financial data on how to reach goals in each category, while at the same time maintaining high levels of municipal service overall.

Thumbing through the statement, it's easy to check up on plans for a major new landfill to be "built to the highest environmental standards," or for a beefed-up recycling effort. There is a remarkably clear section on city finance, from policies on borrowing to strategies of investment.

The Christchurch Strategic Statement is built on the homegrown concept of the "triple bottom line." All policies, projects and expenditures are expected to aim for the three-pronged goal of economic development, social well-being and environmental sustainability. In most American cities, it might seem like so much rhetoric and windy speculation. In Christchurch, it comes out sounding practical. If you look under "city beautification," for example, you find an explanation of how Christchurch plans to deal with drainage issues by taking advantage of natural waterways and wetlands to handle the drainage problem, "instead of laying concrete pipe."

While the Statement sets out the objectives, a companion document, the Financial Plan and Programme, descends further into detail. Not all of it is strictly financial. The FPP will tell you the net cost of water supply for the current fiscal year: $11,285,119, including about $4.7 million in depreciation and $570,000 for "information and advice." It will tell you the exact amount budgeted for grants to a host of community organizations, from the $40,000 earmarked for Table Tennis Canterbury to the $270,000 assigned to the Christchurch Symphony Orchestra.

These expenditure numbers — particularly the ones related to depreciation — are the product of accrual-based accounting that converts them from a wish list to a practical management program. Unlike most local governments in America, Christchurch doesn't hide long-term costs. When it builds a downtown art gallery — as it is currently doing — all the expenses are figured in. The line-item for the gallery that appears in the Financial Plan is not an abstract number that will come to haunt some future set of city councilors — and restrict needed investment in other projects years down the road.

To build the new facility, Christchurch's budget will take a $1 million hit this year, whether it actually spends that amount or not. In every future year, the budget will continue to include accurate numbers for depreciation and maintenance — not numbers that conceal the ultimate cost of the project. It is a system that keeps local officeholders honest when their ambitions start getting bigger than the public purse. It virtually ensures that all new infrastructure gets the upkeep and maintenance it requires.

The remarkable civic consciousness of Christchurch, much like the innovations in finance and management, can be traced back to the late 1980s. Among the reforms enacted by New Zealand's Parliament as a law directing local governments to consolidate. They complied, and with a vengeance. When the dust settled in 1989, 800 local entities — from cities and townships to irrigation and sewer districts — had been reduced to a mere 87.

As might be expected, consolidation wasn't a popular concept in all localities. David Close, who has been on the Christchurch City Council since 1977, remembers the moment well. He recalls that the initial plan for consolidation in Christchurch, put together by a commission of local officials, was essentially a blueprint for the status quo. "It was going to perpetuate divisions and perpetuate inequality," says Close. "It would have left the old inner-city areas impoverished and it would have left the wealthy parts of the metropolitan area with a nice big tax base and nothing to spend the money on." So Close and a few allies set to work drafting an alternative plan designed to connect the whole Christchurch metropolitan area but still preserve local identities. And this is the one that eventually became law.

Under its terms, Christchurch was — and is — divided into six sectors, each with its own city-funded community board. Each sector contains two wards, and each ward sends two members to the city council. All the financial reports are broken down by sector and ward. Flip open the city's capital works budget, and you quickly learn of plans to spend $16,000 on plantings in a neighborhood park in Wigram Ward, and $66,000 for street lights on Bridge St. in Ferrymead Ward. The distribution of resources among different areas of the city is presented much more openly than it would be in most American cities of comparable size, and it is clearly aimed at illustrating for all residents the diffusion of spending citywide.

Technically, Christchurch has a "strong manager/weak mayor" form of government, but the truth is that managers and politicians quietly line up together on most of the fundamentals of governing. "Expecting a hard policy and management split is unrealistic," says Jonathan Fletcher. "If that pothole outside that leading constituent's house spends three weeks unfilled, in the end it's not management on whom that constituent's frustration is going to be taken out, it's the local council member in the next election. And that goes for rubbish collection and any other service."

As with almost all of the successes of Christchurch government, it's crucial to understand the national reforms that helped generate them. In the late 1980s, while the rest of the world was taking slow and tentative steps toward reinventing government, New Zealand was doing it virtually overnight.

A small core of U.S.-trained free-market economists holding sway in the Treasury

Department decided to overhaul what they considered an expensive, unresponsive and flabby governmental system. The reformers were convinced that New Zealanders had come to view government at all levels as the solution to any problem and the employer of first — not last — resort. They had numbers to back up their argument: As of the late 1980s, spending on government represented more than 40 percent of the nation's Gross Domestic Product. And they considered national stagnation to be the inevitable result.

And so, in the State Sector Act of 1988 and the Public Finance Act of 1989, the reformers set out to replace the old system with an enterprise that looked as much as possible like a successful private corporation. Departments wouldn't be run by political appointees anymore but by professional "chief executives," hired for five-year performance-based contracts and subject to termination if they failed to deliver. Budgets would be based on specific sets of "outputs," purchased from the departments by Parliament in order to meet a department's clearly stated strategic objectives.

But for all the tight prescriptions on performance —financial and otherwise — the reforms granted quite a bit of new flexibility. New Zealand's infamous jobs mill — its civic service system — was completely dismantled, and CEs were cut loose to do their own hiring and firing, purchasing and contracting. The New Zealand reforms were — and still are — the most thoroughgoing experiment in market-based bureaucratic reform attempted anywhere in the world.

At the national level, where the ideas were conceived and the need for change was viewed as greatest, the results have been ambiguous, to say the least.

Several of the most important national agencies showed no noticeable improvement in the 1990s under the market-driven system. New Zealand's health care continued to suffer from long waiting lists and accusations of shoddy treatment. On the higher education side, there was one stretch of five years during which professors failed to receive any pay raises at all.

The corporate-style management system has not grafted easily onto the public sector. Critics say it bogs down in measurement of tangible but trivial elements of performance. The Department of Environmental Conservation sought for a while to gauge the success of its reforestation programs by measuring the number of possums missed by possum-reduction efforts, on the theory that the live ones were still out there eating valuable brush and forest seedlings. Social service agencies have found themselves keeping track of minute increments of service rather than tailoring efforts to the specific needs of individuals and families.

Conflicts arose virtually everywhere between CEs and budget analysts. The analysts had been mandated to rise herd on outputs purchased, not to encourage flexible or results-based spending schemes. The CEs considered that a foolish way to go about figuring the cost of hoped-for results. Meanwhile, the entire goal of the new approach — to somehow tie dollars to deeds and results — was subverted by year after year of fiscal squeezing. "It wasn't about performance," says Sue Newberry, a public accounting professor at the University of Canterbury. "It was about 'Did you live within your budget?'"

Even the critics are careful to say that the reforms have had some positive effects. Contracting and purchasing are done more rationally and more efficiently than they were in the old days. And there's no doubt that New Zealand's old approach to public employment would have been difficult to sustain in a competitive global economy.

On the other hand, even the most zealous of the original reformers concede that the results of the experiment have fallen considerably short of what they hoped for in 1989. They feel that way in spite of a second round of reforms in the mid–1990s aimed at pushing management and budgeting more toad bottom-line results. Currently, New Zealand is embarking on yet another round of reforms, again aimed at getting back to the original idea of tracking outcomes, and away from the questionable output-based management and budgeting practices that became common over the past decade.

The great irony of all this, however, is that while the reforms were failing to live up to their promise at the national level, they were quietly generating real achievement at the grassroots. The symbol of that is Christchurch.

Some of the city's good fortune has been simply a matter of good leadership. Indeed, if you press David Close about the importance of government reforms, you get a very candid answer: "I'm a bit of a cynic in regards to something like strategic planning," says Close. "I'm not saying you don't need a framework for decision making, but a strategic plan tells me that I should advance the welfare of the people of Christchurch socially, culturally and environmentally. That's great stuff. But it doesn't tell me whether I should spend $100,000 on this park or half a million on this road or a couple of hundred thousand on health care. That really comes out of the political process, from a perception of what politicians and staff think is needed and is affordable and what the people are saying they want."

What the national reforms did, however, was offer Christchurch and other localities the chance to redesign their systems and their rules, and the incentive to do so. Not all of what the national government mandated was embraced; some of the business-based notions about government that flowed down from Wellington were rejected outright. That was a good thing.

At one point, the market-infatuated national administration tried to mandate that local governments provide every service to citizens on a direct fee-for-service basis, whether it was a library book, a visit to an art gallery or a glass of tap water. Christchurch refused. "If citizens decide they want to pay for t hose things out of general revenues," says Close, "who is the national government to say they can't?"

For example, the national reformers told localities to charge for water by imposing a meter fee on all residential use; Christchurch chose to stick with a flat fee that allows each home as much water as it wants. The meter-based charge might have economized on usage and offset the cost of infrastructure improvements. On the other hand, local residents seem perfectly comfortable paying for water and sewer-related expenses out of general revenues. And the tap water that comes out of the pipes happens to be the cleanest in the world.

For all its successes, Christchurch is facing some difficult issues over the next few years, issues that will test not only its financial and management capacity but its now-entrenched ethic of citizen participation.

The most immediate one is air pollution. In the winter, Christchurch suffers Los Angeles–style temperature inversions that trap the city in so me of the world's worst smog, seriously exacerbated by the fact that most homes are heated with wood. This year, the city council voted to deal with the problem by phasing out wood-burning stoves. But Environment Canterbury, the governmental body charged with handling pollution problems on a regional basis, disagreed with that decision. ECan chose to exert its higher authority in the matter by pushing a go-slow, let's-study-the-issue approach. Even in a place where elected conflicts are inevitable. This one will not be easy to solve.

Meanwhile, sprawl is arriving — later than in much of the world, as with many things — but with increasing momentum. Christchurch is oozing beyond the confines of downtown and into suburban subdivisions, complete with broad swaths of asphalt full of speeding SUVs. Even the lovely Port Hills, which frame the city to the south and help fuel local tourism because of their natural beauty — are developing a bad case of overdevelopment. Partially as a result of this, the city's downtown core, for all its tangible vibrancy and beauty, is beginning to look a little frayed around the edges. The city's economy remains heavily dependent on the uncertain and low-wage tourism industry, as the most transient population in the world rolls in and out, making photo processing and souvenir shops some of the more prominent downtown business fixtures.

This economic development problem may be the toughest of all: Even the most innovative and efficient local government can't wave a wand and create a balanced and thriving local economy.

If history is any indication, though, Christchurch will rise to these challenges. It will do that in part because of the new ways of conducting local affairs mandated by the national government reforms of more than a decade ago. Even more, perhaps, it will do so thanks to the changes in those reforms that the local council successfully fought for in the intervening years.

But the city has an equally important advantage that is much less tangible. Beyond the management and budgeting schemes, beyond the improvements in administration and personnel management, beyond the benefits of contracting out, Christchurch has developed a strength that the vast majority of governments all over the world still lack: leadership that understands how to read citizens' wishes, and then accede to them or buck them, depending on the greater good. It's in handling that balancing act that Christchurch has time and again proved just how well-run a place it really is.

CHAPTER 11

Cincinnati Uses Culture to Revitalize Its Urban Core

Raymond L. Buse III

When Cincinnati-based Procter & Gamble purchased Boston-based Gillette in 2005, the *Boston Globe* dispatched a veteran business reporter to investigate how a medium-sized Midwestern city could claim nine Fortune 500 companies and 18 Fortune 1,000 firms within its midst. After a three-day visit, the reporter, Robert Gavin, came away so impressed with the city's resurgence that his ensuing *Boston Globe* article carried the banner headline, "We may be the hub of the universe, but Cincinnati is eating our lunch."

Cincinnati clearly is working its way up the food chain of U.S. cities with a major investment in both its urban core and its arts and culture. According to local historian Dan Hurley, not since the building of historic Music Hall and the Cincinnati Art Museum in the late 19th century has there been such a push for arts development in the city, accompanied by a wave of urban core redevelopment, including the new Fountain Square, a convention center, and the addition of hundreds of lofts and condominiums, which are pulling young professionals, empty nesters, urbanists, and entrepreneurs to the newly energized downtown.

Development projects representing more than $600 million (€454,373,160) in public/private investment are driving the transformation currently reshaping Cincinnati's center city. In 2005 alone, more than 50 major construction/development actions were initiated, in progress, or completed. The majority of the projects have been independently planned and financed, except for two new sports stadiums on the riverfront, which are being funded by a half-cent sales tax approved by Hamilton County voters.

Development in the arts area has been strong. Since 2002, Cincinnati has opened, or reopened, five museums, including the Rosenthal Center for Contemporary Art, designed by Iraqi-born Zaha Hadid to considerable acclaim. Together with the Aronoff Center for the Performing Arts — designed by architect Cesar Pelli and built at a cost of $82 million (€62,107,269) ten years ago — the Rosenthal Center anchors downtown Cincinnati's Backstage District of restaurants and bistros.

Complementing the Rosenthal Center are four other new or rejuvenated museums, all within walking distance of each other:

• The $45 million (€34,094,571) National Underground Railroad Freedom Center;

Originally published as "Renaissance on the River," *Urban Land*, Vol. 66, No. 4, April 2007, by the Urban Land Institute, Washington, D.C. Reprinted with permission of the publisher.

- The $22.8 million (€17,275,503) renovation of the Taft Museum of Art;
- The $15 million (€11,365,072) Cincinnati Reds Hall of Fame and Museum; and
- The $10 million (€7,576,663) addition of the Cincinnati Wing at the Cincinnati Art Museum, made up of 15 new galleries showcasing 400 objects of Cincinnati art from 1788 to the present.

The National Underground Railroad Freedom Center is strategically positioned between Cincinnati's two new sports stadiums — the $547 million (€414,395,523) Paul Brown Stadium and the $290 million (€219,780,312) Great American Ball Park — on the north bank of the Ohio River, overlooking the John A. Roebling Suspension Bridge, the pioneering cable strand bridge that served as the model for the Brooklyn Bridge. Located a block east of the Freedom Center, the Cincinnati Reds Hall of Fame and Museum offers baseball fans a look into the sports-heralded past of the city's professional baseball team, with exhibit space of more than 15,000 square feet (1,394 sq m). The nearby Taft Museum reopened in 2004 after a renovation and expansion involving a 20,000-square-foot (1,858-sq-m) new wing, which doubled the size of the museum — formerly known as the Baum-Longworth-Taft House — that was built in 1820.

In spring 2003, the Cincinnati Art Museum became the first art museum in the country to dedicate permanent gallery space to celebrating the art history of a city. The Cincinnati Wing: The Story of Art in the Queen City presents the story of Cincinnati's art history with the exhibit of more than 400 objects in 15 galleries summarizing nearly 200 years of art in the Queen City.

The civic epicenter of Cincinnati, Fountain Square, recently underwent a $42 million (€31,852,117) reconstruction to encompass an open accessible plaza, new water features, a new two-story plaza restaurant, and state-of-the-art technology, including a large video screen to support a range of live programming on the square's main stage. The Fountain Square redevelopment — with its total renovation of the underground garage — anchors a new district, which contains retail, dining, and entertainment. The renovation was financed by a $4 million (€3,030,321) city of Cincinnati grant, leveraged by $38 million (€28,799,768) in additional private investment. Property owners surrounding Fountain Square have pledged an estimated $70 million (€53,047,521) in additional private investment to redevelop the Fountain Square District, covering interior/exterior facade improvements and the development of more than 213,000 square feet (19,788 sq m) of new and renovated retail space.

Two blocks west of Fountain Square, the $135 million (€102,266,829) expansion and renovation of the Duke Energy Center — completed last June — now allows Cincinnati's convention center to accommodate 75 percent of the existing U.S. convention and meeting market. Events held at the redesigned Duke Energy Center are expected to generate an estimated incremental increase of $122 million (€92,418,912) annually in direct and indirect spending for the Cincinnati area economy. Demonstrating continued growth and vitality for the Cincinnati hospitality industry, convention attendance reached a five-year high at 228,282 in 2005. In addition, in 2006 the region hosted 156 meetings, translating into 122,737 hotel rooms, and booked 163,194 hotel room nights for future years, which was a 7.8 percent increase over 2005.

Since 2003, investment in the Duke Energy Center has been instrumental in helping the hotels in Hamilton County experience increases in occupancy of 2.2 percent, in the average room rate of 12.6 percent, and in lodging tax revenue of 14.9 percent. Downtown hotels also are investing $16.5 million (€12,496,771) in significant renovations to leverage the new convention center and Fountain Square District.

A block east of Fountain Square, a new Government Square has come online. The hub of the city's bus fleet recently underwent a major $9.3 million (€7,043,589) renovation to enhance accessibility for people with disabilities, and to improve bus transfers and safety.

All this recent development in the city center seems to be resonating with a new breed of downtown resident. Approximately 500 new downtown dwellers moved into newly constructed or renovated condos in 2006, bringing the center city residential population to more than 7,000. Currently, 860 residential units in the urban core are under construction with an additional 215 units breaking ground this year. The downtown apartment market remains in high demand with a 92 percent average occupancy rate.

As far as office space, downtown Cincinnati leads the three-state region in total square footage, and has the lowest vacancy rate compared with the other regional submarkets. The year 2006 closed with a 14.2 percent overall downtown vacancy rate for all office classes.

Representing 33 percent of the region's Class A office space, Cincinnati's downtown office space is renting for $20.20 (€16.78) per square foot, or $238.22 (€180.31) per square meter, leading most of the region and comparing favorably with other similar U.S. markets. Across the three-state, 15-county region, the average quoted rate for Class A office space is $17.21 (€13.11) per square foot, or $186.26 (€140.95) per square meter.

Downtown Cincinnati recently added 180,000 square feet (16,723 sq m) of Class A office space and a new 680-space parking garage to the central business district with 303 Broadway at Queen City Square — the first Class A office building to be built in the central business district in more than a decade. In addition, significant office building renovations are currently underway at 580 Building, 525 Vine, and the Chemed Center.

Across the Ohio River, northern Kentucky is providing inspiration with a multitude of office towers, hotels, floating riverboat restaurants, pubs, and city residences. Chief

among the attractions is Newport on the Levee, a $210 million (€159,078,733) shopping and entertainment complex that draws 6 million people annually. It includes a 20-screen movie theater, the Shadowbox Cabaret, the Funny Bone Comedy Club, GameWorks, and more than a dozen restaurants — all within an urban mall located along the Ohio River.

Complementing the adjoining Newport Aquarium and Levee restaurants and shops is Riverfront West, Covington, Kentucky's collection of restaurants and offices a short distance down river overlooking the Cincinnati skyline. Anchoring the area is the $31 million (€23,482,362) Northern Kentucky Convention Center, which includes adjacent hotels and offices. Nearby, Roebling Row — an expansive rowhouse-style building with 86 apartments — offers panoramic views of the city.

The ever-quickening pace of development on both sides of the river is expected to reach new heights this summer with the completion of the Ascent at Roebling's Bridge, a $40 (€30,005,982) million, 21-floor condominium complex, designed by internationally acclaimed architect Daniel Libeskind.

Connecting the north and south shorelines of the Ohio River is the northern hemisphere's first climbable bridge, the Purple People Bridge Climb, a $3 million (€2,271,587), "over-the-top" attraction that allows climbers to stand 15 stories above the river — with the Cincinnati skyline as the backdrop — and ring a large, ceremonial brass bell cast by the Verdin Co., a world-class brass and clock manufacturer based in Cincinnati.

Connecting the north and south banks is the nation's first interstate Wi-Fi hotspot, joining the assets of three cities in two states with one virtual Internet bridge that spans more than 25 million square feet (2,322,575 sq m) with free wireless access. The riverfront hotspot — which makes it possible "to surf the Ohio River" — was proposed by an all-volunteer Wi-Fi initiative, Lily Pad, driven by young professionals, and made possible by the sponsorship of Time Warner Cable Business Class.

For Teresa Hoelle, a volunteer for Lily Pad, this urban core renaissance initiative and the progressive and inclusive thinking shown by community and business leaders are the principal reasons why she has decided to stay in the region and help combat "brain drain," a major issue confronting Midwest cities of Cincinnati's size and stature.

"Cincinnati's revitalization is as much about heart and soul as it is about bricks and mortar," says Hoelle, a member of the region's new young professional leadership group, C-Change. "It's inspiring to be part of the rebuilding of a great American city in the midst of such significant transformation."

CHAPTER 12

Denver Uses Culture to Stimulate Private Development

Cynthia L. Kemper

Denver's $32 million Museum Residences, a condominium project designed as an architectural counterpoint to the new Denver Art Museum's Frederic C. Hamilton Building, is expected to help rejuvenate the surrounding downtown neighborhood. The new development is part of a complex public/private venture that not only helped Denver's emerging ideals take concrete form, but also opened the floodgates of controversy and debate in a city still struggling to realize a new modern identity.

The $110 million, 146,000-square-foot (13,500-sq-m) Hamilton wing—which opened this past October, and was made possible by a $62.5 million bond initiative approved by Denver voters in 1999—evolved from an idea catalyzed by museum director Lewis Sharp, who had long envisioned building a world-class iconic structure to expand exhibition space for the city's extensive art collection.

In early 2000, Denver Mayor Wellington E. Webb convened an oversight group led by Jennifer Moulton, the city's director of planning and community development, who passed away during the project's planning

phase. Joined by Sharp, the Denver Art Museum's board of directors, and the project's design council, the group initiated a public, international design competition to ensure that the museum provided a "Bilbaoesque" iconography for metropolitan Denver's growing arts district. In June 2000, architect Daniel Libeskind was chosen. "All three of the architect finalists responded very responsibly and thoughtfully, but Libeskind really captivated us," says Sharp. "His energy and optimism were a perfect fit for what the city of Denver was trying to accomplish, and he has exceeded our expectations."

Within the month, Libeskind, now based out of Studio Daniel Libeskind in New York City, sought out architect Brit Probst, a partner at Denver-based Davis Partnership Architects, with an invitation to join him in a 50–50 joint venture to oversee the project's architectural design, technical development, and construction.

The design team's intense planning process—which began in Berlin, where Libeskind was working on the Jewish Museum Berlin, then moved to Denver, where the joint design

Originally published as "Art on View," *Urban Land*, Vol. 66, No. 5, May 2007, by the Urban Land Institute, Washington, D.C. Reprinted with permission of the publisher.

team is still based today — immediately catalyzed a series of additions to the project's scope. Central to the conversation were extensive in-depth planning studies exploring ways to activate the surrounding Golden Triangle neighborhood and the urban fabric.

A nonnegotiable element in the project was a 980-space parking garage to accommodate the museum expansion and replace one and a half square blocks of annexed surface lots. Because placing the garage underground would increase project costs by 50 percent, an above-grade solution was chosen — a decision that ultimately opened the door for the 125,000-square-foot (11,600-sq-m) Museum Residences development, and the complex program of public/private projects still in the process of being developed today. (See "Cultural Assets: Museums Turn to Mixed Uses," September 2006, page 140.)

"From the beginning, the strategy was to make this more than a single building," explains Probst, whose collaboration with Libeskind continues in all aspects of the project's design and construction. "We wanted to create a thriving mixed-use environment to rejuvenate the Golden Triangle neighborhood and connect important parts of the city that were separated by a gulf of asphalt and parking lots. Our planning phase focused on creating a sense of tightness on both sides of the site, surrounded by a mix of uses complementary to a seven-day-a-week, 24-hour-a-day activity pattern."

The genesis of the interrelationship between the new Hamilton wing and the Museum Residences buildings was the six-story Cultural Center Garage — the parking structure located just east of the museum on a site more visually prominent than that of the museum itself, notes Probst. "To best deal with that prominence, we knew we had to face it with active, inviting, and architecturally sensitive uses that would allow us to create a certain level of congestion or density, and a more exciting urban condition," he says.

Adding to the project complexity, the land and all but one floor of the parking garage are owned by the city, while the Museum Residences encasing the garage — as well as a boutique hotel and condominium tower planned for Phase II of the project — are owned and financed privately.

"The garage was a vital part of this strategy, not only because of the lost parking it would replace, but because it provided the skeleton for the entire project, which would eventually wrap three of its four sides," explains George Thorn, president of Denver-based Mile High Development, and one of only two private developers who responded to the city's original request for proposals. "The garage would also provide a home for much of the mechanical and electrical infrastructure that would support the private development. But the very fact that private development was being incorporated into a public parking facility increased our financing challenges exponentially," adds Thorn.

At the time, development of a public/private parking garage — to be faced with high-end condominiums and retail space, and overseen by a heavily invested city — was of little interest to potential local or national financial partners. In fact, the project was declined by as many as 15 potential investment partners during Thorn's two-year search for financing.

The project's insertion of the first luxury, mixed-use player into the still-nascent middle-market Golden Triangle neighborhood and the severe downturn in Denver's real estate market after 9/11 were two key concerns, he says. Because the project could not move forward without an equity partner, regardless of Thorn's commitment, the architectural team continued its design development process on the basis of hope that funding eventually would be found.

"All of my counterparts said I was crazy and that it would never work," reflects Thorn. "The conventional wisdom was that no one would want to live on the plaza. Most developers think you need a traditional streetscape with ground-floor development to succeed."

Thorn figured the location would work because "where else in Denver can you be in the company of world-class architecture?" he says. "Jennifer Moulton was really the only one who 'got it.' Fortunately, she found a soulmate in Daniel, and she had the backing of the mayor," comments Thorn, also developer of the $200 million Wellington E. Webb Municipal Office Building and the $100 million Colorado Center.

An encounter in Steamboat Springs was the break everyone involved in the project was waiting for. Thorn met with William P. Butler, founder and chief executive officer of Cincinnati-based financial investment and services firm Corporex, shortly after Butler had established an office in Denver. "We were looking over several opportunities at the time," reflects Butler. "I realized that other developers and financiers were skeptical of the Museum Residences project, so I studied the plans closely and felt that Corporex could [address] the ... cost-containment challenges." Butler struck a deal with Thorn on the spot.

"Obviously, there were big risks to us," he says. "But, Corporex wanted to make a splash in the Denver metro area [and] there was no better place to do it. More than economics, we were motivated to a great extent by the challenge itself. Our engineers managed to reduce the first bid costs by 35 percent even as units were selling for 25 percent more than George's original pro forma — a home run for both partners. We're now looking to Phase II — a project twice the size of the first."

Denver-based Kim Koehn, president and chief operating officer of Corporex Colorado, notes that his firm's oversight achieved significant cost reductions by changing some building system and design details that took nothing away from the ultimate impact of the structure, but made it easier to build. Examples include switching from steel to concrete when steel prices began to soar, and simplifying the geometry slightly to make the building interiors more livable.

"From the beginning, our priority was to frame a public space in a profound way — to create a dynamic environment that ties Denver's Cultural District to the Golden Triangle neighborhood through an activated pedestrian plaza at its core," says Probst. "By designing a series of inside and outside spaces, with a complementary architectural signature, a powerful dialogue was initiated between the Museum Residences and the iconic work of museum architecture immediately across from it," he explains.

"The condominium buildings are essentially glass boxes, with the greatest amount of transparency and activity possible in the facade," says Probst. "Because the museum has very complex forms, we also integrated a few inventive forms on the condominiums so they would belong in the same vocabulary, yet not be as aggressive as the museum itself. The Hamilton wing and Museum Residences were also designed as two bookends framing the central public space. Colocation with important cultural facilities can indeed be a marketable attraction. Thirty to 40 percent of residents bought because of the architecture; in fact it surprised everyone that the first 25 units sold were all facing the plaza and new Hamilton wing," notes Probst. "Although Libeskind's signature on the project was central to its success, the sales were not merely because of the signature architect," he maintains.

"Architecture matters," concludes Probst. "Value comes from a lot of different areas, but architecture aspires to create that value in a way that the public can participate in, enjoy, and react to — and, in the case of the Museum Residences, be willing to pay to live in," he explains. "A building needs to add to the public domain and reinforce what people find delightful about living and working in Denver, or in a particular neighborhood. People are beginning to realize that architecture can be a central element in establishing that value," adds Probst.

"We achieved among the highest prices ever in our market," says Thorn. "With an initial pro forma of $400 a square foot [$4,300 per sq m], our average sales price of $500 [$5,400 per sq m] exceeded all expectations." Resales of the condominiums have "helped us see what buyers will pay for great architecture," he notes. "Libeskind's name — his image — meant a lot to potential buyers."

Probst agrees. "It's all too easy to set the bar too low in our private developments and not understand the lasting value that can accrue to extraordinarily well-done projects."

CHAPTER 13

Des Moines, Other Cities, Use Libraries to Promote Their Urban Centers

Urban Libraries Council

Economic and physical development often go hand in hand. A variety of place-based strategies have long been at the core of public-private economic development endeavors. Some strategies attempt to create destinations with constant activity by combining office complexes, restaurants, retail spaces, and housing. Other strategies feature cultural districts, which include performance venues, arts organizations, individual artists and arts-based businesses within a larger business or residential district. Still others focus less on buildings more on integrating services and amenities, such as public markets and squares. Many strategies have used public facility investments to catalyze new development and stabilize existing residential neighborhoods and downtowns, increasing property values and commercial tax revenues.

While the case study research for this report was focused primarily on library contributions to human resource development strategies, many examples of how public library facilities act as catalysts for place-based economic development surfaced, and will be highlighted in this chapter. While library facilities are widely recognized as adding safety or amenity value to neighborhoods, public libraries are playing a role in a wide variety of commercial and mixed-use developments as well.

Public Libraries Contribute to Physical Development

- Central libraries as downtown attractions
- Integrating branch libraries into commercial areas
- Building more economically vibrant urban spaces
- Libraries as players in mixed-use developments
- Creating library hybrids

Central libraries as downtown attractions. Center city library developments have received a tremendous amount of attention in recent years. Designed by some of the leading architects around the world, these multi-million dollar facilities have contributed consid-

Originally published as "Public Libraries and the Power of Place" in *Making Cities Stronger: Public Library Contributions to Local Economic Development*, January 2007, by the Urban Institute, Washington, D.C. Reprinted with permission of the publisher.

erable visual appeal to downtown business districts. These dramatic new buildings have added another, less talked about feature as well. They have created vibrant public spaces that attract a steady stream of visitors to areas that often lie dormant after business hours and during weekends. In city after city, new downtown libraries are followed by an immediate and sustained boost in circulation and library use. The Denver Public Library, which finished the expansion of its downtown library in 1995, saw the number of daily visits double from 1,500 to 3,000. The Seattle Public Library, which opened in 2004, draws 8,000 visitors a day, twice the circulation of the old central library facility. Although the Des Moines Public Library just opened the doors of its new Central Library in April 2006, increased demand is already apparent, and they have increased the hours of operation to provide greater accessibility for downtown library customers. While the specific economic impact of the new downtown libraries will certainly vary from city to city, one point is certainly clear: new central city libraries are now attracting visitors to downtown areas in a manner reminiscent of the heyday of the downtown department store.

Integrating branch libraries into commercial areas. Whether located in malls or inserted into corner shopping strips, public libraries are finding a complementary niche by providing a public service in commercial areas. Mall libraries, which in some locations may be open up to 80 hours per week, make books, computers, and other resources accessible to those who may not consider going to a traditional library. For some library systems the mall locations do not function as full service branches but rather as portals into the library system, offering a fraction of the services and amenities that would be available at a branch library. However, some systems are inserting full service branches into malls and shopping strips that until recently were strictly commercial. One of the larger examples of a full service mall branch can be found in Indianapolis.

Indianapolis–Marion County Public Library's Glendale Branch features a full service branch library in the Glendale shopping mall. The 33,000 square foot Glendale Branch library, which opened in October 2000, commands the space of an anchor tenant, with its own dramatic outdoor mall entrance. The Glendale branch library features 37 public computers with Internet access, standard office software and printing services, free wireless Internet access, copy machines, public meeting rooms, and laptops for in-house use and self-checkout.

Building more economically vibrant urban spaces. Thoughtful placement of public library branches can catalyze urban areas in need of economic boost. The Memphis Public Library's South Branch, once located in a quiet residential neighborhood in the south side of Memphis bordering the state of Mississippi, moved to a larger facility located in a commercial shopping strip in an industrial section of town that had lost a considerable number of jobs in the past decade. Six of the eight storefronts were vacant when the library moved in. Now, four years later, the shopping strip is completely full. Though the South Branch library is not the only factor in the revitalization of the South Mall commercial strip, it is reasonable to conclude that local businesses reap a "spin-off" benefit from the 100,000 visitors that stop by the library each year.

Libraries as players in mixed-use developments. Library leaders and private developers across the country are beginning to notice distinct advantages to incorporating public libraries into mixed use, retail and residential areas. In the small town of Atascadero, at the foot of the rapidly growing wine country in San Luis Obispo County, California, a unique partnership has emerged between the San Luis Obispo City-County Public Library and a private local developer. The library, which had sorely needed a new building, has agreed to secure a central area in the new Colony Square development for its new Atascadero branch library. For its part, the library will get a new facility in a more centralized and convenient part of town. The partnership provides the developer, who had tried unsuccessfully to attract two different national bookstore chains, with a steady, long-term tenant. Retailers that are moving into the Colony's 140,000 square foot development are excited about the library partnership because the library functions as an anchor tenant by bringing a considerable amount of foot traffic to the area, without directly competing for commercial sales.

Another example of public libraries being integrated into mixed residential and commercial developments, at a slightly larger scale, can be seen approximately 20 miles north of Washington, D.C. Rockville Town Square is an ambitious $352 million dollar redevelopment effort in the old city center of Rockville, Maryland. The new Towne Square which will offer 644 condominiums, 180,000 square feet of retail and restaurant space, a cultural arts building and a football-field-size town square, will also be the home of the Rockville Regional Library, the largest library in the Montgomery County system. According to Ross Development and Investment, the developer of Rockville Town Square, the housing units are selling briskly, with the cost of some surpassing the $1 million mark. Key amenities identified by early buyers are the mix of shops, ease of access to public transportation and the new 100,000-square-feet state-of-the-art regional library.

Creating library hybrids. Joint-use facilities that combine public libraries with other community amenities are becoming more common in cities and towns across the country. In some cities public libraries are physically part of a local public elementary or middle school. In other communities, public libraries share space with community recreation centers or senior care facilities. Some joint ventures are borne out of economic necessity, as a way to leverage limited development resources or maximize the use of a publicly-owned property. In other communities, joint-use facilities are a product of a deliberate community planning process. The Cleveland Heights–University Heights Public Library — Main Library/Cultural Arts Campus is an example of the latter. After a lengthy community planning process the Cleveland Heights and University Heights Library decided to purchase an old youth services building across the street from its present location and embark on a rebuilding effort that would result in two new buildings connected by a second story walkway. The new library, which will consist of a program building on one side of the street — and a library service building on the other, will meet needs of area residents through expanded library services and targeted programming delivered in partnership with local agencies. The programming building of the new library will house after-school programs, an expanded children's space with a computer area, separate space for teens with a homework center, additional computers and a seating which can be rearranged for specialized programming. The new facility will also feature space for theatrical productions, classes, and programs for children and adults in partnership with a local theater company and an art gallery and studio space for local artists.

Outcomes: How Libraries Contribute to Place-Based Economic Strategies

- Public library facilities are versatile, attractive components in a wide variety of developments — downtown, residential, mixed-use, commercial, and joint-use service sites
- Public libraries in mixed-use and residential developments contribute to safety and quality of life
- Long term tenancy of public libraries reduces some of the financial risk associated with building mixed-use developments
- Public libraries attract foot traffic and can

serve the anchor tenant function in commercial areas without directing competing with local businesses.

Strategies for Broadening the Impact of Libraries in Physical Developments

Demonstrate that public and private services can work together in mutually supportive ways. When voters in local governments are asked to support referenda for libraries, the appeal is rarely supported by a discussion of the potential economic development contributions the library can provide. Integrating libraries into different types of developments keeps resources and services visible and accessible, and the amenity value of public libraries high.

Be proactive in identifying the ways in which public libraries can complement local development plans. Mixed use developments are relatively new economic development tools. Some economic development professionals may be unfamiliar with new development models that combine housing, retail and public services, including public libraries.

Provide data to change developer perceptions. Have library financial and use statistics ready to define the ways in which libraries may contribute to the financial success of prospective projects. Financiers tend to view mixed-use development as complex and difficult. Library financial information speaks to stability of rent and use statistics speak to the all important traffic that benefits adjacent retail businesses.

Understand some of the challenges inherent in shared buildings. Integrating public library facilities into private sector developments can present a number of challenges, because of the different approaches that local governments and private developers bring to the building process. For example, when the city or county wants to develop a civic proj-

ect, architects plan for a 100-year life span, while private residential and mixed-use architects often plan at a different standard. One of the key elements in making this type of partnership work is to work through these different approaches in the early phase of the project. Even when building public joint-use facilities, such as schools and libraries, there are many issues best addressed in the design phase, such as access and security.

Conclusion

While this chapter only touches on the role of public libraries as catalysts for physical development, the past twenty years have witnessed an incredibly wide range of place-based development efforts in which public libraries play a supporting role. In major city centers like Seattle, WA, Des Moines, IA, Minneapolis, MN, Salt Lake City, UT, and Jacksonville, FL, multi-million dollar central libraries manage to make a considerable mark on the look and feel of downtown areas. In inner and outer suburbs, a plethora of new branch libraries and regional facilities are increasingly being integrated into commercial strips and malls, contributing the valued commodity of foot traffic to local businesses, anchoring redevelopment, and providing quality of life amenities to neighborhoods. More recently, developers of mixed-use projects have begun to incorporate public libraries into the initial design along side retail and residential spaces, adding significant public amenity value to burgeoning commercial, office, and residential corridors.

The fact that public libraries fit seamlessly into these vastly different environments is a testament to the versatility of the institution and the high degree of public value it enjoys. Whether located in a center city business district, suburban commercial corridor, mall, housing or retail development, demand for new public libraries, as measured by the circulation and library use statistics, consistently exceeds expectations. One would be hard pressed to identity another public or private development that could operate on such vastly different scales in so many different settings and attract such a diverse stream of visitors and consumers.

Local economies today are in rapid transition, moving from bases of manufacturing and service industries to information and idea industries. Accompanying this transformation are a number of radical changes in preferred work skills, business and service models, local-to-global networks, and definitions of what make places "attractive." Given these changes, communities are reassessing their assets and development strategies in light of what is needed to succeed in the new and next economies.

Strategies for building a strong economic base are being realigned. Human resource strategies are coming to the fore, as jobs created in the new economy require highly educated and technologically-skilled workers. Strategies to keep a vibrant base of small business, traditionally a major source of local job creation, intact and competitive in a very mobile and global entrepreneurial environment are also emerging. Increasingly, physical development strategies are moving away from enticing outside firms with tax abatements and other incentives, to building on local strengths, mixing-up residential, commercial and cultural activities to create vibrant, high quality-of-life cities.

Public libraries are logical partners for local economic development initiatives that focus on people and quality of life. Libraries are widely available, highly regarded public institutions that provide a broad range of information services and support for diverse constituencies. In this era of economic transformation, the business of public libraries is being recast. Public access to digital information and technology is a draw for libraries. Their open structure, combined with the power of new digital collections, technology, and training, position them to help communities make the transition from manufacturing and service economies to high tech and information economies.

Public libraries build a community's capacity for economic activity and resiliency. Many families and caregivers rely on the library to provide important preschool reading and learning. Many people entering the workforce rely on libraries to get them online. Local businesses are increasingly tapping into the library's online databases to keep themselves competitive and to find synergistic new business opportunities. Library facilities often anchor downtown and commercial developments, and are attractive neighborhood amenities.

These are the essential findings uncovered by researchers from the Urban Institute, as they teamed up with the Urban Libraries Council, an association of large metropolitan public libraries, to investigate the impact of public libraries on local economic conditions. *Making Cities Stronger: Public Library Contributions to Local Economic Development* adds to a growing body of research that notes a shift in the role of public libraries — from passive, recreational reading and research institutions to active economic development agents. The study was commissioned by the Urban Libraries Council (ULC) and funded by the Bill & Melinda Gates Foundation and Geraldine R. Dodge Foundation.

Note: To purchase copies of the research publication *Making Cities Stronger*, please contact the Urban Libraries Council at (312) 676-0999 or via e-mail at info@urbanlibraries.org.

CHAPTER 14

Hartford and Other Cities Promote Computer Literacy

Urban Libraries Council

Development strategies have changed dramatically with changes in the workplace over the past ten years. The transition from manufacturing and service industry jobs to technology-based information industry jobs has been rapid. Employers in the growing high-skills sectors report continuing difficulty in finding and keeping a workforce.

New economy jobs call for higher-level skills and a willingness to pursue continuing training to stay competitive. Rapid shifts in the workplace mean that people must anticipate frequent career moves and take responsibility for their own career progression (Porter 2000). Higher wages are strongly linked to some form of post-secondary education and training. Economic self-sufficiency — the ability to support a family — requires education beyond high school.

If local communities are to succeed, they will need more workers with skill levels far beyond those seen in the average worker of the past. As new models of business, products and services continue to emerge, the worker today must continuously "retool" and adjust.

New strategies and networks for building sustained workforce participation are burgeoning, and workforce development agencies are collecting data to better understand the demand for these changing skill sets. They are experimenting with career information centers and sequences services for job-seekers. They are finding new local partners, such as community colleges and local employers, for training and education efforts. They are looking at ways to make local resources and programs more apparent, coordinated, and oriented toward long-term, continuous workforce transitions.

For many communities, the federal Workforce Investment Act of 1998 (WIA) is providing the organizing framework for consolidating development programs and integrating services locally and statewide (NCEE 1997). A cornerstone of WIA is the provision of services through comprehensive One-Stop centers that offer a range of resources pertaining to employment training and education for workers, and recruitment and training assistance for employers. Eight years after the enactment of WIA, it appears that more decisions are being made at the state and local levels, local workforce development agencies have established more formalized partnership arrangements, and there are more collaborative workforce development arrangements

Originally published as "Strategies for Workforce Participation" in *Making Cities Stronger: Public Library Contributions to Local Economic Development*, January 2007, by the Urban Institute, Washington, D.C.

with private sector partners (Barnow and King 2005). There is great variety and flexibility in current local workforce development programs (Eberts and Erickcek 2002).

In this context, public libraries have a host of new opportunities to become more actively engaged in local workforce development initiatives and networks. Indeed job information resources and specialized workforce programs in local libraries have the potential to reach a much wider group of job seekers than One-Stop centers because of their reputation as trusted, quality community information sources, their high volume of use, and their geographic distribution of facilities across the community. Public libraries cover a much broader area than WIA One-Stop centers could ever hope to service. As an example, in the six states with the highest seasonally adjusted unemployment rate in the country in July 2006, there are an average of 83 One-Stop comprehensive centers and affiliates per state compared to an average of 301 library outlets in the same group of states.

Public libraries across the country are answering the call to provide greater workforce support with enhanced job information resources, workplace literacy programs, improved technology access, and staff dedicated to employment services. Seventy-seven percent (77%) of ULC member libraries responding to the survey identified their libraries as having enhanced collections in the area of workforce development. Forty-three percent (43%) of the libraries were investing in digital resources specifically geared toward workforce support, and 31 percent of the libraries were creating web resources specifically designed for job seekers.

A significant amount of workforce development activity in local libraries centers on job search skills, basic computer instruction and workplace literacy. Ninety-two percent (92%) of the libraries answering the survey provide basic computer instruction on a regular basis (at least monthly); 50 percent of the libraries provide workplace literacy instruc-

tion; and 42 percent provide workplace literacy instruction specifically to English language learners. Most of these literacy training and other specialized workshops are provided in library facilities, though often conducted in partnership with local agencies. The section below explores some of the ways libraries are adapting to meet the needs of people navigating today's labor market.

Public Library Strategies for Workforce Development

- Creating Job Information Centers
- Expanding Access to Technology and Tech Training
- Providing Targeted Employment Outreach
- Adult Literacy Training and Community Support Centers

Job Information Centers. Many public libraries across the country are consolidating career resource materials from the shelves and online databases into user-friendly career information centers. These job centers offer resources for job searches, provide training and certification materials, and serve as information clearinghouses for job listings. Many of these centers have special staff available to provide one-on-one assistance and career development workshops. Libraries with dedicated job resource staff often provide assistance in crafting cover letters, résumés, and college and scholarship applications, as well as assessment of skills and interests for clients with little educational experience or for those holding advanced degrees. In some libraries the job information service makes referrals, suggests job listing sites, and works with counselors, community-based organizations, state employment agencies, the Department of Labor, and the Human Resources Administration to help clients realize their educational and professional goals.

Fresno County Public Library– Career Center

The Career Center at the Fresno Public Library provides an excellent example of this type of consolidation effort. In 2003 the library established its Career Center in the Central Library. The new Center provides a wide range of job and career resources in a county that has long been plagued by some of the highest rates of unemployment in the state of California. The new Career Center provides dedicated computing services, a jobs board, enhanced print and digital collections, and a dedicated career specialist/jobs librarian who provides monthly workshops covering online job search basics, building an effective résumé and job interview preparation. In addition to servicing the main library the new career services librarian provides career workshops at area branches and coordinates acquisition and purchasing of career resources for the entire system.

Expanding Access to Technology and Tech Training. Despite the rapid proliferation of home computers, public computers in libraries are still in high demand, serving as an important entry point for new technology users. A recent survey found that 70 percent of people using computers in libraries reported the library was their only way to get on a computer (Hart Research 2006). Another study reports that 95 percent of all public libraries provide some sort of public access to the Internet (Bertot and McClure 2002).

While there is increasing awareness and use of these resources in public libraries, there has been little attention given to how these resources are providing structural, often community-wide, workforce development training and support. Public libraries are providing individual users with access to technology and information resources, as well as structured technology training. From mobile labs to instructional training facilities, public libraries are providing targeted technology training, most often starting with computer basics.

Increasingly, public libraries are working with local workforce development partners, providing local residents with multiple access points for computer training. Libraries that lack staff resources to support formal trainers are entering into agreements with local workforce development agencies to provide instructors and curricula for training facilities located at the public library.

Newark Public Library — Victoria Technology Center

The Victoria Technology Center, a representative example of library training centers, opened in 1999 as part of the community NEON (NEwark Online) initiative, and features eighteen computers for training and Internet access. When classes are not provided, the stations are open to library customers. Free computer classes, which are offered in both English and Spanish, provide detailed training that ranges from computer basics to more advanced word processing and spreadsheet software training.

Targeted Employment Outreach. Libraries with sufficient resources for outreach are providing services in areas of high unemployment and need, working with local employment service agencies that lack resources to provide a full range of employment resource materials and workplace training.

Memphis Public Library — JobLINC

The JobLINC bus is a mobile jobs and career readiness center that helps job seekers locate employment opportunities by providing listings of available jobs and one-on-one assistance in conducting job searches and preparing for interviews. JobLINC provides local job listings and an employment hotline, on-site résumé preparation services, daily JOBFILE listings from the Tennessee Department of Labor and Workforce Development. The initiative began as a targeted outreach to a single neighborhood in Memphis and, due to demand, has expanded to cover the entire county. The JobLINC bus, a 35 foot bus with computers, internet access via satellite hookup, and job reference material, stops at shopping centers, social service agencies, and branch libraries throughout Memphis. The service has been so successful at connecting with residents that employers have even ridden to the bus to conduct on-the-spot interviews to hire prospective workers.

Adult Literacy Training and Community Support Centers for New Americans. Public libraries are an important entry point to community services for new Americans. Programs provided through public libraries can serve as a portal to a wide range of community resources that are vital to a family's economic self-sufficiency. Services to new Americans often involve English language classes; intergenerational literacy, foreign language GED instruction, and other basic skills training. Public libraries often serve as informal referral centers as well, directing immigrants to area support services.

Hartford (CT) Public Library — The American Place

The American Place is an adult literacy and development project serving Hartford's diverse immigrant communities. The American Place program has become an important community service for immigrants in Hartford, a city where over one hundred ethnic cultures are represented and 32 languages are spoken in the public schools. The program provides staff and resources to help people achieve their goals for secure immigration, citizenship and literacy. The program focuses on citizenship preparation, classes for English for Speakers of Other Languages (ESOL) and life-skills workshops. The program, which started as a basic computer-training course, expanded rapidly when staff realized that clients needed English language training in addition to basic computer skills. Programs are provided free of charge and include practical advice for living in the U.S.; classes for learning English; information on becoming a U.S. citizen; and instruction on how to use the library to find information on jobs, health, housing, education and other topics of interest.

Outcomes: Why Library Workforce Development Programs Make Sense

- Expanded individual, and hence, community workforce technology skills and competencies via access to technology and free computer instruction available in public libraries. These technology skills are essential to job seekers of all ages.
- Reduced barriers to employment with one-on-one services, helping job seekers research career options, identify employment opportunities, develop résumés and apply directly for jobs using new technologies.
- Reduced costs to local workforce development agencies by providing a wide range of employment information resources, access to online employment and career certification tests, and training spaces complete with computers and other technology.
- Reduced recruitment costs to employers via contributions to technology and literacy training, and facilitating connections between potential workers and employers.

Strategies for Broadening the Impact of Library Workforce Development Initiatives

Establish strong connections with area workforce development agencies. While public libraries are often aware of other workforce development agencies operating in their service area, workforce development agencies operating in their service area, workforce development agencies are often not aware of the range of programs and information resources available at the local library. Failure to establish connections between area workforce support services effectively limits the range of services available and could lead to costly and unnecessary duplication of resources. Establishing stronger partnerships with other training entities, referral sources, schools, employer associations, and the local One-Stop Career Centers will help people move more quickly from information gathering to action. Stronger institutional connections will raise awareness about the wide range of resources available at the local public library.

Build better employer connections. Creation of comprehensive employment support initiatives in public libraries requires relationships with area employers as well. While the public library will not likely serve as an employment intermediary, program and collections planning will benefit from increased focus on employer needs and standards, as well as a better understanding of the regional labor market.

Know your customers. To better understand how and why people use library career and employment resources, libraries should collect demographic and use information from customers. Data gathered from customer surveys on the needs and behaviors of people being trained or guided to information resources can then feed into decisions about program design, collection development, strategic planning, and partnerships with local agencies and employers.

Know the broader workforce outlook. Keep abreast of broader workforce trends. What are the hot employment sectors globally? Nationally? In the region? What is on the decline? Are there seasonal unemployment trends? If so, in what markets? Understanding these trends, as well as the broader informal and formal network of workforce support providers, helps provide information on how to make the library a more prominent partner, and will help share services and refine the

public library's role in building local workforce strength.

Conclusion

With rapid changes in employment markets and skills, communities are scrambling to build workforce capacity. Public libraries are contributing many resources to workforce development strategies, in concert with other community agencies, education institutions, and private sector employers. The combination of public access technology, enhanced workforce collections and training, and outreach partnerships gives public libraries a unique position as resource to community-wide workforce development efforts.

Libraries are important access points for building technology skills and competencies in communities today. Public access technology, new online resources, and targeted training on computers, job searches, and career development are benefiting both individuals and other workforce development providers.

Libraries are strengthening links between education and employment, as well as building workforce skills and participation. They are contributing training facilities and tailored instruction to a broad base of local residents. There is a great variety in the ways public libraries have developed partnerships and programs that connect job-seekers with employment training and opportunities. Targeted library services such as English language instruction, workplace literacy, and computer instruction are now routine.

Local communities are assessing their human resource base and looking for ways to continuously update workforce skills and assist career transitions. In this context, the attributes of public libraries are not going unnoticed. Public libraries, which enjoy high use rates nationwide, and are broadly distributed across metropolitan areas, are becoming increasingly engaged in local workforce support service networks. By consolidating resources in job information centers, broadening literacy training, expanding access to technology, and conducting targeted outreach to immigrant populations and technology "have nots," public libraries are providing valuable support to building local workforce and resilience.

Local economies today are in rapid transition, moving from basis of manufacturing and service industries to information and idea industries. Accompanying this transformation are a number of radical changes in preferred work skills, business and service models, local-to-global networks, and definitions of what make places "attractive." Given these changes, communities are reassessing their assets and development strategies in light of what is needed to succeed in the new and next economies.

Strategies for building a strong economic base are being realigned. Human resource strategies are coming to the fore, as jobs created in the new economy require highly educated and technologically-skilled workers. Strategies to keep a vibrant base of small business, traditionally a major source of local job creation, intact and competitive in a very mobile and global entrepreneurial environment are also emerging. Increasingly, physical development strategies are moving away from enticing outside firms with tax abatements and other incentives, to building on local strengths, mixing-up residential, commercial and cultural activities to create vibrant, high quality-of-life cities.

Public libraries are logical partners for local economic development initiatives that focus on people and quality of life. Libraries are widely available, highly regarded public institutions that provide a broad range of information services and support for diverse constituencies. In this era of economic transformation, the business of public libraries is being recast. Public access to digital information and technology is a draw for libraries. Their open structure, combined with the power of new digital collections, technology, and training, position them to help communities make the transition from manufacturing and service economies to high tech and information economies.

Public libraries build a community's capacity for economic activity and resiliency. Many families and caregivers rely on the library to provide important preschool reading and learning. Many people entering the workforce rely on libraries to get them online. Local businesses are increasingly tapping into the library's online databases to keep themselves competitive and to find synergistic new business opportunities. Library facilities often anchor downtown and commercial developments, and are attractive neighborhood amenities.

These are the essential findings uncovered by researchers from the Urban Institute, as they teamed up with the Urban Libraries Council, an association of large metropolitan public libraries, to investigate the impact of public libraries on local economic conditions. *Making Cities Stronger: Public Library Contributions to Local Economic Development* adds to a growing body of research that notes a shift in the role of public libraries — from passive, recreational reading and research institutions to active economic development agents. The study was commissioned by the Urban Libraries Council (ULC) and funded by the Bill & Melinda Gates Foundation and Geraldine R. Dodge Foundation.

Note: To purchase copies of the research publication *Making Cities Stronger*, please contact the Urban Libraries Council at (312) 676-0999 or via e-mail at info@urbanlibraries.org.

CHAPTER 15

Germantown Public Officials Save Their Library

Patrick Lawton

When faced with a problem, accept it as a challenge and then pursue the opportunities it presents. That's an attitude that the city of Germantown, Tennessee (population 41,000), followed when county government cut off operating funds for the suburban community's public library. The result is an independent library, managed by professionals at a lower cost and with expanded services.

The problem originated during debate over Shelby County's proposed budget for FY'04. For many years, county government paid for library services for Germantown and other suburban cities around Memphis. The libraries were operated as branches of the Memphis Shelby County Public Library and Information Center (MSCPLIC).

In a budget crunch, the county decided to phase out library funding over a five-year period, leaving it to each local government to pick up the difference and, ultimately, the entire cost of operating its library. The suburban mayors persuaded the Shelby County Commission to give them a one-year reprieve to plan for the transition.

How Do We Pay?

As Germantown began looking at how it would pay for its share beginning in FY'05 and the years beyond, its Board of Mayor and Aldermen and its administrative staff agreed on the challenge: to provide the highest quality services to the community in the most efficient manner possible.

City staff formed an internal committee to thoroughly review the existing library operation and explore all options to deliver service to the customers at the heavily used library, built in 1997 and owned by the city. The committee identified three options to operate the library: (1) contract with MSCPLIC, (2) operate the library in-house as a city library, or (3) contract with a private management company.

Exploring the first option, the committee began a dialogue with MSCPLIC to determine the current cost of operating the Germantown Branch Library. The answer appeared elusive, as Germantown was first given a figure of $1,049,857. After the city questioned MSCPLIC, the figure increased to $1,089,426 — nearly $40,000 more than the

Originally published as "A Challenge with a Happy Ending," *Public Management*, Vol. 87, No. 9, October 2005, by the International City/County Management Association, Washington, D.C. Reprinted with permission of the publisher.

initial quote. There was growing concern from Germantown and the other suburb communities on their ability to obtain accurate and definitive numbers from MSCPLIC.

In September 2003, a meeting was held with Shelby County Mayor A. C. Wharton and staff, MSCPLIC representatives, and the mayors and/or representatives from several of the affected cities. Mayor Wharton formed a committee of the county finance director, a MSCPLIC representative, and a representative from each of the suburbs to determine how much it cost MSCPLIC to run the branches. After several meetings, MSCPLIC issued yet another set of new figures for annual operational costs for each library.

Germantown's new tab was $1,561,632, a staggering increase of nearly 50 percent over what was first quoted. The other localities also received substantial increases. Not only did the MSCPLIC budget include much higher costs than were anticipated but service levels were cut (fewer hours of operation and less spending on materials and automation). Over and above costs directly incurred at the library branch, Germantown's share of system administrative costs weighed in around 40 percent of the total expenses.

While waiting for a cost quote from MSCPLIC, Germantown was checking on the other options. City officials visited several libraries of similar size and operation, reviewing their budgets and the scope of their services. They discovered that it was probably possible to increase services and hours of operation for substantially less than MSPLIC quoted.

Another Option?

At the direction of the board, the city sent a request for proposal for operating the Germantown library to possible vendors and to MSCPLIC. For comparison purposes, the city's research and budget staff developed a budget consistent with goals set by the library committee — goals that emerged from looking for opportunities.

The criteria were framed in fundamental questions: Who could deliver the best services and materials to the citizens of Germantown? What would allow input by the Board of Mayor and Aldermen, city staff and citizens regarding library services, hours of operation, collection development, and programming? How could the vendor provide exceptional service in the most efficient manner?

Extensive review by staff and the research and budget team led to a recommendation to contract with Library Systems & Services, LLC (LSSI), a private library management firm. LSSI's proposal provided Germantown with more services and expertise for less cost, and put the community in control of its library. The MSCPLIC proposal, offering less service, came in at about $500,000 more than the LSSI bid.

The city concluded that LSSI had the experience and qualifications to transition the existing library from a traditional model of branch service to a contemporary community model. The new model had capacity to expand library services, including longer hours of operation, more spending on community-preferred materials, and greater automation. It also accommodated a broader funding base, not just from taxes but also from additional revenue-generating initiatives.

Even as the city moved toward a decision in the spring of 2004, Shelby County was revising the phase-out plan from four years to two years. The accelerated pullout dropped the expected subsidy of $2.3 million over four years to $933,000 over two years. Less than two weeks into FY'05, elected officials appointed a library board and approved a three-year contract with LSSI; the new library board immediately concurred on the contract.

A Problem, a Challenge, an Opportunity

The problem-challenge-opportunity attitude resurfaced the next day and in the weeks to come. The abrupt departure of MSCPLIC staff left the library without personnel, no phone or computer system, and no access to the inventory database. The city closed the library until a new team and cataloging system could be put in place. MSCPLIC voided all library cards belonging to Germantown residents, preventing them from borrowing books from any other Memphis or Shelby County libraries. Eventually, a lawsuit filed by Germantown residents (Lawton v. the City of Memphis) led to the MSCPLIC allowing Germantown residents to purchase a library card for $20.

For the next three weeks, city of Germantown staff, a multitude of volunteers, and LSSI staff worked to inventory, paint, refurbish, reorganize, and redesign areas of the library. As technical obstacles loomed, such as the lack of an accurate database, city officials and LSSI staff huddled to devise solutions. The professional management firm offered a team of experts to handle the many complex issues specific to a library operation.

"We refused to be bogged down by the conversion problems," recalls Mayor Sharon Goldsworthy. "Every time we had to deal with something unexpected or a decision that needed to be made quickly, we shifted into the 'challenge' mode. As an example, fresh wall paint left a couple long gallery-like walls clean but devoid of art. A city employee was sent to snap photos of Germantown residents of all ages and in familiar locations. The photos were enlarged to poster size and hung on the walls. They not only brought great color and life to the spaces, they sent a message that this library was people-centered, focused on community and Germantown."

The problem-challenge-opportunity attitude resurfaced in the weeks to come. The abrupt departure of MSCPLIC staff left the library without personnel, no phone or computer system, and no access to the inventory database. The city closed the library until a new team and cataloging system could be put in place.

Since reopening August 4, 2004, the Germantown Community Library has broadly improved service and expanded opportunities for its customers. The policy-making library board has made library cards available to everyone — for free. So far, 17,000 cards have been issued. Here are other positive changes:

- For the first time, the library is open on Sunday, increasing hours of operation from 60 to 65 hours a week. Sunday is now one of the busiest days.
- The library board is composed of committed, enthusiastic Germantown residents. Under MSCPLIC, Germantown had no representatives on the library board. Previously, Germantown had no say in how the library was operated. The library board now gives direct input regarding the library's collection, activities, and services.
- Before the change, MSCPLIC provided minimal accountability to city officials, although the city was annually providing $150,000 for collection acquisition. LSSI is directly accountable to the library board and city officials.
- Although managed contractually, the city acknowledges and involves the library director, Dr. Sue Loper, as it would a city department director. The relationship encourages cross-departmental collaboration, especially between the library and parks and recreation functions.
- The city's former library commission (an advisory and fund-raising group) is merging with the old branch's Friends of the Library organization, joining efforts in advocacy and fundraising as Germantown Friends of the Library. A Library Foundation (501c3) is being organized for major gift solicitation and the pursuit of grants.
- The community is pleased and supportive of the library's fresh appearance, knowledgeable and friendly staff, expanded collection, and the Sunday hours. On average, more than 1,000 customers walk through the doors each day.

"For all that we've accomplished in just over a year, we view our library as a continuing work in progress," says Mayor Goldsworthy. "Information is dynamic and so are the challenges to present it. We expect and anticipate perpetual change in what our customers want and how we can best deliver it to them.

"Historically, public libraries are managed as a public entity. When we accepted the reality of paying the bill with city tax dollars, we knew we wanted to be making the decisions about how the library would operate," she continues. "We challenged ourselves to not take the routine pathway but to explore all possibilities and seek opportunities to emerge as a far better library."

The city was able to absorb its accelerated share of costs in FY'05. The FY'06 budget was more challenging, as the county's final contribution fell to 25 percent of the library's operational cost. City officials produced a tight library spending plan, trimmed general fund expenditures, and trimmed them again to avoid a property tax increase. "In FY'07, we'll be on our own," the mayor explains. "We'll need more revenue, so we're well engaged in looking at all the opportunities: foundation fundraising, perhaps a coffee shop franchise, fees for certain services, and others."

CHAPTER 16

Indianapolis Uses Libraries to Revitalize Neighborhoods

Anne Jordan

Seattle has long cultivated its reputation as a progressive and literate city. So it was quite a civic embarrassment when, in 1994, a $155 million bond measure — to finance a new central library as well as improvements to some of the system's 22 branches — fell three points short of the 60 percent needed for approval.

This defeat came at a time when library referenda were experiencing great success around the county, and major cities from San Francisco and Denver to Chicago and Cleveland were opening bold new main libraries.

Soon, however, Seattle had a new mayor, Paul Schell, and a new library director, Deborah L. Jacobs, who quickly pushed libraries to the top of the administration's agenda. For months, Jacobs spent as many as four evenings a week attending meetings in all of Seattle's neighborhoods, listening to residents express their library-related hopes and dreams. The concerns turned out to be less about the cost to taxpayers than about how the spending would be allocated: People felt that the emphasis on erecting an impressive central library would shortchange the existing branches out in the neighborhoods.

In 1998, a retooled "Libraries for All" initiative went on the ballot with a price tag of $196.4 million — at that time, the largest single bond issue for librarians in U.S. history. This time, $66.8 million was set aside for the branch libraries, nearly double the amount in the earlier proposal. The second measure passed with 72 percent of the vote.

The commitment is being kept. This fall, when Seattle breaks ground for its new central library, it already will have celebrated the grand re-opening of two branches in low-income neighborhoods. Altogether, 26 new or upgraded libraries are slated for completion by 2006.

Seattle isn't the only city where branch libraries are turning out to have surprising political appeal. Contrary to predictions of their demise in an era of electronic media and mega-bookstores, libraries in almost every metropolitan area are thriving on the changes of the past decade: a huge influx of immigrants; networked technology that gives even the tiniest storefront libraries access to materials from around the world; and the disappearance of other community integrators — groceries, banks, post offices and schools — from the urban landscape. Branch libraries are becoming hybrid institutions that not only offer books and information but foster the social,

Originally published as "Branching Out," *Governing*, Vol. 14, No. 13, October 2001, by Congressional Quarterly Inc., Washington, D.C. Reprinted with permission of the publisher.

cultural and even economic vitality of neighborhoods.

The image of the library as a quiet, scholarly place has given way to that of a "neighborhood living room or front porch — a place where everybody in the community can get together and connect with each other," says Wayne Disher, a branch manager in San Jose and past chairman of the Public Library Association's branch libraries committee. In a growing number of places, it's a literal living room as well as a figurative one. The new 29,000-square-foot Glendale branch in Indianapolis, for example, has a lounge area with a big-screen TV, overstuffed chairs and a fireplace — not to mention a coffee shop.

While libraries have always tried to be welcoming places for all ages and races, they are moving toward "a little bit more comfortable environment conducive to today's lifestyles," Disher notes. "That may even include food and drink, or a space where kids are being as loud and wild and crazy as can be." Not everyone is happy about such changes, but it is clear that branch libraries are responding to their customers' interests and demands in order to remain relevant. Many of them are paying as much attention to the number of people who come in their doors — for whatever reason — as they are to the number of books and other materials that go out.

For more than a decade, the Queens Borough Public Library in New York, with its 62 branches, has had the highest annual circulation of any library system in the country. Last year, 17.2 million items were checked out to 16.9 million customers, and more than half a million people participated in nearly 28,000 programs there. The standard library fare — poetry readings, computer training and puppet shows — is only the beginning in Queens. The 30- to 40-page monthly schedule of programs for adults and children include jewelry-making, yoga, defensive-driving courses, science experiments, cooking demonstrations and asthma screenings, to name just a few.

"We really try to use the branches as a community focal point and a place of destination," says Gary E. Strong, the Queens library director. "So much of what we're trying to do is create neighborhood dialogue." That's no small task in the most ethnically diverse county in the United States. Indeed, the question these days isn't whether people are talking in the Queens library, but rather how many languages are being spoken there.

While Queens operates on a larger scale than most library systems, services similar in scope are being implemented all over the country. Indeed, as their programming has broadened to include art exhibits, concerts, film festivals and Scrabble clubs, more and more branch libraries are becoming full-fledged community centers. One of their most sought-after assets is the free meeting space that they provide for local chambers of commerce, neighborhood associations and other civic groups.

The growth in programs — along with the need to become technologically sophisticated and handicapped-accessible — has fueled a boom in the construction, renovation and expansion of both central libraries and neighborhood branches. Between 1994 and the end of 2000, *Library Journal* estimates, some 1,200 new libraries were built or expanded in the United States — at a cost of $3 billion.

A number of cities that focused on the downtown flagship library in the early 1990s have followed up with comprehensive capital improvements to branches. Since cutting the ribbon on the Harold Washington Library Center a decade ago, Chicago has spent $200 million on 39 new or renovated branch libraries; 25 more are scheduled for completion by 2005, at a cost of $100 million.

The Los Angeles Public Library, which has the largest population base of any system in the nation at 3.8 million, is also in the midst of a huge branch-construction program. In 1989, a $53 million bond issue was approved for 26 new or expanded libraries, and then in 1998, an additional $178.3 million to upgrade

32 more. The master plan calls for nine new libraries citywide for a total of 72 built, renovated and expanded by late 2004.

And last November, by a 75 percent vote, San Francisco approved a $106 million bond measure to make seismic and other structural improvements to 19 neighborhood branches, build a new branch in the Mission Bay neighborhood, and replace four old storefront libraries between 2003 and 2009.

Other cities have decided for political or logistical reasons to refurbish their branches before tackling their central library. Philadelphia is one of those. In the early 1990s, that city was having extraordinary financial difficulties. "We looked at how we could be part of the solution, rather than part of the problem," says Elliot L. Shelkrot, director of the Free Library of Philadelphia. "We knew it was important to do something in these neighborhoods. This is where the quality of life in the city could be affected the most."

So, in 1995, the library launched a fundraising campaign called "Big Change," with a goal of renovating all 52 branches. The city chipped in $25 million and an additional $35 million was raised from private individuals and corporations. Then-Mayor Edward Rendell allowed the money to be turned over to the Free Library Foundation, which oversaw a fast-tracked construction process. All but four of the branches are finished, and the system is just shy of breaking its all-time circulation record set in the 1960s, when Philadelphia had half a million more people than it does today.

Philadelphia's attention is now shifting to rehabilitation of the central library. That's also the case in Indianapolis, which is moving forward with a $103 million downtown library expansion following a $50 million effort to rebuild or renovate more than a dozen of its 21 neighborhood branches.

San Diego has been wrangling for decades over plans to build a new central library. Meanwhile, as the city sprawled, new branches were constructed in fast-growing areas, but little was done to update facilities in the older neighborhoods. Finally, this summer, the city council settled on a site for the $145 million downtown library, but also decided that the plans should include improvements to the entire system.

Seattle's Deborah Jacobs warns that any library debate about downtown versus the neighborhoods is counterproductive. "I wasn't going to allow myself to get into that," she says. Other recent recruits to the library renaissance, such as Minneapolis and Jacksonville, are taking the same approach and tackling both central and branch library projects simultaneously.

When it comes to building new libraries, "it's the opposite of NIMBY," says Los Angeles City Librarian Susan Kent. Every council member wants to have one in his or her ward, and every citizen wants one within easy walking distance.

The sense of pride and ownership that residents feel toward their branch library is something of a double-edged sword for local government. Deep reservoirs of grassroots support can quickly turn into protests against plans to relocate or consolidate facilities in an effort to operate a library system more efficiently.

In a few cities, tight finances and shifting demographics are forcing officials to make those difficult choices. Last year, the Buffalo and Erie County Public Library system explored a consultant's proposal that advocated reducing the total number of branch libraries in the county from 52 to 39. Within the city of Buffalo itself, branches would have dropped from 15 to 8. The idea was to move to fewer but bigger branches that would be open longer hours. In 22 public meetings over four months, residents resoundingly decried the consolidation proposal. In response to intense opposition from the community and its elected representatives, the library board scrapped the plan last fall.

Carla D. Hayden, director of the Enoch Pratt Free Library in Baltimore, unveiled a master plan four years ago to build a regional branch in each quadrant of the city, in addition to the 26 existing branch libraries. Shortly afterward, however, the city found itself with serious budget problems, and this summer, a frustrated Hayden announced that five branches would be shuttered on September 1. They were chosen on the basis of usage, size, condition, renovation cost, proximity to other branches and the library's ability to maintain a presence in the community.

Mayor Martin O'Malley backed Hayden's decision, but in a city where only half of the schools offer any library service at all, and where several schools and fire stations have recently been shut down, residents were outraged. The libraries "are the last sign of government" in these neighborhoods, says state Senator George W. Della, Jr., who represents a part of the city not far from the ill-fated Hollins-Payson branch library. "In this less-than-affluent neighborhood, people cherish that library. They may not have taken out many books, but they used the facility. It's a safe haven for children and seniors."

Della believes that if the library had reached out to the corporate community, some or all of the branches might have been saved. Hayden doesn't think so. "The private sector wants to do public-private partnerships to supplement and enhance services," she says, "but they do not want to replace city dollars just to keep the doors open."

Given the dire fiscal situation, Hayden says she'll be lucky to build two of the four regional libraries in the next decade. Nevertheless, construction is under way on an $8 million, 45,000-square-foot branch in Highlandtown. Supporters believe it will breathe new life into a moribund commercial district. Others are skeptical. "I never have seen a library work as a magnet for business," city council member Nicholas C. D'Adamo, Jr., wrote in a letter to the Baltimore *Sun*.

Other cities, however, have been libraries serve exactly that purpose. In Chicago, Mayor Richard M. Daley refers to them as the "heartbeat of communities" and has been championing them as people-intensive anchors in a larger, holistic approach to the redevelopment of housing, retail, offices, schools and parks in the city's 78 neighborhoods. "The Chicago Public Library," says Eleanor Jo Rodger, president of the Urban Libraries Council, "is in the Chicago business."

The city's library system has all but abandoned the practice of using leased, storefront branches — which tend to be very small and poorly suited — in favor of what Library Commissioner Mary A. Dempsey calls "freestanding 'monumental' buildings that make a bold statement about the city's commitment to these neighborhoods."

Just as Chicago's Harold Washington library spurred revitalization of the South Loop, the city's Near North branch has served as a catalyst for public- and private-sector investment in the long-blighted area around the Cabrini-Green housing project. The library's opening in 1997 has been followed by construction of a new high school, police station, park, several thousand mixed-income housing units and a shopping center that includes a large supermarket and a Starbucks. A diverse mix of people from both Cabrini-Green and the affluent lakeshore area nearby can be found in the checkout lines of both the library and the stores.

In Indianapolis, the College Avenue branch library also bridges two worlds: the Meridian-Kessler neighborhood, an affluent community with large homes on the National Register of Historic Places, and a low-income area with a history of crime and racial tension that culminated in a "mini riot" between police and the black community in 1995. At its opening, Caroline J. Farrar, executive director of the Meridian-Kessler Neighborhood Association, described the branch library as "the most outstanding asset that has come into this neighborhood in a decade."

Several miles away, on Indianapolis' North Side, is the new Glendale branch, which anchors a retail mall. In 1999, the local library was overcrowded but had no room to expand. At the same time, the owner of the city's oldest enclosed shopping center was looking for an infusion of tenants with drawing power and proposed that the library relocate there.

As library officials pondered the six-block move, 1,300 people signed a petition opposing the plan. "It would have been easy to say no. There were people who felt strongly on both sides of the issue," says Edward M. Szynaka, chief executive officer of the Indianapolis–Marion County Public Library system. "But by the time we opened, some of the very citizens who had been the most vociferous critics were saying it had worked out so much better than anything they could have imagined." With some 3,000 daily visitors to the library, he adds, "I know the owner is delighted with the foot traffic."

While Indianapolis' library-in-a-mall is unique, Seattle is emerging as a national leader when it comes to co-location and collaboration, despite the logistical headaches of such an approach.

Seattle opened its NewHolly branch library in 1999 as part of a neighborhood campus/learning center that also houses a branch of South Seattle Community College, a child care center and a youth tutoring program. The surround "urban village" mixes 900 low-income housing units with 200 market-rate homes.

Another branch library, Wallingford, is a $400,000 project in a $5 million building that also houses a family support center, food bank, meeting hall and social services for the homeless. Plans call for the new $6.5 million Ballard branch to be the centerpiece of a six-block stretch with a park, store and housing for seniors. And the International District library will be part of a complex developed by the Seattle Chinatown/International District Preservation and Development Authority. It will include 57 units of low-income housing, a community center, retail space and underground parking.

"We developed a policy that says we prefer a stand-alone library," Jacobs says. "But what we've discovered is that neighborhood by neighborhood there are different needs. Some absolutely demand freestanding libraries. But in lower-income neighborhoods, in order to achieve other goals, they are developing mixed-use buildings and want us to be part of it."

Philadelphia's Shelkrot says the evidence is indisputable that libraries "can change the look and vitality of an area." the role they have to play now, he insists, "is not one of bricks and mortar, but programs, services and technology."

CHAPTER 17

Kansas City Uses Culture to Transform Its Downtown

Howard Kozloff

Kansas City is made up of districts that have been viewed for decades as discrete. Perhaps known best for J.C. Nichols's Country Club Plaza, Kansas City also has the River Market, West Bottoms, and Crown Center, among others. But, as first-term mayor Kay Barnes points out, there has not been a feeling of connectivity among the areas and throughout the city. To change this, she proposes creating the SoLo Performing Arts District, which she envisions as the anchor of an almost seven-mile-long area intended to emulate Paris's Champs Elysées — "a linear boulevard with everything happening on all sides of it," says Barnes.

SoLo — short for South Loop, the southern end of the central business district loop that extends into the Crosstown area of Kansas City — is bounded by, roughly, 12th Street on the north, 17th Street on the south, Oak Street on the east, and Bartle Hall convention center on the west. The proposed mixed-use district, anchored by a $305 million Moshe Safdie–designed performing arts center, will include additional office space, housing, entertainment, and retail. The $1.8 billion redevelopment plan for the 20-block area would not be financed by appropriations, but by private

developers and through innovative state legislation.

Efforts to redevelop the South Loop area are not novel. A previous effort to recreate the area as the Power & Light District, based on creation of a tax increment financing (TIF) district, was turned down by the city council after developers changed the terms and phasing of the project. The former owner of the Kansas City–based AMC Entertainment was the major sponsor of the new district, and the project faded away after his death. As a result, large amounts of disinvestment occurred as doubts about the area's future grew and blight there got worse.

Today, the 20 square blocks are still blighted despite being part of an existing urban renewal area. Vacant parking lots and abandoned buildings line the streets, with occupancy of many buildings ruled out by code violations. One of the major issues highlighting the potential of and need for redevelopment is the difficulty of attracting conventioneers — and their wallets — to Bartle Hall on the western edge of the proposed SoLo district. The lack of diversions in the immediate vicinity forces conventioneers to travel to County Club Plaza about five miles away for entertainment.

Originally published as "Going SoLo," *Urban Land*, Vol. 61, No. 4, April 2002, by the Urban Land Institute, Washington, D.C. Reprinted with permission of the publisher.

Setting the Tone

Bob Marcusse, president of the Kansas City Area Development Council, a regional economic development group, says he is "thrilled by renewed efforts to put a lot of energy and resources behind plans for development and redevelopment." Downtown Kansas City is the "living room of the region," he says, serving as downtown for the entire area. If downtown is not magnificent, it creates the wrong first impression, which has implications for attracting businesses, residents, and visitors. A vibrant downtown, Marcusse adds, is important for the entire region in that it helps to set the tone for the community.

The original strategy for SoLo, created in a May 2001 study by Sasaki Associates, an interdisciplinary planning and design firm of Watertown, Massachusetts, responded to the strengths of the community and, according to Andi Udris, president of the Economic Development Corporation (EDC) of Kansas City, served as "a great concept plan to guide community leadership." The Sasaki study concluded, "The economy of downtown needs to diversify to embrace more residential and cultural uses as a complement to the traditional business and government core." It recommended that "the priorities in the first five years are to set up a development and management entity and to realize significant development in the downtown core."

To this end, Barnes established the Greater Downtown Development Authority (GDDA) as "a vehicle to bring all the key players around the table." GDDA is composed of representatives from EDC; the Greater Kansas City Chamber of Commerce; the Civic Council, an organization made up of CEOs of the larger Kansas City companies; the Downtown Council, which traditionally focuses on the central business district; and at-large members appointed by the mayor. The GDDA, which is staffed full-time by EDC, acts as the development agency responsible for managing, phasing, and implementing the SoLo plan.

Following the Sasaki plan, HNTB, a Kansas City–based architecture, engineering, and planning firm, further refined the concept to offer "an opportunity for Kansas City residents to live, work, and enjoy new amenities in what has been a stagnant area of the city." Calling it a "unique opportunity for a federal-state-city-private partnership to encourage this new, vibrant, urban development," HNTB developed a six-year, market-driven development plan to make the transition from idea to reality. But the energy, confidence, and capital of multiple developers, property owners, and properties will be needed to bring the plan to fruition.

According to HNTB, SoLo's success depends on the area's ability to provide and enhance "linkages between the convention area, the prospective performing arts district, and the balance of the downtown area." Barnes recognizes that Kansas City, as the heart of the region, ultimately supports the economic development of the whole area. Also, despite her desire to create a version of Paris's Champs Elysées where the various districts are interconnected, she is aware of the need for diversity. Because the various districts surrounding SoLo are close to each other, they need to be viewed as a single area for marketing and to have better transportation connections. However, Barnes proclaims, the districts "will always maintain their own identity, but not in isolation from their relationship to the others."

In its current proposed form, the completed SoLo Performing Arts District will include 1,625 new residential units, 455,000 square feet of retail space, 1.6 million square feet of office space, 200 hotel rooms, and 10,788 parking spaces. Phase I will consist of 450 residential units, a 200-room hotel, 100,000 square feet of office space, 425,000 square feet of retail, and 1,500 parking spaces on about three blocks. Two projects already have been identified for Phase I — the President Hotel block and the Kansas City Club redevelopment. HNTB estimates that the potential for increased taxes under the proposed Missouri Downtown Economic Stimulus Act (MODESA) could generate an estimated $8.5 million per year. This could be leveraged to create a bond potential of $85 million, to be paid off over 30 years, for public infrastructure projects that would make SoLo more development friendly. In all, planners believe SoLo could generate more than $30 million in taxes if MODESA legislation passes, which could be used to leverage more than $300 million in bonds to finance the projects.

Udris believes that although the plan has a number of components, the proposal for the performing arts center is perhaps the most critical. The performing arts center, planned as a landmark that will attract investment and philanthropic interest, will define the neighborhood, creating a multiuse district with the specific character of Kansas City. The combination of a renovated, expanded convention center and associated hotels with new residential units, shops, and restaurants will "cater to people going to the theater at night and office workers in the daytime," according to Udris, leading tourists to patronize the area 24 hours a day. In addition, studies are underway to determine the potential for a downtown sports arena in SoLo at 14th Street and Grand Boulevard.

Because an overwhelming percentage of buildings in the area are abandoned, there are no issues of displacement, Udris says. Missouri's strong historic preservation law and state and federal historic tax credits will encourage renovation of some of these buildings, notably older, obsolete Class C and D office buildings that likely will be converted to residential properties. The HNTB plan calls for new housing units to be targeted to all income levels — contrary to some recent nationwide trends that contribute to gentrification by emphasizing upper-income residents. A minimum of 20 percent of the units must be for low- and moderate-income households for housing projects to receive added state benefits; however, the actual percentage could be closer to 40 percent, according to Udris, because recent history shows the success of Missouri policies that encourage development of affordable housing through increased tax credits and funding for developments that exceed the 20 percent minimum.

Udris says SoLo's retail component will try to emulate Nichols's Country Club Plaza. The goal is "to drive the same principles that Nichols saw in his Plaza development to develop strategies for downtown; quality, experience, and tenant mix will create a desirable environment," he says. In so doing, however, SoLo will face the challenge of creating a district that does not duplicate what is already in place five miles away. Instead of bringing in high-end retailers such as Saks Fifth Avenue, Restoration Hardware, or Williams-Sonoma, all of which are at Country Club Plaza, the Performing Arts District will work to create new uses and attract unique tenants as it strives to act as a stimulus for downtown development, says Udris.

Banking on MODESA

Next to private investment, the most significant source of funding for SoLo, and perhaps potentially a significant contribution to a national policy on urban redevelopment, would be the proposed MODESA. Until now, local and federal funds have been insufficient to bring about redevelopment of the South Loop area. Further, without public investment, the private sector is extremely hesitant to risk its own money. To make the public improvements that would attract the private investment needed to make the SoLo Performing Arts District a reality, substantial state funding is necessary.

Because of the massive amounts of capital needed or infrastructure improvements, Barnes is looking to proposed state legislation to provide the economic base from which the SoLo development could grow. MODESA would encourage and emphasize development in blighted areas, which it recognizes as those areas "that [have] not shown growth and development through investment by private investors." MODESA, which calls for no state appropriations, could become law before the end of the summer if it is passed by the state legislature and signed by the governor.

The act would allow state revenue to be redirected to "major-initiative" projects intended to revitalize urban cores and provide economic stimulus for the cities and towns in which they are planned, as well as for the state as a whole. The list of projects that could be considered major initiatives is broad: tourism-related projects, cultural activities, arts, entertainment, education, research, arenas, stadiums, multipurpose facilities, libraries, ports, mass transit, museums, conventions, and business locations or expansions that would create new jobs within three years. The job requirement varies according to a municipality's size: A project in Kansas City would have to create 100 jobs to qualify, whereas a project in a smaller city, such as Springfield, would have to create 50 new jobs.

The idea behind MODESA is a portion of all new state revenue generated by a project, in the form of sales tax and income tax, would be redirected to major infrastructure projects within the development area. Key to the legislation is that taxes could only be applied to public projects, which might include public infrastructure (including parks and open space), parking, remediation of contaminated land, financing and relocation costs, and land acquisition. MODESA would differ from more traditional tax increment financing in that state participation in the project would go only to public infrastructure; private developers would not benefit directly from the state's involvement.

As proposed, 3 percent of the total Missouri sales tax of 4.225 percent and 2 percent of Missouri income tax would remain within project borders. No tax revenues existing before development would be diverted, and the state still would benefit from collecting the remaining 1.225 percent sales tax and an estimated two-thirds of additional income taxes created by new businesses and residents in the area. Net new revenue created by MODESA would be capped at $40 million per year for Kansas City; smaller cities would have lower caps.

MODESA also would create the opportunity for each municipality to establish a downtown development authority (DDA) that would have such powers as eminent domain and the ability to own and transfer property and to borrow funds. Each DDA would bring the project before the Missouri Development Finance Board, where it would have to pass a "but for" test — the project could not be completed but for state participation — to quality for MODESA funds. Each project would have to get local approval, too. Barnes is confident that the legislation will gain approval in Jefferson City, the state capital. Because the bill does not ask for any state appropriations and it applies to cities and towns of various sizes, it has the potential to encourage the redevelopment of downtowns "in a way [not possible] without state participation," says Barnes.

MODESA has the potential to act as a catalyst for further development by the private sector by showing public sector investment and by priming SoLo to emerge as a success story. Although the project costs are high, so, too, are the aspirations. SoLo is in the rare position of being able to stimulate development with little of the social expense often associated with gentrification or displacement. In its potential to contribute to Kansas City as a whole and to establish a citywide relationship, the SoLo Performing Arts District could be poised to have social, physical, and economic benefits for the city, the region, and the state.

CHAPTER 18

Lanark and Other Cities Use Rural Libraries to Promote Community Development

Norman Waizer *and* John J. Gruidl

Many small rural communities are undergoing a significant transition, changing from market centers to bedroom communities for neighboring employment centers. These towns often count on being quiet, attractive places to live in order to retain current populations and, hopefully, attract new residents. Graduates from secondary schools typically move on to better employment opportunities in larger centers, and local retail establishments face more and more difficulty because of shrinking markets.

With increasing frequency, community leaders and local public officials recognize that a positive future for these communities requires local community development initiatives. A vision for the community, a group of committed leaders and an action plan are needed to manage the transition process. Many communities in Illinois have participated in the MAPPING the Future of Your Community program, Competitive Communities Initiative, and/or the Illinois MainStreet program and have succeeded in revitalizing their communities.[1]

Successful communities have identified and incorporated important local resources into an action plan. Typically, community leaders have mobilized these resources into a cohesive unit to bring about an effective strategic planning effort and successful follow through. In some small communities, however, the resource base in thin because elected officials serve part-time, often with little or no remuneration. Because they are employed full-time elsewhere, local officials have limited time to spend on the multitude of tasks involved in successfully managing a city. These limitations make it absolutely necessary for local officials and community leaders to effectively manage local resources and rely on professionals in the community who can contribute to the process.

Public libraries can play a significant role in community economic development for several reasons. First, access to a well-stocked library adds significantly to the overall quality of life in a community. Second, librarians are sometimes the most educated and well-trained community information specialists. Third, libraries frequently have up-to-date computer systems, fax machines, Internet access and in-

Originally published as "Rural Public Libraries and Community Economic Development," *Illinois Libraries*, Vol. 79, No. 4, Fall 1997, by the Illinois State Library, Springfield. Reprinted with permission of the publisher.

formation retrieval skills that are of growing importance in an information-based economy. Businesses recognize the need for these services, but, unfortunately, often do not know that they are available in the local library.

Many local librarians and library boards have recognized the potential for the library in community development efforts and see positive results for both the community library from these efforts. (See Benefits to Public Libraries from Economic Development Activities.) In 1993, the Illinois Institute for Rural Affairs, with a grant from the Illinois State Library, started a series of workshops for local librarians to help them better understand the role for libraries in community economic development. More than 100 librarians participated in these regional workshops and follow-up activities. Many have continued their efforts. This article is based on a mail survey of libraries participating in the project to determine the extent to which libraries are actively engaged in local economic development efforts and how they perceive the benefits.

Participation in Community Development Efforts

Statewide, 39 rural librarians responded to the survey mailed in November 1996. Most of the respondents had participated in the economic development workshops. The vast majority (84.2 percent) of respondents reported that their library actively supports local economic development activities. When asked about reasons for not actively supporting these efforts, the most common response was that they had not been asked. The fact that 82.1 percent (32 librarians) reported spending less than 10 percent of their time on community development and/or business retention activities should alert community leaders that additional help may be available if they contacted the library board or librarian.

An intended outcome of the economic development seminars was to encourage greater participation in local community activities. Half of the responding librarians (17 librarians) reported being more active in local development efforts now than prior to the workshops. Likewise, 60 percent reported that the percentage of their time spent on community development or business retention had increased compared with three years ago. Only 8.6 percent reported that the time spent had decreased.

For involvement in local development efforts to be sustained, libraries must see benefits. Respondents were asked about the efforts of participation on their libraries. The vast majority (88.8 percent) of respondents reported that the library had received at least "limited benefits, or benefits well worth the effort." Only four respondents said that there had been no effects.

A related question asked if the respondents would prefer the library's involvement to "increase, remain the same, or decrease" in the future. About two-thirds (65.8 percent) of the respondents said they would prefer an increase in their involvement, and 34.2 percent said the efforts should remain at least at the current level.

These findings suggest that a majority of the librarians responding to the survey have found local involvement beneficial to the library and that they, perhaps, would be more involved if opportunities arose. This should be welcome news to local economic development groups.

Involvement of Librarians

Respondents were asked about the local economic development efforts in which they had participated during the previous year and were provided with a list of activities to be checked:

• During the past year, in which local economic development activities have you been involved?

- Many presentations on library services to business groups or social organizations
- Invited groups or committees to hold meetings in the library
- Inventoried library business collection to see if it meets community needs
- Attended all meetings of economic development groups or the Chamber of Commerce
- Joined the Chamber of Commerce or local economic development organization
- Promotion of library service such as FAX and Internet to business
- Provided or collected information to support economic development activities.
- Hosted a program for local businesses at which library resources were displayed
- Created media program to inform businesses of library resources/activities
- Library staff have taken a leadership role in community development projects
- Hosted training programs on library resources for business personnel
- Surveyed local businesses about information needs
- Formed an advisory group with members from business and/or economic development organizations to help on library issues

Presentations to Groups and Organizations

Most often reported were presentations about library services to business groups and social organizations. Making potential clients aware of library services is one of the most important outreach efforts that librarians can perform. The availability of information services has increased so much that many small business owners are not fully aware of the potential for their use. Just being aware of the services may, in some instances, help some businesses better recognize the potential uses of the information.

Presentations to business and community groups also offer several advantages to librarians. In particular, interactions with business personnel can help librarians understand the needs for library services within the community. When librarians are perceived as being an integral part of community efforts to expand, they are more likely to receive support, financial and otherwise. In essence, librarians are a valuable community resource and many residents do not fully understand the value of the services available, especially given the explosion in availability of data and business-related information. Better marketing of library services and more exposure in the community can reap significant and immediate dividends.

One example of this community support is in Mt. Vernon where the C.E. Brehm Memorial Library needed a local match for a grant to provide Internet access. The local Nations Bank office provided $15,000 to help the library obtain a Southern Illinois Regional Information Network (SIRIN) grant. Many local agencies and groups now have access to Internet because of the library's involvement.

Hosting Groups and Meetings

Librarians in this survey have actively hosted meetings of groups or committees in the library. This service offers several advantages. First, the library is often viewed as a neutral location, making it especially attractive for discussions of controversial issues. Second, having residents in the library offers librarians an opportunity to market the services available, e.g., a new business data source, Internet access, and a variety of other items with which residents may not be familiar. Third, interactions with community groups may identify needs for other services, some of which may generate additional support for the library.

The Lanark Public Library has hosted the Women's Club for a workshop on the Internet. The librarian recognized that a substantial number of attendees were elderly, and she started a program to help them communicate with their grandchildren who were in college. The library also hosts an open house associated with the high school homecoming. Pictures, scholastic achievements, and other activities are provided during these sessions. The local chamber of commerce pays for the advertising needed for this event.

Inventory Business Collection

Responding librarians also assessed their potential for meeting business needs by inventorying the business collection. There is a multitude of data and information available that is, at least potentially, useful to the business community. Some of the information and sources are beyond the current library budget and may be too specialized for use by many businesses. A major contribution of the local librarian, however, is to know the resources available and to make businesses aware of them.

The cost of reference information and limited local library budgets make it imperative for librarians to engage in partnerships and cooperative purchasing efforts. Several libraries can jointly purchase a data set or participate in a regional effort through their System Library and stretch scarce resources, while providing high quality services to local businesses. The Internet is very important in this regard because much of the census data in the future will be provided only on an electronic format.

Attending Economic Development Meetings

Librarians responding to the survey also were active in attending meetings of the economic development organization and chambers of commerce in their communities. In many small communities, these organizations have few resources and librarians can be of substantial assistance in organizing the overall effort, providing necessary information and serving a clearinghouse role or as a contact point for outreach efforts. At the very minimum, a local library can have a designated area containing community information and brochures so that visitors and residents have ready access.

The Lanark Public Library, for example, houses much of the information about proposals for alternative uses of the Savanna Army Depot. Grant applications for uses of the land are housed in the library for public review. Other materials, including city government reports, are also available in the library. Comments from librarians indicated that they are gaining familiarity with local institutions and becoming more actively involved in community efforts. In some instances, this involvement has translated into tangible support by the library board and residents for expanding the library collection and/or for providing specialized services.

Ten Ways a Public Library Can Get Involved in Community Economic Development

1. Establish the mission of the library. What is the library's role in community economic development? What support is the library willing to make to engage the library in community development?

2. Review available state and regional resources for community development. The Illinois Economic Resource Directory can be obtained from the Rural Economic Technical Assistance Center, Illinois Institute for Rural Affairs (800–526–9943). The Rural Development Resources Guide is available from the Department of Commercial and Community Affairs (217–782–7500).

3. Visit with community leaders, including the major, city council members, chamber of commerce director, local development organization members. Find out what economic development projects are underway and what information is needed.

4. Attend meetings of the economic development group and chamber of commerce.
   The library should become a member of
   these organizations, if possible. Be prepared
   to spend at least 10 percent of your working time in activities outside the library
   building. Find out whether the community has developed a strategic plan for community economic development. As you
   learn more, search for the niche that the library might play in implementing community projects.

5. Explore ways of working with your
   economic development group and/or
   chamber on community projects. Don't
   hesitate to contact state and regional organizations for assistance or to identify
   other communities that have dealt with
   similar issues.

6. Develop an outreach program to local
   businesses. Host in-house events to promote and explain your business collection
   and services. Develop a media campaign
   to inform businesses of your services.

7. Develop a core collection of materials.
   Form an advisory group consisting of
   business and community leaders. Work
   with other librarians in the region to develop cooperative collections. Investigate
   the potential for becoming an access point
   for the Internet.

8. Invite groups and committees to hold
   their meetings in the library. Partner with
   the Small Business Development Center
   or SCORE chapter in offering a business
   workshop.

9. Make presentations about library resources to service clubs, development organizations, the chamber, and other business groups.

10. Be committed to serving the information
    needs of businesses and economic devel-
    opment groups. Remember that informa-
    tion is key and that you know how to find
    it.

Summary

This survey of librarians yields several fit-
tings. First, libraries are active in community
development efforts and they view these activities as an important part of the library outreach program. Second, respondents reported
that, at least in some instances, outreach efforts have brought increased support for the
library and have better integrated the library
into community activities.

The benefits from increased involvement
by librarians are not limited to the library,
however. Small communities usually do not
have sufficient resources to employ a full-time
economic development staff. Data collection
and limited analyses, a repository or clearinghouse for information, a meeting place for
community leaders, and serving as a contact
point for external agencies are important functions provided by libraries. These activities involve additional time spent on the community
activities but may not represent significant additional outlays of library funds.

Benefits to Public Libraries from Economic Development Activities: Summary

- Libraries gain greater visibility and stature
  among the business community and local
  government.
- Libraries contribute to the viability and
  growth of their towns.
- Public-private partnerships (e.g., with the
  local chamber of commerce) are formed or
  strengthened.
- Library collections, particularly business resources, are enhanced.
- Services are expanded to non-traditional
  users.
- Donations of money and equipment to the
  library increase.
- Library-to-library cooperation increases
  through resource sharing.
- Libraries help businesses and local organiza-

tions become better consumers of information.

Successful community development, especially in small rural cities, depends heavily on identifying important local resources, charting a reasonable future for the community, and having groups follow through on assigned tasks. All too often, local librarians are overlooked in this process. The growing importance of information in the economy and the increased access to this information through the local library makes it a key resource in attracting certain types of businesses.

In an even more general way, prosperous local libraries add significantly to the quality of life in rural communities and this quality of life is increasingly important in business location decisions. Thus, local libraries can play a direct role in local economic development efforts as well as enhancing the attractiveness of a community to prospective residents. The survey findings reported in this article show that librarians are succeeding in many of these efforts and some would like to be even more involved.

NOTES

1. Robin Hanna and Steve Kline. 1997. *Mapping the Future of Your Community: Strategic Visioning for Community and Economic Development* (Macomb, IL: Illinois Institute for Rural Affairs).

CHAPTER 19

Little Rock Focuses on Cultural Assets to Restore Its Riverfront Area

Robert J. Gorman *and* Nancy Egan

Little Rock, Arkansas, is enjoying a makeover. The national press has focused its attention on the arrival of the Clinton Presidential Center, the nation's next presidential library. But the real story begins with the vision of local government and its residents. Strong, creative leadership and civic involvement have reshaped this quiet southern river town in the last decade. When Bill Clinton became president in 1992, Little Rock drew national attention for the first time since the desegregation of Central High School in 1957. This is the story of how citizens of Little Rock leveraged their existing assets with the political momentum of the Clinton election to create a more attractive and dynamic city.

Ten years ago, Little Rock's central business district — like that of many other cities that suffered from the ground-zero approach to redevelopment prevalent in the 1960s — was the requisite collection of office and parking towers and "soon-to-be-developed" vacant lots. Although there did exist a handful of historic structures and several buildings of architectural significance, the downtown lacked the focus and vibrancy that results from a thoughtful urban plan. With Clinton in Washington, Little Rock was on camera. Local leaders recognized the economic prize that the presidential library represented and committed to creating an environment for this once-in-a-lifetime, urban development opportunity.

As this was not the city's first attempt at revitalization — earlier efforts had failed — Little Rock officials realized that a long-range vision and specific, short-term development objectives were needed. George Wittenberg, director of the Donaghey Project for Urban Studies, the urban planning arm of the University of Arkansas at Little Rock, recalls, "The City was ready to get serious. We looked around the country at other cities to see what had been done, and we took a very hard look at what we had failed to do before. There was a new confidence in Little Rock following Clinton's election, and we were able to translate that into a sense of urgency." Business and civic leaders represented by the Downtown Partnership worked with the Donaghey Institute and MRA International, a Philadelphia-based development strategy firm, to define and

Originally published as "Revitalizing Little Rock," *Urban Land*, Vol. 60, No. 9, September 2001, by the Urban Land Institute, Washington, D.C. Reprinted with permission of the publisher.

accomplish their goal: to develop a business strategy to enhance Little Rock's competitive position as a business center and regional leisure destination.

Facing Facts

The consulting team's 1994 study revealed both the challenges and the potential gains of an accelerated economic development program. First the tough realities — Little Rock is the center of a region with a relatively small population, and competitor cities within a 150-mile radius boast entertainment and recreational offerings that the city cannot match.

However, the city's natural riverfront location offered an attractive physical asset on which to build a strategy. Little Rock possessed substantial vacant land and, while there was little public financial support available to initiate development there, a few privately funded projects were beginning to create a critical mass. A revitalized River District would provide an identifiable destination within the city and would reconnect the downtown to the historic riverfront and its geological formation, the little rock, from which the city derives its name.

A number of existing assets in the River District needed upgrading: The Central Library and the Museum of Science and History were due for new facilities; and the Convention Center, the Camelot Hotel, and River Park needed attention. Finally, a number of "missing assets" were identified that would give the River District a distinctive draw and enhance the existing properties.

Inventing the River District Area

Barry Travis, the executive director of the Little Rock Convention Center and Visitors' Bureau, describes the redevelopment process: "Like pieces of a jigsaw puzzle, Little Rock is re-creating itself as new projects are finished

and other projects are announced. This is a very exciting time." Today, the majority of the facilities outlined in the 1994 plan are in operation. Development has recaptured the waterfront to create a busting hot spot in the heart of the city.

The River Market. The lively farmers' market has become the rallying symbol for the transformation of the entire district. Its food stalls, eateries, and year-round events — from the seasonal farmers' market to holiday ice-skating — have changed the way both locals and visitors view the River District. The initial $5 million investment in the market served as a catalyst for further development in the River District.

Operated by the Little Rock Parks and Recreation Department, the market comprises 18 businesses in the Market Hall and two 7,500-square-foot pavilions on its river side. The pavilions, including the plaza area, houses more than 100 vendors and host many other events throughout the year. They attract approximately 75,000 visitors to the farmers' market ach year. Started in 1974, the market, which has been in other locations, continues today to be very successful during its six-month run each year from May through October.

The Alltell Arena. This state-of-the-art facility originally was slated for the River District. The decision to locate it in North Little Rock directly across from the Arkansas River from the River Market in Little Rock was made, in part, to reinforce the concept of the two-sided riverfront destination. Today, the arena draws hundreds of thousands of people to the central Arkansas area, increasing the vitality of the entertainment/recreation sectors on both sides of the river.

Costing approximately $7 million to build, the arena provides seating for more than 18,000. It opened in October 1999 and during its first year hosted 30 concerts, eight Arena Football League games, 35 Arkansas Razorblade hockey games, 22 basketball games, and 100 meetings and reception events, attracting more than 711,000 people. The local economic impact already is estimated to be more than $2 million.

Statehouse Convention Center. The $23 million expansion of the Little Rock Convention Center and Visitors' Bureau doubled the size of the convention center, increasing it to 192,000 square feet and making it a strong, regional contender. The existing center already was drawing 450,000 to 500,000 visitors per year. Now, the expanded center has the size and flexibility to compete on a new level.

Little Rock Central Library. The new, $15 million facility provided a needed boost to the River District revitalization efforts. The Little Rock Central Library was a pioneer, having made an early commitment to renovate and occupy an existing warehouse. Since its opening in the fall of 1997, the number of visitors has doubled.

Museum of Discovery. This museum has been a Little Rock institution for more than 70 years. Relocated in another refurbished warehouse, the museum contains 50,000 square feet — three times the original size. The $10.6 million expanded museum attracts 200,000 visitors per year.

The Riverfront Amphitheater. This tented structure has been home to warm-weather events for a number of years. Recently, permanent seating, restrooms, and performer facilities have helped enhance the amphitheater.

The Doubletree Hotel. Doubletree Hotels, along with a local development group, completely renovated the former Camelot Hotel, investing $8 million to bring the facility up to the standard of its competing hotels, the Capitol and the Excelsior. The remodeled hotel provides an entryway to the main spine of the River District.

Seeding the Future

The fast-track redevelopment program began to pay off in 1997, when the city selected the Little Rock River District over other sites, including the University of Arkansas at Fayetteville, as the home for the Clinton Presidential Center. Little Rock's City Board of Directors approved the use of $1.2 million from its 1998 economic development budget to pay for the first year's estimated debt service on $15 million of a total $22 million revenue bond issue. This move did not increase taxes. The bonds are earmarked for the acquisition of land for the center, the removal of railroad tracks, and the transformation of the Arkansas River's Rock Island Bridge into a pedestrian bridge.

James L. (Skip) Rutherford, who has been responsible for organizing the planning of the center, comments, "This commitment to urban development creates a catalyst that will influence additional community development on both sides of the Arkansas River. We see the Clinton Presidential Center as part of a larger vision of the future of Little Rock." With a solid commitment to action, a coalition of the Downtown Partnership and city leadership, including the mayor's office, the Convention Center and Visitors' Bureau, the Greater Little Rock Chamber of Commerce, Fifty for the Future (an organization of senior business executives), and private investors, has changed the image of the city. Each project, whether it is a public or private initiative, is an impressive contributor on its own.

As local businessmen and civic leader Jimmy Moses says, "Our first decisions are still reverberating as additional projects expand our original vision. We are filling the gaps and re-developing older properties to take advantage of the real estate value that has been created. And I wouldn't rule out another major new project based on increased interest in the city."

The timing of the River District's redevelopment could not have been better. Little Rock's economy mirrored the nation's, giving locals and out-of-town visitors more disposable income to spend. Major national trends toward downtown living gave a boost to several older properties in the district as they were converted to residential lofts. A variety of new businesses have flocked to the area — now a flourishing collection of restaurants, florists, retail outlets, and even a satellite studio for a local television station — which hosted more than 250,000 visitors in 2000.

With their success in revitalizing the historic River District and securing the Clinton Library as the centerpiece for an expansion of the area, Little Rock's leaders — all dedicated citizens — are celebrating a renaissance in their community. They are committed to the quality of life, as they are to the economic vitality, of their city. They understand that urban renewal requires the improvement of both and have included them successfully in tie revitalization of Little Rock.

Observers are stunned by the turnaround. The community leadership defined a vision, created a plan, and followed a clear strategy for implementation with remarkable speed. Little Rock's story provides a compelling scenario for other cities hoping to renew their urban core.

A Checklist for Success

Towns and cities across America share a dream of revitalizing their downtowns, their forgotten waterfronts, or faded retail districts. All too often, pursuit of a single magic project that is expected to turn everything around — be it an aquarium, a planetarium, or a museum — sidetracks civic leaders. Little Rock could have waited for the arrival of the Clinton Library. However, cities that have been successful in attracting a blockbuster project usually begin with a series of smaller, related projects that build confidence without breaking the budget, thereby creating a platform of support for a large-scale attraction. Although each opportunity is different, the lessons of Little Rock's success can be readily extrapolated to suit other locales. Essential criteria include:

- Long-term political and community leaders with the patience and perseverance to nurture a plan over time.
- A clear sense of the possibilities scaled to the place, and a marked sense of "optimistic realism." These will keep doubters at bay in the critical early stages.
- A vision articulated in a way that captures the imagination of the community. Professional planners and other advisers often can sell the concept more successfully than the local support team.
- A strategic plan for implementing the vision. It is important to have a tactical game plan as well as a compelling goal — dreams fade when no visible action exists.
- A management entity that can "act" and take responsibility for implementing the plan. Most cities have term limits for elected officials, making it imperative to have an organization that will ensure continuity.
- Early successes that can enhance the community's ability to maintain a sense of momentum. Realistic first targets and an integrated marketing program help to set a sustainable pace.
- Borrowed successes. Linking the plan through shared amenities to initiatives already underway (i.e., streetscapes, transport systems, or marketing programs) accelerates the sense of achievement.
- Critical mass. If the program encompasses too much territory it ceases to be a precise destination in the eyes — and feet — of the visitors.
- Funding through a variety of sources. The dream should be realizable to a certain degree when taken in smaller steps that can be financed quickly.

CHAPTER 20

Memphis and Other Cities Use Libraries to Promote Literacy

Urban Libraries Council

Libraries have long been recognized as one of the most important community institutions for adult and child literacy development. However, new research in the area of child development is now uncovering a strong connection between early literacy investments and the improved school outcomes of young children. Researchers are showing that children who begin kindergarten with greater literacy skills resources are more likely to test well in reading and basic mathematics at the end of kindergarten and the start of first grade (Denton and West 2002). Early literacy, along with early numeracy, and building social-emotional competence, is seen by many researchers as a key strategy for developing of school readiness in very young children (Brooks-Gunn and Markman 2005; Foorman, Anthony, Seals, Parlakian 2003; Mouzaki 2002; Whitehurst and Lonigan 1998).

In the past, little importance was placed on what children experienced in the first years of life. Reading instruction took place primarily in elementary school. Formal instruction and curriculums emphasized the teaching of reading and writing to children when they reached school age and not before. However,

the current research-based understanding of early language and literacy development is providing new and early pathways for helping children learn to talk, read and write. Current literacy development theory emphasizes the more natural unfolding of skills through the enjoyment of books, the importance of positive interactions between young children and adults who read, and the critical role of literacy-rich experiences.

On another track, researchers in the field of economics are beginning to identify child development investments as the most cost effective strategies for long-term economic development. In a recent study, researchers from the Minneapolis Federal Reserve Bank identify investments in early education as yielding a financial return that far exceeds the return on most state funded economic development projects (Rolnick and Grunewald 2003).

Researchers at the University of Chicago, identify early education investments as more efficient public investments because their benefits tend to compound, by creating a solid foundation for later human capital investments, such as education, youth development and job skills training (Cunha and Heckman

Originally published as "Improving Early Literacy and School Readiness" in *Making Cities Stronger: Public Library Contributions to Local Economic Development*, January 2007, by the Urban Institute, Washington, D.C. Reprinted with permission of the publisher.

2003; Currie 2001, Karoly, et al. 1998). This work finds that the return on investment decreases as investments move from early literacy and child development, to youth programs, to adult education and job training programs.

"Learning and motivation are dynamic, cumulative processes; skill begets skill; learning begets learning. Early disadvantages lead to academic and social difficulties later. Early disadvantages accumulate; just as early disadvantages do."

The Productivity Argument for
Investing in Young Children,
Working Paper 51
— Committee for Economic
Development, October 2004

There is also evidence that the important of early childhood investments is beginning to take hold among policy makers at the various levels of government (Katz, Dylan, and de Kervor 2003). Since 2005, the National League of Cities' National Municipal Policy has had a major initiative to highlight practices and catalyze investments in early learning to build stronger local economic capacity long-term. The National Governors Association has also adopted a policy position that calls for greater support of early literacy programming, and has established a small grant program designed to build more comprehensive early childhood development systems at the state level (NGA Education, Early Childhood and Workforce Committee ECW-04).

Children's literacy services in public libraries are being recast to this end. In cities large and small, libraries are expanding traditional story-time activities, retooling children's literacy programming to meet developmentally appropriate standards, and creating more comprehensive child literacy support services for parents and child care providers. Libraries are now making much deeper resource investments in early literacy training. Indeed, for many communities they are the lead agencies for early literacy services and training for

young children. In the survey conducted among Urban Libraries Council members, over 90 percent of responding libraries identified their library as providing special programming in the area of early literacy. Of these, 92 percent had enhanced their collections with materials specifically related to early literacy promotion. School readiness and child development activities included family and intergenerational reading development programs, parenting programs, and support services for child care professionals. Among the libraries providing early child development programming 70 percent provided early literacy workshops on a weekly or monthly basis, and just over 60 percent provided workshops for childcare workers and early education teachers.

As children's programming has grown over the years so too has the need for specialized education and training on the part of library staff. Survey results highlighted a strong commitment on the part of public libraries to providing specialized services with appropriately trained personnel. More than half of the libraries surveyed identified someone on their children's services staff as having an early childhood education certificate. At this point computers do not appear to play a major role in direct provision of early literacy services. Less than 13 percent of the libraries indicated that they used computers as an integral part of their early literacy activities. However, public libraries do appear to be using their websites as a way to collect information resources for parents and caregivers to learn about early learning. Over one-third of the libraries responding to the survey indicated that they had developed websites specifically for early literacy/early learning.

Based in part on the programs highlighted in that survey, a group of public libraries were identified for further investigations into how early literacy collections and services were mobilized at the local level. Strategies observed in the field studies range from citywide information campaigns to the provision of tailored technical assistance to childcare agencies. The overall goals of these initiatives are consistent — improving child social and development outcomes through literacy and providing essential building blocks for school readiness. In many of the communities in this study, the public library was the only agency promoting early literacy programming.

The following descriptions of early literacy/school readiness strategies are followed by an examination of the impacts, and thoughts about how the public library could stretch resources and strategic investments further.

Public Library Strategies for Building Early Literacy

- Public education campaigns
- Parental training workshops
- Tailored technical assistance for childcare and other children's service agencies
- Implement model literacy programs

Public Education Campaigns for Early Literacy

Effective public education campaigns use media, messaging, and an organized set of communication activities to shape behavior toward desirable social outcomes (Weiss & Tschirhart 1994). They will often combine broadcast media campaign messaging with a wide range of marketing and program strategies meant to bolster the "marketing mix" (Balch & Sutton 1997). A common strategy for public education campaigns is to coordinate media efforts with a diverse mix of other communication channels, some interpersonal and some community-based, in order to extend the reach and frequency of the campaign's messages and increase the probability that messages will successfully result in a change (Dungan-Seaver 1999). Public libraries have been engaged in literacy campaigns for years. However, some public libraries are drawing

on this experience to build more targeted campaigns, which focus specifically on the promotion of early literacy. These strategies broaden the early literacy messages to the widest possible audience. By delivering the messages in multiple languages and through a variety of media, public libraries are extending the reach of their programs to community residents who may not even know where to find their closest branch library. An example of an ambitious multi-lingual public information campaign, which combines media outreach with informational workshops for parents and caregivers, is Brooklyn Public Library's campaign, Brooklyn Reads to Babies.

Brooklyn Public Library — Brooklyn Reads to Babies Campaign

Brooklyn Public Library's (BPL's) citywide literacy campaign, which targets both parents and caregivers of babies and toddlers, includes informational brochures and materials, produced in six different languages, which are distributed through the library and community partners; a web resource with information about early literacy; library programming on early literacy for children from birth to age five; and direct outreach to a wide range of children and family service agencies throughout Brooklyn. The campaign has cast a wide net by connecting with area service providers to get the word out to the community. Flyers and posters are available at area beauty parlors, clinics, schools, hospitals and markets. BPL has also made informational brochures available for family court. Area health providers, such as Coney Island Hospital, assist by providing Brooklyn Reads to Babies program information and library card applications in new infant goody bags. Start up resources for the program, which were covered by an initial donation of $1 million, included development and production of marketing pieces, board books in the branches, child size furniture for creating child-friendly areas in local branches, and purchasing program learning tools for area libraries. While it may be too early to measure direct impacts of the program, the demand for workshops and materials speaks to the need for this type of children's programming.

Early Literacy Training for Parents

Libraries across the country are augmenting children's services to provide intergenerational programming workshops that promote early literacy to parents. Workshops in some libraries are run directly by children's service librarians or in partnership with local child development agencies. Most workshops offer hands-on activities and supervised practice sessions that guide parents through a range of developmentally appropriate educational activities.

The Providence Public Library — Ready to Learn Providence Partnership for Parents

The Providence Public Library, in partnership with Ready to Learn Providence, provides a wide range of early literacy support services for young children and their parents and caregivers. The Cradle to Crayons initiative, a free nine-week program available at most Providence Public Library branches, focuses on literacy development of children ages 1–3. The program, which is funded by Ready to Learn Providence and CVS/Pharmacy Charitable Trust, is designed to introduce young families to the library in a comfortable setting and to develop early literacy skills through songs, rhymes, storytelling and play. Library staff members offer tips that can be used at home to encourage an early interest in reading and learning.

The program also invites local child service agency professionals to attend some sessions to share information on child development, health and safety. Bilingual staff (English/Spanish) attend most sessions, and materials are available in both languages. Families also receive free books through Reading Is Fundamental twice during the nine-week session. In addition to Cradle to Crayons, the partnership offers a three-hour program (in both Spanish and English) to teach adults how to share children's books, rhymes and songs with infants and toddlers. A third component of the parenting education program is the Learning and Reading Kits (LARK Kits). Created jointly by Providence Public Library and Ready to Learn Providence, the LARK kits contain 10 books, music, visual aides such as puppets and flannel boards, and educational games. The activity folder in each kit offers a choice of activities, helping educators to teach thematic curriculum units in a developmentally appropriate way.

The kits for use with preschool-age children, which can be checked out at branch libraries, are in English only and bilingual (English-Spanish) versions. There are also kits especially designed for use with toddlers. There are now over 200 LARK kits available through the library.

Technical Assistance/ Staff Development for Child Care Facilities

Sixty percent (60%) of the libraries providing early literacy programs in the ULC member survey identified their institutions as providers of technical assistance to child care agencies in their area. These training workshops, which are free through local libraries, provide staff development training to agencies that, due to resource constraints, might not otherwise make this type of business investment. In some communities these trainings have been incorporated into the broader network of accredited agency support and educational services. In these communities, participation in library early literacy workshops provides a portion of the credits necessary for annual accreditation or recertification. The Memphis Public Library has a program that combines traditional story times with detailed instruction to childcare staff about age appropriate literacy programming.

Memphis Public Library — Training Wheels Program

In the summer of 1999, the Memphis Public Library (MPL) held a series of focus groups with day care and other children's service providers in the Shelby County area to help structure a new mobile children's service. Though library staff had initially thought the focus groups would provide more detailed information about ways to deliver direct services to children, the greatest need identified by child care staff was for on-site, staff development programming. In response to this call, MPL developed the Training Wheels program, which provides on-site, customized training for those who care for young children (ages 0–6). The training is designed to improve caregivers' skills in developmentally appropriate practice, especially as it relates to early literacy.

The Training Wheels bus, which is staffed by children's librarians and early childhood specialists trained in adult education, visit a site and give "annotated" demonstration story times using the site's own children. In so doing, the program operates on two levels. Children at the local centers receive the care and attention of a librarian through traditional story time activity. As the library staff person is working with the children on one end of the bus, a second staff person is providing "color commentary" to day care staff, identifying key elements of the instruction, highlighting developmentally appropriate activities. This is a particularly important staff development activity for agencies that generally cannot afford to pay for continuing education training for their staff. After the story time demonstration activity, library staff works with caregivers to identify additional learning materials and tailor staff development activities to their specific needs.

Materials used in the story time demonstration are available for fully-automated checkout from the vehicle. The free Training Wheels workshops, which are certified by Department of Human Services of the State of Tennessee and provide child care workers with accreditation credits needed for annual recertification, are delivered to over 200 day care centers a year across the Memphis/Shelby County area on a rolling basis at visits scheduled during the regular business hours of the day care center.

Implementing Model Literacy Programs Locally

Public libraries provide a ready network for disseminating innovative program services. The adoption of early literacy services models such as Raising a Reader and Every Child Ready to Read @ Your Library provide excellent examples of the ways in which best practice models can spread in public libraries. The Raising a Reader program, which features bags filled with four multilingual and multicultural children's books, a literacy instructional video for parents, and a teacher training curriculum, started in 1999. Since that time the program has grown to over 118 affiliates that have implemented the program in 32 states. The Every Child Ready to Read @ Your Library, an early literacy curriculum developed by the Public Library Association and the Association for Library Service to Children, is another early literacy program that has spread rapidly. The program, which was designed as a trainer program, provides the basic curriculum, training and evaluation tools necessary for children's service librarians to incorporate early literacy training into their local regimen of children's services. Over the past two years, the Every Child Ready to Read program has provided 82 trainings for librarians at public libraries across the country.

San Luis Obispo Public Library — Raising a Reader Program, Oceano Branch Library

The Oceano Branch of the San Luis Obispo (SLO) City-County Public Library system is the first (SLO) branch library to implement the Raising a Reader Program. The newly opened branch, which is situated on a site next to the Oceano Elementary School and an adult learning center, is well positioned to provide services to both parents and their children. The program, which is partially supported by First 5 of San Luis Obispo and the San Luis Obispo County Office of Education, targets children and their families living in the predominantly Hispanic community surrounding Oceano Elementary School. The project is part of a broad initiative to provide educational support to parents, provide preschool and childcare, operate kindergarten transition programs, coordinate existing health and social services, and encourage schools to be ready for children, and vice versa. A preliminary review of the program results conducted by First 5 of San Luis Obispo indicate that the program is having a significant impact on the way parents approach learning in the household. Parents surveyed after three months of program participation reported statistically significant changes in the amount they read to their children (from 59 percent at baseline to 85 percent), their perceived importance of such reading (from 8.9 percent at baseline to 9.8 percent), and their increased use of the library system (from 38 percent at baseline to 69 percent) (First 5 SLO 2005).

Outcomes: Why Investments in Early Literacy Programming Make Sense

Early literacy programming in public libraries contributes to elevating young children's levels of literacy and engagement in learning, thereby contributing to school readiness and school success.

Public library literacy programs reduce the cost of doing business for area agencies by providing free staff development opportunities and in some places, certification credits.

Public libraries are strengthening the community child care support network by expanding learning resources and improving the quality of child care through literacy training.

Strategies for Broadening the Impact of Early Literacy Initiatives

Discussions with library staff, community partners and local development professionals revealed a set of strategies that could expand the capacity of programs to even broader participation by parents or area caregivers, bolster existing literacy partnerships, and strengthen community resources for child development.

Broaden Support for Outreach

Though a wide range of early literacy program models are now available, children's services divisions will require significantly more financial support to expand outreach services to parents and area caregivers. Whether providing services via a library book mobile or at the branch level, community outreach requires significant staff investments.

Establish Strong Partnerships with Area Child Service Providers

Library staff should identify ways to connect early literacy activities to other education services in the area to broaden the impact of literacy programming. While many libraries provide literacy programming through open workshops within the library, fewer libraries take the additional step of establishing formal partnerships with child care centers and Early Head Start programs to provide these services directly to caregivers on site. These formal partnerships represent a stronger commitment by both parties to program services, and provide library staff with a more detailed understanding of the needs of area service providers. Library staff also talked about the importance of making stronger connections between early literacy education staff and teachers at area schools. These connections provide area teachers with a better sense of the range of community educational services and can help librarians articulate programming to better prepare students for the reading strategies that are taught in area schools.

Continually Elevate Early Literacy Programming and Collect Information Over Time

Relatively few libraries were found to be tracking individual literacy program participants to determine the impact of their services over time. However, demonstrating the value of these programs requires this type of detailed information about participants (young and old) over time. There are many tools librarians can use to determine whether or not the services they provide have a lasting effect. Most require the systematic collection of information about individual program participants. This type of information is especially important when libraries are incorporating a standardized service model in a new setting. Because model programs are developed in other communities, sometimes with very different service populations, there may be conditions in the new "host" community that could affect the outcome of the program. Furthermore, local assessments could reveal important changes that are needed to better target services and improve participation.

acy to long-term education and economic success continues to mount. Through public awareness campaigns, more targeted program services, and collaborative training with other child care providers, public libraries are introducing many more children to books and reading before they enter school, greatly improving their chances of academic success. Library early literacy resources and programs are benefiting individuals and the community at large.

Investments in these areas are not without challenges, however. Sustained investments are necessary to build comprehensive, consistent pre-school literacy experiences and services both in and outside the library. Despite the challenges, public libraries across the country are retraining staff and retooling services to be in line with effective practices being defined in the new research, and are working with broad and diverse kinds of child care providers.

As libraries make deeper investments in the area of early literacy and school readiness support, the one area that will need greater attention is measuring impacts. Demonstrating the impacts of public library programs is not without difficulties. Voluntary drop-in visits do not lend themselves to traditional evaluation methodologies. Library efforts are impacted by other context factors, such as family, economic, race, school and other social aspects. Nonetheless, demonstrating the comparatively small but effective return on early literacy investments has the potential to yield even greater investments and payback.

Note: To purchase copies of the research publication *Making Cities Stronger*, please contact the Urban Libraries Council at (312) 676-0999 or via e-mail at info@urbanlibraries.org.

Conclusion

Public libraries across the country are responding as the evidence linking early liter-

CHAPTER 21

Minneapolis Uses Arts and Culture as Economic Development Incentives

Wendy Wheeler

The arts industry, especially in Minnesota, has in the past and will continue in the future to prove itself a fundamental contributor to our economy, not only through the jobs it sustains but also in the economic activity generated by arts organizations.

Major arts building projects are often the centerpiece of renewed and revitalized economic activity and can become cultural icons that define a city. Therefore, a lot of responsibility rests on the shoulders of organizations that take on such subjects. "the question of investing millions of dollars in a new building project is often the single biggest financial decision an arts organization will face," says Peter Kitchak, president of Keewaydin Real Estate Advisors of Minneapolis. Cultural organizations like the Guthrie Theater have turned to Keewaydin for advice on making these decisions, and for help building their own future.

The Guthrie's $125 million theater campus on the Mississippi River, which will include three major performance spaces, will not only further define Minneapolis as a cultural destination, but like many other proven projects, will also play a significant role in Minnesota's economy through its own economic business contribution and through its influence on other developments in the city.

Building Economic Activity

Communities across the nation have discovered two things: that culture is good business and that investments in the arts make sense. A 2002 study by Americans for the Arts noted that the total economic activity of nonprofit arts organizations in the United States in 2000 totaled $134 billion, and that these organizations generated 4.85 million full-time equivalent jobs in that same year.

An economic impact statement prepared for Guthrie by Anton, Lubov and Associates of Minneapolis states that the construction of the new Guthrie complex will be a one-time addition of $336 million in economic activity and will add the equivalent of 1,831 full-time jobs to the state's economy for two years. Once complete, the theater will be able to expand its programs and increase its annual economic impact to more than $82 million each year be-

Originally published as "Arts Serve as a Catalyst for Economic Development," *Minnesota Real Estate Journal*, March 17, 2003, by the Real Estate Communications Group, Chicago, IL. Reprinted with permission of the publisher.

ginning in 2006, a number that includes tourist spending of more than $15 million per year. Furthermore, the expanded operations will add the equivalent of 200 full-time jobs to the state on an ongoing basis.

Building Business

The creative economy brings benefits that extend beyond direct employment and tourist spending. One of the greatest strengths of a vibrant arts community is its ability to attract other business and encourage neighborhood development. Richard Florida of Carnegie Mellon University, author of "The Rise of the Creative Class," says: "...Talent has become the single most critical factor of production. In the knowledge economy, those places that have talent thrive, while those that do not decline."

Culture helps build community by influencing commercial and residential development, which in turn attracts workers and residents. When companies make decisions to relocate, they seek markets with concentrations of talented workers. In turn, the power of industry to attract talented workers depends largely upon a city's quality of life. Florida says that "quality-of-place" is vital to maintaining an advantage in the marketplace. In his report, "Competing in the Age of Talent: Quality of Place in the New Economy," he says, "Simply put, regional advantage accrues to places that offer the lifestyle advantages required to attract talent, as well as the economic and career opportunity and the ability to attract firms and industry."

Building Communities

Arts and cultural amenities in urban areas also attract city dwellers, specifically young professionals and empty-nesters, to upscale housing. To these groups, proximity to cultural activities is an important factor in their choice of location. They want to be in a neighborhood that doesn't shut down at 5 P.M., one that offers dining and entertainment choices within walking distance and a vibrant street scene at all times of the day.

The new Guthrie Theater and the Mill City Museum are two important cultural elements of an ongoing effort to revitalize one of Minneapolis' oldest neighborhoods. The Minneapolis Riverfront Development District represents a partnership between civic entities, real estate developers and cultural organizations that aims to convert the area from a utility to a vital public amenity. The district, which spans both banks of the Mississippi River between interstates 94 and 35W surrounding downtown Minneapolis, includes 4.6 million square feet of commercial, industrial and cultural space, more than 600 hotel rooms, 3,400 residential units, and 9,800 parking spaces. In an area recently dominated by surface parking lots, condominium developments started after the announcement of the Guthrie project are being occupied at prices ranging from $317,000 to $1.5 million.

Other cities like Philadelphia, Seattle and Fort Worth, Texas, have experienced booms in overall economic activity after new arts venues moved in. The Kimmel Center and other new and renovated theater venues along Philadelphia's Broad Street have helped to revitalize the city. The office vacancy rate along Broad Street has dropped from 40 percent to 7 percent. More than 2,500 residential units were added to the area. National retailers have moved in, and the city has experienced 167 percent growth in restaurant business. In addition to its positive impact on Philadelphia's economy, Kimmel has helped to establish Philadelphia as an international arts destination, welcoming more than 1 million visitors since its opening in December 2001.

Building Public and Private Partnerships

In a 2001 brief, the National Governors Association advised members to consider the role of arts in economic development. "Governors can position their states to use the arts effectively by promoting new partnerships among state agencies, communities, and the business sector and by harnessing the power of the arts and culture as tools that unite communities, create economic opportunity and improve the quality of life," the brief said.

Kathy Ehrmann, a principal with Keewaydin, says that looking at examples like Philadelphia, where the interests of civic leaders and arts organizations combined to create Kimmel Center, are especially useful in showing how partnerships can benefit the entire community. "The community leaders want to strengthen their cities, and the arts organizations want to improve and expand their cultural offerings, but they need help from each other," she says. "It's often our job to get everyone singing off the same sheet of music."

Keewaydin has not only been involved with the Guthrie Theater in developing partnerships, but the firm has expanded its arts consulting business nationally. Last year Keewaydin completed a study for four performing arts organizations in Portland, Oregon, to help them determine the feasibility of a new performance venue for their city. The study resulted in a Master Plan for the Arts, which includes construction of two new venues within a seven-year period and capital improvements to two existing venues, all at a cost of approximately $200 million. Keewaydin recommended a crucial first step in the process: The establishment of a Community for the Arts Task Force made up of civic officials, community leaders, and arts representatives.

Why Invest in the Arts?

So in an era when public and private coffers are depleted, it's easy to ask why arts investment should be a priority. With more than $500 million dedicated to projects like the Guthrie Theater, the Walker Art Center, the downtown Minneapolis Public Library, the Children's Theater and the Mill City Museum, Minneapolis is an example of a community building for the future. Minnesotans understand that every dollar spent on such projects yields many multiples of payback in direct economic activity from jobs and tourism. More importantly, we know that cultural enhancements are a catalyst for long-term economic vitality, attracting the knowledge workers who influence commercial and residential developments that build solid foundations for our future.

CHAPTER 22

Miramar and Other Cities Use Libraries and Cultural Amenities to Create Town Center

Mike Sheridan

Mixed-use town center developments are becoming increasingly a must-have for suburban and exurban communities across the country.

In the once-sleepy bedroom community of Sugar Land some 20 miles west of Houston, developers are constructing the Sugar Land Town Square, which will feature high-rise buildings with residential lofts, as well as office, retail, and restaurant components, all anchored by the new Sugar Land City Hall. "We are seeing a number of municipal buildings, such as a city hall, now being included in new town center projects," says David Lewis, president of Houston-based Lewis Realty Advisors, a valuation and advisory services firm. "When you are trying to create a main street feel in suburban America, there's nothing like the presence of an authentic city hall, the heartbeat of a community. People crave the feeling of community that many small towns have given us in the past, with the county courthouse being the center of town and social life."

About a thousand miles to the north, in West Des Moines, Iowa, General Growth Properties' Jordan Creek Town Center has introduced a broad selection of shopping and entertainment activities to central Iowa. The 2 million-square-foot master-planned development includes a two-level enclosed shopping center, plus a 3.5-acre lake surrounded by bike trails, pedestrian walkways, and a boardwalk. The development also has a collection of large and specialty retailers in an open-air lifestyle center design. "Shopping centers are evolving into more than just retail," says John Bucksbaum, chief executive of General Growth Properties. "We are creating experiences at our centers. Jordan Creek Town Center is the blueprint for our new developments and redevelopments moving forward."

In Miramar, Florida, city officials have approved construction of a town center that will include municipal uses such as a new city hall, a public library, a cultural center arts park, and an educational facility, all surrounded by residential, retail, office, and entertainment space. A joint venture of Rockefeller Group Development Corporation and Kimco Developers, Inc., is slated to purchase the land earmarked for the mixed-use retail,

Originally published as "Centering Towns," *Urban Land*, Vol. 64, No. 4, April 2005, by the Urban land Institute, Washington, D.C. Reprinted with permission of the publisher.

office, and residential components of the project. The new development will be a "genuine town center with arts, commerce, social, civic, and government activity," says Mayor Lori Moseley.

The town center concept is changing, developers say. Consumers now demand places offering more urban, walkable facilities that serve as gathering spots for individuals and provide a sense of community through a well-thought-out, cohesive design. Called town centers, transit-oriented developments, urban villages, or main street developments, these new offerings seek to create unique places with lasting value. Already such developments have challenged conventional wisdom about consumers, retailing practices, building design, parking arrangements, and housing types. The desire of Americans to live in neighborhoods that provide a higher quality of life is expected to result in the creation of even more town centers in the years ahead that integrate housing, office, retail, and entertainment space.

John Torti, president of Torti Gallas and Partners, an architecture, planning, and urban design firm based in Silver Spring, Maryland, says his firm is working on a half dozen town center developments in several areas. Each development is unique to the area, he explains, and developments include what he characterized as the "true" town center, the "fill the hole in the doughnut" town center, and the "build it and they will come" town center.

A true town center — an area that is, in fact, the governmental and civic core of a municipality — is being built in south Florida's Miramar community, whose new city hall is the centerpiece of its town center. "Miramar does not enjoy the beaches of a Fort Lauderdale or a Palm Beach, but it had profitable tax generators such as big-box and industrial users," says Torti. "Because the city was running out of space in its present city hall, it decided to build a new mixed-use town center neighborhood and purchased a parcel in the geographic middle of the town for its new city hall and a new performing arts center to make

the once-moribund area a desirable live/work/play environment." The city is selling the surrounding parcels to private developers for office, housing, and retail uses to animate the center and to help defray some of the costs of buying the land and building the city hall, he says. "It's very unusual and very exciting. Miramar is a real, honest-to-goodness town center."

In contrast, at Orlando's bustling Baldwin Park is an example of another type of town center — an effort to "fill the hole in the doughnut." The developers of Baldwin Park have transformed a 1,000-acre set of neighborhoods, once the Orlando Naval Training Center, into residential, office, and retail space. "The surrounding area has existing infrastructure and people are already living there. The development, however, is in search of a central place — a civic heart, if you will — in the midst of the new neighborhoods," says Torti. "In this case, the town center is in an area where a full-size Publix supermarket is located on a new main street of shops and restaurants with housing above. It is essentially a fourth neighborhood with a main street used as a town center."

The Twinbrook development in Rockville, Maryland, is a similar infill town center. "Its generator is the existing transit station surrounded by well-established residential, employment, and retail neighborhoods," says Torti. "This transit-oriented development creates a new town center of 2.5 million square feet of mixed-use new urbanism where old, underutilized warehouses once existed along the tracks."

Torti says a third category of town center is greenfields development, in which a new town center is used as the generator or marker of the development. An example is Disney's Celebration community in Florida, he says, where developers built the town center first "as a stake in the ground" to identify the place, and it, in turn, became the generator for housing development. "They built the town center upfront and it became an identifiable symbol of the town: a very handsome place that operates on the same set of principles as a town center with wonderful mixed uses — a place where you could live, work, shop, and enjoy. The town center was used as a generator for the residential development that followed."

The keys to a successful town center, Torti explains, are numerous high-density mixed uses and an appealing public realm designed especially for pedestrians and their activities. It needs to have good connections to neighborhoods and the region so that people can come and enjoy it, and it must have a mix of activities so it is full of life not only in the day, but also during evenings and weekends. "Thus, today's new town center becomes a place people want to go to as a reflection of their lifestyle," says Torti. "We are basically remaking suburbs that were built over the past five decades to create more intimate, interconnected areas."

The town center concept can be expanded to encompass plans to relieve traffic congestion as well, notes John Ellis, principal at WRT/Solomon E.T.C. of San Francisco. Transit-oriented developments (TODs) as well as town centers are popular in many cities and towns on the West Coast because municipalities are realizing that they need to offer an opportunity for growth without necessarily increasing traffic congestion or continuing sprawl into greenfield sites.

"Transit-oriented development is a hot-button issue today because people realize that as our communities get bigger and our highways become increasingly congested, it makes sense to build higher-density developments around transit networks," says Ellis. In the San Francisco Bay area, for instance, transit-oriented development is being planned along several of the region's transit corridors, including the 72-mile Bay Area Rapid Transit (BART) network, the Caltrain system, and Amtrak's Capitol Corridor. "At many of those stations, the huge surface parking lots that have been destructive to the life of the surrounding community have been rebuilt as mixed-use developments," he says.

Recognizing that marrying mass transit and real estate development could be a smart move, forward-thinking California communities such as Hercules, Hayward, and Mountain View are embracing TOD to revitalize neighborhoods.

"Several communities have turned surface parking lots into structured parking areas and then built high-density multifamily developments," says Ellis. "Recent examples include the Fruitvale BART mixed-use development and downtown Hayward, where, as master planners, we proposed the new city hall, multifamily housing, and new retail next to the BART station." In Mountain View, WRT/Solomon E.T.C. designed a TOD/residential infill project that demonstrates how development can occur successfully in an upscale suburb while responding to the local context and the needs of the community. "A big part of this plan is obtaining community acceptance," emphasizes Ellis.

One of WRT/Solomon E.T.C.'s most recent projects was a study that reimagined the Hacienda Business Park in Dublin, about 30 miles east of Oakland. The business park consisted of a huge arterial road network with acres of surface parking surrounded by isolated low-density office buildings. Originally planned in 1985 and adjacent to a new BART station, Hacendia Business Park is a good candidate for a mixed-use community rather than one with a single use. "We worked within the constraints of the existing infrastructure to create a new network of streets and blocks," says Ellis. "Since some 65 percent of the land in the business park was surface parking, we suggested creating a parking district and building parking structures. In addition, we proposed reducing the width of some of the roadways and liberated land for development."

Such reconstruction is occurring all over the United States. "We must continually come up with new ideas for places that have reached the end of their natural economic cycle, such as dead shopping malls, empty business parks, or defunct brownfield sites, and create more compact, mixed-use communities that are smarter and more sustainable," says Ellis.

Near the Fruitvale BART station in Oakland, for example, San Francisco's Patri Merker Architects is designing a mixed-use development that consists of residential condominiums and retail lease space. Piero Patri, a principal at Patri Merker, says the idea is to be as flexible as possible with new TOD developments. "Many cities are grappling with similar problems, so it's an interesting challenge," he says. "Our key idea is to offer flexible space in a development that will evolve over time."

As a result of the increasing popularity of public transit and the importance of smart growth initiatives, the land surrounding transportation hubs has grown significantly more valuable, continues Nate Cherry, a vice president in the Los Angeles office of Baltimore, Maryland–based RTKL Associates' planning/urban design group. Consequently, developers and municipalities are looking to increase the density and to diversify the uses around these hubs. "What used to be just retail is now retail, office, and residential," says Cherry. "For example, in Anaheim, California, the downtown redevelopment project that began 20 years ago has evolved to accommodate a changing economic climate. As traffic woes have heightened in the region, development has demanded more than an office base. Today, residential is a major component in Anaheim's town center redevelopment plan."

Cherry says he is also seeing changes in how TOD projects are being created. "There's significantly more diversity in the kinds of developers getting involved in a single project, and public agencies are playing a far more proactive role in assembling a good development team," he explains. "In California's San Gabriel Valley around Pasadena, developers are scrambling to get involved in these transit projects because they want to take advantage of the high-density options. It took the market ten to 15 years to realize that transit is a plus, and now these are some of the best projects to be involved in."

This kind of development has a promising future, Cherry emphasized, adding that businesses are beginning to support transit routes, which suggests a heightened awareness of the financial benefits of transit. "Consecutive federal transportation laws are increasingly broadening funds to support transit projects," he says. "And, with every success, developers and planners are growing more knowledgeable on how to successfully implement this crucial new type of development."

A number of other developers throughout the country have latched on to the new development concepts. Simon Property Group of Indianapolis and Atlanta's Ben Carter Properties recently opened St. Johns Town Center in Jacksonville, Florida, a mixed-use town center development that will include 225 townhouses, 225 luxury apartments, two hotels, and 1.5 million square feet of retail, restaurant, and entertainment space.

Lewis notes that developers will continue to create town centers, transit-oriented developments, and other new developments designed to transform suburbs from satellite communities into more self-sufficient areas that have urban complexity without urban concentration.

"Town centers and transit-oriented developments are a way for developers and municipalities to create their own center, their own identity," says Lewis. "It is an attempt to make a development stand out, while at the same time give residents a main street feeling. The concepts will continue for some time to come."

CHAPTER 23

Pekin and Other Cities Use Libraries to Enhance Economic Development

Norman Walzer *and* Karen Scott

This chapter has four main parts (1) the "New Role" curriculum on local economic development principles and practices provided to participating librarians is described; (2) the involvement and participation of librarians in local economic development before and after the "New Role" training program are analyzed; (3) eight key strategies useful to local librarians assisting in the development efforts are identified — these approaches are drawn from case studies and anecdotal information provided by participating librarians, along with their perceptions of the impact of involvement; and (4) future directions using technological advancements for expanding library services to pursue economic revitalization, especially in small rural Illinois communities are considered.

The recession in the early 1980s brought major economic and population declines in rural areas, and Illinois was no exception. Farm consolidations and declines in agricultural employment robbed many small towns of markets that they had traditionally served. Displaced farm families, secondary school graduates, and others who had lost jobs during the period of high unemployment in rural areas left in search of better employment opportunities.

The exodus of this rural population caused many small communities to literally wither away as stores on main streets and factories closed. While the adverse impacts on central business districts were obvious to most observers, what was not as fully recognized was the loss of local leadership and the capacity of communities to assess the options available for developing a plan of action to improve local conditions to re-invent themselves in a changing environment.

Small towns must take advantage of available resources in order to improve economic conditions. Many local elected officials serve part-time and typically lack experience with local economic development practices. Typically, these officials are employed full-time in the private sector and do not have sufficient time to attend education and training programs to upgrade their community leadership skills. Because of this, they may not always recognize the resources available within the community to assist in economic development efforts.

Originally published as "Enhancing Economic Development Through Libraries," July 1998, by the Illinois Institute for Rural Affairs, Western Illinois University, Macomb. Reprinted with permission of the author.

Local librarians in small communities often possess skills and knowledge useful in assisting community leaders to chart a course of action to improve local economic conditions. In the past, however, they have not been active in these or other civic activities. They often do not realize their potential for involvement and the opportunities available to them to work with community leaders for community betterment. Lack of unfamiliarity with business practices and relatively little formal training in economic development activities have prevented librarians from active involvement in local economic development organizations and programs.

The inactivity of librarians in local development efforts is especially unfortunate for communities since much of the economic growth in recent years has been in the information economy where libraries have a special advantage: "The 'intellectual property' segment of the U.S. economy is growing at twice the rate of other growth" (Schroeder, 1988). In many small communities, libraries offer one of the few publicly available fax machines and, in some instances, they are one of the few places with public access to a computer. They also may offer special training programs to bring residents up to date on computer techniques, especially during the summer months when schools are closed.

Increasingly, astute librarians have recognized that their future will be spent in collecting and processing information needed by business and residents. Librarians also are being asked to evaluate information and data since they are in a position to know about its origin. This task requires that they are in tune with local issue and concerns.

The Illinois State Library set as one of its goals "to implement partnerships between various types of libraries and the economic community" (Illinois State Library, 1994, p. 47). The potential contribution of local libraries as a key resource in improving economic conditions and the potential for local librarians to expand their role was recognized by the Illinois State Library. It initiated a program, "Library Partners," that encouraged local libraries to partner with chambers of commerce to become more active in economic development. This program helped open the door for librarians to engage in public discussions and expand the visibility of their services to the business community.

In the early 1900s, the need for more active participation by public librarians in local economic development efforts was recognized in Illinois and a training program for librarians was started. When the "Preparing Librarians for a New Role in Economic Development" also known as "New Role" seminars were taught across Illinois, the major planning document of the American Library Association (1987), *Planning and Role Setting for Public Libraries*, did not include the library's role in supporting business or economic development. The Illinois State Library funded the Illinois' Institute for Rural Affairs (IIRA), located at Western Illinois University, to initiate a training program that prepared librarians to aggressively support local economic development efforts. The "New Role" seminars, funded with a Library Services and Construction Act (LSCA) grant, validated the concept that supporting business and economic development efforts was a legitimate role for librarians in Illinois. The "New Role" program included seminars, teleconferences, guidebooks, and on-site technical assistance from university faculty working with more than 100 local librarians. This training effort and its effects on the involvement by local librarians in development efforts are described below.

Businesses benefit greatly from increased library services and these services will be even more important in the future. Significant savings exist when library subscription costs, both on-line and in print, are shared rather than duplicated by businesses or community leaders and when specialized information sources can be obtained by libraries on interlibrary loan. The time needed to search for essential market information can be drastically reduced when skilled librarians assist local business leaders.

The market for libraries in many small communities is shifting from a place where residents mainly check out books and read newspaper to a community information center serving a broad cross-section of residents, including businesses. Part of this expanded role includes informing residents of the information available as well as training them to access it.

The "New Role" approach in Illinois required an investment of time and money in public librarians to broaden their horizons and enable them to assist community leaders in designing effective strategies for the future of the community. It is a recognized principle that community development with local human resource capacity-building must precede or at least accompany economic development. Libraries, as a major institution in many small towns, can play an effective role in bringing the community together and helping residents make informed decisions about their future.

Armed with knowledge and skills, local librarians can engage in public discussions with business and community leaders to help select appropriate strategies for their community. Librarians have access to materials about strategic planning and are encouraged to undertake long-term planning in their operations (Himmel and Wilson, 1998a). In some instances, librarians participating in this project have played an active role in planning and development efforts and, in a few instances, have assumed leadership roles or initiated development efforts. Shifting librarians from their traditional roles of providing library services and making them economic developers, however, was never the intent of this program. Rather, it was intended to help broaden and strengthen the services provided by libraries and to encourage better marketing of library services.

Traditionally, at least in rural Illinois, local librarians were not active in economic development practices in the past. This does not necessarily reflect poorly on librarians because many small communities in Illinois did not have an organized approach to economic development in which librarians can participate. As more communities start organized development efforts, additional opportunities for library involvement will exist.

Another reason for the relative inactivity is that many local public libraries in Illinois are small. They also may not have the financial resources to support additional services, and in some instances, may not have the support of the library board of trustees. These characteristics are verified in the 1994 survey of libraries, which generated 182 responses. Of the 148 libraries responding to the question of size, 61 reported an average of 1,617 people served and only 47 reported serving a population of 10,000 or more. Responding libraries reported an average of five full-time employees, but these are mainly in libraries serving a population of 10,000 or more. Two-thirds of the libraries reported between one and two full-time staff, and two to four part — time staff. In libraries with so few personnel, it is unlikely that librarians have much time to work on projects beyond tradition library services.

The 1994 mail questionnaire requested information on reasons for libraries not supporting community development activities. The largest number of librarians (21.3%) reported that the main reason was that "the library had not been asked." Community leaders may not perceive librarians as having expertise on development issues, or perhaps librarians did not express their interest in these efforts.

Nearly one-fifth (18.1%) of responding librarians reported no involvement because "organized community development efforts are not underway in their community." This is especially true in small communities with limited professional staff. Ironically, the smaller communities may be those in which the potential for library personnel to make a significant contribution is greatest since there are relatively few paid professionals in public agencies in these locales.

Time and money constraints were also reported as important in preventing library involvement. As noted previously, many local libraries in Illinois have few full-time employees with limited or no expertise in community development. It is difficult to keep the library open with limited funds, and a high priority is placed on summer reading programs and more visible library services that directly benefit residents.

Equally interesting, however, is that only a few librarians (5.9%) reported that the director and staff do not have the appropriate skills. It is possible that they did not fully understand the economic development process and therefore did not know what fully participating in this arena requires. At the very least, they need to know the terminology and concepts used by the economic development profession. In Illinois, many librarians have participated in strategic planning processes in their libraries. The techniques that they have used for their libraries, such as environmental scans and a SWOT (Strengths, Weaknesses, Opportunities, and Treats) analysis, could be readily applied to community betterment projects.

The main objective of the "New Role" project was to prepare local librarians for an expanded role in the development efforts and the starting point was to identify potential participants. Illinois has more than 2,429 libraries, but the main purpose of this project was to work with public libraries in non-metropolitan areas (University of Illinois 1996). This reduced the number of libraries to 625.

It was decided that training seminars on community development were needed.

To attract a potential clientele for this project, IIRA enlisted support from the 12 library systems in Illinois. These systems employ professional consultants to work with local libraries in multi-county service areas. Many system consultants were interested in becoming involved in community development issues and saw this as an opportunity to work with clients to broaden their vision and to become more directly involved in community efforts. A statewide advisory board of library consultants and staff of the Illinois State Library was formed to guide the project and evaluate the potential for librarians to benefit from the program.

Participants were self-selected in that those expressing an interest and willingness to participate were accepted into the program. More than 100 librarians attended at least one of the seminars and many attended all three.

In total, three day-long seminars, involving development issues and concepts, were repeated at three locations across Illinois in 1994 and 1995. In addition, resource materials for use in working with community leaders were prepared. A more detailed description of the project is available elsewhere (Walzer and Gruidl, 1996). Seminars were also provided for library consultants on several occasions as well as presentations at professional meetings such as the Illinois Library Association annual Conference. The meeting topics and agendas were designed to build capacity in local librarians and to empower the library system consultants to provide technical expertise and support participating libraries.

Topics covered during the seminars involved the following:

Basic community and economic development concepts and issues were presented so that participants became familiar with concepts and terminology used in discussions of economic development. These presentations were made by IIRA faculty and economic development practitioners. Case studies showing successful involvement by librarians in development efforts were included to encourage participants to try new approaches. The seminars were usually held in library system offices and in community colleges, places with which local librarians were familiar and comfortable.

Considerable time was spent in the seminars outlining possibilities for involvement by librarians in community decision making in general. Librarians currently engaged in similar projects in Illinois made these presentations. Learning about opportunities and successes from peers was an important element in the program. Each presenter provided resource materials and models encouraging participants to become more actively involved in local issues. Speakers also mentored participants to get them started in community efforts. The fact that the library consultants attended the meetings and participated in the discussions provided another layer of support in the library community.

Internet materials and resources useful in economic development activities were identified and presented. Librarians, especially from larger areas with major collections, presented the types of materials they had found most useful in working with community issues. Collections of reference materials, ways to market library resources to the community, ideas for business seminars held in the library, and the growing use of on-line databases were included in these presentations. Participants also learned about special collections within their region that could be accessed through interlibrary loans. Librarians received materials to use as models for marketing purposes and library programming.

Participants were shown approaches used by other libraries across the state to become better integrated into the community decision making process. Examples include hosting chamber of commerce meetings in the library, serving as a resource center for economic development information, chairing economic development committees in community organizations, and participating directly in the community development or business recruitment process.

Seminar participants were also introduced to the Library Partners program initiated by the Illinois State Library. This program obtained signed partnership contracts between local public libraries and chambers of commerce. The links between the chambers of commerce and other business organization are especially important in opening doors to local library involvement in the community on a variety of issues. More frequent contacts between business leaders and library staff can assist in helping to analyze and expand business collections.

Because the Illinois Secretary of State had recently introduced a program to expand the availability of computers and to provide access to CD-ROM and Internet products in public libraries throughout Illinois, special attention was paid to Internet resources potentially useful to businesses. Up-to-date computer equipment and Internet access are important resources for libraries to use in supporting economic expansion and business development. Participating librarians were encouraged to take advantage of these resources in marketing library services. It is equally important for librarians to know how to transform large quantities of data into efficient packages of pertinent information that the business community can use in developing markets or otherwise enhancing their operations. The seminars paid special attention to accessing community information through electronic means. After these sessions, librarians became regular users of this information.

Other supportive efforts in the seminar series included developing a list of resources available from the library, state agencies, and universities on economic development issues. Librarians who had built or expanded business collections discussed their experiences and provided ideas regarding which approaches worked best for matching collections with community needs.

Large libraries in metropolitan areas regularly host training programs for the community at large or for targeted business groups. In some instances, the library invites external speakers from agencies such as SCORE (Service Corp of Retired Executives) and the Small Business Development Centers (SBDCs). This approach can make the library a major resource for economic development training in the community for relatively little cost.

Finally, a set of guidebooks was prepared

to help participants just starting to support local economic development initiatives. These educational materials, prepared by librarians experienced in these activities and economic development practitioners, were distributed to participants in the training programs. The guidebooks include ideas and ways to host a meeting of community development groups in the library, successful approaches to surveying local businesses, a collection adequacy analysis, and development practices or principles.

Following the seminars, an IIRA project staff member provided on-site technical assistance to groups of participating librarians working on related projects. An effort was made to group libraries by region to facilitate cooperation and learning from each other. At these meetings, librarians were encouraged to contact development organizations, express an interest and a willingness to help, and invite organizations to meet in the library to see what was available. In the interim, participating librarians were provided with information about the economy of their region in tabular and graphic form to use in working with the economic development groups. They also received training in community strategic visioning efforts to assist in working with the development organizations.

Outcomes

The success of the "New Role" program can be measured by increased library activity in the economic development arena. Accurately measuring outcomes is complicated by two factors. First, gaining acceptance and becoming involved in community efforts takes time, especially where libraries have not been active in external affairs in the past. In some instances, economic development efforts are organized and conducted by a select group of business leaders or public officials. Gaining acceptance into this group is not always easy. If librarians are not well-integrated into the community decision-making process, it may take a while to become involved in a meaningful way.

Second, community and economic development projects typically take several years to reach fruition. Thus, ultimate outcomes or results from the project cannot be accomplished within a year or two. Actual involvement by librarians in community development efforts can be documented, however, and IIRA conducted periodic mail surveys of participating librarians to collect this information (Walzer and Gruidl, 1977).The mail survey responses and telephone interviews are the basis for the following comparisons and analyses.

Librarians can engage in community development efforts in several ways. For this report, we have used eight basic strategies listed below (in no specific order of importance) to categorize the efforts. Certainly, librarians are not expected to participate in each strategy, but based on phone interviews and personal contacts, these strategies capture most of the ways that librarians in this project have become more involved with the community affairs:

1. Assume new library responsibilities for economic development
2. Raise visibility of librarians in the community and market library services
3. Expand current library holdings and data collection
4. Serve as a hub for community Internet access
5. Become directly involved in community development efforts
6. Preserve community history and serve as information center
7. Establish library as a community training center
8. Redesign and customize library product line and delivery methods

Librarians differ widely in their efforts within each strategy. The specific approaches that have been more effective depend upon opportunities in the community, the abilities and experiences of the librarians, and community needs. Activities range from making presentations about library services to offering new services to holding offices in economic development or business recruitment organizations.

In general, three common outcomes from the project were reported by responding librarians. First, they made presentations to business and social organizations and/or hosted meetings for these groups in the library. While these efforts may not cause an immediate impact on community and economic development, they provide opportunities for community leaders to become acquainted with library services and personnel.

Second, librarians reported joining the chamber of commerce or community development groups and participating in the meetings. Informal conversations at such meetings may help community leaders or development group members become familiar with library resources, thereby increasing their use. The personal contacts with community leaders can produce substantial benefits both in usage and financing.

Finally, hosting seminars on local development issues allows librarians to aggressively market their services and expertise to community leaders because these officials are probably unaware of the services available and may not feel completely comfortable accessing the resources on their own. Librarians should follow up the initial contacts to increase the impact.

For a librarian to contribute extensively to local community development efforts, additional training in programs such as "New Role" seminars described in this report may be required. Librarians must at least know the terminology used in economic development discussions and they should be aware of various state and federal programs. While they need not be experts on these topics, being conversant raises their credibility and allows them to offer ideas about options for their cities.

It is important for librarians to be visible in the community and to market library services to community leaders. Librarians have found several ways to increase their visibility as shown below:

• Write columns for a local newspaper — The emphasis here is that newspaper articles, as well as library brochures, should not merely list library resources and assume people know what they contain. Rather the resources should be listed with an explanation of what they contain. The library can use the newspaper to inform the town and businesses about library acquisitions. They can also be told to access the library home page to learn more about planned library programs. The library can also place articles in the chamber of commerce newsletter tailored for the business community.

• Participate in radio and television shows — Staff can create radio and TV public service announcements and interviews. The library can also form a partnership with local public access television.

• Participate in community festivals — This not only markets the library, it shows support for activities that are important to the community and to local business.

• Participate in chamber business expo — The library can have a display booth at the annual business expos sponsored by the local chamber of commerce. Off-site reference service using web access to the library's catalog demonstrates the services the library can provide.

The libraries can expand current library holdings and data collections. Librarians collect information about the community and make it available to development groups or the chamber of commerce. In some instances, this involved purchasing census materials and related documents, if the library is not a state data center. In other instances, librarians contact a university, community college, or regional planning council to obtain detailed information that otherwise is not readily available to community leaders. Maintaining a current database can be an important service provided by librarians because it is time-consuming to find information which is not readily available from other local sources.

Librarians have also been innovative in serving as a depository for locally generated community information. Community brochures and profiles, directories of businesses and services, and other forms of information are useful to visitors or prospective business investors. Librarians can work with local chambers of commerce, if they exist, to make sure that accurate and up-to-date information is available.

Serving as a local depository for regional information is an excellent, low-cost role that librarians can play in community development. According to survey responses, 20.2 percent of the libraries had made a conscious effort to collect information to support community development efforts. In some instances, however, librarians must become better acquainted with data availability and interpretation.

A librarian in Iowa who spoke at the "New Roles" seminars reported that a visiting business owner stopped in the library in the evening when other agencies were closed. He obtained a packet of information about the community that at a later date brought a Fortune 500 company with 200 jobs to the city. This role is not expensive for the library and, at least in this case, clearly benefited the city. Distributing information for the chamber of commerce can also increase traffic through a library and broaden its clientele.

A major element of the "New Role" seminars was to acquaint participating librarians with an electronic community development and planning database sponsored by IIRA. Librarians with computers can access this database and obtain detailed demographic information for a city, county, or region at the cost of a telephone call. Librarians have become significant users of this system in their work with community leaders and business groups.

A guidebook prepared for the "New

Role" seminars explained the steps to take in building a better business collection. In the guidebook, it was suggested that an environmental scan of both the library and the community can help identify the strengths of the current business collection as well as the needs of the business community.

Both surveys and focus groups can help determine community needs. Information about economic development needs and practices should be considered as well. If economic growth is part of the community vision and the only new jobs created require a level of skills that few residents possess, a gap between the vision and reality has been identified. A gap is need. The library should determine which needs it can fill based on its strengths, weaknesses, and budgetary constraints.

The next step is to develop a local collection of print materials and to determine other types of sources to supplement the print collection. Public libraries are active in answering questions for the business community and have estimated that in 1995, they went on-line for approximately one-third of their questions (Tenopir 1998).

Libraries also house specialized data collections. The Pekin Library, for example, works with local employers to maintain a specialized collection. The important point is that local librarians identify their potential role(s) in these efforts and have the courage to move forward and make the necessary contacts, Developing strong relationships and partnerships takes time, but it can pay off in the long run as libraries gain more community support, especially when a tax referendum is on the ballot. Better community linkages also can bring gifts of collections or dollars to expand library services.

Not every library can be self-sufficient, nor should it be in this age. Illinois offers membership in a library system to all public, school, special, and academic libraries. The Alliance Library System (Pekin, Illinois) began to develop a shared database or LLSAP (Local Library System Automation program) of multi-type member holdings 15 years ago. There are now more than three million records on the RSA (Resource Sharing alliance) database. Libraries may choose either on-line or CD-ROM access to RSA.

The most cost-effective way for a local library to provide many on-line information sources is through a shared licensing agreement within the library system or from the Illinois State Library to help contain costs of on-line database access. Staff training should be negotiated in these contracts.

The Illinois State Library provides "First Search," an on-line database of periodicals and professional journals. More than 30,000 requests per month are made from the alliance Library System alone. Of all the "First Search" requests across Illinois, 75 percent are from academic institutions. However, in Illinois, even the smallest libraries have access to "First Search." In addition, the Alliance Library System has negotiated reduced rates for group access to the "Electric Library," which many school libraries find especially useful.

The Internet offers major opportunities for local libraries and these opportunities will increase dramatically with the growth of Internet services. Several options are described below.

Hometown Countryside Connection (HCC) is a community information network that enables rural communities in central and western Illinois to provide Internet access for patrons. Community information networks are also electronic information systems established and maintained by community members and organizations. HCC information is part of the World Wide Web (WWW) and is accessible to others throughout Illinois, the United States, and the world. Funding for the project was provided through a grant awarded by the Secretary of State and the Illinois State Library.

In addition to providing public Internet access, the libraries involved took a leadership role in developing sources of community information on the Internet. Twenty-four public or district libraries, serving 63 communities in 14 countries, participated in the initial project in 1996.

Each library provided training and technical support for community organizations to develop their Internet presence. The library served as the hub for coordination and initiator of the project in each community. When the grant began in 1996, most organizations did not have computers on-site and had to use the library's computers for data entry. Special software was designed to make community data entry possible by anyone, even "html illiterate."

The director of the Eureka Public Library District expressed enthusiasm about participating in HCC because it established community partnerships with the public library. "The businesses and organizations really perceived that this was a great opportunity provided by the library to the community. This project stands on its own. It fosters the image that the library is "ahead of the curve" with technological innovations" (Bell & Cloyes 1997).

Major changes in the ways the 2000 Census of Population will be distributed will offer libraries new challenges and opportunities. Much of the information at the sub-state level will not be available in print form. Consequently, libraries can offer a service in which they print basic information from the Census for users or can provide computers with access to the Census data. From a research perspective, the internet offers many new ways for libraries to serve communities, but many librarians need considerable training to effectively use the Internet as a research tool.

Librarians have also taken leadership roles in local community development activities. In fact, 31 libraries (16.5%) responding to the mail survey reported this activity. The "New Roles" seminars were not designed to significantly alter the primary mission of local libraries; however, the number of volunteers in small communities with expertise in strategic planning is small. Evaluating a community's future options requires accurate data and an understanding of local needs. Because of their familiarity with planning for internal purposes, librarians often can make important contributions to community development exercises. This contribution is enhanced by librarians' familiarity with data sources and availability. Very early in a strategic visioning and planning process, community leaders must take stock of trends and assess the need for action. Librarians have comparative advantage in providing this data.

Most librarians who have participated in the planning process, *Planning and Role Setting for Public Libraries,* understand strategic planning. When participating in communitywide and countywide economic planning, many librarians are pleasantly surprised at how many of the thought processes are easily transferable. Librarians should be confident that they can adapt their strategic planning experience using focus groups and advisory groups at the library too community and county planning efforts. Several steps in the strategic visioning and planning process depend heavily on local data. Environmental scans, for example, require statistics and demographic information. Librarians are typically comfortable and skilled in data collection and organization.

Librarians who complete the steps in *Planning for Results* will have developed skills that can be adapted to economic development planning. Librarians who attend training sessions offered by a library system on *Planning for Results* should realize that they will be simultaneously helping their community.

Librarians responding to a questionnaire were asked about changes in their work programs and the percentage of time spent on community development activities. Overall, 78.5 percent of respondents reported participating in community projects such as festivals, business expos, and similar events. However, relatively little time was actually spent on these efforts. As part of the "New Role" program, librarians were encouraged to spend at least 10 percent of their time on develop-

ment issues. This commitment, of course, requires concurrence by the library board, and that support is not always available. In fact, several librarians reported that their board was opposed to a direct involvement in community affairs. They see the library in a more traditional role — loaning books, providing summer reading programs, and answering reference questions for clients.

It is encouraging that 46.9 percent of respondents reported that the library involvement in community economic development activities had increased — either slightly or substantially — following the "new role" seminars. This figure compares with the 51.4 percent reporting that the involvement had remained the same, and 1.7 percent reporting declines in involvement. Following are several approaches used by local libraries in Illinois to increase their direct involvement in community development efforts.

A chamber of commerce is often the "nerve center" of the local business community. Joining the chamber or other economic development organizations is one of the most widely practiced strategies of "New Role" participants.

The director at Fondulac Public Library District in East Peoria hosts "Eggs and Issues," a breakfast symposium for chamber members. She is currently an officer in the chamber and will be its president in 2001. The library director at Alpha Park Library district in Bartonville, is a member of the recently formed local chamber of commerce. She plans to host a Business-After-Hours at the newly remodeled library. The director of the Odell Public Library in Morrison says "I am a chamber member. Our chamber of commerce is just great and if anyone needs my help, they just ask."

The director at the Eureka Public Library was asked by the local business association to serve on a taskforce for revitalization of the downtown area. Not every community has a local chamber, thus, knowing the alternative association is vital for librarians. "The library is seen as a viable business in town in its own right. I promote the library as such. That is why I believe I was asked to serve on the taskforce," says the library director.

The Mt. Morris Public Library Director provides an example of a librarian taking a leadership role in economic development efforts. A group interested in the economic development of the community was just starting when she began attending the "new Role" seminars. The library director helped organize the group, soon became an officer, and often hosted the meetings in the library. Many other dynamics have affected Mt. Morris since the inception of the group. The immediate consolidation of schools with a neighboring community, election of a new mayor opposed to the group's power, and sale of a major employer to another company all focused attention on the need for a consistent community approach. A capable, trained and willing librarian can do only so much. Willingness does not guarantee smooth sailing. "I will be ready to continue the activities I learned at the "New role" seminars when the time is right in my community," reported the librarian.

In the mail survey, librarians were asked whether the percentage of time spent on community development or business retention had changed in the previous three years. Approximately one-third, 34.2 percent, reported that the time spent had increased, compared with 63.6 percent reporting that they spent approximately the same percentage of time as before. Only 2.2 percent (four libraries) reported decreases. These findings are encouraging and suggest that the training efforts have been positive.

Tourism is a major industry in Illinois. In fact, Illinois leads many Midwestern states in tourism growth, and clearly tourism is becoming a major factor in rural revitalization. Many of the most popular tourist destination sites in Illinois are based on their historical uniqueness.

Main Street communities, which receive technical assistance from the Lieutenant Governor's office in Illinois, stress the historical preservation aspect of revitalizing small town character and ambience. The local library is typically the sole source for preservation/collection of information about local history.

According to the director of the Brehm Memorial Public Library, "We heavily promote our extensive genealogy collection placed in our library by Illinois Daughters of the American Revolution — Several local bed and breakfasts have been restored and opened for business in Mt. Vernon." Staff from the Savanna Public Library District report that, "The Main Street committee created their logo for everything from sweatshirts to stationery from the library's collection of historical photos."

Several libraries in the Alliance Library System have digitized information on early Illinois women and they placed this information on the WWW. The libraries have received grants for computers and scanning equipment for this project. All Illinois First Ladies are included as well as many local women who helped found local libraries, colleges and organizations. This collection attracts many visitors. Local tourist events such as the Women's Walk, a cemetery walk, have been designed by adapting materials used for the Early Illinois Women's homepage.

Libraries can serve many clientele in providing access to information and in helping clients learn how to improve their workforce skills. Some programs involve basic education, such as literacy enhancement, while others may involve assisting residents in upgrading their workforce skills. In some instances, libraries provide little more than a meeting place, while in other cases they may locate materials to be used by program participants. Several programs are described below.

Literacy Training for Welfare-to-Work participants. Librarians can assist community members seeking entry-level jobs. The library can provide a learning environment, specialized materials, and access to trained tutors to help people reach their personal literacy goals. The library may provide specifically designed facilities with private areas for tutoring and access to instructional technologies that enhance the effectiveness of tutoring efforts. Multimedia computers and software designed to encourage independent learning may be provided.

Information Literacy Instruction. "Information literacy" addresses the need for skills related to finding, evaluating, and using information efficiently. With electronic sources of information, just as with print sources, the consumer must know how to evaluate the reliability of information sources. Books, periodicals, videotapes, sound recordings, television, radio, and on-line information resources can all be used to help people understand how to find and critically evaluate information (Himmel and Wilson, 1988b). While an information literacy service involves more than just computer literacy, training in locating and evaluating on-line resources is often a major component.

Training Centers in Libraries. Training centers are built into many of the new and remodeled libraries in Illinois. According to the director of the alpha Park Public Library district in Bartonville, Internet classes are taught by the local Internet service provider and the library staff in the library training center. "Classes are still very popular, enrollment is full, and SeniorNet group members often help teach classes." Classes are held for one hour twice a month. Allowing reference staff time to become familiar with Internet sites — both through formal training and informal practice time — is necessary.

Video conferencing in Public Libraries. Video conferencing theaters were first added to individual libraries in Illinois during the most recent round of construction grants. These theaters will not doubt become more common as each library system headquarters now has a video conferencing training center, and local librarians will become familiar with this technology as they attend video conference training in library systems. As such theaters become common in more local libraries, small businesses can "borrow" the theaters for staff training.

Distance learning Facilities. The Bloomington Public Library is often used as a downlink site for video conferencing training. The Illinois State Library offers monthly statewide training sessions via this medium. Currently, this training is library-to-library and the equipment stands idle much of the time. As librarians become more acquainted to this technology, they will see the benefit of offering this service to the public as well, especially since not every small business needs on-site distance learning capabilities. Small businesses may want to "borrow" this service from the local public library, sine infrequent use often does not justify the cost of ownership. Institutions of higher education in Illinois are starting to coordinate and make efficient use of distance leaning capabilities. Partnering with higher education will expand the educational offerings that libraries can make to the public.

Survey Follow-Up

Participating librarians were surveyed again in 1997 to determine whether they had continued with the efforts they started after the "New Role" seminars. Several librarians had changed employment or retired, but the overall results are encouraging, nevertheless. The vast majority of respondents who had participated in the seminars reported that their library actively supports community development activities. When asked about the reasons for not actively supporting the efforts, the most common response was still that they had not been asked. This finding suggests that additional work is needed to help librarians be more aggressive in marketing their niche in community development efforts.

When asked to compare levels of participation in development at the time of the survey with the time prior to the workshops, 50 percent reported increases. Only 8.8 percent (3 libraries) reported less activity. Apparently, a significant number of librarians had found a niche and work with local development groups.

While the benefits to the communities of having another experienced player in the development effort can be many, libraries also benefit from more involvement in these and other community efforts. More interaction with community leaders often elicits greater support from these officials during the library budgeting process. All too often libraries become somewhat isolated and the value of their services is overlooked or minimized. By becoming an important part of the community economic development effort, they build greater support for library needs.

The Kewanee Public Library district passed two library referenda simultaneously in the last election. One for a major library building renovation project and another for a general operating funds levy. The Kewanee librarian joined the local chamber of commerce after attending the "New Roles" seminars. The Chatham librarian reported similar referenda success: "holding an office in the chamber of commerce made a difference, following an earlier failed referendum."

Building community support, however, requires an aggressive approach by librarians and it is not sufficient for librarians to simply "be available for service." They must be proactive in communicating with business and community leaders and in working with them to explore the potential contributions of the library. Expanding the business collection,, for example, can bring significant returns in terms of community support because it not only provides a direct service to business leaders, but it also brings more people into the library to see other services they might find useful. The interaction with this larger number of potential clients can also help librarians assess community needs and identify potential new services. Identifying and adapting new services by using innovative technology can be explored jointly by library staff and library users. In each case, however, broadening services and becoming more involved in the community require that librarians actively engage in community efforts and take an active position in identifying community interests and needs.

The recently published Public Library Association document, *Planning for Results: A Public Library Transformation Process*, endorses this very approach. According to Himmel and Wilson (1998a) "*Planning for Results*" emphasizes the important connection between needs that exist in a community and services that a library offers.... In determining library service responses ... areas where the library's strengths and the community's needs seem to overlap ... the library could address" (pp. 5, 24).

A constraint on library involvement in community development efforts raised several times during the project is that the library board is not directly involved in economic development efforts and, therefore, does not see the immediate value of library involvement. In these cases, the board does not wish to raise the funds (taxes) needed to support economic development. Permitting a librarian to be away from the library attending training and economic development organization meetings can bring problems, especially with limited staff. Ironically, having librarians active in community affairs may build greater interest by board members when they see what can be accomplished.

To help librarians educate their boards regarding the contributions that librarians could make, a statewide teleconference aimed at board members was held as part of the "New Role" project. This teleconference provided several case studies of librarians who had succeeded in working with community groups. In Sterling, Illinois, the downtown revitalization project involved leveling and redeveloping several city blocks surrounding the public library. The library remained the linchpin for the restored area. The library simultaneously received a LSCA library construction grant and a grant to automate its circulating system.

Librarians responding to the 1997 survey were asked about the effects of participation in community development efforts on the library. For responding librarians who had participated in both the seminars and in the survey, 44.4 percent (16 libraries) reported that the benefits were well worth the effort, and an additional 44.4 percent reported that limited benefits to the library had occurred. The 1997 survey took place more than one year after the seminars had been completed and, as noted previously, immediate results were not reported. However, the amount of benefits realized will definitely depend on the level of service provided by the library and the extent to which the librarian(s) engage in public discussions and activities. Some librarians (23.1%) reported that business section usage had increased more than other sections. The Pekin Public Library reported significant increases in usage following a personal survey of business users. It takes several years for (1) the library to gain acceptance as a participant in community development efforts, and (2) for the library budget to increase sufficiently to expand the business collection.

Summary and Conclusions

The "New Role" seminars raised several issues. First, librarians seem interested and willing to assume new roles in supporting economic development when, and if, the library board allows them to participate and raises the necessary funds to so. During a phone survey of librarians in 1998, many mentioned the validation they received from their boards after sharing seminar handouts suggesting librarians might spend 10 percent of their time outside the library interfacing with community organizations. One librarian stated, "it actually raised my own guilt level about not being more active in my community and not necessarily 'hawking' the library's services to the community." Also clear, however, is that at the start of the "new Role" seminars, economic

development support was new to many librarians, a concept with which dew were familiar.

Second. There is clear evidence that librarians have a serious role to play in supporting local community efforts. In some instances, they have assumed leadership roles. The precise involvement, however, usually depends both on the personality and interests of librarians as well as on opportunities for involvement in the community. For instance, if no organized development efforts are underway, it is unlikely that librarians will initiate them.

Third, where librarians have actively supported local development efforts, both the library and the community benefited. Support for the library increased, and local officials gained additional support in the community development efforts. There is every indication that the interaction will increase in these communities in the future.

Fourth, continued success will require that librarians receive additional training in local development practices as well as inn data analysis, presentation, and marketing techniques. Traditionally, librarians do not have expertise in these practices and may not see the opportunities available or even feel comfortable in becoming involved locally. This is especially the case in small libraries where the few personnel are already busy with summer reading programs and a host of other valuable services that the community expects.

The rapid growth of the Internet and its potential for information processing are quickly changing the role played by public libraries, especially in small communities. Even their traditional role of providing basic information is being challenged by the relatively easily alternative access to sometimes better sources at lower cost. Students in secondary schools are being introduced to the Internet as a basic research tool, and as they enter the workforce, will rely on information obtained from the Internet more than from the traditional local library. The challenge for the librarian is to work with this advancing technology and make sure that the library has a niche.

The Internet's increasing popularity does not mean that it will replace local libraries; however, these libraries certainly must change the way they process and deliver information if they are to remain relevant to their communities. Libraries certainly must adopt and embrace electronic data processing and look for ways in which they can increase the value added if they are to continue attracting public support.

Data are retrieved in bits and bytes. Enough bits and bytes of data appropriately related become useful information. Public officials and business people need librarians with expertise in retrieving appropriate information from reliable, authoritative sources whether in print or electronic format. The librarian has a role as an educator, as well as a retriever. A librarian provides an "interface" between the information consumer and the ever-expanding, increasingly complicated myriad of data available. Prosperity in the future requires that local librarians obtain additional training in assembling data used for public policy decisions and in ways to present it as information, rather than data, to public officials.

Helping businesses and community leaders find accurate and appropriate data efficiently is still the basic role of the information specialist or librarian. The major question re-

mains "Do community leaders perceive librarians as the appropriate authority to ask for help, and do librarians feel confident enough in this role to promote their expertise aggressively?"

References

American Library Association, 1987. *Planning and Role Setting for Public Libraries.* Chicago: American Library Association

Bell, Lori and Kay Cloyes. 1997. *Hometown Countryside Connection Final Report.* Pekin: Alliance Library System.

Bleiweis, Maxine. 1997. *Helping Business — The Library's Role in Community* Economic *Development.* New York: Neal-Schuman Publishers, Inc.

Dent, Harry S. 1993 *The Great Boom Ahead.* New York: Hyperion.

Himmel, Ethel and William James Wilson. 1998a. *Planning for Results: A Public Library Transformation Process.* Chicago: American Library Association.

Himmel, Ethel and William James Wilson. 1998b. *Planning for Results: A Public Library Transformation Process, the How-To-Manual.* Chicago: American Library Association.

Illinois State Library. 1994. *The Illinois State Library's Long Range Program Utilizing Library Services and Construction Act Funds 1994–1998.* Springfield, IL: Illinois State Library.

Schroeder, Pat. (Former Congresswoman). 1998, March 13. *Keynote Speech at Public Library Association.* 7th Annual Conference in Kansas City.

Tenopir, Carol. 1998 "Online Databases." *Library Journal* 123 (8): 32–33.

Vavrek, Bernard, 1995, "Rural Libraries and Community Development." *Wilson Library Bulletin 69 (5): 42–44.*

University of Illinois. 1996. *Illinois Public Library Statistics: A Guide for Librarians and Trustees.* Champaign, IL: Graduate School of Library Science and Information Science Library Research Center.

Walzer, Norman, and John J, Gruidl. 1996. Winter. "The Role of Small Public Libraries in Community Economic Development." *Illinois Libraries* 78 (1): 50–56.

Walzer, Norman, and John J, Gruidl. 1997, Fall. "Rural Public Libraries and community Economic Development." *Illinois Libraries* 79 (4): 178–181.

CHAPTER 24

Philadelphia and Other Cities Use Museums as Vehicles to Promote Urban Development

Susan Breitkopf

Downtown Denver is booming. Nearly 2,000 residential units are under construction, and more than 5,000 are in the planning stages.

With a flurry of housing being built in and around downtown, developers are getting creative about luring residents to their projects. "The developers are starting to dissect and understand the demographic groups interested in downtown and tailoring their projects to those groups," says Ken Schroeppel, creator of DenverInfill.com, which tracks projects in and around downtown.

Developers are attracting these new residents with fine restaurants, appealing retail, upscale hotels, and even museums.

By 2009, Denver will have three major new museum buildings in its downtown. Two of these projects — the new wing of the Denver Art Museum (DAM) and a new space for the Museum of Contemporary Art — are the anchors for mixed-use developments. This has as much to do with developing a rich cultural landscape as it does with attracting to the downtown area wealthy residents who have a lot of disposable income and will contribute to the tax base.

The old model for museums involved a white-marble institution set back from the street with dozens of stairs. That changed starting in 1939 with the groundbreaking for the Museum of Modern Art (MoMA) in New York City. Breaking a long museum tradition, according to Marjorie Schwarzer's book *Riches, Rivals, and Radicals: 100 Years of Museums in America*, MoMA moved toward the city's commercial core. Not only was it located away from the city's Museum Mile district, visitors entered directly from the sidewalk through a set of glass doors. Gone were the giant staircases that set most museums apart from the bustle of everyday life.

These days, museums in cities such as Louisville, Kentucky; Washington, D.C.; Charlotte and Raleigh, North Carolina; and Philadelphia are finding themselves as anchors in or centerpieces of mixed-use residential developments. If shopping malls, movie theaters, and restaurants can anchor a development, why not a museum?

"Museums realize they aren't isolated islands [and are] making themselves part of a vibrant community," notes social theorist

Originally published as "Cultural Assets: Museums Turn to Mixed Uses," *Urban Land*, Vol. 65, No. 9, September 2006, by the Urban Land Institute, Washington, D.C. Reprinted with permission of the publisher.

Richard Florida. As Florida wrote in his 2002 book *The Rise of the Creative Class*, "Place is the key economic and social organizing unit of our time." With that idea in mind, museums are capitalizing on people's desire for community and a high quality of life.

Although Denver is a city known for its outdoor pursuits, it is banking on its cultural institutions to diversify its leisure offerings as well as attract residents for downtown. The city and its business sector are investing heavily in arts and culture, which generate more than $1.3 billion per year in economic activity in the Denver metropolitan area, according to a 2004 Colorado Business Committee for the Arts study.

Denver is rallying around museums in such developments because it wants to attract what Florida calls the creative class — the people who work in research, the arts, or any other knowledge-based profession — which he contends is the force behind the country's booming economic regions. Cities that have large contingents of the creative class want to keep them and attract more; those that do not, want them.

"Creative people's scarcest resource is time," says Florida, who has written extensively on the creative economy. "They demand spaces that are close to everything. People don't want to sit in traffic."

In his research, Florida saw repeatedly that the creative class wanted more in a community than watering holes and shopping malls. "We found that people wanted experiences that weren't self-destructive," says Florida. "The real thing to understand is people want stimulation in their lives."

The Denver Art Museum worked with the city and local firm Mile High Development on the building adjacent to its new museum space, slated to open in October. The city built a 980-car above-ground parking garage badly needed for museum-goers and downtown visitors, and the developer constructed Museum Residences, a 56-unit residential and retail development that wraps around two sides of it. This structure and the museum, both designed by star architect Daniel Libeskind, are so close to each other that the jagged spires of the museum are a mere 35 feet from dining tables in some of the residences. The units sold out in their first few months on the market; among the buyers were the city's head of economic development and the DAM's director.

Those buying into the development are largely the empty-nester crowd, says George Thorn, president of Mile High Development. "You need a location that's unique," he says. "It's got to be a site that's good for museum [-goers] but has to be where people want to live."

Also planned just a block away is the Clyfford Still Museum, a $10.5 million project dedicated to the late abstract expressionist painter. The museum announced in July that it had selected five architects as semifinalists for design of the building, scheduled for completion in 2009.

Across town, the Museum of Contemporary Art (MCA) is anchoring a development that broke ground in late spring. Mark Falcone, CEO and founder of Denver-based Continuum Partners, a development company that specializes in large-scale, mixed-use projects, and his wife donated the land for the museum. The Falcones, longtime MCA patrons, also decided to live in the mixed-use development that will surround the museum. "We both knew we wanted to relocate downtown, and we integrated that into the museum process," says Mark Falcone.

It is the first time Continuum has included a museum in a development, but Falcone says it is a natural fit. "The kinds of neighborhoods we like to develop have unique centers of gravity that include commercial, civic, and cultural activity within them," he says. "Value is established by streets and neighborhoods rather than individual houses."

In this case, money was not the primary motivator. "MCA was a more personally motivated decision and an act of patronage. [We are] helping advance an important cultural asset," says Falcone. But, he concedes, anchoring the development with MCA will be enormously beneficial to his company in the long term. And in the short term, "having a museum located on the property helps sell the residential developments."

In Louisville, the nearly $400 million, four-skyscraper Museum Plaza development will dramatically alter the city's skyline and offerings. Connecting the buildings will be an island that will float 22 stories above ground and house the city's contemporary arts museum. The complex will also contain restaurants and stores, 85 luxury condominiums, 150 lofts, a 300-room hotel, office space, and a 1,100-stall underground parking garage.

This project is the next step in a downtown revitalization plan more than 20 years in the making. Over that time, the city has been aggressive in giving incentives and pitching in its own resources to make downtown a cultural district. Several museums already exist in the neighborhood, including the Muhammad Ali Center, a museum and cultural center dedicated to the boxer's legacy that opened last year, and the Frazier International History Museum, a military history museum that opened in 2003.

"Almost 2,000 units of housing are being constructed as we speak," says Mayor Jerry Abramson. "It is a very exciting time to be in our community. It's becoming more and more of a 24/7 neighborhood."

In Washington, D.C., construction is underway at the new site for the Newseum, a museum of journalism. New York City–based Polshek Partnership Architects has designed seven levels of galleries, theaters, a food court, a two-level Newseum store, an 11,000-square-foot (1,020-sq-m) conference center on two levels, a three-level space slated for a Wolfgang Puck restaurant, and more than 140,000 square feet (13,000 sq m) of residences.

When looking to relocate from suburban Arlington, Virginia, in the late 1990s, the museum was not set on a mixed-use environment. But the site — the last undeveloped property between the White House and the Capitol, according to museum president Peter Prichard — was designated for mixed use by Washington's master plan to attract residents to live downtown. "There's some prestige associated with living on a museum site and near the great museums of Washington," says Prichard. "[And, in turn,] it will be nice to have people living next to us. A good building brings value to everyone."

The museum and its affiliated nonprofit foundation, the Freedom Forum, own the building and will collect rent from the residential dwellings and restaurant space. Despite the arrangement, Prichard says the museum will never break even, given the costs of producing the highly technical exhibits.

Museum involvement in real estate transactions is not new. MoMA was one of the first museums to get into the mixed-use business, selling its air rights in the 1970s — to a residential developer that built a 44-floor condominium tower — to fund an expansion that opened in 1984.

The MoMA project was not without its share of battles, Harold Snedcof wrote in his 1985 landmark study *Cultural Facilities in Mixed-Use Development*, published by the Urban Land Institute. State legislation allowing creation of a museum trust that would administer the real estate project went through several incarnations before being passed in 1978. "Fears that an involvement with commercial real estate would compromise the integrity of the museum have thus far proven groundless," wrote Snedcof. "The museum has been kept at a distance from the commercial aspects of the tower's construction and the sale of its apartments." In the end, it was a wise financial decision for the institution, enabling an expansion without crippling the museum financially.

These days, museums involved in real estate have fewer qualms about the financial gains. The Museum of Life and the Environment, which will anchor Kanawha, a 400-acre

(162-ha) tract of land in York County, South Carolina, located seven miles (11 km) south of Charlotte, will get its endowment in part from residential property sales. The community around the environmental history museum will include about 750 single-family homes; several hundred multifamily units; about 50 acres (20 ha) of retail, office, and institutional buildings; and possibly a sustainable organic farm. The entire project, which is being designed by William McDonough, whose firm is based in Charlottesville, Virginia, will be constructed and operated according to the U.S. Green Building Council's Leadership in Energy and Environmental Design (LEED) guidelines.

The money from sales of residential properties in the surrounding development will be distributed to the property's subcorporation, according to Van Shields, director and CEO, Culture and Heritage Museums, which operates the Museum of Life and the Environment. Those funds then will flow to the museum's foundation through dividends, which in turn will fund the museum.

Shields is enthusiastic about the setup because of the solid footing it will establish for the museum for the future. "Museums need to understand that meeting their missions means being able to pay for it," he says.

Cynthia Nikitin, vice president of Project for Public Spaces, based in New York City, agrees that such arrangements constitute sound financial planning. "If you invest in a building and sell apartments, that's money free and clear," she says. "That's like taking the gift shop to a whole other level in terms of a funding stream."

"It provides them a lot of ready cash to cover their expenses," she adds. "They are being driven by a robust real estate market and the ever-shrinking pot of public and private dollars."

In Raleigh, Charlotte-based Grubb Properties is developing a visual arts complex on a half-acre (0.2-ha) site occupied by a 20,000-square-foot (1,860-sq-m) warehouse in a project that likely will include residential units, artist studios, retail space, and the city's Contemporary Arts Museum (CAM). "It's the first time we have had a museum as part of a mixed-use development," says Steve Biggerstaff, Grubb's vice president for marketing. "It will be a little of everything in a neat little corner in the warehouse district of Raleigh."

The CAM bought the empty warehouse about a decade ago, but did not have the money to renovate it. Since then, CAM, which spun off its fundraising activities into the Contemporary Art Foundation, has raised enough money to begin the construction process. In addition, last year it received a $1 million grant from the city.

"Grubb Properties saw the intrinsic value of this development — that a museum connected to condos could increase the value and excitement for our prospective residents and funders," says Linda Satterfield, board chair of the Contemporary Art Foundation.

The entire property, currently owned by the foundation, will be sold to Grubb, Satterfield explains. The foundation will then buy back the museum space and act as a landlord to the museum. The money from the sale will help pay for the museum building's operating expenses. "It will enable us to bring our mission to life," says Satterfield.

The planning is still in its infancy, and the involved parties are deciding whether to tear down the warehouse. Either way, the site will include a mix of affordable housing for artists and market-rate housing, underground parking, office space for the museum, and possibly office space for other cultural institutions. "This is about bringing life and residents into this district, which doesn't have much residential," says Paul Ostergaard, a principal of Pittsburgh-based Urban Design Associates, which held a charrette for the project.

In Philadelphia, Alon Barzilay, partner and vice president of development of the Klein Company, is working on a luxury high-rise of 150 condominiums along the city's Museum Mile, home of the Philadelphia Art Museum and the Franklin Institute. Museums contribute to a snowball effect in creating and revitalizing neighborhoods, such as the one surrounding the museums, says Barzilay.

"We see them as a great source and anchor," he says. "It's not just about art hanging on the walls. There are social activities and events. Museum are great places to meet people and should be a daily experience."

Like many other developers, Philadelphia-based Klein Company's target audience is young professionals and empty nesters, both of which are moving to cities more and more. "They're bored of the local experience they've had a million times," says Barzilay. "They're coming into the city to experience something new."

Robert McNulty, president and CEO of Washington, D.C.–based Partners for Livable Communities, says these audiences are the new focus of community and developer attention. "Any community that's wise will appeal to baby boomers and 18- to 34-year-olds," he says. "Any institution we would call an amenity is crazy not to form partnerships with these demographic groups."

In particular, the baby-boom generation is viewed as a cash cow. "Baby boomers have more money, live longer, and are better educated than any other group in history," he says.

DenverInfill's Schroeppel agrees that the most sought-after demographic is empty-nester baby boomers, followed by the young professional crowd. "You're starting to see projects really targeting demographics that haven't been targeted up to this point," he says. "It leads to a higher probability of presales."

With all these partnerships under way, it is difficult to see any downside for the developer or the museum. Snedcof foresaw a few caveats in his study. "Only when mixed-use projects make financial sense apart from the arts should plans be made for including cultural components," he cautioned. "This comprehensive planning ... will guarantee that all the project uses, revenue producing and non-revenue producing, will support and augment each other."

Denver's leap into the museum/mixed-use realm is a well-planned one the city has placed a lot of stock in. Denver Mayor John Hickenlooper is pleased with what is taking place in his city and sees the museum-developer partnerships as being beneficial in yet another way. "Those people [living near the museum] are going to be part of the buzz — not just when the building opens, but every time there's a new show," he says. "They're part of the marketing team, not just for the museum but for the city."

CHAPTER 25

Phoenix Uses Museum as Focus for Renewal in Its Downtown

William Fulton

The unfinished superstructure of the Bank One Ballpark towers 20 stories above downtown Phoenix like a gigantic empty barn, awaiting the retractable roof that will make it possible to play baseball in the desert heat.

When the building is ready, at the start of the 1998 season, Maricopa County residents will see what they have purchased with the $350 million in sales tax money the project is costing them. If things turn out the way local leaders hope, they will have more than a stadium. They will have a full-fledged urban theme park. Bank One Ballpark — known affectionately to the locals as BOB — will include a baseball museum called Cooperstown West, two restaurants overlooking the field, a swimming pool and picnic areas in center field, and a sports-oriented entertainment center for kids.

In fact, Phoenix planners and politicians see BOB as the last important piece that will make downtown Phoenix into one of the leading arts and entertainment centers in the country. The new stadium is within a block of two major museums and two major concert halls. It's just a short walk from Arizona Center, the upscale retail complex where the

Diamondbacks have their own store and a full-scale stadium model. And BOB is across the street from the America West Arena, home of the Suns basketball team and Coyotes hockey team, and Phoenix Civic Plaza, the city's convention center.

The stadium's completion will give downtown 325 "event nights" a year — meaning that something big will be happening in downtown Phoenix virtually all the time. "We get 4 million visitors a year to these venues downtown," says David Krietor, the city's economic development director. "When the ballpark opens, that will double to 8 million."

Phoenix is about as unlikely a place as anyone can imagine for all this to happen. Having grown from 100,000 people in 1950 to more than 1 million today, Phoenix is the classic spread-out Sun Belt town — a suburban-style city better known for ranch-resort tourism than for downtown vitality. Located in the middle of a flat, dry valley, downtown Phoenix has no distinguishing topography and little historical cachet. In other words, there's no particular reason why anybody would want to be downtown in Phoenix as opposed to anywhere else.

Yet unlikely as it may seem, downtown is

Originally published as "Planet Downtown," *Governing*, Vol. 11, No. 7, April 1997, by Congressional Quarterly Inc., Washington, D.C. Reprinted with permission of the publisher.

now the city's focal point, drawing tens of thousands of people every night. And while it has been more aggressive than most cities in building new facilities, Phoenix isn't unusual. All across the country, sports arenas, multiplex cinemas, restaurants and other theme-type diversions are converging on America's central cities, making night-time entertainment the newest symbol of hope in the never-ending struggle for downtown economic recovery. For decades, planners have dreamed of reviving downtowns with nightlife. Now, some of them are finding to their own astonishment that it is actually happening.

Indeed, the whole idea of combining entertainment-oriented retail trade and downtown settings has become an industry unto itself. The Urban Land Institute has not only given the phenomenon a name — urban entertainment districts, or UEDs — it has even started a newsletter (The E-Zone) to keep track of developments in the field.

And there are lots of developments to keep track of. In Los Angeles, small suburban downtowns such as Santa Monica, Pasadena, Burbank and Glendale have blossomed as active centers of round-the-clock recreational activity. In mid-sized industrial cities, such as Kansas City and Baltimore, a whole new generation of entertainment centers is being built. Even in the granddaddy of all entertainment districts, New York's 42nd Street, the city has turned to no less than the Walt Disney Co. to clean up and revive the area with new attractions. "We see phenomenal growth in all forms of entertainment," says David Wilcox of Economics Research Associates in Los Angeles, a consulting firm that specializes in leisure-oriented projects.

To any older city that has lost its central department stores and confronts half-empty downtown office buildings, all these developments will seem almost too good to be true. In the end, they may be. Many of the entertainment districts are basing their strategies on construction of huge movie theaters — 20 to 30 screens — yet there is little doubt that the exhibition companies are overbuilding and a shakeout is coming. Meanwhile, shopping center developers are modifying the suburban mall to create strong competition for entertainment-oriented downtowns.

Perhaps most important, it remains to be seen how durable any entertainment-led revival will be if it is not accompanied by a resurgence in office employment and broader retail trade. Without those components, even the glitziest entertainment center stands to end up a little more than a new species of amusement park. "If downtown is just the ULI flavor of the month, then it runs the risk of every real estate fad since urban renewal," says Rick Cole, the former mayor of Pasadena, California, who presided over the rise of one of the strongest downtown entertainment districts in the country. "In the end, people simply won't care about it as a place."

The idea of the city as a stage for human drama is as old as the city itself. Indeed, the great urbanist Lewis Mumford believed the city's most basic role was as a backdrop for performance. "The ancient city," he once wrote, "was above all things a theater, in which common life itself takes on the features of a drama, heightened by every device of custom and scenery, for the setting itself magnifies the voice and increases the apparent stature of the actors."

This notion of a public space where ordinary people could participate in a great spectacle was one of the driving forces behind the first great era of American urban entertainment: the period between 1895 and 1920, when movie palaces, baseball parks and other amusements drew urban dwellers out of their dingy apartments and into the brightness of newly electrified cities. As historian David Nasaw explained in his book *Going Out: The Rise and Fall of Public Amusements*, electric lighting eradicated the public perception that cities were dark and dangerous, and technological advances — such as moving pictures — created new amusements people could not obtain at home.

Many analysts believe that the current urban entertainment fad is the result of similar conditions. After a long period of hibernation at home, Americans are now changing their once-dreary perceptions of downtown areas and seeking out new amusements in "public" settings. In the past decade, entertainment and recreation spending has grown at twice the rate of overall consumer spending. According to Philadelphia consultant Michael Rubin, Americans now spend almost as many of their leisure dollars on "congregating" activities, such as amusement parks and movies, as on "cocooning" activities, such as VCRs, books and home computers.

"A whole generation of Americans are starved for social interaction because they didn't grow up in cities," says Michael Beyard of the Urban Land Institute. "They grew up in private domain, and now they want something more." At the same time, they are increasingly reluctant to spend scarce disposable income on long and costly vacations. A larger share of leisure dollars is being spent close to home. Downtown, as a regional attraction that can be "hit" quickly and frequently, is well positioned to benefit.

The modern idea of using downtown as a self-conscious entertainment venue first began to surface some 20 years ago, when Maryland developer James Rouse revived both Boston and Baltimore with "festival marketplaces." These colorful retail centers, which combined boutique-style shopping with an intensely urban fun-oriented experience, have served as the cornerstone of downtown revitalization for cities all over the country. They have not worked everywhere. Smaller and less affluent cities, such as Toledo and Flint, have built festival marketplaces and found them to be expensive, well-publicized failures. But in the larger metropolitan areas, with bigger markets to draw on, Rouse-style projects have planted the idea of entertainment as the ultimate downtown solution.

Meanwhile, the use of sports and innovative movie theaters as engines of development has been spreading around the country. In Cleveland, Baltimore and Denver, old-style baseball "parks" have replaced older and less inviting stadiums and provided an anchor for downtown recreation. Downtown Baltimore attracts more visitors every year than Walt Disney World. In New York and San Francisco, high culture and popular culture are working together to bring about a renaissance that even these two sturdy poles of urbanism couldn't have foreseen. In both cities, for example, Sony is opening facilities that combine movie screens, an IMAX–style theater and "reprogrammable" attractions that can be changed via computer. Entertainment retail has helped revive the Lincoln Center area in Manhattan, while in San Francisco the Sony project has been combined with the convention center and museums to complete the 30-year-old Yerba Buena redevelopment project.

In city after city, huge multiplex cinemas now anchor retailing districts that typically include restaurants, bookstores, coffeehouses, newsstands and other complementary businesses. Retailers such as Virgin Records and Incredible Universe have attracted shoppers by transforming a visit to their stores into an entertainment experience. Increasingly, IMAX movie theaters, Sega super-arcades and various purveyors of "virtual reality" experiences have sought to take urban entertainment one step beyond mere moviegoing — not just in New York and San Francisco but in smaller cities as well.

For real estate developers crippled by the savings-and-loan debacle of the '80s, urban entertainment has been a gateway to a new source of capital: the entertainment industry — a darling of Wall Street currently awash in so much money that it is ravenously seeking new business opportunities. For many local governments, the entertainment district phenomenon has amounted to an unexpected fiscal opportunity that dropped from the sky.

In Phoenix, Mayor Skip Rimsza says his biggest problem these days is "complacency." With something like $1.5 billion in investment in downtown venues in the past decade, some critics simply don't believe that the city should be subsidizing additional facilities, such as a new luxury hotel. "People think things are going so well that we shouldn't do anything," Rimsza laments, "but we need to stay the course." The city is putting $13.5 million into the hotel.

In the Los Angeles area, where entertainment has always been a part of the social fabric, smaller downtowns that seemed uncompetitive just a few years ago are sharing in the windfall, as new facilities attract entertainment-seekers drawn to the historic architecture and intimate scale. Santa Monica's Third Street Promenade and Pasadena's Old Town have been enormously successful. Their main fear is that the coming of the megaplex theaters to the downtown streets will disrupt the tranquility of their small-town lifestyle. In fact, however, there are other clouds on the horizon.

On a vast swath of land at the intersection of two freeways 40 miles east of Los Angeles, the Mills Corp. of Virginia has created what might be the biggest existing threat to the L.A. urban entertainment boom. Ontario Mills is a 134-acre shopping center (with 88 acres of parking) that combines all the current fads in the retail world: multiplex theaters, entertainment-oriented stores and "offprice" outlets that sell high-class goods at a discount.

At a time when old-fashioned regional malls are dying, Ontario Mills is attracting some 60,000 visitors a day — double the number that will come to downtown Phoenix even after the Bank One Ballpark opens. Divided into eight different "neighborhoods" with different design themes, Ontario Mills seems like a shopping mall on steroids. Its 1.7 million square feet of space include most major offprice retailers, such as Burlington Coat Factory, Bed Bath & Beyond, and Off 5th (the Saks Fifth Avenue Outlet).

Grafted to the "outlet mall" concept, however, is a whole slew of entertainment-style businesses: a 30-screen AMC Theater, a Virgin Records Superstore, a Wolfgang Puck restaurant and a food court three football fields long. Video monitors throughout the store blast an MTV–style "Mills TV," with music videos and commercials. "I've never opened a shopping center so strong," says general manager Jim Mance, a Rouse Corp. veteran who has previously managed downtown retail projects in Seattle and elsewhere. The buzz on Ontario Mills has been so strong that Southern California cinema impresario Jim Edwards is building a 22-screen theater on a separate piece of land across the parking lot, giving the project more screens than any other location in the country.

Only the first of several large projects being planned by Mills Corp., Ontario Mills is one of several high-profile attempts to survive in suburban retailing by imitating the formula that has worked for urban entertainment. Other examples are close at hand. Some 30 miles to the south, the Irvine Co. has created another nationally recognized example — Irving Spectrum, a built-from-scratch entertainment district seeking to take advantage of the half-million drivers whizzing past its location every day on the freeways. And at Universal Studios in Los Angeles, MCA Inc. has gathered recognizable movie icons from throughout the city and reproduced them in its CityWalk retailing center — just as "New York, New York" and other theme attractions have done in Las Vegas and Orlando.

Ontario Mills and the other suburban centers show the vulnerability of entertainment-oriented downtowns — not just because they represent competition but because they reveal just how fad-driven the retailing business has become. Regional malls built 10 to 15 years ago are in trouble now because they are neither huge and cheap, like Wal-Marts, nor exciting, like entertainment retail centers. Eight-screen multiplex theaters a decade old seem comically out of date, with uncomfortable seating and bad sound. Even festival marketplaces have come to strike most consumers as last year's model. Seeking to cater to the fickle tastes of American consumers, the retailing business is metamorphosing faster than new buildings can be built. "The problem with retailing," says Peter Katz, a real estate marketing consultant and executive director of the Congress for the New Urbanism, "is that nobody knows what the next T.J. Maxx's is going to look like in five years."

Cities have begun subsidizing downtown multiplexes the way they once subsidized office buildings and hotels. Yet it's hard to know just how "sustainable" the aggressive expansion of movie screens is. Oddly, the expansion is coming at a time when the movie studios themselves are producing fewer films, not more. The new multiplexes don't show a greater variety of films, but, rather, show the same films more often.

Once the orgy of building is over, a shakeout appears inevitable — just as a shakeout in office buildings occurred after the savings-and-loan orgy of the '80s was halted by corporate downsizing in the '90s. And movie theaters are just one aspect of the market. Retailing in general appears to be overbuilt, despite aggressive expansion by some companies. The question is not whether entertainment-oriented retail will crash and burn. The question is who will survive — and whether downtowns will be among the winners.

The Rouse Corp. is continuing to bet heavily that they will. Seven years ago, a few blocks from the future site of Bank One Ballpark, Rouse opened Arizona Center, a downtown project of boutiques and restaurants overlooking a landscaped courtyard designed to stay cool during the summertime. In seven years, Arizona Center has become the state's fourth most popular tourist attraction. Still, the company has decided to change its focus, away from general retailing and toward entertainment. Rouse has kicked out several major clothing chains and is now building restaurants, a 24-screen AMC theater and a hotel.

But in order to work as an entertainment complex, Arizona Center will have to establish better connections than it now has with the streets around it. Although linked to the nearby sidewalks by a handsome row of palm trees, Arizona Center is still somewhat self-contained, oriented more toward visitors arriving from the adjacent parking garage. "It's totally introverted," says Michael Dollin, associate director of the Arizona State University Joint Urban Design Studio, whose offices are a half-block away. Arizona Center has yet to define its relationship to the arena, the ballpark, the convention center, and the museum and theater, all located within about six blocks.

In other words, for the downtown Phoenix entertainment district to succeed, it will have to succeed as a neighborhood, where different facilities and uses connect and interact with each other in a positive way. Because so many of Phoenix's downtown projects are built on a huge scale, this will not be easy to accomplish. But it may happen. All the new facilities are being overlaid on an old-fashioned downtown grid, and city officials are now placing a high priority on the creation of more housing and more office space that will put people within walking distance of Arizona Center and the other attractions. "A block is a mile in a downtown," Mayor Skip Rimsza says.

This, in a nutshell, is the challenge for downtowns as they face the inevitable shakeout in entertainment and retail trade. It is a difficult challenge, but it is not an impossible one, because most older downtowns — with their history, intimate scale, and variety — are much better stages for urban drama than suburban malls. "Downtowns definitely have a competitive advantage," insists Michael Beyard of the Urban Land Institute. "Much of the current generation grew up in the suburbs and is bored stiff."

For many real estate development specialists — and even for downtown advocates — this requires a major shift in thinking. By nature, downtowns are not simply suburban malls in a different location. They are messy places, filled with decades-old animosities, truculent property owners, homeless panhandlers and other complicating factors. A whole generation in the ruthless world of commercial development has learned to treat these facts as liabilities.

Yet even the skeptics realize that downtowns have a history, a sense of place that resonates with people, and — at their best — a reason for being that goes beyond separating people from their money. After decades of false starts, these assets are finally strong enough in may downtowns that are on the ropes. "For years, we've been teaching downtowns that they must learn from suburban malls," says Rick Cole, the former Pasadena mayor, "and all the time suburban malls have been dying."

In the years ahead, the trick will be to use entertainment in the service of downtown survival — not simply to turn downtowns into theme parks. Office-based businesses, especially government, must be nurtured to continue providing a daytime population. Local merchants must be reassured that their businesses will continue to be valued even as the boutiques and cinemas go in around them. Civic destinations such as museums and libraries — facilities everyone can use and relate to — need to play an important role in assuring that people come downtown as citizens, not just as consumers. In the end, if downtowns succeed in the entertainment era, it will be because the drama of day-to-day life in the city remains just as compelling as the drama in the movie theaters, the sports arenas and the theme restaurants that can be located anywhere.

CHAPTER 26

Portland and Other Cities Use Libraries to Promote Their Downtowns

Anne Jordan

Without question, 1995 was a landmark year in Denver. In a span of four weeks last spring, the Mile High city witnessed the grand opening of three immense public projects: the largest airport in North America, a major league baseball stadium, and new central library.

Two of the three generated national news coverage, but the news was not entirely positive. Denver's $4.9 billion International Airport was 16 months behind schedule and $3 billion over budget, and its debut generated relief rather than rejoicing. And Coors Field, the $215.5 million home of the Colorado Rockies, came in at more than twice its original estimate.

That may have been one reason why 13,000 people turned out on a chilly Saturday in March to revel in the dedication of the other member of the trio: the seven-story, $71.7 million structure described in the city's own promotional brochures as "The Big New Library." Perhaps some of those spectators wanted the reassurance of seeing the city actually finish one of its public edifices within budget. But there was another reason to show up as well. For all the hype about the airport and the sta-dium, it was the library that had become the architectural talk of the town.

From the outside, the Denver library is a striking collection of multi-colored geometric shapes — cubes, cylinders and pylons. Its creators call it a dynamic little "village" on a downtown city block. Critics deride it as an awkward mishmash of forms topped by an ungainly copper crown. But there is no question that it has quickly taken on the status of the cultural monument city officials envisioned.

On the inside, the building is more comfortable than controversial. Natural-finished solid maple is everywhere: in the pillars, paneling, windowsills, handrails, bookcases, tables, chairs — even the desk lamps. Virtually everything was custom-designed by the principal architect, Michael Graves. All around the building, but unseen by visitors, are more than 50 miles of fiber-optic cable and copper wire, hidden in the ceilings, walls and floors. "We didn't want the building to come across as a piece of machinery," says Brian R. Klipp, the associate architect. The only clue to the high-tech nature of the building is thousands of four-receptacle electrical outlets.

Originally published as "Library Renaissance," *Governing*, Vol. 10, No. 1, January 1996, by Congressional Quarterly Inc., Washington, D.C. Reprinted with permission of the publisher.

Denver's new building is part of a full-fledged national library boom. There are or soon will be brand-new central libraries or major additions in more than a dozen large American cities, and many of them, like the one in Denver, are as notable for their architectural boldness as for the services they provide. In a decade when new city halls and airports are a rarity, when most convention centers are little more than utilitarian boxes and correctional facilities soak up much of the capital construction budget, libraries are the one great exception to the drought in creative design. They are turning out to be the showpieces of urban public architecture in the 1990s.

No one would have predicted this a decade ago. The first hint of what was to come surfaced in 1991, when Chicago threw open the doors to the $144 million Harold Washington Library Center, the nation's largest municipal library at 756,000 square feet. Its massive red brick façade and crafted metalwork echo the Beaux Arts style of Chicago's first architectural Golden Age while paying tribute to the city's first black mayor.

Sacramento and then Los Angeles — with great fanfare — followed over the next couple of years. But it was the near-simultaneous opening of new libraries last year in Denver, Phoenix and San Antonio that made the library renaissance a widespread reality. And more are on the way: San Francisco, Cincinnati, Cleveland, Memphis, San Diego and Portland, Oregon.

All the excitement is especially remarkable because public library architecture has not always been a great crowd-pleaser. The classical-revival style of the early 20th century, characterized by white marble, Greek columns, grand staircases and elaborate ornamentation, seemed cold and intimidating to many library users. The International Style Modernism of the 1950s produced stark, boxy structures of glass and concrete that were difficult to distinguish from office buildings.

And in order to maximize space, the libraries of that era were designed to house most of their collections — in Denver's case 75 percent — in closed stacks. While this enabled them to cram many more books into compact shelving units, it also meant that patrons had to depend on staff to retrieve them. Many people came to think of the buildings themselves as little more than warehouses.

The libraries of the 1990s are changing that image in a dramatic way. Denver's ratio of open to closed stacks, for example, has been reversed. "Libraries have finally progressed from the medieval notion of precious books that had to be protected," says Joey Rodger, president of the Urban Libraries Council. "Now a book becomes valuable when people use it."

There are a host of reasons why a library boom is occurring at this particular moment. Some of them have to do with the natural cycle of construction over the past century.

Given their heavy usage and the fact that collections have tended to double in size roughly every couple of decades, the normal life span for library buildings has been 30 to 40 years. In most cities, the first public libraries — many of them among the 2,500 financed by Andrew Carnegie — were built early in this century. That is why, by the 1950s, most cities were ready for a new round of construction. And it is why, by the end of the 1980s, many needed to build again.

With all the recent talk about libraries becoming "virtual" in the age of cyberspace, some questioned why so much money should be invested in new buildings. But it was easy for library supporters to demonstrate that publishing was continuing to increase at an unprecedented rate and that printed matter remained "the driving force in the space requirements," in the words of Cleveland Public Library Director Marilyn Gell Mason.

Meanwhile, the growth in electronic technology had created practical problems of its own. Online card catalog systems, microcomputers, printers, fax machines, CD-ROM jukeboxes and sophisticated telecommunications infrastructure were overloading the electrical capacities of many of the '50s-vintage library buildings. Forced to configure their work stations around existing power sources or to string more wire, many libraries had electrical spaghetti everywhere.

Besides making the libraries look junky, this practice was a headache for the many buildings that were already woefully out of compliance with local fire codes. Often the only fire-suppression device was a pumper truck from the nearest station house. Indeed, Los Angeles had just begun discussing the possibility of a new facility when two arson fires gutted its historic central library and destroyed 400,000 books in 1986.

Luckily, as the needs were growing more acute in the late 1980s, the national economy was booming. All of the libraries that have opened so far this decade were given the green light before the early 1990s recession took hold. In the most prosperous years of the '80s, according to Library Journal, voters approved more than 90 percent of all referenda for public library facilities. But even in the more cautious fiscal climate of the 1990s, roughly three-quarters of all library construction ballot measures have won voter approval.

At a time of widespread distrust of government, libraries have succeeded better than almost any other public entity at escaping public hostility. Voters who would indignantly refuse to spend money refurbishing the city council chambers are often willing to look favorably upon improving the library, an institution they understand and often view as personally theirs.

Phoenix is a case in point. In 1988, then–Mayor Terry Goddard led what he calls "a popular revolution" for a $1.1 billion bond program of which the new library was a crucial part. "The prevailing wisdom," says Goddard, "was that residents didn't want to see any public money spent on infrastructure for arts and culture." Despite pundits' predictions to the contrary, the bond issue passed handily. "I place its success squarely on the doorstep of mothers with young children," he says. "They weren't noisy, but they were passionate."

What may be most remarkable about the new libraries is how different each one looks from the next. All the International Style libraries of the 1950s and 1960s tended to look more or less alike. Each of the new ones seems to reflect the symbols and traditions of the place that built it.

The architects of Chicago's Harold Washington Library, for example, borrowed design elements from other famous city landmarks. San Francisco's exterior is an interesting hybrid, integrating gray granite Beaux Arts design on the two sides that face the government center with a modern style for the sides that front on the commercial district.

Los Angeles' Central Library continued its tradition of defying easy description. To the original 1926 building — part Modern Spanish Revival, Byzantine and Egyptian — was added the eight-story Tom Bradley wing, with numerous cultural motifs reflecting the city's ethnic diversity.

Denver incorporated its historic Burnham Hoyt library into the new structure, which evokes the Southwestern landscape with soft shades of red, green and buff-colored limestone. An enormous "derrick" sculpture made from the rough pine timbers of an old mill dominates its Western History Reading Room.

San Antonio's library is ... well ... loud. The outside is painted Enchilada Red (the winning entry in the local newspaper's name-the-color contest; submissions ranged from Liberry Red to Dried-Blood-of-Taxpayers Red). One of the outdoor terraces has a water display reminiscent of irrigation ditches in pioneer days. Mesquite flooring covers the Texana and genealogy room. Elsewhere, purple carpet and upholstery and yellow walls echo colors found in Mexican art and native Indian clothing, according to its architect, Ricardo Legorreta. The new library's motto: "Shhh? No Way."

But Phoenix is probably the most unconventional — and arguably the most successful — in terms of design. Its library is the handiwork of local architect/sculptor William P. Bruder, who Terry Goddard boasts has "forever rid libraries of their dowdiness." Clad in 100,000 pounds of copper, it plays off the state's most dramatic resource: the sun. Mirrored skylights in the suspended roof create little balls of light that move around the one-acre Great Reading Room. Two ends of the building are eight-story glass walls outfitted with computer-controlled louvers and fabric sails to adjust the amount of light streaming inside.

At the center is the "Crystal Canyon," an atrium six stories deep. The open steel-and-glass interior, which reveals the mechanical systems and fiber-optic nerve center, gives people an unusual glimpse of its inner workings and the sense of a busy place. All partitions are movable. "Flexibility is the key word," says City Librarian Ralph Edwards. "We cannot predict how we will use any space in the building. So each floor was designed to be as open as possible and as near to a square as possible so we could reorganize to meet changing needs."

Not all the architects have chosen to do it that way. Denver's library, nearly twice the size of those in San Antonio and Phoenix, sacrificed some flexibility in order to create a collection of smaller, friendlier spaces within a huge building. The design of Cleveland's 10-story addition, which is still under construction, was changed from a square to an oval tower in an effort to lessen the height impact on downtown neighbors.

Despite wide variations in style and material, on the inside these libraries have some key features in common. To create an orientation point for the public, each has a multi-story atrium in the center. And nearly all of them have escalators, as in an old-fashioned department store, meant to introduce visitors to the diverse functions of the library and, as Denver City Librarian Rick Ashton puts it, to encourage "serendipitous discoveries."

It is hard to say how long the construction craze will continue, but one thing is clear:

Large amounts of capital, even for popular public causes, will be much harder to come by in the next few years than during the years when Denver, San Antonio and Phoenix laid their big plans. Cities hoping to duplicate such achievements will need to find creative means of financing.

Seattle officials found that out the hard way in 1994 when their $155 million ballot measure for a new downtown library and renovation of 22 branches garnered only 57.7 percent of the necessary 60 percent vote. "We're hoping to go back to the voters with a downsized and better-leveraged package," says Librarian Elizabeth Stroup.

The city need look only 125 miles to the north for some ideas. A stunning new main library opened last year in Vancouver, British Columbia, with a mix of public and private financing. Among the interesting aspects of the deal: The top two floors of the library — its future expansion space — have been leased to the provincial government as offices for the next 20 years.

The financing schemes in Los Angeles included the sale of tax increment bonds by the Community Redevelopment Agency and fees paid by private developers for the right to build on sites near the library at a greater density than would otherwise be permitted. In addition, the new wing was set aside as a separate property for financing purposes. The Municipal Improvement Corp. of Los Angeles issued a lease-revenue bond to be paid out of the city's regular operating budget. In San Diego, the Centre City Development Corp. is purchasing the land for the new central library, and money for construction will come from a hotel room tax (originally targeted for a sports stadium) and private donations.

Private contributions are, in fact, making an enormous difference to all the new libraries, especially when it comes to furnishing them. San Antonio and Denver raised private donations of $10 million and $6 million, respectively, for enhancements such as a landscaped outdoor plaza, marble floors and customized light fixtures. And a host of rooms and galleries, named in honor of their wealthy benefactors, contain special collections. Phoenix is in the middle of a $3 million private capital campaign to put seats in its auditorium and get rid of the decades-old vinyl furniture it moved into the new building.

But San Francisco has taken library fundraising to another level altogether. Through the formation of various affinity groups representing roughly one-sixth of the local population — gays and lesbians, African Americans, Chinese and environmentalists, among others — more than $30 million has been raised for individual centers that will be devoted to the groups' history and literature.

What a capital campaign cannot do, of course, is guarantee that the city will have enough money to operate its extensive new library on a long-term basis. Given their size and heavy electrical demands, the buildings generate huge security and utility bills. "We don't have a good handle on what our utility costs will be," admits Denver's Rick Ashton. "The old library didn't have air conditioning, and a lot of times in the winter it was so warm in there that we turned off the heat. Until we've run the building for a couple of years, who knows?"

But staffing represents the biggest expenditure, typically accounting for between 70 and 80 percent of operating budgets. "People think that libraries spend most of their money on books, when it's really more like 8 percent," says Rodger of the Urban Libraries Council. Although it might seem that open stacks would require fewer employees, in fact, the more information that customers have access to — on the shelves or online — the more help they seem to need finding it. San Antonio found it necessary to double the size of its public-service staff when its new building opened.

No one wants to wind up like Dallas. When its new central library opened in 1982, it was considered the premier library system in the nation in terms of technology and serv-

ices. But when the local economy soured in the mid–1980s, the library suffered mightily. Its budget fell from $16.6 million in 1985 to less than $14 million in 1987 and remained stagnant for the next seven years.

Because the library hasn't been able to afford many new materials, the expansion that the architects planned for hasn't occurred. Its physical structure has deteriorated too. But Dallas' dark decade appears to be drawing to a close. Last October, the city council approved the library's largest operating budget in 10 years. In addition, the city accepted a challenge to match a $250,000 donation from a private donor for capital improvements to the central library building.

San Francisco, on the other hand, has managed to engineer long-term support. In 1994, the city's voters overwhelmingly approved a charter amendment that increased the library system's hours by 46 percent and its total budget by nearly 70 percent — from $20.8 million to $35 million — through a guaranteed general-fund set-aside and 2½ cents from every $100 the city collects in property tax revenue over the next 15 years. The voters made it clear, says City Librarian Kenneth E. Dowlin, that they wanted "a world class facility filled with books and computer access and open as many hours as possible."

For all the enthusiasm of the library renaissance in San Francisco and other cities, the new designs have provoked some critics who say they are headed in the wrong direction. Stephen C. Davies, vice president of Project for Public Spaces Inc., calls most of the snazzy new libraries "too formal and uninviting."

In his view, they all lack a "front porch" area that generates visible activity and attracts people to a site. "If the library is to become a great gathering place," Davies says, "this has to start from the outside." His remedy for deserted plazas and blank walls is the creation of an urban oasis with such things as drinking fountains, movable benches, shade trees, window displays and cafes.

But if the new buildings are uninviting,

the popular reaction in most cities so far does not show it. Every one of the new libraries has become THE hot spot in town for after-hours galas and other social events. On a rainy afternoon last fall, the Denver library's three-story Schlessman Hall was bustling with white-jacketed caterers setting up tables of hors d'oeuvres and microbrews. Bins of yellow peppers and avocados lay everywhere, clashing incongruously with the subdued dignity of the polished wood and marble surroundings. Denver's Junior League was renting out the atrium for a buffet to promote its new cookbook.

It is not just fundraisers that have been keeping the new library busy. In its first few months of existence, the Denver library has hosted a wedding and a memorial service, and generated a constant demand for what Rick Ashton calls "convention center–type services." Ashton has had to hire a meeting-room coordinator to take reservations, approve caterers and collect fees, which range from $25 up to $2,000. Meanwhile, the Denver Art Museum, which sits next door, is paying the new building what may be the most tangible compliment of all: It is digging a tunnel to the library to connect itself with all the action.

CHAPTER 27

Prince Rupert and Other Cities Use Libraries to Promote "Smart Communities" Movement

Trina A. Innes

In the summer of 1999, the Southern Interior Forest Extension and Research Partnership (SIFERP), and its member organizations, made arrangements to hold an international conference on "Economic Development, Libraries and Smart Communities" in Toronto, Canada. SIFERP prepared a summary of the highlights of this conference, which are presented in the following pages. It should be noted that SIFERP is a non-profit society consisting of over 50 member organizations. SIFERP's goal is to integrate science, indigenous knowledge, and natural resource information to promote sustainable ecosystem management.

Attended by over 160 delegates, this major international conference was largely focused on examining the role of libraries in community economic development. Participants from Canada, the United States, Australia and Europe represented a variety of sectors. While largely comprised of public and specialty librarians from urban and rural centres, federal, provincial and municipal government representatives, economic develop-

ment planners, the information technology industry, public policy experts, information science schools, community networks, and groups working with information and smart communities also attended.

Over 30 speakers presented in a combination of plenary and concurrent sessions. Topics presented at this conference included: contributions of special libraries, creation of regional networks, development of rural information services, techniques for providing and marketing information services, the development of smart communities, opportunities for federal government funding, strategies for building partnerships and methods/techniques for measuring the impacts of information initiatives.

The papers represented are an exceptional collection of thoughts, experiences, and approaches. Proceeds of the conference will be published and made available by the Canadian Library Association.

Keynote speakers and concurrent sessions focused on the experience of using technology in communities, introducing and inno-

Originally published as *Economic Development, Libraries and Smart Communities*, Report 99–4, 1999, by the Southern Interior Forest Extension & Research Partnership, Kamloops, BC, Canada. Other publications are accessible online at *www.forrex.org*. Reprinted with permission of the publisher.

vating smart communities, highlighting sources of available funding, and promoting economic development. They presented papers that discussed the important role and links between librarians, libraries, technology and communities.

An overview of the main issues, experiences and opportunities identified in this conference are outlined in the following sections. Highlights of important points and internet addresses from selected presentations are also provided.

Role of Libraries

Libraries were identified as the focal point of communities. They are a place for meeting and sharing ideas. Libraries are considered leaders in the area of economic development. This is of great importance to the Partnership because in British Columbia natural resources drive the economy.

Organizations interested in providing an information service should build partnerships with their local libraries. Librarians are natural leaders in building partnerships in communities. Keeping librarians informed is key to meeting the information needs of the community.

Speaker Notes

Mark Deacon, President of SMART Toronto, Toronto, Ontario

- Virtual reference libraries are the book mobile of the next millennium, and computer technologists are the "mailroom staff" of the next millennium.
- People are the ultimate search engine. It is important that we do not separate service and human support from technology.
- Small rural communities often don't have technology. There is a need to place technology in these locations and ensure the training is provided to use it wisely. There

are many opportunities to access funding through federal initiatives.

Ensuring an Effective Information Service

Many presenters shared their experience in adopting, adapting and implementing information services in their community. Smart communities are generally "plugged in" to technology so the bulk of the ideas and approaches are related to the provision of web sites.

The best information services ensure links and participation from a variety of partnering organizations. They have a strong sense of their users' information needs and know the strengths of their partners. They demonstrate that they "know information," and that they can be trusted to support and deliver on information requests.

The best source of assistance is youth that are closer to technology. Further, there are many government funding opportunities in place to subsidize their work.

Information services should focus on providing service and support to partnering agencies, and while libraries are often considered the ultimate search engine, specialization of purpose lends itself to better results. Effort must be placed in tracking the volume of use, participation and trends in usage over time. This requires dedication, but the costs of this work produces results that can be used to demonstrate effectiveness.

Ideas and approaches under several topic areas are outlined below:

Publicity

- Take all opportunities to promote your service.
- One of the main keys to ensuring an effective information service is publicity. Building networks, involving the com-

munity and providing opportunities for interactive feedback is critical.

- Providing a space for testimonials about the service on a web site helps build publicity and demonstrates the usefulness of the service.
- Partnering with an organization with a widely recognized logo can assist with drawing people to your service.
- Publicize unusual business activities (if it is a good story, put it on the net).
- Marketing, training and education on how to use these systems are considered equally as important as content on the web site.

Service

- To be effective requires active servicing of user needs.

Attractions

- Multiuse sites, let people do more than one thing.

Partnerships

- Lone rangers will fail.
- Building partnerships with other organizations will help ensure both the quality of your site and its survival. Some suggested partnering with universities or using students and Industry Canada grants to maintain your site at low cost.
- Keep partners involved. Circulate draft documents for their information.
- Vision is essential (partners best involved in the development of a vision).
- Only bring supporters to the table.
- Advisory group roles must be clear.
- Be alert to opportunities, write proposals, record agreements.
- Recruit moderators to assist you.
- Allow for fair remuneration of partners; some things can be billed to the project.

Sustainability

- Revenue is often critical to sustainability. Building revenue-generating schemes into the service will be of benefit. Consider building and hosting web pages for other organizations for a fee.

Training

- Internet training should include: email, discussion groups, ftp, and web authoring.
- Building First Nations capacity is important in some rural areas.
- Offer mini-conferences that address: content (information services, systems, and products), speakers (government, industry and commercial). Conferences should be designed for all sorts of people including industry, consultants, academics, students, extension officers and librarians. Conferences should demonstrate how to use technology.

Non-Connected Customers

- Prepare packages to direct to people who are not connected.
- Deliver information to desktops of those who do not have access to the internet by CD-ROM (e.g., copy technical notes and distribute to key organizations at low cost).
- Make copies available to libraries. Librarians aware of the availability of this information can make it available to their clients.

Interaction

- Online request forms will ensure that you get feedback regarding your site. This feedback ensures that your site is constantly changing. Change attracts clients.
- Next wave in the information world is not about giving information, but about creating opportunities for interaction and reaction. Discussion groups and other op-

portunities for information exchange and feedback should be explored.

Purpose

- Put purpose into short sound bites.

Leadership

- Keep visionaries.
- "Visionaries can often be identified by the arrows in their back."

Specialize

- Staff need skills and knowledge (money must be made available for professional development and conferences.
- Staff can bring back summaries of conferences and give results to organizations.

Security

- Use the universities if security is an issue. Colleges often best deal with these issues because they must keep the smart students out of their system.

Speakers Notes

Ken Roberts, PIC Hamilton
- Group items on your web site by service, not institution.
- Develop a shared mall where each agency has a shop.
- Insist on introducing a mature site.

Allan Wilson, Chief Librarian, Prince Rupert Public Library, Prince Rupert, British Columbia
- Resource economy = knowledge economy
- Add value beforehand (before asking for money to support your project, make sure it has something substantial to see and say).
- STUMPERS —file the hard to get information so others have access to it.

- First Nations oral histories; file them online (they can be digitized).
- Provide referrals documents, brief bibliographies and customized information products.

Cathy Campbell, Manager, Library Services, Queensland Department of Primary Industries, Queensland, Australia
- Provide initiatives such as internet training in rural communities, web services (provide a framework for sharing information, and operate an information supermarket.
- Consider a mobile training room (portable laptops).
- Provide web services support in content development, information infrastructure, technical infrastructure.
- Provide online forms for searches, and consider a small fee for service.

Wendy Newman, Brantford Public Library
- CHANGING a model for building a smart community.
  - ➤Challenge-attending meetings in other cities, communities
  - ➤Honour Partnerships
  - ➤Alliances — Build them
  - ➤Needs and Vision (work together on this)
  - ➤Goals and Outcomes (promoting involvement, sharing resources)
  - ➤Identify Roles and responsibilities
  - ➤New directions
  - ➤Go forward

Dr. Todd Sands, Regional Networks for Ontario
- Suggests that organizations such as nonprofits use secondments from partnering organizations.

Brenda Herchmer, Niagara Centre for Community Leadership
- Provide one stop source for information in specialized area.
- Bell Canada is a good partner, even for the logo (grabs attention).

- Human Resources Development Canada seems to have a lot of money.
- Key to obtaining funding is building community capacity.

Greg Salmers, Estevan Public Library, Saskatchewan
- Information is extracted from Knowledge.
- Knowledge is anything that is known.

Smart Communities Initiative

The World Foundation for Smart Communities is a non-profit educational organization founded to promote the concept and facilitate the implementation of "smart communities" which are leaders in the use of communication and information technology. The Government of Canada is very interested in using our current industry-leading skills in these areas to place Canada as a world leader in the concept of smart communities.

The Smart Communities Demonstration Project initiative is a nation-wide competition designed to select one "world-class" Smart Communities Demonstration Project in each province, one in the North and one in an Aboriginal community. Created and administered by Industry Canada, the goal of this program is to help Canada become a world leader in the development and use of information and communication technologies for economic, social and cultural development.

The Government of Canada plans to invest $60 million over the next three years in support of this project. Announced June 9, 1999, communities, through a local or new non-profit organization, are invited to submit a letter of intent by August 3, 1999.

More information on the Smart Communities initiative, both nationally and internationally can be found through the following links:

➤www.sto.org
➤www.multimediator.com

➤www.a4s.org
➤www.smartcommunities.org
➤smartcommunities.ic.gc.ca

Government Initiatives/ Funding Sources

Several programs are in progress that may be a source of funding for introducing training and technology into local communities. Programs offered by Industry Canada include:

- Connecting Canadians and the Smart Communities Demonstration Project
- Community Access Project
- Rural Access Project (soon)
- VolNet

Human Resources Development Canada was also identified as a major source of federal funds. Speakers stressed that applications stressing partnerships and capacity building, as well as focusing on services rather than technology, are most successful in obtaining funding.

Measuring the Impacts of Information Initiatives

Dr. Charles R. McClure, Frances Eppes Professor of Information Studies at Florida State University, gave an excellent paper covering methods for measuring the impacts of information initiatives. Readers are encouraged to consult McClure's web site for additional background on this topic (*http://istweb. syr.edu/~mcclure*). McClure highlighted that gaining political visibility is one of the most effective tools for ensuring the survival of a site. Visibility and quality measures of impact will attract continued support for the project.

It is very important to have measures for measuring performance. If expected levels of performance can be defined by an organization (e.g. response time), it can make it easier to measure performance.

McClure stresses that it is "better to collect bad data and use it wisely than collect no data at all." Further, it is better to collect data that will sell your initiative (e.g., contact hours, invitations to do work by others, inquiries, number of and type of collaborations with other organizations, revenues generated, attitude changes). To be effective, everyone in the organization must be dedicated to effective record keeping.

Measures may include:

Extensiveness

- Counts, how many (e.g., web page visits, number of inquiries).

Efficiency

- Track the costs and time related to providing services.
- Very important to count volunteer hours included in the provision of services.
- Account for all in-kind contributions.

Effectiveness

- Degree to which program meets objectives.

Service Quality

- Measure how well service activity done (e.g., percent of transactions in which users acquired the information they needed).
- Consider using Likert scales.

Usefulness

- Degree to which service is appropriate to user.
- Have you designed something that meets with user needs?

- Relevance is more important than access.
- Relevance = smart (not wired).

Impacts

- Describe how service has made a difference in some activity or situation.

Growth Opportunities for Partnership

The Partnership plans on exploring or implementing the following ideas and initiatives based on the Economic Development, Libraries and Smart Communities conference:

- Developing enhanced measures for assessing the information service.
- Improving interactivity of web site.
- Building Partnerships with libraries throughout the southern interior of British Columbia.
- Offering support for any community in the southern interior interested in submitting an application to the Smart Communities Program.
- Investigating identified and other funding opportunities for funding of technological infrastructure and training.
- Improving use of Partners in information service.

NOTES

1. The *Natural Resources Information Network* (NRIN) was launched in June of 2001 by the Southern Interior Forest Extension and Research Partnership (SIFERP). The NRIN is an online network of information libraries made possible through a collaboration of natural resource organizations. It is managed by SIREP. NRIN operates like a virtual library where the owners of information fill the shelves.

2. The website for NRIN (*http://nrin.siferp.org*) and its founding organization, SIFERP (*http://www.siferp.org*), provide valuable online information services to citizens throughout the world.

3. The actual conference took place on June 15 and 16, 1999, in Toronto, Ontario, Canada.

CHAPTER 28

St. Louis Places Monetary Value on Public Library Services

Glen E. Holt, Donald Elliott, *and* Amonia Moore

Like the other public-sector institutions facing today's current conservative fiscal climate, tax-supported urban public libraries are increasingly subject to fiscal scrutiny. As urban schools, hospitals, police, and other essential public services are subjected to skepticism and to formal assessment procedures, many libraries get caught in similar demands for measures of their success. While claiming to be essential to the social fabric of urban communities and, therefore, worthy of precious public resources, libraries also must now respond to the cries of fiscal gadflies who say, "Prove it!"[1]

In the face of these new demands, public library leaders face the challenge of making credible "bottom line" estimates of the net value of their services to their users and to their communities as a whole. That challenge to "prove it!" brought the St. Louis Public Library (SLPL) Services Valuation Study into existence. With never less than four lawyers on its board of directors, in a city where voters since the mid–1960s have approved only a handful of tax increases, and in a region where nearly all large donations come from major corporations, SLPL staff have often encountered demands to furnish quantitative measures of their institutional worth.

SLPL management shared that challenge with the leaders of many other library systems in January 1994 at the ALA Midwinter Meeting in Los Angeles. The discussion that kicked off the St. Louis project took place at a meeting of the Strategic Directions Committee of the Urban Libraries Council; the dozen directors in attendance stated their need for a statistical methodology they could use to quantify the benefits of library services and communicate that value to elected officials, board members, and donors.

During the meeting SLPL Director Glen Holt expressed the belief that economists could develop a methodology to estimate the value of public investment in library services.

Goal of the Study

The goal of this research has been to develop and test a practical, conservative methodology that large urban public libraries can use to estimate and communicate the direct return on annual taxpayer investment in their organizations. To achieve this goal, the economic methodology must be conceptually and empirically sound, cost-effective to administer,

Originally published as "Placing a Value on Public Library Services," *Public Libraries*, Vol. 28, No. 2, March/April 1999, by the American Library Association, Chicago, IL. Reprinted with permission of the publisher.

pragmatic in its objectives, and simple to interpret and communicate.

By the spring of 1998 the research team had met this goal for the St. Louis Public Library. With no hesitation, it is now possible for SLPL spokespersons to tell board members, city officials, civic leaders — and even economists — that the library's users are receiving more than $4 in direct benefits for every $1 of tax revenues that the public is investing annually to the institution. For economists who work with methodologies like those used in this study, the $4-to-$1 benefits-to-tax ratio is a substantial return on public investment. Moreover, this result is based on conceptually and empirically sound methodology, and it meets the other goal criteria as well.

Although the methodology that produced this $4-to-$1 benefits-to-tax ratio worked for the SLPL system, it is not yet transportable to other systems. To be transportable, the methodology has to be tested in other libraries with different demographics and environments. The strategy for making the methodology transportable is outlined in the last section of this article.

Economic-Impact Analysis and Cost-Benefit Analysis

At the outset of this project, the principal investigators considered two different measurement methodologies. These were economic-impact analysis and cost-benefit analysis.

In economic-impact analysis, the magnitude of an institution's impact on the regional economy is directly dependent on the extent to which it attracts new dollars to the region. For example, a major museum attracts visitors from other regions. While visiting the museum, these tourists or convention-goers stay at local hotels, eat at area restaurants, and shop in area malls. When visitors spend in this way, a museum like the Art Institute of Chicago or the St. Louis Art Museum generates a significant net impact on the area econ-

omy.[2] Similarly, when a museum receives national or international grants to engage a local construction company to add a new wing, the institution stimulates employment and income in the regional economy.

Most public libraries do not attract substantial numbers of visitors or extensive funding from outside the region and, thus, do not attract new dollars into the region. Because they are locale-serving institutions, most public libraries have little short-term net economic impact on their communities. The wages they pay, the services they purchase, and the buildings they construct or remodel merely recycle local dollars. For the most part, such local tax dollars still would have been spent in the region.

However, like school districts, community colleges, and area universities, libraries are critically important to the long-term economic health of the regions they serve. Along with these other critical education and information institutions, libraries sustain the human capital that enriches a region in the long run. Cost-benefit analysis (CBA) is a more appropriate tool than economic-impact analysis for measuring the benefits of the services a library delivers in carrying out its mission.

Economists use cost-benefit analysis to evaluate the benefits of education, pollution control, and locks and dams — to name only a few applications. The SLPL project researchers chose CBA because it matches the way public libraries deliver services and the way benefits flow from them. The methodology also tends to fit the way citizens think about the taxes they invest in public-service organizations.

CBA Estimates Two Different Benefits

CBA involves estimating two different kinds of benefits.

Direct benefits. First, CBA measures the "direct value" to those who use or who have access to the services being measured. Economic scholars recognize a number of methods to determine the direct value of services. The SLPL study used three different ways to assess the direct benefits of library services. The library provided materials and services directly to its users. Those users benefited directly from those services. Hence, they received direct benefits.

Indirect (third-party or societal) benefits. The second part of determining value in cost-benefit analysis is estimating "the indirect benefits" or "societal benefits" from the services being studied. These are the benefits that third parties or the population as a whole derive when individuals use the services of a public institution.

Library services implicitly yield indirect benefits. When users get the help they need (the information to start a business, help in learning to read, or the material for an important speech to be given to a community organization), society benefits indirectly. These indirect benefits accumulate when a new business hires unemployed or underemployed residents, when children grow up to become literate voters and productive workers, and when a community leader is successful in getting a bill passed that stabilizes a community's neighborhoods.

To sum up, libraries — in carrying out the social mission for which they were chartered — provide users with services from which those users receive direct benefits. And, because good things happen as a result of residents' use of the library's services, others benefit indirectly from the library's operations.

Since the opening of the first publicly supported library in 1833, public librarians, library boards of directors, local government officials, and philanthropists from Andrew Carnegie to Bill Gates have recognized that these two sets of benefits — direct and indirect — flow from public library services.[3] This easy fit with the library's ongoing relationship with its users and its community makes CBA an ideal tool to measure both the direct and indirect benefits of library services.

Difficulties in the Measurement of Indirect Benefits

The greatest problem with indirect benefits is the difficulty in measuring them. Indirect benefits are hard to identify and even more difficult to estimate.

For example, scholars have calculated the benefits to society when a youngster knows how to read vs. being illiterate. What portion of that indirect-benefit estimate can be claimed for the library because the child used public library services and materials?

Or, suppose that the youngster who learns to read is the daughter of an inner-city welfare recipient, but when she becomes a mother, she teaches all her children to read even before they go to school. In the process, both the mother and her children make heavy use of library materials to climb out of poverty. What contribution can the library claim for helping this generation move up economically? Lynn A. Karoly and others have attempted this examination for early-childhood intervention programs but not for library-based programs.[4]

Examples of other indirect and collective benefits include community-building enhancements — because a library functions as a neighborhood center — or the possible effects of library youth programs on reducing area crime. Peter Greenwood provides one such study.[5]

Because indirect benefits of such situations are extremely difficult to estimate, the SLPL Services-Valuation Project team focused only on direct benefits.

Important Characteristics

From the outset, the principal researchers in the SLPL Services Valuation Project have sought to develop a reliable methodology that has the following characteristics:

- **Simplicity.** Most voters understand the concept of a rate of return. The SLPL researchers sought a methodology that would communicate the library's value in a short sound bite: "For each dollar of taxes, city residents and businesses respond that they receive more than a dollar and ten cents in benefits." A measurement of direct benefits to users provides a solid, simple statement about direct returns flowing from public library tax revenues. Articulating direct benefits is relatively simple.

- **Credibility.** The SLPL Services Valuation Project methods are intentionally designed to provide a lower bound, not the highest estimated value. The inclusion of indirect benefits would substantially increase the value estimates, but without more knowledge about the flow of direct benefits, such estimates of high indirect benefits would strain credibility. It is possible to set lower bounds for indirect benefits, but library practitioners seeking creditable measurements needs to be cautious using these calculations. Creditable public communication occurs when a public official does not overstate the case for the institution. To be credible, the SLPL project focused only on direct benefits.

- **Rich detail.** The methods used in this study can be employed to delineate the benefits of particular categories of services for different categories of users: "SLPL general users receive far higher benefits from using the library's adult books than they do from attending its special events." Such flexibility enables library spokespersons to study benefit flows and express those benefits to specific constituent audiences. Estimates of benefits by category of service also can assist administrators in budget allocation and strategic planning. Moreover, the survey methodology used in the study resulted in a rich store of user quotations that can help spokespersons define the meaning of the benefits in human terms.[6]

To sum up, the SLPL CBA project focused on developing and implementing a methodology by which practitioners can estimate the lower bounds of direct benefits from public tax investments in library services. This tool allows practitioners to measure and to communicate that value in a simple, credible way for the public library investment as a whole and for individual services as well. The time for estimating indirect or societal benefits will come, but it should come after more is known about the measurement of direct benefits.

Methods to Measure Direct Benefits

Consumer surplus was the first measurement selected. Consumer surplus is used frequently by economists in policy studies. Consumer surplus measures the value that consumers place on the consumption of goods or services in excess of what they must pay to get them. Although library services typically are "free," patrons do pay by the effort they exert and the time they spend to access those services. This time and effort represent an implicit price to patrons. Moreover, many alternatives to library services are sold in the marketplace. For example, households can buy novels rather than check out the library's fiction books. Businesses can purchase CD-ROM databases or subscribe to online information services rather than use staff time to undertake library research.

Basing the study on such assumptions, the SLPL researchers moved through the following steps to estimate consumer surplus from library use. In a telephone survey, interviewers asked patrons about the number of books they borrow from the library, the books they purchased, and additional books that they would buy if they could not borrow. By comparing the number of books a patron borrows with the number of books he/she would buy at an established market price, it is possible to calculate the value that library patrons place on borrowing materials above and beyond any cost of traveling to and the time involved in using the library. This value is a dollar measure of the net benefits provided by the library's borrowing privileges. Such estimates can be made for each patron and each service used. The estimates can be summed to provide an estimate of total direct annual benefits measured in dollars. Economists refer to this set of calculations as determination of consumer surplus.

Contingent valuation measures, though controversial, have been used extensively, even in judicial proceedings, to value environmental conditions. Two alternative approaches are available. In the willingness-to-pay approach (WTP), the researcher asks respondents how much they would pay to have something that they current do not have. In the willingness-to-accept approach (WTA), the researcher asks respondents how much they would accept to give up something that they already have. Generally, WTA estimates of benefits are higher than WTP estimates. WTA estimates are usually considered less reliable than WTP estimates.

In applying contingent valuation analysis to libraries, many alternative hypothetical situations can be used. For example, library patrons (or the general public) can be asked how much they would be willing to pay rather than forego library usage or, if libraries did not exist, how much they would be willing to pay (for example, in taxes) to enjoy the library privileges they have today. Alternatively, patrons can be asked how much they would accept to give up their library privileges or how much of a tax cut they would accept in exchange for closing all public libraries.

Note that the willingness to pay and the willingness to accept measures elicit some appraisal of indirect or social benefits of public libraries while the consumer surplus measure focuses solely on benefits to individual households. Because the contingent valuation measures elicit some sense of indirect or social benefits, usually the different methodologies produce divergent estimates. With that weakness clearly understood, the SLPL team decided to use both WTP and WTA as methods to appraise the direct benefits of SLPL services.

Cost of time. Because patrons must exert effort and spend time to access library services, the value that users place on library services must be at least as great as their sacrifice in accessing and using them. By valuing patrons' time in traveling to a library service point and in actually using library services, cost-benefit researchers can obtain a third estimate of the value of library services. The sum of these time-cost estimates for all patrons provides another estimate of total library benefits. Cost of time also was added to the SLPL valuation methodology.

Each of these approaches has its strengths and weaknesses. Ideally all three approaches provide identical estimates of benefits. In the absence of such convergence, however, the alternative methods provide a range of values from which to infer the magnitude of benefits. That range of values in itself provides significant information where none now exists.

To sum up, the researchers decided to use three different measurements to construct a range of values rather than stake everything on the estimation of one value. The rationale was simple: It did not cost much more to undertake multiple measures rather than one, and, if all the methods were used, much more could be learned about how to construct a nationally transportable CBA methodology for public libraries. As the next two sections demonstrate, this strategy worked reasonably well.

How the Methodology Was Tested

Inevitably the calculation of direct benefits had to involve an extensive user survey. The preparation for and carrying out of the survey involved many steps.

Construction of the Service/User Matrix

The initial step, the development of a Service/User Matrix involved staff discussions and library-user focus groups. The development of the matrix began with SLPL's mission and goals. Within this context, the matrix makes explicit the relationships between services and users.

By identifying classes of library customers (i.e., general users, teachers, and businesses) the matrix is customer-focused. By arraying customers against the library's portfolio of services (e.g., reference and reader's advisory, adult collections, visits to daycare centers, etc.) a library's service and user categories become visually explicit. Each cell of the matrix represents a stream of benefits from a library service to a particular class of customer.

When arrayed in this way, the matrix becomes the basis for a series of value estimates in which customers describe how much of which services they use. In some cases, customers need little prodding to assign a specific value to the services they receive. In other cases, users have no sense of the value of the services they use but are able to articulate the number of pieces of material they use or the amount of time they are involved in using a service. In either case, measuring services used by customers and cumulating their value are the basis for the consumer-surplus method of estimating the value of direct library services.

As with other aspects of this study, the Service/User Matrix is designed conservatively. By intent, some worthwhile but hard-to-measure collective values (e.g., the library as a safe place for children, as a neighborhood center, or as a family recreational center) were dropped from the matrix. The quantification of such indirect and collective benefits is complex. To pursue these in detail would have exhausted respondents' patience and reduced user responses to questions estimating the direct individual benefits — the focus of the SLPL survey. Instead, some time in the survey interviews was devoted to qualitative exploration of these collective benefits. As suggested previously in this paper, numeric estimates of such values can be made part of later calculations of indirect benefits.

Development of Survey Instruments: Use of Focus Groups

To test the Service/User Matrix and to refine the language of the proposed telephone survey, project staff organized some of the library's heaviest users and its best friends into seven focus groups: two with "general users," two with "teachers and caregivers," and three with "business users." The third focus group with business users was necessary to work through difficulties encountered in delimiting questions that would identify anything like a full range of library business uses. Further discussion of problems with business users can be found in the concluding section of this article.

Members of the focus groups proved extremely helpful. Group comments helped transform arcane library terms into easier-to-understand terms ("audio-visual" became "videos," "CDs," and "audio or music tapes," and "outreach services" became "visits to daycare centers"). Focus group participants also offered good advice on how to get the most accurate answers from survey questions. To enhance the validity of the focus groups, SIUE Marketing Department students facilitated the group discussions. SLPL staff observed indirectly over closed-circuit television. They were not present to influence focus groups to speak in positive ways about library services.

Consumer Surplus Valuation of Services: Pricing Market Substitutes for Library Services

The focus groups also helped test the accuracy of the prices the research team established for individual library services. In completing the Service/User Matrix, the research team finally settled on fifteen services to address in the telephone survey. Those fifteen services were: children's books, adult books, videos/films, audio/music, magazines, newspapers, toys, parent-teacher materials, reference and research services, special events, craft and activity programs, social skills/etiquette training, computer skills training, encyclopedias, and, finally, dictionaries and almanacs.

This methodology requires measuring library use of each service and contrasting that use with hypothetical purchases of similar services at market prices. The pricing of market alternatives to library services required considerable research. Whenever possible, the research team used published prices of comparable items or services. Book values came from the *Bowker Annual*. That publication became the basis of assigning a value of $8 to the purchase of each children's paperback book and $14 for the price of each book that an adult patron would have purchased if borrowing privileges were not available.[7]

Some library activities, like special events (author lectures, which the library and area bookstores provide free, and children's storytime, which is also provided free by several area bookstores) were valued at zero because researchers simply could not find any way to set a reasonable price. Remember that the intent in this project was to price everything conservatively. Replicating the SLPL research for other libraries operating under different cost situations undoubtedly will result in the pricing for some services which were assigned zero values in the SLPL study.

The hardest library service to price — and as it turned out, the most critical — was "Reference and Research Services, including Readers' Advisory." After much time on telephone calling both within the region and to other cities throughout the middle part of the United States, the research team priced this service conservatively at $50 per hour.

In the discussions which library professionals have had with Dr. Holt during his many presentations on the CBA project, only one person has objected to this $50 per hour figure — because that person's hourly salary was lower than $50 per hour. The objection misses the point. In St. Louis and in larger cities throughout the middle United States, $50 is a conservative figure. When this CBA study is replicated in smaller libraries, the value of substitutes for staff time can be valued higher or lower depending on local or regional circumstances. Moreover, the study method is to ascertain the benefits that users perceive they derive from a service. Users may perceive service benefits as lower, higher, or the same as the costs of providing them. In short, service prices can and should be adjusted to fit individual institutions.

Organization of the Telephone Survey

The St. Louis Public Library Automation System (SLPLS) cardholder database was used to select the survey candidates. On the day that staff pulled the cardholder sample, the database contained more than 72,000 "active cardholders" — those who had used their cards within the past twelve months — residing at 39,444 unique addresses.[8] Each address was considered a separate household or institution that received library services. From that database, Technology Services staff pulled a random sample of the names of 2,350 "general" cardholders, 400 "teacher" cardholders, and 100 "business" cardholders. If a youth card was selected, the survey addressed the parent(s) or guardian(s) of the cardholder.

Then, in his capacity as SLPL's executive director, Dr. Holt wrote a letter to all 2,850 persons selected for inclusion in the survey asking if each was willing to be interviewed by telephone about library services. In the letter, Holt gave certain assurances: first, that the study was intended to improve SLPL's ability to serve users. Second, that a grant from the Public Library Association — not local tax funds — was paying for the nationally significant study. Third, that for completing the telephone survey, the library would provide a choice of premiums: a Friends of the Library tote bag, a set of Friends' coffee mugs, or a choice of one-of-two SLPL commemorative posters.

Finally, the letter stressed finding a convenient time for library representatives to talk to the user. A mail-back sheet asked the user to check the correctness of the personal name and address, provide a correct phone number and choose various weekday evening times (Monday through Thursday) when the user would be available to take a call from a library representative.

Sixteen percent of general users receiving invitations agreed to participate in the survey. Twenty-three percent of invited teachers and 29 percent of invited businesses agreed to participate.

Trained interviewers of the SIUE Center for Regional Research and Development Services conducted the telephone interviews. All had participated previously in phone surveys, and all were coached specifically for administering the SLPL–CBA telephone survey.

If the surveyors did not reach the interview subject on the first call, three more attempts were made. With this follow up, interviewers completed 235 "general" interviews, 75 "teacher" interviews, and 25 "business" interviews. Measured against those who had agreed to participate, the response rate for completed interviews proved to be 64 percent for "general" users, 83.3 percent for "teachers" users, and 86.2 percent for "business" users.

Checking and Improving the Survey's Statistical Reliability

As with any new survey, this one had to be checked for statistical reliability. A special concern was the low number of general users who accepted the invitation to participate. Chi-square tests, however, demonstrated the overall statistical validity of the survey sample relative to the known characteristics of the cardholder population.

To test further the validity of the sample of general users, members of the research team also checked for non-response bias by race and income level — characteristics not available from the cardholder database but which could be inferred from census tract data which SLPL uses regularly as part of its services planning. Not surprisingly, in the sample, whites were over-represented and African-Americans were under-represented, while higher income levels were over-represented and lower-incomes were under-represented. Moreover, those from the outer ring (generally higher income) zip codes of the city and the library's out-of-district suburban users were over-represented while inner-ring (generally lower-income) city dwellers were under-represented. The research team mathematically adjusted the survey results to correct for these biases.

After the adjustments, the weighted sample matched the presumed race, income level, and geography demographics of the SLPL user population as a whole. Reassuringly, the valuation estimates from the weighted sample varied little from the valuation estimates from the original data, suggesting in one more way the validity of the survey.

The Estimated Benefits — Survey Results

The survey produced dramatic results. The consumer-surplus methodology produced an estimated value of $47 million on SLPL's annual taxpayer investment of $15.3 million, and this figure was only for general users. In other words, benefits on public investment just for services used by general users were estimated to be more than $3 to $1.

Just as important from the standpoint of library practice was the source of the value in the consumer surplus measurements. Four library-service categories produced 94 percent of the total estimated value.

The SLPL researchers are eager to test the CBA methodology in other library systems to see if the strength of these categories is sustained. Also, in the nearly two years since completion of the telephone survey, SLPL has nearly doubled the number of public computers at its locations, and circulation of electronic materials continues to escalate. It is important to find out in replicating this study how these changes affect the absolute and relative value estimates of the various service categories.

The project's second benefits measurements — willingness to accept and willingness to pay — also produced intriguing results. As with the first measurement methodology, these estimates are only for general users.

The specific survey question used to elicit a response on willingness to accept was as follows:

> The next question is hypothetical, but very important. Please take a moment to think about it before you respond: Suppose that in the next election the ballot contained a referendum on closing all public libraries. The referendum states that all public libraries in the region will close, and the budgetary savings will be used to lower taxes or provide annual cash payments to households. Under these circumstances, would you vote to close the libraries if the yearly tax savings or cash payments to your household were an amount ranging from ? to ?

The pay-back ranges provided to respond to the question ran from a low of "between $1 to $100 to "over $2,500."

When the research team extrapolated the values from the question on willingness to accept, the cumulative population value was $136 million. Another way of reporting this finding is that when confronted with the closing option, cardholders responded that it would take a $9 payback for every $1 in current taxes to get those users to close libraries.

The problem with this conclusion is that it was produced by a very small percentage of total survey respondents. Only about 12 percent of those who completed the survey were willing to consider closing the St. Louis Public Library at any reasonable price.

The project team had anticipated this refusal and had a follow up question for those who would not answer it. The question was, "Why would you vote 'NO' to closing public libraries regardless of tax savings or cash payments to your household?"

Other and still-smaller groups of respondents provided different answers, but the tenor of all objections was the same: Lots of users talked for many minutes, as survey takers filled pages of notes, with their comments about the value of libraries, and their belief that they should not be closed at any price. As stated previously, WTA responses appraise not only the value of library services to the individual household, but also value to society (i.e., third-party and indirect benefits). Thus, the WTA estimate should have been higher than the consumer surplus estimate, which focuses only on the value of services used directly by the household itself.

Along with willingness to accept, the researchers also asked about willingness to pay. The question was posed in the following way:

> We have been discussing how the St. Louis Public Library benefits your household. Suppose, however, that no libraries had ever existed and taxes for libraries had never existed. How many dollars of taxes or fees would your household be willing to pay annually to create and maintain the St. Louis Public Library as it exists today? Please round your estimate to the nearest $100.

The literature on cost-benefit analysis methodology suggests that willingness to pay should produce the most conservative results. The question is intended to make people ask, "If these services did not now exist, how much would I budget from my household expenses to purchase them?"

The population estimate of value derived from responses to this question was $15,170,000. Thus, the most conservative valuation methodology produced an estimate of $1 returned in willingness to pay for ever $1

SLPL currently receives in tax revenues. Again, no secondary or indirect benefits are included in this 1:1 ration of dollar invested to dollar-value returned.

The third estimation methodology, that for time valuation or opportunity cost, produced a valuation of $90 million of over $5.50 in direct value for ever $1 paid to the library in taxes. Again the methodology was conservative. One of the last questions on the survey asked respondents to furnish family income figures. The cost of each respondent's time and of an employed spouse's time, if the spouse used the library, was calculated based upon the income figures provided. The time of stay-at-home spouses and teens (12–17) was valued below minimum wage by using the midpoint of the lowest income bracket in the survey ($5,000 annually or $2.40/hr.). The time of younger children was valued at zero and not included in this estimate.

Measurement of Benefits to Businesses and Schools

Estimation of the valuation of benefits to caregivers (primarily preschools) and teachers (public and parochial) uses contingent valuation. Teachers were asked to estimate how much their budgets would have to increase to provide the same services for their students if the library did not exist. This is a WTA formulation. Unlike general users, teachers found the WTA formulation easy to answer. They appeared knowledgeable about alternatives and the costs of acquiring replacement materials or services.

Estimation of the valuation of benefits to business users was more problematic. Several methods were attempted: replacement services, WTA, and WTP. Despite the use of three focus groups to frame the survey questions, actual respondents had difficulty identifying and valuing replacement services. Also, respondents were reluctant to state how much their businesses would be willing to pay in property taxes to support library services. They were somewhat more responsive in replying how much their businesses would have to be compensated to give up library services. Those estimates are reported in the next section.

Results of the SLPL Study

The weighted data, corrected for all survey biases, produced the estimates of value returned on public investment. Remember that the annual tax income of the St. Louis Public Library in the year of the survey was $15.3 million.

When we summed up the benefits of total patron benefits on the public investment of $15.3 million, we obtained the range of benefits.

SLPL spokespersons can now claim that every $1 in public investment in the institution produces direct benefits to users of more than $4. This figure is conservative and therefore creditable.

One must be careful, however, in interpreting and publicizing or discussing these results. Given the business orientation and private-sector experience of many library board members, rates of return to current library tax investment of the magnitude above may be viewed with skepticism. Explaining to the board that the ratios incorporate benefit streams accruing not only from current operating outlays, but also from past accumulation of library capital may assuage such concerns and reinforce board members' appreciation for the library as a critical investment in the community's infrastructure.

The benefits accruing to users annually are produced not only by current tax-funded operating outlays on staff, subscriptions, maintenance, and other items, but also by past public investments in buildings and collections. Current users are reaping returns not only from current public funds supporting the library, but also from the foresight and generosity of past tax and philanthropic support.

Yet no matter how generous or lavish the past investments, it is current tax support that permits users to access collections conveniently, receive staff assistance to find and use collections effectively, and ensure that the collections built up over time through past investment will continue to be preserved. The ratio of benefits to current annual tax support reflects how much the community is reaping from past and current investment as it provides annual operating revenues to the library.

Beyond the knowledge gained and the talking-point benefit for SLPL spokespersons, the research team believes that public librarians generally should be heartened by the results of this study. An established economics methodology applied conservatively — weighted to account for nonresponse bias associated with low-income and other social and geographical characteristics, and measuring only direct benefits — has produced a lower bound for benefits that SLPL policy makers feel safe in defending to board members, elected officials, and conservative donors. That figure is substantial. SLPL is a good investment for the people of St. Louis.

Limits, Needs, and Prospects: Toward a Transportable Valuation Methodology

What has been done at St. Louis Public Library is possible in other libraries, but there are important qualifications.

First, the SLPL Services Valuation Study is no simplistic formulation that other libraries can pick up and apply simply without thought to derive the benefits of investment in their own situations. If employed correctly, the methodology can be applied to other systems but not without effort or costs.

Second, particular user categories need more detailed attention than they could be given in this study. The research team believes it has a handle on how to measure educational use, but is less certain about business use.

Third, this project did not address walk-in use by individuals who are not library card-holders. A recent survey of walk-in users shows that as many as 20 percent of the daily visitors at the Central Branch do not have current library cards. Future research should attempt to incorporate benefits to these users as well as to cardholders.

Fourth, other special-user audiences deserve specific attention in estimating the benefits mix. SLPL, for example, spends a great deal on outreach services to seniors living in group residential settings and services for those that are blind and/or otherwise physically challenged. St. Louis also has large, specialized educational and cultural communities who use rich collections of fine arts (architecture and architectural history, art and art history, music and music history). Many genealogists travel hundreds of miles to use the library's collection, as well. All of these collections are expensive to maintain and service. Can their benefits be estimated and expressed in useful form? The SLPL researchers think so, but much more study is needed.

Fifth, in order to validate the SLPL benefits-valuation methodology, the project researchers need to replicate the study of the SLPL system. A September 1998 National Library Leadership from the Institute for Museum and Library Services will carry this work forward. The two-year $208,000 IMLS grant allows the SLPL to partner with Baltimore (Md.) County Library System, Birmingham (Ala.) Public Library, King County (Seattle) Library System, and Phoenix (Ariz.) Public Library in the refinement of a transportable cost-benefit analysis methodology that can be used by other public library systems.

Sixth, to make it transportable, the methodology needs to be tested in library systems with different governmental, demographic, racial, and economic characteristics from the St. Louis system. A September 1998 National Library Leadership from the Institute for Museum and Library Services will carry this work forward. The two-year

$208,000 IMLS grant allows the SLPL to partner with Baltimore (Md.) County Library System, Birmingham (Ala.) Public Library, King County (Seattle) Library System, and Phoenix (Ariz.) Public Library in the refinement of a transportable cost-benefit analysis methodology that can be used by other public library systems.

Seventh, as these studies continue and are completed, an effort needs to be made to document and estimate the indirect and collective benefits that society receives from library services.

The SLPL Services Valuation Project team members are certain that they are on the right track in valuing the benefits of public investments in library services. The heartening results, however, cannot be extrapolated for public libraries as a whole. The research base needs to be widened. More systems need to be surveyed. Methods need to be refined. There is much more to do.

Still, there is a new fact. In St. Louis — a far from wealthy city with an adult population whose "reading problems" rate equals 38 percent — it is possible for administrators and board members alike to respond to the latest "prove it!" by saying "We have! And what we have proved is that on average for every dollar the public has invested in library services, the direct benefits just to library users is $4."

In St. Louis, the public is getting a good return on its investment in its public libraries.

NOTES

1. Glen E. Holt, Donald Elliott, and Christopher Dussold. "A framework for evaluating public investment in urban libraries." *Bottom Line*, 9:4 (Summer 1996), 4–13. This article contains a substantial body of footnotes supporting the rationale for this study and the use of cost benefit analysis as a methodology. The authors did not repeat those footnotes here.

2. Developmental Strategies, Inc. The economic impact of museums and performing arts institutions. Prepared for the Museums and Performing Arts Institutions Committee [of RCGA] and the St. Louis Regional Commerce and Growth Association (Sept. 1988); Developmental Strategies Inc. The community and economic impact of museums, performing arts and other cultural institutions on the St. Louis Metropolitan Area. Second in a series prepared for the Museums and Performing Arts Institutions Committee and the St. Louis Regional Commerce and Growth Association (July 1994); Stephen G. Taylor. Economic impact of cultural institutions on the St. Louis region, 1994/95. RCGA (St. Louis Regional Commerce and Growth Association) (March 11, 1996).

3. The sense of direct and societal benefits is articulated both implicitly and explicitly on the Gates Library Foundation home page, and on the homepage of its linked Gates Center for Technology Access.

4. Lynn A. Karoly and others. *Investing in our children: What we know and don't know about the costs and benefits of early childhood interventions.* Santa Monica, Calif.: Rand (1998).

5. Peter Greenwood and others. *Diverting children from a life of crime: Measuring costs and benefits.* Santa Monica, Calif.: Rand (1996).

6. Glen E. Holt. "As parents and teachers see it: The community values of a public library." *Bottom Line*, 10:1 (1997), pp. 32–35.

7. Wherever possible, a rental price was used for the market substitute. Subsequent to the completion of the study, a local retail establishment began to offer rental audio books.

8. SLPL defines an "active" cardholder as a person who has used his/her card within the last 12 months. Any card without utilization is dropped automatically from the base after one year. When an "inactive" cardholder makes a card-based transaction, the computer automatically adds the name to the "active" category. The use of this conservative, automated approach creates a "clean" user database, a significant policy issue because of SLPL's continual efforts to upgrade cardholder services and benefits.

CHAPTER 29

St. Paul Uses Branch Library to Anchor Mixed-Use Development

Ellen Perlman

Pajamas will likely be frowned upon, but about this time next year, some residents in St. Paul will be able to roll out of bed and into the library. That's because they'll be living in apartments directly above their local branch library, in a new complex currently being constructed on land where an X-rated movie theater once stood. Apartment dwellers in Portland, Oregon, and Seattle already have the books-with-breakfast option, residing in units above the stacks. Library projects already underway in San Francisco and Kansas City also involve similar mixed uses. San Francisco's will include a grocery stores, along with 14 apartments. Kansas City is building a nine-story office building along with the Plaza Branch library, with plans to add housing later.

In a different twist, Salt Lake City's new Main Library, which opened in early 2003, has retail shops within it, providing space for a dozen or so businesses that further the library's mission. The idea of combining library and commercial space is being bandied about in several other metropolitan areas. "It's the best of urban renewal," says Gina La Force, director of the St. Paul Public Library. "When

you have two groups contributing funds, there are economies of scale allowing us to build a bigger and better library than if we had done this alone."

These mixed-use projects are not always cheaper for government entities, however. In fact, in some cases, the arrangements end up costing more. And the process can drag on longer than if the library were a stand-alone facility, as the private and public sectors negotiate and jump through their different hoops for approvals. "It probably slowed it down," says Rick Crawford, a planner in San Francisco. "We had some design issues and city planning had to work through this. It made it a little more challenging."

Nevertheless, interest in the idea among cities and counties is growing as libraries shed their dusty-shelf and shushing-librarian image and become vibrant educational, cultural and social centers. Supporters of public-private partnerships cite the many benefits to tucking libraries into communities in this way. Business is driven painlessly to the collection from apartment complexes or stores sharing the space next door or above. In the case of hous-

Originally published as "Library Living," *Governing*, Vol. 18, No. 14, November 2004, by Congressional Quarterly Inc., Washington, D.C. Reprinted with permission of the publisher.

ing, the library becomes the heart of an emerging residential community. "We like to take our libraries where the people are," says Carol Brey-Casiano, president of the American Library Association. Surely no bookmobile has ever made it closer to the people than underneath their dwellings. And such close proximity to a library is proving to be an amenity to many renters or condo buyers.

A Tricky Merger

In St. Paul, the developer worked with library staff and brought architects and contractors to the table to make sure the two purposes meshed and the facilities were compatible. Because the major street out front is designated for a future light-rail line, it made sense to build denser housing. The final product will be a structural layer cake, with library parking underground, a street-level library and parking above that for the mixed-income housing to be built above it all. The city is using bond money to fund its share and will get a more substantial building than if it built a stand-alone facility. The best part is that officials were having trouble finding a site to place a large enough library for the community, and the partnership solves that.

Multnomah County, Oregon, didn't plan specifically to combine housing with libraries either. Rather, the idea there is to build housing with anything and everything. "It's one of the areas of real need," says June Mikkelson, who was the library renovation manager for the most recently constructed facility. The county commission passed a resolution that any new county building must undergo a feasibility study to see if housing, particularly mixed-income housing, could be built along with it.

Three new libraries in the county passed the test. One that opened in 2001 has four market-rate apartments above it. The second, opened in 2002, has market-rate apartments above it and retail next door on half of the

ground floor. The library leases its space in each of these cases.

But the third facility — the Hollywood Library and Bookmark Apartments — sits on county land. The library portion was built and paid for with general obligation bonds. A developer bought the air rights above it to erect 47 mixed-income units. The deal was not a money-saving proposition for the county. There were costs associated with the partnership that would not have existed in a stand-alone library project.

Since it was the first building financed and constructed in this way, there were legal issues to wrangle with, including working out a two-party condominium agreement between the library and the developer. In addition, in order to build four stories high, the foundation of the structure had to be stronger than if there were nothing above it. And negotiations for how and what to build extended the planning process beyond the timeframe necessary to build just a library.

Merging such different uses can also create architectural challenges. Seattle seems to have successfully built a housing-library project with a split personality by pulling the pieces together with architectural elements. "We wanted to build a library that had that civic quality that people often look for in libraries, a sense of durability, using masonry," says David Kunselman, capital projects manager. The city had money available from a 1998 bond referendum.

The affordable-housing side, however, had different rules, regulations and expectations. Because there are stringent cost-per-foot limits, for example, the housing portion was built with siding rather than masonry. Before getting underway, the two entities had to find a middle ground for melding the two concepts. The result is hosing units set back a little so they're not flush with the library, leaving room for some planters that also help to mark the separation between the public library and private living quarters.

Like Multnomah, Seattle came up with a

two-party condo arrangement so that each entity owns its particular share of the building. "We wanted to make sure each organization was getting what it needed, since we were projecting longevity," Kunselman says.

San Francisco has split its project into a three-party condo arrangement, with a grocery store as a separate owner from the library and an apartment dweller. Not everyone was happy with the fact that the library portion is being sent upstairs. There's a lobby presence on the ground floor with an elevator and a display but some officials felt the library was given secondary status. Still, it will save the city as much as $10 million to have the developer build the outer shell of the structure. Kansas City is getting a similar shell deal in exchange for the use of its public land.

Some cities have not been able to overcome a challenge more daunting than the legal and architectural arrangements — opposition from citizens who simply aren't able to accept the idea that libraries might share space with private development. In West Palm Beach, a proposal to build six floors of condominiums above a 115,000-square-foot library recently was nixed. "It seems a group of people out there in our community think libraries have to be stand-alone buildings from Andrew Carnegie times, which would be nice except that no one has the money to do that," says Nancy Graham, executive director of the Downtown Development authority and former mayor.

In Washington, D.C., the two-story Tenleytown library, long overdue for renovation, sits on a highly valuable corner of real estate across from shops and restaurants and near a subway station. Last year, residents said no to the idea of a development above the library. It wasn't so much that they were opposed to a mixed use; rather they were afraid that scheduled renovation of the library might end up being delayed. "It was short-sighted," says Andrew Altman, director of the D.C. Office of Planning. "We could have had a library and housing right at a Metro stop."

Currently, two other D.C. libraries are being considered for mixed use. Altman points out that it's not just about the real estate. Many libraries are underutilized and short on resources. A private partner could bring financial help and make libraries the center of a community. "It's a tool to bring resources to a library system that is severely strained," he says. "If we capture that development and reinvest in the library — what an opportunity."

Shoppers and Tourists

Salt Lake City has taken a different tack on its relationship with the commercial sector. Its new library does not include housing but business tenants that support and enhance the library's mission. When designing the new Main Library on a 10-acre block where the old one once stood, the architects included retail space, both inside and outside of the soaring structure. The library retained the right to subjectively choose shops that would provide and support library services; they are not "formula" establishments with required standardized décor or uniforms; or that have a nonprofit or community-based focus.

The result is a ground level "urban" area with little shops, including a deli and a coffee roaster, a garden shop, a film center and a radio station. Now, when people come to a library event straight from work, they can grab a sandwich and a drink before the program begins. Or they can buy a notepad and pen without having to leave the building.

The film center provides films and documentaries to the library. The radio station sometimes broadcasts lecture series and the mayor can walk across the street, from city hall, to be interviewed for programs on community building. The garden shops offers programs with patrons on caring for plants. A bookstore sells the books that are the focus of library events. And a comic book and graphic novels shop emphasizes programs for reluctant readers and literary programs in schools and has brought in speakers and illustrators for library programs, including the illustrator from *The Simpsons*. The library on its own couldn't have paid to bring in someone of that stature. But it was able to provide room for the 3,000 people who showed up over four hours.

The financial contribution from the businesses is small since there's only a small portion of private space that can be leased when a government entity floats a bond to pay for the facility. In this case, it's only 10,000 square feet

of the 200,000-square-foot structure. But it goes a ways toward satisfying a city council mandate to get creative about bringing in revenue to support the unrelenting demand for library growth and develop. And it enhances the library's mission of bringing people in. "It helps us enliven the space, offers variety and makes it that much more of a destination," says director Nancy Tessman. The library now is the second-most-popular destination in the state, with 3 million visitors last year, many of them tourists.

CHAPTER 30

San Jose Builds "Green" Library

J. Lindsey Wolf, Loraine Oback, *and* Jane Christophersen

Although Dr. Seuss's book *Green Eggs and Ham* is a popular children's title, that's not what prompted the City of San Jose to make its new West Valley Branch Library "green." Rather, the building was conceived and constructed as a model of "green" building design, using 30 percent less energy and 50 percent less irrigation water than standard buildings. It also incorporates natural day lighting and a variety of chemical-free fabrics and materials to improve indoor air quality and the comfort of library patrons. What's more, at least 25 percent of the materials used during construction were made from recycled products, such as soda bottles, and 20 percent of the building materials were manufactured locally.

But that's all inside. Outside, the preservation of mature redwood trees, a drought-tolerant landscape, and a mix of carefully shaded windows with clerestory windows and skylights signal that this is not a typical library building. And that's what attracted the attention of the U.S. Green Building council (USGBC), which recently recognized San Jose's West Valley Branch Library as the nation's — and the world's — first green library.

The nation's foremost coalition of leaders from across the building industry, government and other organizations, USGBC is working to promote buildings that are environmentally responsible, profitable, and healthy places to live and work. Half of the projects registered with USGBC are located in California.

San Jose Invests in Going Green

The West Valley Branch Library is the city's first building to achieve the special USGBC distinction. Approved under the city council's green building policy, its design and construction represent a successful collaboration between three city departments — Public Works, the library system and Environmental Services.

"We are very proud of this significant investment in green building," said City Council Member Linda J. LeZotte, the council's leading proponent for energy efficiency. "San Jose is taking positive steps toward sustainability. Designing more buildings like West Valley will help the city reduce long-term operating costs while increasing community satisfaction."

California Cities Lead in Green Building Design

Three Los Angeles–area buildings have recently received a Leadership in Energy and Environmental Design (LEED™) Platinum Certification from the USGBC — the highest possible level of sustainable design. Developed by the USGBC membership and launched in 1999, the LEED Green Building Rating System is a national system for designing, constructing and certifying the world's greenest and best buildings. Eight nations (Canada, Mexico, China, India, Japan, Spain, Italy and the United States) have registered projects with LEED, which is the accepted industry standard for evaluating and certifying green buildings.

Only four projects worldwide have earned the Platinum rating, and three of them are in California.

Inland Empire Utilities Agency (IEUA) Headquarters, Chino

IEUA was the first to achieve a LEED Platinum certification with a project cost *below* industry standards. It is the only public agency to have earned this LEED distinction.

The headquarters complex is one of the largest public landscapes in Southern California to use California-friendly plants and to have integrated state-of-the-art stormwater management on the property. Planting more than 10,000 native and drought-tolerant trees, shrubs and ground cover throughout the site further reduces water consumption.

"Our facility incorporates many of the most innovative and progressive technologies addressing urban sustainability in the workplace — at a price of less than $160 per square foot for the building envelope and the hardscape and softscape," said IEUA's Project Manager Eliza Jane Whitman. "Our administrative headquarters demonstrates how using recycled building materials and state-of-the-art energy efficiency can create a better environment, save on our electricity bills, conserve water and contribute to the restoration of native landscapes."

Natural Resources Defense Council (NRDC) Office, Santa Monica

NRDC's Southern California office building reclaims water and generates electricity from sunlight, is built from recycled or recyclable materials, makes the most of natural light and sea breezes to minimize the need for artificial lighting and cooling, and reuses already urbanized property in a part of the city that encourages walking and the use of public transit.

This three-story, clapboard structure, named after NRDC Trustee Robert Redford, reflects its Santa Monica surroundings. Among its more striking features are three multi-level atria with rooftop monitors that diffuse sunlight and send fresh air throughout the building, evoking the feel of a lighthouse.

Audubon Center at Debs Park, Los Angeles

The first project to receive a LEED Platinum Rating, the Audubon Center employs renewable energy sources, water conservation, recycled building materials and native landscaping. The 5,023-square-foot building is the first in the City of Los Angeles to be powered entirely by onsite solar systems. The building also uses significantly less water than a conventional building of its size. More than 25 percent of the building materials were locally harvested, and more than 50 percent of the materials were locally manufactured.

Why Build Green?

The built environment has a profound impact on our natural environment, economy, health and productivity. According to the U.S.

Green Building Council, buildings for the United States account for:

- 36 percent of total energy use and 65 percent of electricity consumption;
- 30 percent of greenhouse gas emissions;
- 30 percent of raw materials use;
- 30 percent of waste output; and
- 12 percent of potable water consumption.

The advantages of building green are numerous and include:

Environmental Benefits:

- Enhancing and protecting ecosystems and biodiversity;
- Improving air and water quality;
- Reducing solid waste; and
- Conserving natural resources.

Economic Benefits:

- Reduced operating costs;
- Enhanced asset value and profits;
- Improved employee productivity and satisfaction; and
- Optimized economic life-cycle performance.

Health and Community Benefits:

- Improved air, thermal and acoustic environments;
- Enhanced occupant comfort and health;
- Minimized strain on local infrastructure; and
- Contributions to the overall quality of life.

For more information, visit the U.S. Green Building Council website at *www.usgbc.org*.

Green Buildings Make Good Sense Financially

In October 2003, the State of California released an in-depth analysis called *The Costs and Financial Benefits of Green Buildings*. The reports presents the most comprehensive study ever done on the cost benefits of green buildings and concludes that the financial upside exceeds the cost by a factor of 10 to 1. This report, available online through the USGBC website at *www.usgbc.org/Docs/News/News477.pdf*, includes that:

> The benefits of building green include cost savings from reduced energy, water and waste; lower operations and maintenance costs; and enhanced occupant productivity and health. ... [The] total financial benefits of green buildings are over ten times the average initial investment required to design and construct a green building. Energy savings alone exceed the average increased cost associated with building green. Additionally, the relatively large impact of productivity and health gains reflects the fact that the direct and indirect cost of employees is far larger than the cost of construction or energy. Consequently, even small changes in productivity and health translate into large financial benefits.
>
> "Green building makes good sense," said Carl Mosher, San Jose's director of environmental services. "In the next 10 years, San Jose will be building up to 30 new libraries and community centers. If we pursue this path, we can reduce operating and maintenance costs by saving energy, water and other natural resources in addition to reusing certain materials."

CHAPTER 31

San Jose Creates Joint City and University Library

Lorraine Oback

In the mid–1990s, the city of San Jose and San Jose State University (SJSU) faced a similar dilemma: They both needed to build new libraries to replace their old ones, which were too small and technologically outdated, and both entities had limited financial resources.

Extensive Planning for Building and Operation

Implementing the project involved years of planning and community input. Teams of staff from both libraries were established to review building specifications for functional design and create operational plans for the transition and management of the joint library. Consultants were hired to assist with technology planning and customer satisfaction benchmarking. The two libraries had very different organizational cultures, so determining how to merge their operations was challenging; from choosing what type of library automation to purchase to how to share coverage of reference and circulation desks. Multiple change management tools were employed to inform

and encourage integration of staff. Planning for the move of 1.5 million items was time intensive and complex, yet the phased move-in took a mere 2.5 months.

Architectural Excellence

At 475,000 square feet, the joint library is the largest all-new library west of the Mississippi.

The architects were challenged to create a large building that would be appealing on a human scale — distinctive but compatible with campus and downtown revitalization. Their design centers around an eight-story atrium, through which natural light pours in. A ground floor promenade links the public and campus lobbies. The most popular and widely used materials are located on the first four floors. Special collections are on the fifth floor, and the university's academic research collections fill the top three floors. A large reading room on the eighth floor offers a spectacular view of San Jose.

The goal of making the Dr. Martin Luther King Jr. Library a center for intellectual and creative thought extended to the process of creating 33 pieces of public art for installation throughout the library. Internationally renowned artist Mel Chin engaged the community in lively discussions about how art should be used to reflect the diversity of the community.

Funding and Cost Savings

The King Library is a large-scale example of resource sharing among public entities. The project cost of $170 million drew on public and private sources: $70 million from the city, $86 million from the State of California fund for California State University capital projects, $5 from SJSU and $9 million from private funds.

Savings for the City of San Jose and State of California taxpayers have been significant. Eliminating the need for two stand-alone library buildings (155,000–180,000 square feet each) saved approximately $24 million on construction and reduced annual building maintenance costs by an estimated $1.5 million.

According to PG&E, the energy efficient design of the library is saving 1.5 million kilowatt-hours (kWh) per year, well above California's Title 24 Energy Code requirements. High quality glazing and new technology in lighting design and control systems have reduced the cooling requirements of the building by 44 percent and the heating requirements by 31 percent.

Improving Service Delivery

Residents now have easier access to the university's intellectual resources while the campus community has convenient access to the public library's collections of popular books and media. Additional benefits include:

- A landmark downtown building whose distinctive architecture and size transform a quiet campus corner into a bustling center of activity;
- Expanded hours of operation plus 24/7 online access to extensive electronic resources and research databases;
- Multilingual collections for San Jose's highly diverse ethnic populations plus separate resource center space for African, Asian-American and Chicano collections;
- Equal access for all, from an undocumented day laborer with limited English language skills to an internationally renowned professor with multiple academic degrees; and
- An intellectual and cultural center for the city, reflecting the unique creativity and energy of Silicon Valley.

Effect on Community

The vision of the Dr. Martin Luther King Jr. Library is being realized: a world class library serving the lifelong learning needs of both the city and the university.

Whether they have attended SJSU, some other college or no college at all, residents feel comfortable in the King Library and experience it as a welcoming place where they can read, learn, research, think, create, relax and enjoy new ideas and information.

Most public agencies are caught between the need and/or desire to improve the delivery of service to constituents and limited financial resources. The King Library is an excellent example of how public agencies can pool their resources to develop community assets that are mutually beneficial. It is also a unique collaborative model for library design that could be replicated in many regions of California and throughout the United States.

CHAPTER 32

Seattle Builds Public Library to Attract Private Investment to Its Downtown

Urban Libraries Council

Approaches to local economic development have traditionally focused on tax abatements and credits, preferential financial rates, provision of land and, often, facilities to attract business and boost employment in local markets. However, the new knowledge economy has altered the landscape for many business decisions. Recent studies of location decisions of "high performance firms" reveal that a number of these businesses prefer to locate in areas with higher wages, a labor force with plentiful high school graduates, responsive and efficient government, good schools, and a decent quality of life (Doeringer, Terkla, Klock 2002).

Responding to these shifting factors for economic success, local economic development strategies that once focused narrowly on highlighting assets of a given location or access to major transportation are giving way to strategies that promote quality-of-life environments and strong community capacity for economic growth. Business attraction strategies that once focused narrowly on landing large "outside" firms are now identifying ways to nurture local small businesses, and to build clusters of competitive industries, linked in regional networks, that create new growth and income. Employment-centered economic development strategies that once focused on job creation, even if many were at minimum wage, are now focusing on developing comprehensive skills to build workforce competitiveness and creating career paths to quality jobs and higher wages.

As local economic development practice broadens to include strategies for building human, social, institutional, and physical resources for stronger, self-sustaining local economic systems, there is an approach for a much wider range of community organizations to identify when and where their assets contribute to making cities stronger and building better local economies. This shift in strategies provides an opportunity for public libraries to identify specific ways in which library services contribute to broader local economic strategies.

The new Seattle Public Library, located in the center of downtown, attracts some 8,000

Originally published as "Linking to Local Economic Development" in *Making Cities Stronger: Public Library Contributions to Local Economic Development*, May 2007, by the Urban Institute, Washington, D.C. Reprinted with permission of the publisher.

visitors a day. This is twice the number of daily visitors that visited the old main library downtown. This new inner city attraction, which was completed in 2004, has created "public space" and, at the same time, stimulated local economic development.

A Trusted Public Place

Few community services enjoy the type of public support that is generally given to public libraries. In a recent national survey conducted by Public Agenda, people were more likely to rate library service as excellent or good than the service they receive from their local police department, public schools or their local media (PA 2006). In a national public opinion survey conducted for the American Library Association, over 90 percent of the total respondents said they believe libraries are places of opportunity for education, self-help, and offer free access to all (KRS Research Associates 2002).

Many demands challenge public library leaders to continue to provide services in a manner that meets the high expectations of the public while operating in an environment of constrained state and local budgets. Despite high regard for public libraries as an institution, leaders in many public library systems are facing difficult choices because of a decline in public funding. Additionally, rising costs of new materials, such as online journals, databases, and operations has forced libraries nationwide to cut services, or to find more money by dipping into budgets for books, audiovisual materials and programs. Further, many library systems across the country are in desperate need of capital support to upgrade or repair existing buildings or build entirely new facilities to adequately service communities where the local population has swelled.

Amidst these competing demands, library leaders across the country have also felt increasing pressure to justify the investment in public libraries given the growing volume of content on the Internet, increased computer ownership in many American homes, and market competition from private book vendors.

Measuring the Economic Impacts of Public Libraries

An increasing number of economic research tools are now being used to measure the public value of libraries, including the cost-benefit impacts and return on investment that public libraries generate. These studies consistently identify positive economic impacts made by libraries at the national, state and local levels:

• At the national level, Liu (2004) examined the causal relationship between public libraries, literacy levels, and economic productivity measured by gross domestic product per capita using path analysis. This study found that public libraries contribute to long-term economic productivity primarily through literacy programs.
• Recent studies at the state level have found significant economic benefits as well, including significant returns on public investment and generation of gross regional product (Barron, et al. 2005, McClure, et al. 2000). There have been tremendous short-term local economic spin-off benefits from construction alone, as expenditures for state and local library construction doubled from $948 million dollars in 2000 to just over $2 billion dollars in 2005.
• Positive economic impacts are also evident at the city level. A recent study conducted by the Carnegie Mellon University's Center for Economic Development (CMU) for the Carnegie Library of Pittsburgh found the library to be the most visited regional asset, attracting 500 thousand more visitors than the Carnegie Science

Center and the Pittsburgh Steelers combined. CMU researchers estimate that the library generates a return of more than $91 million in combined economic output and sustains more than 700 jobs. Using a different methodology, the Seattle Public library found substantial economic returns to the city and local business immediately following the development of the new downtown library. They found the net new contribution to the local economy to be approximately $16 million during the first full year of operation alone (Berk & Associates 2004).

This study seeks to follow the links between libraries and economic development benefits. It looks at how layers of special program resources and activities in public libraries intersect with specific local economic development strategies already in motion. Return on Investment (ROI) studies alone do not identify the ways in which library services are benefiting students, job seekers, employers, small businesses and entrepreneurs. This study takes a closer look at the layers of targeted programmatic benefits, and investigates and articulates the ways in which public libraries are addressing the needs of individuals and agencies, within the context of broader formal and informal local economic development networks.

Special programs, which have always been a part of public library services, have increasingly taken on local community development challenges in the past decade. Public libraries are now working with local schools to create a more integrated set of services for children (Saunders 2001), coordinating with workforce development agencies for job and career information services (Durrance 1994), and collaborating with local chambers of commerce to improve business information services for micro and small businesses (Wilson and Train 2002). These special program services are broadening the impact of traditional library information resources by networking with the efforts of other groups in the community.

Modeling Public Library Benefits

Figure 1 provides a model that summarizes the multiple ways in which public library resources, programs and services impact local economic development conditions.

Traditional Service Benefits. Public libraries provide direct service benefits to individuals. These include the cost savings of public access resources over market costs of goods and services, as well as the self-identified benefits of getting information or access to technology, for example.

Benefits of Business Operations. Public libraries are large organizations, particularly in metropolitan settings, and thus, provide significant business-related spin-off benefits to the local economy that include employment and wage contributions, purchasing of supplies and materials, contracted services, library construction and even the effect on local business resulting from increased foot traffic. A recent study of the economic impact of South Carolina public libraries estimated that the libraries contributed close to $126 million in spending on wages, supplies, books and related materials, construction, and other business related expenditures (Barron, et al. 2005).

Program Related Benefits. Public libraries contribute significant community-level benefits, particularly as they relate to program services. Library resources and programs contribute capacity to local strategies that seek to strengthen human capital, reduce service costs to complementary local agencies, and broaden the reach of local partner organizations.

Programming in public libraries is highly local, and touches on many community development agendas — from school success to financial literacy to public health. In this report, the focus is on three program areas that are core local economic development strategies:

- **early literacy**— initiatives that promote reading, prepare young children for school and raise levels of education.

- **workforce initiatives**— efforts that increase workforce skills, provide career training, and facilitate employment and career search.
- **small business support**— strengthening the small business sector through the provision of business information resources, workshops and training for both new and experienced business owners.

The case study research examines specific library program strategies that support current practice in the field of local economic development. It highlights the range of short-term and long-term economic outcomes that were either identified by program participants or could be identified and measured in future research. Finally, the report provides suggestions about ways public libraries can stretch resources and programs further, providing even greater impact.

Note: To purchase copies of the research publication *Making Cities Stronger*, please contact the Urban Libraries Council at (312) 676-0999 or via e-mail at info@urbanlibraries.org.

CHAPTER 33

Tacoma Uses Museums
to Promote Its Culture

Juli Wilkerson

In the mid–1980s, Tacoma, Washington, was considered by most to be a city on the decline. Crime was rampant and the city's downtown waterfront — a federally designated "Superfund" site — sat wasting away. Pulp mills choked the air, drug dealers solicited openly on street corners, and gangs and prostitution abounded. Most investment went north to Seattle and retail left downtown for the mall. Foot traffic downtown was virtually nonexistent.

Today, this community of just under 200,000 has become the region's "cultural corridor," with several museums and theaters clustered in the city's downtown. Clean air is back and crime is down. Students move between University of Washington classes located in artfully restored buildings. The downtown area offers new market-rate housing, a bridge of glass, a light rail line, and a new convention center that will be completed this year. Moreover, business is returning to Tacoma, which has earned a new reputation as "America's #1 Wired City."

What was the formula that this mid-sized city used to turn itself around and create a thriving community? It was one of investing public dollars in order to spur private invest-

ment in major projects. Of course, a great many communities have spent public monies on projects like this over the years. What made Tacoma different was a "can-do" attitude that provided the energy and enthusiasm necessary to bring all parties together, and a spirit of collaboration that enabled both the public and private sector to work together to overcome the political roadblocks that often stand in the way of projects like these. By relying on this approach, the City of Tacoma has become a model for other U.S. cities seeking to revitalize their communities.

Rebirth of a Waterway

One of the biggest projects o the city's capital project was cleaning up the Thea Foss Waterway, Tacoma's downtown waterfront. In the early 1990s, the city had taken a careful look at this Superfund site and determined that no private sector developer was going to take on the project — and the liability that went with it. So the city purchased the 26-acre tract of land with the long-range goal of cleaning it up and seeking private investment.

Once the clean-up was complete, a

Originally published as "Public Investment Promotes Tacoma's Rebirth," *Government West*, July-August 2004, by Colt Stewart Inc., Sacramento, CA. Reprinted with permission of the author.

group of local leaders decided to build an architecturally spectacular museum on the Foss. To make it a reality, the city donated the land and built the parking garage upon which the building would stand. The private sector added to this effort with $63 million to build the Museum of Glass, now deemed by Conde Nast Traveler as one of the "Seven Architectural Wonders of the World."

The next key to redeveloping the Foss was finding a way to move people from the city's recovering downtown over an interstate highway to the new museum and the waterway. The city government worked closely with Tacoma native and renowned glass artist Dale Chihuly to make it happen. The result was the Chihuly Bridge of Glass, a project unique in the world, with $12 million of Chihuly's glass installed across the new bridge.

Private investment has followed in the wake of these public activities. For instance, a group of local investors built Thea's Landing, a $40 million mixed-use development of luxury waterfront condominia, apartments, restaurant space, and retail next to the Museum of Glass.

Making the Public/Private Model Work

Tacoma has made the public/private model work in other projects, too. In 1997, for example, Tacoma Power invested nearly $100 million to build "Click! Network," a 700-mile network of fiberoptics and cable covering every city block — part of the largest city-owned telecommunications infrastructure in the nation. The private sector followed with its own $200 million in telecommunication investments, and today Tacoma is more "wired" than nearly any city its size.

In 1999, the city embarked on a marketing campaign aimed at capturing the unique selling point of being "wired" and began billing itself as "America's #1 Wired City." That new image has taken hold, and is reflected in the private sector's confidence in investing in Tacoma. From 2001 to 2002, while Seattle lost 23,000 jobs, Tacoma gained more than 7,000 jobs.

Tacoma has also added to its transportation infrastructure. Earlier this year, Sound Transit, the largest public transportation organization in the State of Washington, opened the state's first light rail line in Tacoma. The $80.4 million public investment in this project is proving to be a magnet for private investment. Buildings near the line are selling and being renovated, and businesses looking to locate in Tacoma are signing leases because their employees can take "The Link" to work.

The bottom line: Tacoma has found that public investment — combined with a can-do, business friendly attitude — is a strong catalyst for generating private investment and long-term economic renewal.

CHAPTER 34

Tallahassee and Other Cities Place a Value on Cultural Amenities

Glenda E. Hood

It is my pleasure to present the results of recent economic impact studies generated by the Florida Department of State's Office of Cultural and Historical Programs and the State Library and Archives of Florida. These inquiries examine the return on investment that Florida taxpayers enjoy as a result of our cultural, historical and library program activities.

While it may not seem obvious to some, cultural, historical and library services positively contribute to Florida's economy through increased tourism, enhanced education, community revitalization, rural development, strengthening of families and by allowing us to celebrate our state's diversity.

Enterprise Florida, a not-for-profit public-private partnership dedicated to boosting Florida's economic development, identifies the arts and culture as statewide priorities in its recent strategic plan, labeling them integral to the state's economic diversification efforts. Further, the Florida Chamber of Commerce, the state's largest business group, in *New Cornerstone: Foundations for Florida's 21st Century Economy*, defined specific growth strategies, emphasizing cooperation among Florida's government, academic and business communi-

ties. The importance of creative communities to the economy as a whole was one of the key components noted.

We have long maintained anecdotal and empirical evidence that our cultural, historical, and library programs stimulate economic growth in Florida. This brochure corroborates our assessment with the facts. Please join me in continuing your support of our cultural, historical and library programs, and know that by doing so you are helping to make Florida a better place for all of us.

The Arts & Cultural Industry

Florida's cultural arts industry is among the fastest growing in the state. Enterprise Florida, a not-for-profit partnership between state government and the private sector dedicated to boosting Florida's economic development, identifies the arts and culture as statewide priorities, labeling them integral to the state's economic diversification efforts. This growing awareness among the non-arts sector is tangible evidence that the arts and cultural industry is being acknowledged as one of Florida's principle economic engines.

Originally published as *Return on Investment: Florida's Cultural, Historical and Library Programs*, 2004. Published by the State of Florida, Tallahassee.

The Florida Cultural Alliance, with funding from the National Endowment for the Arts and the Florida Department of State, recently commissioned Dr. William Stronge of Florida Atlantic University to document and analyze what is prompting this trend. In his *Economic Impact of the Arts and Cultural Industry*, Stronge examined data collected from 2,914 not-for-profit organizations and the cultural programs of 57 colleges and universities during the 2000–2001 fiscal year. Programs of such as these comprise a major component of Florida's cultural Industry. The study revealed the following:

- The total impact of Florida's cultural arts industry, including performing arts organizations, museums and galleries, science museums and zoos, festivals, service and support organizations, presenting organizations, and cultural councils, totals $2.9 billion on Florida's gross state product every year.
- The cultural arts industry created 28,302 jobs in FY2001, adding $877.8 million to income statewide. As the cultural arts industry is labor-intensive, it depends on a variety of skilled individuals such as performers, artists, administrators, stagehands, designers and technicians. These jobs were created through expenditures totaling $1.2 billion.
- More than 400 million people, including 7 million out-of-state tourists, attended cultural events in Florida during 2001. The majority (192.7 million) attended performing arts events, while 38.6 million visited museums and galleries, 5.9 million visited science museums and zoos, and 2.5 million attended culture festivals. A total of 96.3 million individuals either sponsored such events or were presenters, while 70.3 million represented service and support organizations.
- The 7 million out-of-state tourists noted above spent an average of $588.30, totaling $4.5 billion.

- The total impact of these expenditures on the state economy amount to **$9.3 billion**, creating 103,713 jobs and incomes (primarily payrolls) of **$2.6 billion**.
- Since 1976, over 18,000 state cultural affairs grants have been awarded to projects in every Florida county, representing an investment of $497,761,646.

Clearly, the cultural arts industry impacts Florida's economy daily and as such it should be afforded the incentives and devices derived by other similar economic catalysts.[1]

Historic Preservation

The Division of Historical Resources is the primary state agency responsible for promoting the historical, archaeological and folk culture resources in Florida, and oversees the state's legislatively-funded preservation grants-in-aid program. In 2002, the *Economic Impacts of Historic Preservation in Florida* study was released, representing the input from 60 local government officials and individuals involved in historic preservation and more than 30 Florida communities. The study was financed with historic preservation grant assistance provided by the National Park Service, U.S. Department of the Interior, administered through the Florida Bureau of Historic Preservation and was conducted by the Center for Governmental Responsibility, University of Florida Levin College of Law and the Center for Urban Policy Research, Rutgers State University.

- The total impact of historic preservation in Florida is $4.2 billion a year. This encompasses the impact of job creation, income generated, increased gross state product, and increased state and local taxes.
- The impacts were created in 2000 from historic preservation activities in the sectors of manufacturing, retail trade, services and construction. State officials estimate that between 60 percent and 70 percent of

the budget for a historic rehabilitation project is expanded on labor, which benefits local workers. Furthermore, historic preservation added $2.7 billion to statewide income in 2000.

- Approximately 42.9 million tourists visited the state's more than 135,000 historic sites, historic museums, state parks and archaeological sites. These tourists spent a total of $3.7 billion. Additionally, more than one-half of Florida's museums are historical, welcoming more than 9.7 million visitors in 2002, according to the Florida Association of Museums.

- Historic preservation activities help to maintain property values in historic districts. In a survey of 18 historic and 25 non-historic residential districts across Florida, historic preservation was never found to depress property values. In fact, historic preservation contributed to greater appreciation of property value in at least 15 cases. An example of this can be found in Jacksonville's Springfield Historic District where property values have doubled due to rehabilitation efforts.

- Public funds invested in historic preservation grants are matched many times over with private funds in local rehabilitation projects. Since 1983, state historic preservation grants have been awarded to projects in every Florida county, representing 2,751 projects and a state investment of $212.1 million. The Secretary of State's office estimates funding is more than doubled by leveraged public and private funds in these local communities.[2]

Public Libraries

In 2004, the State Library and Archives of Florida contracted with a research team consisting of representatives from the University of Pittsburgh, the University of North Carolina at Chapel Hill and Florida State University to measure taxpayer return on invest-ment in Florida's public libraries. Over 2,380 individuals and 169 organizations participated in this groundbreaking study which was the first of its kind ever completed in the state.

Researchers used an input-output econometric model called REMI (Regional Economic Modeling Inc.) to assess the return on investment. The study was funded under the provisions of the Library Services and Technology Act, from the Institute of Museum and Library Services, administered by the Florida Department of State, State Library and Archives of Florida.

- Florida's public libraries return at least $6.54 for ever $1.00 invested from all sources, including local, state and federal dollars. The economic benefit can be seen in jobs created, increased wages for Florida's residents and positive impact on Florida's gross regional product.

- Florida's public libraries provide total direct economic benefit of $6.0 billion per year to Florida's communities and population. The total revenue investment in Florida's public libraries is $449 million. This includes federal, state and local public funds ($2.3 million, $34 million and $387 million respectively); other funds such as grants ($20 million); and funds that support the multitype library cooperatives ($6 million).

- Florida's public libraries, by their very existence, stimulate an economic ripple effect. The statewide gross regional product is estimated to increase by $4 billion as a result of publicly-funded library expenditures in the state. These direct instate expenditures by public libraries include books, periodicals, electronic equipment and resources, as well as large capital projects such as library construction and renovation.

- In 2003/2004 there were 68.3 million in-person visits to public libraries in Florida and at least 25.2 million remote Internet connections to public libraries.

- For every $6,488 of public support (federal, state and local) one job is created. An estimated 900,000 jobs were created in 2004, generating wages of $5.6 billion.
- The direct economic contribution of Florida's public libraries to the state's education is $2.1 billion annually.
- The benefits of Florida's public libraries to their users can be measured in terms of savings in both time and money. In the past year, users indicated a total of 57.6 million hours or $2.4 billion saved. Florida's citizens save both time and money by accessing the resources available through their public libraries, whether they use them for personal, educational or work-related purposes.[3]

Summary

In summary, the economic return on the investment in the State of Florida's cultural, historical, and library facilities and programs is extensive. The direct economic benefits are nearly twenty billion dollars. Nearly 300,000 jobs are provided by these sectors. The annual payroll for those employees working in these sectors is eleven billion dollars. In the aggregate, over 500 million people visit these facilities throughout the year.

A more detailed overview of these economic benefits is highlighted below.

- The cultural arts, historic preservation, and library services industries in Florida have a combined impact of **$19.5 billion** per year on the state's economy.
- Over 295,655 jobs are created by these industries in Florida.
- Over **$10.9 billion** in personal income is generated annually by the jobs created in cultural, historical, and library related industries in Florida.
- **511.2 million people** visit public libraries, visit historic locations, and attend cultural events every year in Florida!

CHAPTER 35

Toronto Embraces Museums for Its Cultural Renaissance

Albert Warson

"To have any one of these projects is phenomenal, but to have so many of them at the same time is a unique and historic moment for Toronto," says Rita Davies, the city's executive director of culture. "There was practically no money spent on cultural infrastructure in Toronto for a number of decades," she explains, "and to have so many of these projects coming on stream at the same time is a legacy of that pent-up demand."

Though widely dubbed a "cultural renaissance," given the often obsolete, dowdy, generally neglected state of the city's cultural stock, it could also be called a cultural "naissance." For sheer scale, Davies maintains that there is nothing going on like it in all of North America. Not only does the cultural renaissance include the National Ballet School and the Young Centre for the Performing Arts, both of which opened a few months ago, but also it will include the Royal Ontario Museum (ROM), the Art Gallery of Ontario (AGO), the Gardiner Museum of Ceramic Art (the Gardiner), the Four Seasons Centre for the Performing Arts (an opera house), the Royal Conservatory of Music, and a Toronto International Film Festival (TIFF) headquarters, all of which will be opening sporadically over the next two years.

The federal and Ontario governments funded about one-third of the C$1billion (US$870 billion) total cost, in cash or land value. "None of these projects would have gotten off the ground without an initial government investment," Davies says. The private sector money that followed — the most ever raised in Toronto for cultural development — floated in on a wave of civic pride, and large checks. Much of the money was for naming rights, which also energized the fundraising; the "Four Seasons" stamp on the opera house is named for the Toronto-based international hotel chain.

Davies describes the overall architectural design as "astonishing," rendered by the likes of native son Frank Gehry for client AGO, and by former Torontonian Daniel Libeskind for the ROM expansion. These two projects were heralded in 2004, she says, by British architect Will Alsop's nine-story-high "flying tabletop" building perched on 12 slanting legs at the Ontario College of Art and Design, around the corner from the AGO.

The C$207 million (US$235.3 million) AGO expansion is designed to add 47 percent more viewing space for a total of 190,000 net square feet of renovated space, including

Originally published as "Toronto's Cultural Renaissance," *Urban Land*, Vol. 65, No. 3, March 2006, by the Urban Land Institute, Washington, D.C. Reprinted with permission of the publisher.

97,000 square feet of newly built space. It will allow the gallery to accommodate more and larger art exhibits, more programs, and more areas for art restoration, storage, art classes, and research. Attendance is expected to increase from 600,000 to 800,000 visitors a year when the project is completed in spring 2008. The most visible exterior feature of Gehry's design will be a 600-foot-long facade 70 feet above the main street.

Less than a ten-minute drive north, on the perimeter of the University of Toronto campus and overlooking a stretch of Bloor Street West that is Toronto's answer to Park Avenue, the ROM's C$211 million (US$184 million) expansion and heritage renovation project will add 40,000 square feet of exhibit space for a total of 300,000 square feet. Ten new galleries opened in December; the soaring crystalline ROM addition and other construction will be completed this summer.

With few exceptions, Toronto's architecture is regarded as rather bland and forgettable. The city's characteristic restraint is summed up in Gehry's remake of the AGO, which lacked the budget that could have afforded his initial scheme. This factor, along with site constraints, made it impossible for Gehry to fulfill his vision of the gallery that he visited as a boy and that was on the same block where he grew up. As a result, he has said that the AGO project is his last project in Canada.

Peter Clewes, a Toronto architect, says the city "is somewhat averse to supporting cultural institutions, unlike Montreal and cities in western Europe." The "City of Toronto's Culture Plan Report," dated November 2005, states that in 2003 Toronto spent C$15 (US$13) per capita on arts and culture, compared with municipal per-capita spending of C$18.4 (US$16) for Vancouver and C$36.8 (US$32) for Montreal — both with far smaller populations — C$18.4 (US$16) for Chicago, C$62 (US$54) for New York, and C$100 (US$80) for San Francisco. Clewes also says he doubts the accuracy of the oft-repeated marketing hype that Toronto has the third-largest number of theaters after London and New York.

While the cash-strapped city — the municipal budget will fall short this fiscal year by C$500 million (US$435.8 million) — is not likely or able to spend much more on arts and culture, the eight cultural expansion projects alone are expected to attract more than 4 million visitors a year, says Matthew Teitelbaum, the AGO's director and CEO. According to Teitelbaum, that number will fuel "an engine that's already producing more jobs for more people. Cultural institutions create 600,000 jobs for Canadians and more than C$39 billion (US$34 billion) in annual revenues" [on a national basis]. "Over the last decade," he continues, "Ontario witnessed an 18 percent increase in cultural sector jobs. Toronto's cultural sector alone generates more than C$9.2 billion (US$8 billion) annually and accounts for half of Ontario's cultural revenues," notes Teitelbaum.

Realistically, says Bruce Kuwabara, a partner in Toronto-based Kuwabara Payne McKenna Blumberg Architects (KPMB), the provincial government's financial largesse is motivated by the expectation that supporting cultural tourism will in turn have an economic benefit for Toronto. KPMB also designed the Gardiner, TIFF, and the conservatory.

Kuwabara notes that his firm was working on a master plan for the conservatory at least ten years ago, and that Goldsmith Borgal and Co., KPMB's joint venture partner in the design of the C$100 million (US$87.2 million) ballet school, also was working on that project some ten years ago. But, their work, for the most part, was the manifestation of visions that had been "percolating," as he put it, over the years and that had been brought to life by government and private sector funding. "They started at different places, but are coming to fruition at the same time," explains Kuwabara.

Jack Diamond, a partner in Diamond and Schmitt Architects Incorporated, Toronto, which designed the opera house, agrees that Toronto may be taking its own hype too seriously. "In a way, Toronto has protested too much that it's a world-class city simply because it has a clean subway that runs on time. It also has an opera house in a rented hall [Hummingbird Centre], which gives a few opera and ballet performances occasionally. But now, there will be national opera and ballet companies in repertory [in the new C$207 million (US$180 million) opera house], as the perception of the city shifts. The city is finally providing the venues or facilities for that highest of aspirations — art," Diamond says. "Helsinki has two opera houses in a city of half a million people. We're just now starting to catch up."

The number of projects is a "manifestation of the wealth and complexity of this city." As for the influence of the architecture represented in the cultural projects, Diamond says it has definitely raised the bar for future projects of different categories, which is yet "another aspect of the maturation of the city."

CHAPTER 36

Valencia Focuses on Museums and Libraries to Create a "Sense of Place"

Thomas L. Lee

In the 1980s, when the New York Islanders hockey team won the Stanley Cup four years in a row, the team's triumphant motorcade was reduced to circling around the suburban Nassau Coliseum parking lot as loyal fans cheered them on. There was nowhere else to go. That sad scene could soon change as "place making"—a new development trend discussed at ULI's first place-making conference held a year ago last June in Chicago—drives the reinvention of dozens of suburban communities across the country as well as new development, creating places where there were none.

"Places" take many forms: from old-fashioned main streets and town squares, to traditional big-city downtowns, to newly developed suburban town centers. Each creates a public realm that gives a community its heart, its character, its identity, and, most important, a place where all kinds of people can come for a wide variety of everyday activities, from early in the morning until late at night, seven days a week.

As lifestyles become more mobile, computerized, and hectic, many people are finding that they crave connection. They also crave reality and are turning away from overstructured, formulaic places that do not look or feel real—such as could-be-anywhere shopping malls—and turning instead to real places such as downtowns and town centers.

Many declining 1950s and 1960s inner suburbs see place making as one way to create an easily recognizable—and marketable—identity and character that can attract new businesses, residents, and development, increase property values and tax revenues, and help them compete with their newer, shinier counterparts in the outer suburbs.

Also fueling the place-making trend are changing retail patterns, the increasingly powerful smart growth and new urbanism movements, and more forward-looking developers who are willing to take a chance on new products that serve both the community and the bottom line.

Place making is by necessity a cooperative process in which developers, local governments, architects, businesses, and residents work together—from formulating a vision, to gaining approvals and financing, to construc-

Originally published as "Place Making in Suburbia," *Urban Land*, Vol. 59, No. 10, October 2000, by the Urban Land Institute, Washington, D.C. Reprinted with permission of the publisher.

tion and leasing. As a result, place making has turned real estate developers into city builders. They no longer are constructing isolated projects, they are building large-scale multidimensional places that will last for generations. In becoming city builders, however, developers have found that longstanding rules of development are changing. So are the determinants of success.

Because place making extends far beyond constructing a single stand-alone project, it requires a broad vision that encompasses streets, sidewalks, buildings, open spaces, and people. In formulating a vision, developers "must capture the public imagination, or it won't happen," notes Michael Sizemore, a principal at Sizemore Floyd Architects of Atlanta. "If the vision doesn't catch your breath, it's too dull." But he adds an important caveat: "If the vision isn't founded in reality, it won't work. You've got to walk the fine line between the two."

"Balancing vision and practicality is essential" to place making, says George de Guardiola, president of de Guardiola Development Ventures of West Palm Beach, which is building Abacoa Town Center in Jupiter, Florida. "Vision should guide the place-making master plan, but practicality must structure and sell it." When de Guardiola was leasing buildings at Abacoa Town Center, he did not meet any prospective tenants who asked questions about town planning issues. They wanted to know about traffic counts, circulation, and parking — just as they would about any conventional development.

The following criteria must be met for successful place making:

Location. Place making may be a new development trend, but it has not supplanted that tried-and-true real estate axiom: location, location, location. Whether the town center is in a new community or in a reinvented inner suburb, its location must be easily accessible and best serve the community and the market. Ideally, the location should be underserved by retail, office, and other uses in order

to lure tenants. "Reston [Virginia] is eight miles from Tysons Corner, the largest retail concentration in the Washington, D.C., metropolitan area, which meant we faced tremendous competition," points out Thomas D'Alesandro, vice president of Terrabrook, which owns Reston Town Center. "Yet there is little retail between Tysons and Reston. We couldn't get anchor department stores," he adds, "but we could offer something else, like distinctive retailers and entertainment, to a market that didn't have many nearby options."

The place-making location also can fill a niche. In Valencia, California, outside Los Angeles, Valencia's Town Center Drive complements the regional mall, which anchors the eastern end of the half-mile-long street, by creating a pedestrian-friendly main street environment, providing more upscale retail stores and restaurants, and including offices, a hotel, a conference center, and housing.

Site Plan and Streets. A town center should not stand in splendid isolation, surrounded by surface and structured parking lots. To be successful, the site plan must integrate the town center into the surrounding community, both visually and physically, through compatible massing and scale, roads, and transit lines. The town center streets, for example, should connect with the existing street and sidewalk layout and actively encourage pedestrian uses, not just move cars as quickly as possible, which means avoiding overly wide streets. Anything wider than 60 feet usually encourages high-speed traffic, which creates a pedestrian-intimidating atmosphere, defeating place making at its most basic level. To calm through traffic, streets should be designed for two-way, single-lane traffic. One-way streets encourage faster traffic, no matter what the posted speed limit, and that can destroy a street's pedestrian-friendly character.

On-street parking should be included. Whether angled or parallel, on-street parking buffers pedestrians from traffic and also serves to calm traffic. Bike lanes should be set aside to encourage greater bicycle use and to slow traffic. In addition, streets should be designed so that they can be closed for several hours twice a week to accommodate a farmers' market and remain open the rest of the time.

Sidewalks. Sidewalks, like streets, knit buildings and open space into a public realm that people can share. Therefore, a town center's sidewalks should be wide enough to allow groups of people to stroll together and to stop and gaze into shop windows without blocking others. They also should be wide enough to accommodate sidewalk cafés in good weather. Flashy, expensive sidewalk treatments that require considerable maintenance should be avoided in favor of simple, durable, high-quality paving materials that wear well and provide a simple backdrop for the buildings, people, and activity on the street. Dark paving materials should be avoided, particularly in northern locations, since they create a gloomy atmosphere in winter.

Plentiful shade trees, planters, and flower boxes are important place-making components, bringing color and a touch of nature to the street throughout the year. In the winter, trees can be strung with lights to create a cheerful and inviting street scene. In selecting street furniture, the latest, trendiest benches, kiosks, and transit shelters are not always the best. They may be eye catching, but they are not always comfortable or useful, and they can quickly begin to look dated. Simple, durable street furniture that serves its purpose well and complements the overall design of the street, sidewalks, and buildings should be selected instead. Particular attention should be paid to the placement of street furniture. Pedestrian patterns and sightlines should be studied carefully and kiosks and shelters placed accordingly.

Buildings. When people think of a place, one of the first things that comes to mind is its characteristic buildings, like the steepled white frame church on a New England village green or a courthouse on a Southern town square. As a result, a number of municipalities and developers are constructing one or more signature buildings in their town centers to create a stronger identity. The Celebration Company, for example, invested heavily in icon architecture for its new town, Celebration, Florida: Philip Johnson designed the town hall; Cesar Pelli designed the movie theater; and Michael Graves designed the post office.

At the same time, successful and profitable place making requires more than architectural landmarks. To reflect its region, a town center should use local architectural designs, some regional materials, and local scale and massing, but it is not necessary to have a uniform design. Buildings on the older main streets and town squares are not of a single hand, but instead were built over the years in a variety of styles, notes Richard Heapes, a partner at Street-Works, a developing and consulting group in Alexandria, Virginia. A single hand, no matter how skillful, will create a town center that feels overdesigned, he adds. A new town center therefore needs several different architects to create a variety of regionally appropriate styles that, together, create a genuine place.

Because town centers will be in constant flux as tenants, users, and markets come and go, buildings should be designed to anticipate change and redevelopment. Some developers are constructing buildings flexible enough to accommodate housing, offices, or retail, depending on market demand. Landscaping also is important and can serve to unite the disparate elements of a town center into an attractive whole. Again, landscaping should be appropriate to the geographical area, as well as durable and easy to maintain.

Design and Development Guidelines. Because town centers are so complex, developers must set strict design guidelines to create — and protect — the all-important sense of place. Poorly planned streetscapes and buildings can harm both a project's popular appeal and the developer's bottom line. In Schaumburg, Illinois, near Chicago's O'Hare Airport, for example, the retail and office buildings on the south side of the several-year-old town square are not double-loaded. The building fronts, with their large, pedestrian-pleasing windows, face the parking lot behind the town square. The less appealing building backs — which have windows, blank walls, and somewhat intimidating steel service doors and emergency exits — face the town square.

To avoid such mistakes, master plans should require the ground floors of all buildings to have retail uses, including restaurants, to maintain a continuous level of activity and visual interest and to generate the street energy to attract pedestrians. The master plan also should focus on "build-to" lines, rather than setbacks, to allow pedestrian-friendly window shopping and to create a true town center ambience.

Parking. A true place is filled with people, not cars. But since most people are going to drive their cars to a town center, carefully located and designed parking is an essential component of place making. Although street parking can be used to slow traffic and provide immediate access to shops and other uses, most parking areas should be tucked away behind the buildings.

Both surface and structured parking lots have their advantages and disadvantages. Although surface lots are much easier, faster, and cheaper to construct than structured parking, they consume valuable land that could be devoted to buildings and open space. They also create large, empty spaces that separate buildings and uses, leaving holes in the town fabric that can disrupt its coherence. Some developers, however, use surface parking as land banks to be redeveloped later into structured parking and other uses.

Parking structures can hold many more vehicles than surface lots, and they can be integrated into the town center's everyday life. For example, the ground floors of parking structures can contain low-cost retail spaces for shoe repair shops, pet groomers, and appliance repair shops, thereby providing a location for these services and enlivening the otherwise dull parking garage.

The Right Uses. "A town center is not two strip malls facing each other," comments Gary A. Bowden, senior vice president at RTKL in Baltimore. A successful town center must have a wide variety of uses if it is going to create a true public realm that attracts people from early morning until late at night. Basic guidelines for planning town centers include the following:

• *Civic Uses.* Libraries, post offices, educational institutions, and town halls are essential for building a genuine place. They can bring legitimacy and strong pedestrian traffic to a town center, and they are permanently popular, points out Terry Shook, president of Shook Design Group in Charlotte, North Carolina. Unlike retailers and other users, they will not pack up and leave in a few years, creating holes in the overall development. But not all civic uses are created equal. A post office, for example, will be used primarily during the day. Libraries may be the best civic use of all, attracting a broad spectrum of residents and workers at all times of the day and into the evening. Some suburban libraries attract more than 1 million users a year, making them excellent anchors for town centers.

• *Retail Uses.* Retail, ideally a mix of local and national retailers, is "the glue that holds a place together," says Donald Hunter of Hunter Interests of Annapolis, Maryland. For Southlake Town Center in Southlake, Texas, for example, project developer Cooper & Stebbins programmed a 60/40 split between national and local retailers when leasing space to avoid creating a "chain row."

While not discounting the importance of local retailers, de Guardiola believes that it is vital to sign national anchors for a town center project at the start. Nationally known stores make development financing easier to obtain, attract other national retailers and local merchants, and lure customers to the town center. To help establish an upscale identity for Phillips Place in Charlotte, North Carolina, and to differentiate its town center from nearby shopping centers, Peter A. Pappas, president of Pappas Properties of Charlotte, says he lured national restaurateurs and retailers that wanted only one outlet in the Charlotte market, including the high-end Palm restaurant and the Dean & Deluca gourmet food store.

Not all national retailers work in a town center. The typical big box is anathema to this pedestrian-oriented environment, because the huge building and its acres of surface parking destroy the human scale that is the center's foundation. Still, with careful site planning and building design, some larger retailers can successfully fit hybrid stores into town center developments and reap the benefits of a strong customer base. When Crate & Barrel considered locating in Southlake Town Center, the retailer originally wanted a standard 40,000-square-foot building. Cooper & Stebbins, however, persuaded the national retailer to compromise on a two-story building with several distinct facades to break down the otherwise overwhelming building mass.

- *Entertainment and Culture.* Say the word "entertainment" to town center developers, and they immediately think of movie theaters. Cinemas generate significant pedestrian traffic, but they are just one form of entertainment, and one that is now standard in most shopping malls. Other forms of entertainment, such as cultural facilities, need to be included as well.

    Like civic uses, cultural facilities legitimize a place and put people on the street both day and night. A new town center does not need a Carnegie Hall, but it can benefit from live theaters and studio spaces for actors, artists, dancers, and musicians. Similarly, a town center does not need a major museum, but it can take part in a new trend that is putting branch museums in towns across the country. For example, Silver Spring, Maryland, will soon have a branch of the American Film Institute. (See "The Synergy of Mixed Uses," page 36, July *Urban Land*.)

- *Offices and Hotels.* Office tenants provide jobs for nearby residents and daytime customers for town center restaurants and stores. Offices also bring many people to a town center to conduct business who might otherwise not venture there. Some forward-thinking companies already have discovered that town centers offer the ideal combination of a close-to-home suburban location and a pedestrian-friendly, mixed-use environment. During lunch hours, employees can walk — not drive — to a restaurant, a bookstore, a dry cleaner, or a doctor's office. AT&T Wireless, for example, was attracted to Redmond Town Center near Seattle because of the development's pedestrian-oriented mixed uses. And for round-the-clock activity, a town center needs a hotel. A hotel is a destination unto itself, and guests create an important spillover effect, especially in the evening.

- *Housing.* Housing in or near a town center supplies customers and workers for retail and commercial uses. It also provides that all-important pedestrian traffic, which creates a feeling of safety and of movement and excitement on a street. Market demand is growing for housing in new town centers, particularly from young singles, childless couples, and seniors. In Celebration's town center, second-floor apartments above retail stores are popular. The high-end Montecito apartments that anchor one end of Valencia's Town Center Drive leased up faster than originally expected, and at the highest rents in the area.

Financing

Because place making is a new trend, many developers have had problems arranging financing from cautious lenders. Two banks in Charlotte, North Carolina, refused to provide financing for Phillips Place's specialty retail component. Pappas kept looking and finally found a willing bank in Alabama. De Guardiola offers some advice for pitching a town center to a potential financial source: Keep the financing separate from the placing making vision. "Make sure that someone who understands the project inside out presents the concept to the financing source. Then, have the financial people make a separate presentation about everything that lenders need to know." He says that he followed his own advice when he successfully pitched Abacoa Town Center to GMAC, which previously had never backed a town center.

Most lenders are not used to making loans for mixed-use developments, so it is best to create several plats in a site plan. In effect, platting can be used to create a series of comfort zones to the lender. For Abacoa Town Square, de Guardiola says that he had a plat for the common areas, including parking decks; a plat for stand-alone apartments; and a plat for each commercial building. Thus, the lender was asked to lend money to particular plats, not a complex place-making development.

Overcoming Hurdles

One-half to two-thirds of planned place-making projects eventually will fail because developers choose bad locations or a bad mix of uses, spend too much money on the development, or have too much ego, according to Robert J. Gibbs, president of Gibbs Planning Group in Birmingham, Michigan. Even if developers can avoid those problems, they still must overcome a number of other hurdles:

Development Codes. Many building and zoning codes require projects that create the antithesis of place. Initially, Cooper & Stebbins was told that all of the buildings in its 130-acre Southlake Town Center had to be set back from the street if they were located in a suburban office park, every building had to have berms, and the land adjacent to two existing roads had to be developed with the highest value, leaving 60 to 70 percent of the site in an interior location with limited use.

First, "town center developers should go to the appropriate officials and tell them why this project is different from others in the community," advises Steve Kellenberg, a principal in the Irvine, California, office of EDAW, a planning and landscape architecture firm. "If you show people that it's a new conceptual approach and that it's focused on the pedestrian experience, you can often get alternative design standards approved. If that doesn't work, developers can go to the planning commission itself and work from the top down to get the commission to buy into the project."

Traffic codes also can wreak havoc with the best-planned town centers because they usually insist on overscaled streets that discourage pedestrian use and diminish the quality of life for residents, shoppers, and workers. Changing traffic codes is doubly daunting because they are enforced by both traffic engineers and fire officials; however, developers often can secure alternative street design standards by negotiating with these authorities. If that does not work, they can designate the town center's streets as private thoroughfares, which often have more flexible standards.

Complying with traffic codes soon could become less difficult. The influential Institute of Transportation Engineers (ITE) recently released new street design guidelines for traditional neighborhood developments (TNDs), including town centers. These proposed guidelines, notes de Guardiola, have been issued for discussion, though not adopted formally by the ITE.

Distinctiveness. Many town centers will have some of the same retailers, restaurant chains, and entertainment venues that fill shopping malls. The challenge is making town centers distinctive and keeping them fresh so that people will return to them again and again. Regional architecture, civic institutions, and cultural facilities are three ingredients.

Developers also must create a truly local identity that makes their town center different from formulaic shopping malls. A real place has space for local professionals such as doctors and lawyers, local entrepreneurial shopkeepers, and local everyday services like hair salons, dry cleaners, and pet groomers. These local uses should not be relegated to one end of the street or around the corner. They should be interspersed among the national uses to avoid a could-be-anywhere chain row.

Phasing. Most developers and municipalities do not have the luxury of building everything at once, as the Disney Co. did in Celebration's town center. Instead, they usually must develop the town center in phases to meet market demand and budget requirements, thereby stretching the development process over several years or more.

Of course, phased development sets up an immediate challenge: How can the initial critical mass necessary to launch a town center successfully be created quickly? Some developers subsidize initial retail tenants through various measures, such as substantially reduced rents. Above all, developers should not be overly ambitious in the first phase of their town center. "Your first priority is creating continuity at the sidewalk level, so that you have a welcoming pedestrian connectivity from place to place," says Kellenberg. "If you must trade off a skyline or density to have that village feel, it's worth it. Many great pedestrian streets have one- and two-story buildings. So, in the beginning, it's better to be modest and go low rise — and create a successful critical mass — than to attempt a higher density, have lots of gaps in your town center, and fail to achieve a pedestrian scale and critical mass."

Another challenge is holding back prime sites in anticipation of future growth, thereby allowing the developer to respond to changing markets and keep a town center fresh by bringing in new buildings and uses. One approach is to structure a joint venture with the site's original landowner or the project lender, says Brian R. Stebbins of Cooper & Stebbins. "We have legal control over the entire 130 acres at Southlake Town Center, but we don't have to take down the parcels for the next 15 years until we are ready, through an agreement with the original land owner," he explains. "We are driven by the marketplace, but we don't have to do things because of interest pressures."

Looking Ahead

Place making is the very essence of a real estate development. As people choose one place over another, the place of choice attracts a higher valuation and sells at a premium. Desired places are ones that appeal to all of the senses — sight, sound, smell, taste, and touch. It is a rich mix of aesthetic design, the activities offered, the quality of providers, and price. Successful place making is therefore about meeting the demand from the local community. It is not a formulaic real estate product or the latest fad. Therefore, developers should exercise a high level of conceptualization and market matching in their place-making activities.

Remember the fate of festival marketplaces? Once a red-hot trend, many quickly declined or died after they became formulaic and the fad wore off. If developers build a fad, rather than a true town center, they will fail. If, however, they build for the community, if they focus on people and place, they will create a lasting legacy, not to mention reap greater profits.

CHAPTER 37

Wakefield and Other Cities Use Libraries to Stimulate Neighborhood Renewal

Richard Bertman *and* Alfred Wojciechowski

Updated programming has turned libraries into multipurpose destinations, in turn revitalizing surrounding neighborhoods.

By embracing the very trends that seemed to predict their demise — the rise of the Internet and the decline of communal activities — public libraries have once again put themselves at the heart of civic life. While headlines tout the remarkable success of a new generation of buildings, such as the Rem Koolhaas–designed Seattle Public Library where visits have doubled and circulation is up more than 50 percent since it opened a year ago, older libraries across the country are reinventing themselves for the 21st century.

Among the most notable examples of the resurgence of public libraries are the historic libraries established during the first wave of library building around the turn of the last century. From the 1880s to the 1920s, at the same time that Andrew Carnegie was funding some 2,500 libraries, communities of all sizes rallied public will and financing, as well as private support, to create some of the finest civic buildings in the country. At the time they were built, these libraries were an important part of community life, providing even small towns with a gathering place, books, and access to knowledgeable librarians.

Fast forward 100 years to a society in which Amazon, Barnes & Noble, Starbucks, and Google might have all but displaced these quaint, albeit historic, buildings. Instead, culturally alert librarians have allied themselves with their loyal library patrons, various friends of library groups, civic leaders, and local governments to reinvigorate their programs and facilities. All of these individuals and groups recognize that the need for free, public access to information available in books, magazines, and now, on the Internet, is more important than ever. So, too, is the need for a community center that welcomes people of all ages with programs designed for everyone from prekindergarten children and preteens to students and seniors.

Updated programming has turned the library into a multipurpose destination. "Community libraries are antidotes to the social isolation that Robert Putnam described in his book Bowling Alone," notes Mary Wilson, library director at the Harvard Public Library in Harvard, Massachusetts. "Because we offer a

Originally published as "Historic Libraries Transformed," *Urban Land*, Vol. 64, No. 11/12, November/December 2005, by the Urban Land Institute, Washington, D.C. Reprinted with permission of the publisher.

place where everyone in town can come together for programs or meetings or just to hang out, we are busier than ever." The town of 6,000 is in the middle of a relocation and expansion of its library to a historic property, in part, she explains, because its activity levels are those of a town of 15,000 residents.

The once familiar "Ssh!" of the traditionally silent library has been replaced with bright and lively children's areas that have been relocated front and center. There is now room for young adults to congregate surrounded by age-appropriate reading, as well as meeting rooms for literacy programs, reading groups, or civic gatherings. Traditional stacks and the periodicals' reading room are still there as well, along with new computers.

"Technology happened. We had to adapt the library to be a part of the change," says Sharon Gilley, library director at Lucius Beebe Library in Wakefield, Massachusetts. Internet access draws those library patrons who do not have computers at home or who appreciate the extra research guidance offered by the librarians. As libraries have expanded their offerings to include a wide range of communications, there now are programs for the visually impaired providing books on tape, and library lending now includes videos and CDs, in addition to books.

Adapting 19th- and early-20th-century buildings to support today's programming and technological demands, as well as making them accessible to handicapped patrons, creates a challenge for both the libraries and the communities they serve. In New England, where historic library buildings are situated on the town square or on the main street, the Massachusetts Board of Library Commissioners (MBLC) has developed a program to assist local libraries with capital improvements and additional space. While the program supports the development of new facilities in addition to improving existing properties, the renaissance of the state's historic libraries owes a great deal to the guidance and funding provided by the MBLC.

"Since its founding in 1890, the Board of Library Commissioners has worked hard to help local libraries meet the needs of their communities," explains David Gray, director, Communications and Public Information for the MBLC. "In the last 15 years, there has been tremendous pressure to accommodate technology and increased use. Our public library construction program is designed to help libraries obtain grants — first for planning and design, then for construction and renovation."

The planning and design grants assist in the preliminary planning stages. Funds may be used to develop the library building program; architectural studies, including feasibility and schematic design; cost estimates; and soil and site studies. There is a $20,000 cap on these awards, which must be matched by the town. The grants for new construction, additions and/or renovations assist libraries with the design, development, and construction stages of projects.

Funding for construction/renovation projects is based on eligible costs, which include the purchase price of the land; consulting, architectural, and engineering fees; actual construction costs; and costs of fixed equipment. The state share is awarded on a sliding scale and ranges from 35 percent of a larger project to 60 percent of a project under $1.2 million.

Since its inception, the program has provided aid to 200 communities out of the 370 eligible. The process can take years as towns gather the political, social, and financial capital to renovate and expand. Ray Moffa, a library trustee and cochair of the building committee for the Harvard Public Library, calls it the "the perfect storm." "In gaining support to adapt and expand the 'Old Bromfield' school as the library, we found three willing groups: the people who love and believe in libraries, the preservationists who wanted to protect the historic building, and the citizens who saw that reviving the old school building would help preserve the culture and character of the town. It has taken eight years, but we are ready to go."

The ability of a community to leverage the popularity and location of its historical assets contributes to the success of local libraries in raising funds and securing support. The buildings have long been sources of immense pride, but many of them suffer from deferred maintenance, lack of space, and lack of adequate parking. Frequently, the surrounding neighborhood has declined as traditional downtowns lose business to suburban malls.

Recognizing the drawing power of libraries as activity centers and architectural presences, local governments see the opportunity to revitalize entire districts with the renovation and expansion of their historic libraries. Quincy, Massachusetts's former mayor, John Sheets, championed the renovation and expansion of the Thomas Crane Library. "I had been mesmerized by the library since my first days in Quincy and understood that by preserving and expanding the building, we would also encourage the revitalization of downtown. The library serves as an anchor and magnet in attracting new development."

Quincy's most recent development is the Residences at Presidents' Place, a ten-story, 200-unit luxury residential project being developed by Intercontinental Real Estate Corporation (IREC) of Boston. Located at 10 Faxon Avenue adjacent to the library, the building will have views to the historic H. H. Richardson–designed building with grounds designed by Frederick Law Olmsted.

The restoration and expansion of the historic 1922 library in Wakefield, Massachusetts, helped to stabilize the civic/commercial district. Nancy Bertrand, chair of the Wakefield chamber of commerce and executive director of the historical commission, cites the city's "enormous pride in the library" as a factor in the development of other projects in the city. "The renovation of the library showed that we could do it — we could come together as a city and support a project that was important to all of us," she explains.

Once the city focused on redeveloping the well-used library as its first project, revitalizing the historic civic core of the town proved to be a bellwether, lifting the fortunes of other businesses in the years following the 1998 renovation. Even today, as Wakefield has felt the effects of a less robust economy, the library and its surrounding neighborhood remain healthy and encouraging to the citizenry, notes Bertrand.

Much the same story holds true in the Cape Cod town of Harwich, where the town's decision to renovate and expand the Brooks Free Library was also a vote to reinvigorate the center of the town as a place for businesses. The 19th-century building bookends the town's main street with the equally historic Brooks Academy at the other end. The townspeople feel that the local library contributes significantly to local economic well-being.

"The town has never refused the trustees of the library anytime we have asked for support," comments Joann Green, an active member of the board of trustees. "City officials, as well as the citizens, know what the library provides to the community and want to see it continue." As a vacation destination, Harwich's population of 12,000 triples during the summer months, exacerbating the need for strong community services and a memorable identity — areas in which the Brook Free Library excels, says Green.

The present-day success of such historic libraries is founded on two potentially contradictory strengths. First is a societal desire to connect with history. Ann McLaughlin, library director at the Thomas Crane Library in Quincy, recalls the fundraising for the renovation, noting, "We raised $920,000 from the community and many pledges were for $5,000 or less. It seemed that everyone had a story that connected them to the library. The townspeople — from Mayor James Sheets to the average citizen — cherish the building," she notes. "No one ever questioned funding the quality that was required for their beloved structure."

Second is the level of imagination that the coalition of librarians, state and local governments, preservationists, and architects have demonstrated as they reprogram, reuse, and expand these historic institutions. The proof of their far-sightedness is in the numbers. As happened with Koolhaas's shiny new building, usage of the historic brick and clapboard library buildings has exploded. Librarians report that the number of visits and the circulation have doubled. If, as Mayor Sheets says, "Preservation pays our debt to the future," it appears that these libraries are making a serious investment for all of us.

CHAPTER 38

Urban Design, Culture, and the Public Realm

Charles Lockwood

What constitutes good urban design and a strong public realm, and what role can good urban design play in city planning today? Moderator Michael D. Beyard, a ULI senior resident fellow, posed these questions to participants in a roundtable at ULI's fall meeting in Los Angeles last November.

A wide-ranging discussion by the five panelists followed, touching on topics ranging from correct definitions for terms like public to how to address sprawl, with the panelists talking in broad strokes rather than in details and interjecting anecdotes from their personal experiences.

Finding revenue to support the public realm is a worldwide problem, declared Sir Stuart Lipton, chairman of London-based commercial property developer Stanhope plc. "Why do we love our cities? It is because of their civic facilities. The fact that we don't want to pay for them is perverse," he said. "We're going to a football game and paying a lot of bucks for a ticket, but we wouldn't do the same for a public space we enjoy every day, or for a public building."

The panelists offered several financial strategies, such as partnering on public spaces with the private sector — developers, business improvement districts, and community associations. Audience member Mary Murphy, a board member of the Presidio Trust, discussed Lucasfilm's development of the recently opened Letterman District within the Presidio of San Francisco national park, which included construction of and a commitment to maintain an eight-acre public park. "The quality of the park work was superlative," she said.

Dennis Pieprz, president of planning and design firm Sasaki Associates in Watertown, Massachusetts, however, cited the growing concern that a private company that develops and owns a public space may see fit to ban social and community activities there that it finds objectionable — from political gatherings to neighborhood block parties that are the heart of a true public realm.

Much of the roundtable was devoted to a discussion of the ingredients critical to creating a successful public realm and executing high-quality urban design once funding is in hand.

Simplicity. "Be very clear and simple about the nature of the space," advised Joseph E. Brown, president and CEO of San Francisco–based EDAW, Inc., an international

Originally published as "What Makes a Great Public Realm?," *Urban Land*, Vol. 65, No. 3, March 2006, by the Urban Land Institute, Washington, D.C. Reprinted with permission of the publisher.

planning and design firm. "Be more modest. Don't fill it all up. Don't overdesign it. Get it simple, get it universal, then let's see what happens next, and we'll adjust. And let's not make them too expensive."

The panelists cited European public spaces like Paris's Place Vendôme and London's Belgrave Square as examples of the power of simplicity.

Scale. The scale — of buildings, streets, trees, street furniture, activities — can make or break a public realm. "What's interesting about London to me is not just the great spaces that the city is known by, but the incredible streets," said Howard F. Elkus, a principal of Boston-based Elkus Manfredi Architects. "There is a scale about the street and a continuity of fabric that creates an inclusionary city."

Lipton pointed out that in older cities, changes to scale must be made gradually. "London is full of people who'll say they've got to build 50-story towers," he noted. "But if you build 25-story towers, you're already 100 or 200 feet above most other buildings. London is ten stories tall. At 25 stories, you're a hero. At 50 stories, you're a bum."

Time. This issue came up repeatedly in discussions covering everything from scale to the development of new cities. "If you think back to the Campo in Sienna or St. Mark's Place in Venice, these are places that evolved over hundreds of years, one building at a time toward a larger idea," said Pieprz. "But today we have an instant urbanism where everything is built at once. How do you get to a more authentic kind of public realm when the kind of public spaces that we're making today don't easily acknowledge time?"

The key, the panelists agreed, is to build time into each public realm. Rather than design a finished product, leave space for new buildings and uses to be layered in over the years in phases. Plan for layers to be removed, as well. Low-rise buildings, for example, can be replaced over time with high-rise buildings, as Manhattan has demonstrated for

decades. A temporary landscape installation can provide an amenity today while saving a site for development in the future.

Details. Essential to the success of a public realm, the panelists agreed, are the many features, large and small, that help create and define how people experience that space. Details include everything from specific building materials to street furniture, artwork, the size of trees, and how each building and space in the public realm relates to the others.

"To me, the most important detail is sun," said Lipton. "Are we going to get sun in that space, and what are the shadows going to be like? The second most important detail is where people will walk. What are their natural sight lines? Do they feel comfortable walking from A to B?"

Programming/activities. "There's a raging debate in the urban design/landscape community about programming public spaces," said Pieprz. "Should there be a whole array of programmed activities, or should public spaces be designed in a way that is a little more abstract, a little more reliant on spontaneous activity? I think there should probably be a balance of the two."

The panelists generally agreed that a great space provides opportunities for a broad spectrum of activities — social, political, recreational, and other types — from political demonstrators gathering in a city square to workers eating lunch there and neighbors participating in tai chi classes. A city square with a band shell can be the site of concerts, children's plays, and lectures.

"In my opinion, the town square is all," declared Lipton. "The town square components — the library, health facility, town hall — are all a part of great cities. These components are coordinated, they're acting together, they're kind of family, and that's surely where the strength is."

Pieprz believes that the integration of uses is far more important than the mix of uses. He pointed to CityPlace in West Palm Beach, Florida, as an example of a place where retail space, commercial space, and housing are integrated by the street and the public realm. "I think that seamless connectivity and those seamless relationships are absolutely critical," he said.

Sports and recreation. The question of programming sports and recreational activities for a public realm sparked considerable discussion. Organized sports, from soccer to youth hockey, draw children and their families to the public realm, starting the whole process of community participation, which is what the public realm is all about.

Resistance to active recreation, however, crops up frequently, partly because some sports venues, like baseball diamonds, are only used seasonally, leaving large dead zones in the public realm for long periods. Some people also believe that active recreation may attract people interested in violence and drug use.

Access/connection. How people get to the public space — be it a town square or a park — and how that public space connects to the rest of the city are vital considerations mentioned by each panelist. A great public realm provides easy, natural access for people, and has seamless connections and seamless relationships between each space and building, making users feel as though they are a part of the greater city.

Access and connection were at the root of differing opinions among the panelists regarding Chicago's Millennium Park, which is notable for its monumental attractions, like the Frank Gehry–designed 120-foot-high, stainless-steel Jay Pritzker Pavilion.

Elkus called Millennium Park "one of the great urban parks of the world," noting, "It is accessible all the way across the city. It's also kind of an invitation and a stepping stone into a greater resource for the community: Grant Park."

Lipton had conflicting opinions of this public realm. He thinks the variety within Millennium Park is wonderful, he said, but because the park is elevated, it hinders easy,

seamless access and severs direct connections to surrounding uses.

Brown has deeper concerns. "I find Millennium Park very worrisome," he said. "I think there are some beautiful aspects to it, but the least successful part is, I think, Frank Gehry's pavilion. It is such an extravagant and rigid fixed expression — and they apparently don't have the money to maintain it. I am very worried about Millennium Park as a precedent for good public realm design."

Engagement with users. A successful public realm engages its users through its design, attractions, details, and connections. "In the end, it's about the user and the value of the public realm to the city dweller," said Elkus. "If you design the space for the people who live there, the others will come. That's your first priority."

The design of the public realm should stir the emotions and create a sense of ownership of the space among its users. "The emotional attachments — whether it be a mother and child, or boy and girl — are very simple things," Lipton said. "But there is a trend to make them very grand — to just throw money at them. You walk around Bunker Hill in Los Angeles, and every known recent sculptor has a piece there. To me, none of them has any meaning. They're just expensive pieces of kitsch."

Quality, not style. Often when planning a public realm, the project team focuses on architectural style. The roundtable panelists, however, declared that high quality was more important than style. British newspapers, for example, routinely criticize the architectural style of the new town of Poundbury in England. But Poundbury has high-quality materials, a good plan, a good mix of uses, and a successful energy conservation program. It is generally accepted now that the new town works.

Flexibility. The public realm should have the flexibility to adapt to changing needs and uses over the years. Flexibility does not have to be complex. It can turn on simple strategies like the movable chairs provided in midtown Manhattan's Bryant Park.

Human flexibility is also critical. That a place changes over time is not negative; it is positive if the changes follow a bigger purpose. "There are mistakes that have to be rectified if we are going to return cities to their greatness," said Lipton. "There are dramatic pieces of demolition that need to be done, and people seem very shy about this. No one wants to talk about the essential demolition."

Security. The panelists identified four elements that can go a long way toward creating a safe public space:

- **Design.** Studies have proved that well-designed spaces have less crime because of their focus on the details. A public space, for example, should not have hidden areas that cannot be observed by general visitors. In addition, visual connections to the surrounding city district should be created so that the public space is part of the larger community.
- **Activity.** People create safety. Programmed activities, a snack kiosk, or a clean and staffed public restroom, for example, attract people, which enhances security.
- **Maintenance.** Desired users are usually scared away if a public realm looks run down, dirty, or uncared for. It is perceived as a threat.
- **Observation.** This can include kiosk workers, maintenance workers, officers at a police substation — even video cameras.

A design for the people and the place. Design for the public realm should reflect the climate, region, and culture, and the values and needs of the people who use the space. A public realm that works in Europe or the United States, for example, will not necessarily succeed in Asia.

"In Ho Chi Minh City in Vietnam, we're developing a plan for a new urban district," said Pieprz. "People in the city spoke about public spaces having a culture of noise. I'd never heard this before. But that city is hot, it's humid; people come out in the evenings. Ho Chi Minh City has 6 million people and 3 million motorbikes flying around. It's an active, vibrant, urban culture that is very different from the kind of passive parks and quiet squares that we think of in other places of the world."

Pieprz also expressed concern about China importing U.S. and European mistakes that Western cities are now trying to undo. "What we're seeing in cities like Beijing and Shanghai are mega-private realms — megablocks with no streets and a kind of mystery green space in the middle that's closed off to the public," he said. "That causes a disconnectedness, a separation of the classes. I'm concerned that China is undermining its own culture — or the potential of it — by importing ideas from the West that are now discredited here."

Did panelists come up with the "magic formula," particularly for today's "instant" megadevelopments, to create what Prince Charles at the first World Cities Forum in London last June referred to as "great and lasting cities that are worthy of our humanity"? Not in a one-hour roundtable discussion. The panelists, however, did agree that the key is to lay a foundation of great urban and public realm design at the very beginning of a project — and then provide a framework for future adaptation and change.

CHAPTER 39

Urban Planning and the Future

Philip N. Loheed *and* Brandy H.M. Brooks

General planning in the 20th century can be summed up in one word: isolation. It began with the sweatshop-era idea of isolating uses — residential from industrial, office parks from retail districts, swaths of green space from everything else — so that, through the wonders of the automobile, where we live has no relation to where we work, shop, or play. From 20th-century America evolved the view that we should live without regard for connecting places, extending the sense of isolation not only to zoning districts but also to specific sites, so that what was created on one site need not relate to anything on surrounding parcels. Each site became a self-contained world of its own, reaching out only to the collector road nearby.

A series of at-risk site studies recently commissioned by the town of Lincoln, Massachusetts, illustrates some effects of isolation. At each of several large properties, the existing uses — based on 20th-century, car-based practice — are compared with possible alternative uses: single-family residential within the default two-acre zoning limits; affordable housing (using Chapter 40B, Massachusetts's anti-snob zoning law); mixed use (retail/office/restaurant, church, private school); and so on. Only wetlands and steep slopes are considered a constraint on any of these uses. Typically, the only access to these properties is from a state highway. The town may easily be forgiven for rejecting all of these options as simply scattered pockets that would eventually consume the entire land base with disconnected "pods in the buffer network." Further, these pods would tend to be "set pieces" created by a single developer and design team — for example, buildings surrounded by parking lots surrounded by buffer plantings connected to highways; or layer upon layer of privatized turf, embedded in remnants of the landscape. Even the various new urbanist communities tend to assemble such suburban projects, modified by a series of trendy "looks" to create pseudourbanism — all with plenty of parking "out back."

As we move deeper into the 21st century, however, the name of the game has changed; instead of isolation, we are faced with the pressing reality of a single, rapidly evolving, global and multiethnic culture. The global culture dominates the biosphere with a logarithmically escalating effect; connections and relationships cannot be ignored, because what happens in one part of the world, whether economic, political, cultural, or environmental, affects all other parts. The built environment requires sustainable solutions that meet the needs of a network of people. Through it all,

Originally published as "Land Writes: New Places for a New Age," *Urban Land*, Vol. 65, No. 3, March 2006, by the Urban Land Institute, Washington, D.C. Reprinted with permission of the publisher.

the biosphere must remain functional and intact. Unfortunately, current development regulations and design strategies remain legacies of the era of isolation. How might planning and settlement patterns be altered to house this integrated world?

Any network, whether made up of spaces or people, has three key components to consider: the parts, the core, and the relationships. The parts have a series of distinct elements, each with its own characteristics. To bring the parts together requires some sort of core — a common resource, a central idea, an organizing element — that brings the parts close enough to connect with one another. These connections, or relationships, can take two forms: the relationship of the parts to the core, or the relationship that individual parts may develop with each other or with other parts that touch the network. The key concept in any network is shared connections. Pooling of resources in a networked community makes the whole far more capable and competitive than any one part could be if isolated.

Possibly, neighborhoods can be designed deliberately as people and production networks, and interconnected internally and to the biosphere; or as places that encourage serendipity and creativity and maximize diversity, and that celebrate their relationship to the landscape they inhabit. Our new development strategy allows for unexpected maverick parts to be present while simultaneously protecting the network and its environment. Most important, this strategy needs to be fully mobilized and to enable all of the people in the network. To succeed in the global economy, all people in the network must be connected.

To build an urban fabric that works, we must first have the pieces. However, a single developer or designer cannot create them wholesale at one time. What is needed instead is old-fashioned microinvestment — a varied collection of individuals bringing their skills and resources into the community and contributing to its development. Enter the mavericks — buildings that are flexible in use but

designed to coordinate with one another to create coherent public environments.

To illustrate the possible nature of maverick buildings, consider a street like Newbury in Boston, a neighborhood like Adams Morgan in Washington, D.C., or the row buildings of the Haussmann-era of Paris. From all of these areas evolved a complex mix of residential, commercial, artistic, and institutional uses in buildings that are "networked" by relating to one another, creating and defining important parts of the public realm, and, less frequently, important natural areas. In each of these examples, the maverick buildings, along with public and natural areas, establish a pattern, and were built lot by lot.

In this hypothetical urban fabric, macro-investment is directed toward building the core elements that bind together the community. Large public and private investors provide both the attractors and the efficient resources for the mavericks of the urban neighborhood: a train station complex, multifaith forums, public markets, urban parks, and so on. When large parcels are developed, the master developer itself should not design more than 10 to 20 percent, and instead should market parcels to, and manage the coordination of, the mavericks.

The common core is as essential to the urban community as the maverick investors are. First, it creates neutral territory where participants can function freely without invading anyone else's space. This is necessary for building the relationships that form the community network. One of the biggest problems with 20th-century isolationist planning was that it provided no public place for the casual social interaction required to build relationships with strangers. In *The Death and Life of Great American Cities*, Jane Jacobs made the case more than 40 years ago that these passing interactions are key to building public trust and a shared responsibility for the neighborhood. Without a common reason to meet and a common place to meet in, relationships in the network of an urban community are never established, and the community will not be competitive with those that have this advantage. Examples of this sort of public environment include any of the world's great streets, and, in particular, places of public hospitality — such as Union Station in the District of Columbia and Grand Central Station and the redeveloped Bryant Park in New York City — which allow residents and visitors alike to be fully mobilized and functional in spite of any cultural or class differences among them.

Large public/private investors can help build a public place. For a resource to bring a community together, (1) it must be shared, public, and open; (2) it must meet the needs of a variety of users within the community; and (3) it must allow all users to feel a sense of welcome, belonging, and citizen participation. Neutral places can include market spaces, cultural spaces, recreation facilities, centers of knowledge and communication, or spiritual places. Whatever the type, it must meet all three of the qualifications listed above.

Neutral places are the least understood and often the most problematic of the requirements of our new system. Not only must a neutral place be available or provide diverse services, but also it must allow users to feel that they have a right to use its resources. The signals that indicate a user does not belong are subtle but powerful: language, codes of behavior and appearance, separation of special needs, and barriers that make services difficult to access are all implicit but clear indicators that those who do not fit the norm may be tolerated, but are not invited. The destructive isolation that results breaks down the communication that builds the community, effectively blocking out the full range of skills and resources that could be provided by those who have been socially shut out.

To understand, in practice, how mavericks and neutral places have worked, it is instructive to examine one of the world's great places that was built using this model.

Early in the 19th century, the British Crown dispatched an emissary in the person of Colonel Stamford Raffles to the Far East to establish a viable trading base to compete with the Spanish and Portuguese in Hong Kong and Macao.

The various ethnic Kampongs (neighborhoods) of Singapore began to evolve after a "trading factory" agreement was signed between Raffles and the Sultan Hussein as part of a plan for a free port in 1819. The "clientele" for the free port consisted mainly of migratory pirates from a wide variety of ethnic groups all over the region, who needed a the free port that was convenient, and who were entirely capable of enforcing their will through violence.

In June 1819, Raffles developed a plan to divide the town into communal areas for the various pirate traders, which culminated in his instructions of November 4, 1822.

"The Instructions included directions that streets were to be laid out in regular right-angled grids wherever possible. Houses were to have a uniform front and 'a verandah open at all times as a continued and covered passage on each side of the street,' stipulations which were to result in the singularly unique character of Singapore and, later, Malaya." — *The Singapore House* by Lee Kip Lin.

Today, the Kampongs are among the world's more stable ethnic neighborhoods — and perhaps constitute the world's largest collection of live/work (shop/house) residential buildings. They give the city virtually an unparalleled and celebrated range of ethnic foods, languages, schools, religious institutions, costumes, theaters, retail, cultural traditions, and the like.

The success of the trading factory was based on the dual concepts of convenience and neutral territory: all the pirates found it convenient to have a place where they could sell their loot without having to fight their way in and out of town past their piratical peers. Such economic and social mobility enjoyed by traders and their celebratory attitude toward diversity have carried over to their descendants.

The information age is enabling members of the global culture to understand their relationship to the planet and to each other, and to adjust their behavior to suit it. We have entered into a time of reflective consideration: What global impacts are we having on our society and the environment? Can the negative impacts be slowed, stopped, or reversed? Is an economy possible that fits the available resources of the biosphere? What better ways to create places are available? Will violence continue to be a dominant force in the future?

We are in a struggle to prosper within new rules. To succeed, we will need to mobilize every resource of human intelligence available — we must learn to "fire on all cylinders" culturally. In this regard, the diversity of our people is a precious competitive resource that must be conserved. Maverick microinvestment and neutral places can play a useful part in achieving this goal, providing spaces for the new ideas and new people who will help build sustainable solutions for the future.

CHAPTER 40

Urban Creativity, Culture, and the Future

John M. Eger

Cities across the globe are struggling today to reinvent themselves for the postindustrial economy anticipated by sociologist Daniel Bell and others in the 1960s.

Many communities have been adapting their communications infrastructure to meet the needs of an age in which information is the most valuable commodity. Most of these initiatives, such as the U.S. National Information Infrastructure and Singapore's Intelligent Island, focus on the technological aspects of the postindustrial economy.

San Diego even commissioned a City of the Future Committee in 1993 to make plans to build the first fiber-optic-wired city in the United States in the belief that, just as cities of the past were built along waterways, railroads, and interstate highways, the cities of the future will be built along "information highways"—wired and wireless information pathways connecting every home, office, school, and hospital and, through the World Wide Web, millions of other individuals and institutions around the world.

These new information infrastructures are undoubtedly important. But creating a twenty-first-century city is not so much a question of technology as it is of jobs, dollars, and quality of life. A community's plan to reinvent itself for the new, knowledge-based economy and society therefore requires educating all its citizens about this new global revolution in the nature of work. To succeed, cities must prepare their citizens to take ownership of their communities and educate the next generation of leaders and workers to meet the new global challenges of what has now been termed the "Creative Economy."

At the heart of such an effort is recognition of the vital roles that art and culture play in enhancing economic development and, ultimately, defining a "creative community"—a community that exploits the vital linkages among art, culture, and commerce. Communities that consciously invest in these broader human and financial resources are at the very forefront in preparing their citizens to meet the challenges of the rapidly evolving, and now global, knowledge-based economy and society.

Cyberspace and Cyberplace

The mammoth global network of computer systems collectively referred to as the In-

Originally published in *The Futurist*. Used with permission from the World Future Society, 7910 Woodmont Avenue, Suite 450, Bethesda, Maryland 20814. Telephone: 301–656–8274; *www.wfs.org*.

ternet has blossomed from an obscure tool used by government researchers and academics into a worldwide mass communications medium. The Internet is now recognized as the leading carrier of all communications and financial transactions affecting life and work in the twenty-first century.

Internet usage statistics point to one billion users worldwide, with a growth rate of 15 percent per month. The World Wide Web, the Internet's most popular component, is being integrated into the marketing, information, and communications strategies of almost every major corporation, educational institution, charitable and political organization, community service agency, and government entity in the developed world. No previous communications advance has been adopted by the public so widely so rapidly.

Many people are concerned about where this phenomenon ultimately will lead. Predictions range from electronic "virtual communities," in which individuals interact socially with like-minded Internet users around the world, to fully networked dwellings in which electronic devices and other appliances respond to the spoken commands of residents.

In recent years, people habitually have referred to the domain in which Internet-based communications occur as *cyberspace*, an abstract communications space that exists both everywhere and nowhere. But until flesh-and-blood humans can be digitized into electronic pulses in the same way that computer scientists transform images and data, the denizens of cyberspace will have to continue living in some sort of real physical space — a home, a neighborhood, and a community.

Many communities, often without being directly conscious of it, are beginning to design the initial blueprints for the cyberplaces of the twenty-first century. As early as 1976, the French government launched an aggressive plan called Télématique, which sought to place computers on every desktop and in every residence in France. Singapore's Intelligent Island plan includes the world's first nationwide broadband network, Singapore ONE. Japan is working toward an electronic future known as Teletopia, with 150 municipalities transforming themselves into "cybercities" specializing in various industrial applications of information technology. Dubai has launched its Internet City, and Torino, Italy, has its Infoville initiative. In the United States in the mid–1990s, the Clinton administration unveiled the ambitious National Information Infrastructure Initiative, with the goal of linking every school and school-age child to the Internet by the turn of the century.

The state of California in 1996 launched its statewide Smart Communities program, recognizing that electronic networks like these will play an increasingly important role in the economic competitiveness of its municipalities. The underlying premise of the California initiative is that smart communities are not, at their core, exercises in the deployment and use of technology, but rather active tools in the promotion of economic development, job growth, and higher living standards overall. In other words, technological propagation in smart communities is not an end in itself, but rather a means to a larger end with clear and compelling benefits for communities.

We have learned a great deal about the challenges that cities face in a new global "information economy," an economy based on something other than the production of goods and services or agriculture. Although these basic industries continue, the new economy relies on the production, use, and transfer of information and knowledge.

In fact, one distinct possibility is that cities of the future will not be cities in the usual sense, but rather powerful regional economies. Kenichi Ohmae, author of *The Borderless World* (1999), suggests we are witnessing the resurgence of the age-old concept of the city-state or, as he prefers, "region-state." The new region-state has the power and authority to take ownership of its own future and establish a governing process reflecting a new model of government for the digital age.

Civic engagement and new civic "collaboratories" (collaborative projects and endeavors) will also be needed to help reinvent our great cities to reclaim the sense of place and civic pride they once possessed, as well as to ensure that no one is left behind. In *The Magic of Dialogue: Transforming Conflict into Cooperation* (1999), David Yankelovich argues that there is a "struggle between two one-sided visions of our future: the vision of the free market and the vision of the civil society." Citizens need to create the "social capital" that distinguishes their communities, and in the process close the gap between the electorate and those they elect, as Robert D. Putnam put in his seminal work *Bowling Alone* (2000).

Cities of the future no doubt will be "creative communities" in the sense that they recognize art and culture as vital, not only to a region's livability, but also to the preparedness of its workforce. Future cities will understand that art-infused education is critical to producing the next generation of leaders and workers for the knowledge economy. While art, music, and all things cultural have been enjoyed and appreciated by every generation, there has often been an often unspoken assumption that they were nonessential, even frills. Today, the demand for creativity has outpaced the ability of most nations to produce enough workers simply to meet their needs.

Jobs in the Creative Age

Worrying about the lack of qualified workers in this day and age may sound odd. With the globalization of media and markets in full bloom, America, for example, is beginning to see the outlines of yet another outmigration of jobs, unleashing new concerns about rising unemployment. Many economists are alarmed that the latest round of losses, unlike the earlier shift of manufacturing jobs to Taiwan and less-developed East Asian countries, will have a dramatic impact on America's wealth and well-being.

Twenty years ago, it was fashionable to blame foreign competition and cheap labor markets abroad for the loss of U.S. manufacturing jobs, but the pain of the loss was softened by the emergence of a new services industry. Now that the service sector has also widely automated itself, banking, insurance, and telecommunications firms are eliminating layers of management and infrastructure. The traditional corporate pyramid is disappearing, replaced by highly skilled professional work teams. State-of-the-art software and telecommunications technologies now enable any kind of enterprise to maximize efficiency and productivity by employing foreign workers wherever they are located, making the service-sector jobs even more precious. Forrester Research Inc., a market-research firm, estimates that some 3.3 million service jobs will move out of the United States over the next 10 to 15 years. Others put that number at 15 million and say the results will be devastating for the U.S. economy.

While CEOs, economists, and politicians are telling us that these are short-term adjustments, it is clear that the pervasive spread of the Internet, digitization, and the availability of white-collar skills abroad mean potentially huge cost savings for global corporations. Consequently, this shift of high-tech service jobs will be a permanent feature of economic life in the twenty-first century — but this does not necessarily mean the news is all bad for workers in the United States and other developed countries.

Some economists believe that globalization and digitization will improve the profits and efficiency of American corporations and set the stage for the next big growth-generating breakthrough. But what will that be?

A number of think tanks, including Japan's Nomura Research Institute, argue that the elements are in place for the advance of the Creative Age, a period in which free, democratic nations thrive and prosper because of their tolerance for dissent, respect for individual enterprise, freedom of expression, and recognition that innovation, not mass production of low-value goods and services, is the driving force for the new economy.

The new economy's demand for creativity has manifested itself in the emergence and growth of what author Richard Florida has termed the Creative Class. Although Florida defines this demographic group very broadly, he does a convincing job of underscoring the facts of life and work in the new knowledge economy. As he points out, "every aspect and every manifestation of creativity — cultural, technological, and economic — is inextricably linked."

By tracking certain migration patterns and trends, Florida did a huge service for those struggling to redefine their communities for the new knowledge economy. However, many questions remain. Can the community, through public art or cultural offerings, enhance the creativity of its citizens? And if the new economy so desperately demands the creative worker and leader, what should schools and universities do to prepare the next generation of creative people?

Recent U.S. Initiatives

U.S. investing in the arts themselves is already a $134 billion industry, according to the Washington, D.C., based advocacy organization Americans for the Arts. But the real benefit is that the arts are "a potent source for economic development," according to a report by the National Governors Association. NGA credits Philadelphia, Newark, and Charleston, South Carolina, as cities that "have used the creation of arts districts as centerpieces in efforts to combat increasing crime and suburban flight by restoring vitality to downtown areas."

The governors' report vividly showed that arts funding reliably generates positive revenue. For example, Virginia collected $849 million in arts-related revenue in 2000. That year, more than 245,000 arts-based jobs were created in the six states of New England.

Michigan earned a tenfold return for every dollar invested in the Council for Arts and Cultural Affairs.

In the last three years, the Los Angeles County Board of Supervisors has developed Arts for All — a Regional Blueprint for Arts Education. The program's objective is for every public-school student in the county to receive an effective K–12 education, of which the arts are an important component. Under this plan, each school district will acknowledge that exposure to and participation in the arts strengthens a child's academic development and growth as an individual, prepares the child to feel a part of and make a positive contribution to the community, and ensures a creative and competitive workforce to meet the economic opportunities in both the present and the future. Thus, sequential instruction in multiple arts disciplines will be scheduled into each school day and accounted for in the budget of every Los Angeles County school district.

I first realized that we were doing something fundamentally wrong in K–12 education when I was asked to chair California's then governor Pete Wilson's Commission on Information Technology in 1996. About the same time, the governor had a subcommittee on education technology, which I also chaired. Participating in that effort were such luminaries as one of the founders of the personal computer industry, Alan Kay; Larry Ellison, founder and chairman of Oracle Corporation; Joanne Kosburg, former president of Californians for the Arts and secretary of state and consumer affairs under Wilson; and Jeff Berg, chairman and CEO of International Creative Management Inc.

Early on in our deliberations Larry Ellison suggested our goal should be "to put a personal computer in the backpack of every K–12 student by the year 2001." It was a big, startling idea and captured everyone's attention regarding the enormity of our task. California in 1996 was about fiftieth among the 50 states in computers per pupil.

But Alan Kay shouted across the room, "Would you give five pencils to a school, Larry?" The computer, Alan argued, was nothing more than a pencil. What about the paper, he asked, and more importantly, what about the ideas that must come when we ask the student to put pencil to paper? Our challenge, he said, was to better understand how students learn, what they needed to learn to survive and succeed in today's knowledge economy, and what our teachers in private and public learning institutions were doing abut it.

Later that year I was asked to meet with a senior vice president of the Los Angeles based Alliance of Motion Picture and Television Producers, who were asking Governor Wilson to declare a "state of emergency" to help Hollywood find digital artists. Silicon Valley, we learned, also wanted the governor to lobby Washington for more foreign visas for the same reason. There were people aplenty who were computer literate, they claimed, but could not draw. In the new economy, they argued, artistic talents are vital to all industries dependent upon the marriage of computers and telecommunications.

Sadly, we discovered that art and music had been cut out of most California schools over 20 years ago in our zeal to be number one in the world in math and science. At the time this decision was made, the United States was about eleventh in the world, according to the Organization for Economic Cooperation and Development. Now, the United States ranks abut twenty-fourth in the world while Singapore, Sweden, Denmark, and Finland are in the top 10, in part because they have found a way to underscore the linkages between music and math, art and science.

One institution working to prepare its students for the challenges of the new millennium and the information age is the University of California at San Diego's Sixth College. The new college's themes are art, culture, and technology. Students will study the progress of the human species and its varied cultures and will explore watershed events in history in which art, culture, and technology converged. Provost Gabrielle Weinhausen has noted that the rediscovery of perspective during the Renaissance enabled architects and artists to collaborate on the creation of maps. The key to studying events like that, Weinhausen says, is learning how to ask the questions that illustrate relationships and patterns.

Until recently, there has been only limited evidence of the connection between education and appreciation of the arts and success in the post-industrial age of information. But now it is becoming increasingly apparent that arts initiatives will be the hallmarks of the most-successful and vibrant twenty-first-century cities and regions. One key to this vision is that we must acknowledge the current out-migration of high-tech jobs as a challenge to the status quo. As former Hewlett-Packard CEO Carly Fiorina told a panel of governors a short time ago, "Keep your tax incentives and highway interchanges; we will go where the highly skilled people are."

Those communities placing a premium on cultural, ethnic, and artistic diversity, and reinventing their knowledge factories for the creative age, will likely burst with creativity and entrepreneurial fervor. These are the ingredients so essential to developing and attracting the bright and creative people to generate new patents and inventions, innovative world-class products and services, and the finance and marketing plans to support them. Nothing less will ensure a city's economic, social, and political viability in the twenty-first century.

CHAPTER 41

Placing an Economic Value on Our Cultural Heritage

Susan Mourato *and* Massimiliano Mazzanti

In recent years, the demand for cultural destinations has become a major force in the global economy (Greffe 1990, 1999; Pearce and Mourato 1998). Tourist traps typically include cultural heritage elements that range widely, from a journey to a historical town center to a visit to a museum or a stroll around a historic garden. Visitors benefit from the expectations, experiences (educational, visual, recreational), and memories offered by heritage assets; while nonvisitors may benefit indirectly through magazines, films, or, increasingly, the Internet (virtual visits). Even if one does not use a cultural asset at present, investing in its conservation and maintenance retains the possibility of being able to use it at some point in the future. The *option value* of cultural designations is akin to an insurance premium.

Furthermore, people may attach a value to the conservation of cultural resources for a number of reasons — without ever using or visiting them. There may be altruistic feelings associated with the knowledge that other people may enjoy cultural heritage. Or there may be bequest motivations accruing from the desire to conserve cultural goods for future generations. Or there may even be existence val-

ues — that is, benefits that come from the knowledge that cultural heritage is being conserved for its own sake. These *nonuse values* are thought to be a significant proportion of the *total economic value* of cultural heritage, which may well extend beyond country borders.

Yet despite its obvious benefits to society, cultural heritage is increasingly threatened with degradation and destruction. While some risk factors result from natural environmental causes (such as earthquakes, landslides, volcanism, floods, avalanches, and coastal dynamics), human activities are arguably the main pressures behind the decay and loss of cultural assets. These include tourist and user pressure, unplanned urbanization, destructive development projects, theft, vandalism, war, air pollution, vibration, and plain neglect.

Part of the problem is that many cultural assets are not traded in markets: they have a "zero price" and can be enjoyed by many without charge. In other words, these so-called nonmarket cultural resources are valued by society but in a way that is not translated into any market price — i.e., they are external to markets. The impacts on conservation of this

Originally published as "Economic Valuation of Cultural Heritage: Evidence and Prospects" in *Assessing the Values of Cultural Heritage*, 2002, by The Getty Conservation Institute, Los Angeles, CA. Other publications are accessible online at *www.getty.edu/conservation/publications*. Reprinted with permission of the publisher.

"market failure" can be severe: underfunding, with insufficient funds generated to finance conservation; strong reliance on government support and public subsidy, which leaves the conservation of many important cultural assets at the mercy of political whims and over-stretched government budgets; overuse, with resulting wear and tear, congestion, vandalism, and theft; and inability to compete on the same level with alternative development projects, as the economic value of cultural assets appears to be zero of very small. A notorious example is the recent loss of the ancient city of Zeugma in Turkey, which was flooded because of the construction of a dam. The discovery on site of some of the most beautiful Roman mosaics in the Near East did not prevent the complete destruction of the city remains.

Paradoxically, underuse of cultural resources can also be detrimental for conservation. This is the case, for instance, when the goal of preserving a site is pursued by implementing only defensive policies, such as listing, without investment in integrated strategies of valorization: conservation, restoration, and demand-oriented policies.

Even when cultural goods and services are marketed, like many cultural destinations where visitors are required to pay an entry fee, more often than not there is a failure to practice optimal charges — namely, fees that would maximize visitor revenues without compromising targets for number of visits and feeds that could subsequently revert to conservation (Steiner 1997; Hett and Mourato 2000; Beltran and Rojas 1996). For example, in the case of the Historical Sanctuary of Machu Picchu in Peru, where both foreign and national tourists are charged the same, Hett and Mourato estimate that 80 percent of all visitors would be willing to pay higher fees (Hett and Mourato 2000). A policy of price differentiation between foreign and national tourists was found to increase the profitability of the site by more than 150 percent while simultaneously increasing visitation rates of national visitors by about 15 percent.

Statements in the existing cultural heritage literature that attempt to motivate conservation policies by reference to large "cultural values" are commonplace (Feldstein 1991; Couper 1996; Hutchinson 1996), and the deterioration or disappearance of any term of this heritage is thought to constitute a harmful impoverishment of the world heritage of mankind as a whole (UNESCO 1972). However, apart from what can be inferred from data on visitors and from maintenance and restoration expenditures, little is known about how changes in quality affect the value of these resources. Somewhat surprisingly, there has been little effort to demonstrate these values in practice.

But there is some good news. In the last two decades, economists have developed techniques to assess the economic value of changes that are external to markets. In recent years, a number of these nonmarket valuation methods have gained increasing popularity among academics and policy makers, particularly since a panel of experts led by two Nobel laureates in economics ruled that, under certain conditions, they were reliable enough to be used in a U.S. court of law in the context of natural resource damage assessment (Arrow et al. 1993). Following this historic decision, survey methods like contingent valuation (Mitchell and Carson 1989) have flourished and have been widely used in environmental decision making at various levels (Bateman et al. 2002). A contingent valuation questionnaire is a survey instrument that sets out a number of questions to elicit, among other information, the monetary value of a change in a public good or service. Most interestingly, its use has slowly but inexorably extended into other fields, such as health, transport, social, and, notably, cultural policy.[1]

The estimation of the economic value of cultural heritage conservation has increasingly been recognized as a fundamental part of cultural policy (Frey 2000; Throsby 2001; Maddison and Mourato 2002; Creigh-Tyte, Dawe, and Stock 2000; Darnell 1998; Navrud and

Ready 2002; Nuti 1998; Pearce and Mourato 1998; Davies 1994). Empirically, there are at least two powerful arguments for using economic valuation to inform macro and micro decisions in the cultural heritage sector. On the one hand, public institutions are increasingly being required to justify their expenditure decisions or requests for funding in terms of generated "consumer benefits," and those that are unable to do so might find their budgets cut. Furthermore, in a world where potential visitors are spoiled for choice, time constrained (rather than income constrained), and getting more sophisticated, cultural destinations are having to renew and market themselves to compete and survive. A consumer-oriented approach has increasingly taken over traditional supply-driven approaches to cultural heritage management and conservation, leading to ongoing market research studies to understand demand, strong marketing to generate awareness and attract new visitors, and a focus on building "brand" loyalty and encouraging repeat visits, essential for long-term survival. For these reasons, discussed in more detail in the following sections, demand-led approaches, such as economic valuation techniques, might quickly form an integral part of the new lexicon of the cultural analyst tool kit. Economic value as defined here does not deny the importance of other value dimensions but has a specific, and arguably special, role to play in cultural policy toward heritage fruition, enhancement, and conservation.[2]

In essence, neglecting to take into account the economic value of cultural heritage conservation and the full costs and benefits of policies, regulations, and projects with cultural components can lead to suboptimal allocation of resources in the sector, investment failure, and continuous degradation of the world's cultural assets. Clearly, these are complex issues that need to go beyond the financial aspects and be understood in the wider context of raising adequate financing for conservation and renewal, while, at the same time, reaching out and encouraging a demand to

visit and appreciate cultural heritage. This chapter argues that economic valuation is a necessary (although not sufficient) stage to achieve the sustainable use of cultural resources and to help reach a balanced, optimal mix of preservation, conservation, and access, while assessing the relative opportunity costs of each component.

The rest of the chapter is organized as follows: The next section, "Economic Valuation: Principles and Tools," presents the basic principles of economic valuation and examines a range of economic tools for the evaluation of cultural heritage, explaining their advantages and disadvantages. In the following section, the authors discuss the role of economic valuation techniques for microanalysis of cultural policies and cultural institutions and argue the need for measuring (nonmarket) economic flows to inform cultural policy and management; some cultural targets that economic valuation tools might help to achieve are also suggested. The following section reviews the current evidence on the application of economic valuation methods to cultural goods and discusses its main findings and implications. The final section proposes a new framework for the valuation of cultural heritage, based on recent developments of economic measurement tools and on a more integrated approach for socio-economic-cultural evaluation. Conclusions and suggestions for future research are also presented.

Economic Valuation Principles and Tools

Basic Principles

In line with standard economic theory, human well-being is determined by people's preferences. A benefit is defined as anything that increases human well-being, and a cost as anything that decreases human well-being. Measurement of preferences is obtained by finding out individuals' maximum willingness to pay (WTP) for a benefit or for the avoidance of a cost, or their minimum willingness to accept (WTA) compensation for tolerating a cost or forgoing a benefit. The rate at which individuals are prepared to trade off goods and services against one another corresponds to the total economic value of a change in the price or quality of a good or service.[3] This is because it forces people to take into account the fact that they are being asked to sacrifice some of their limited income to secure the change and must thus weight the value of what is being offered to them against alternative uses of that income. In this sense, WTP is a much more powerful measure of value than an attitudinal statement. While people may say, in response to an attitudinal question, that they "care about" many things, in practice they will only be able to pay for a much smaller subset of these things.

WTP is normally expressed in the marketplace. The market equilibrium between demand and supply of goods and services is a reflection of people's preferences and is characterized by an optimal quantity and price. Consumers who are willing to pay the market price of a good or service will buy it: For those willing to pay exactly the market price and no more, the cost of buying the good or service — i.e., the money they spend — is just equal to the benefit they get from the purchase — i.e., the well-being generated by the good; while those consumers who are willing to pay more than the price will also buy that good and get a net gain from the purchase, a "consumer surplus," measured by the excess of WTP over price. When the price of the good exceeds the price that people are prepared to pay for it, there is no corresponding welfare loss, as people simply do not buy that good.

A large proportion of cultural goods and services are traded in markets: cultural tourism, performing arts, antiques, paintings, and books are just a few examples of cultural goods for which thriving markets exist. But even in these cases, pricing policies are many times controlled, noncompetitive, and arbitrary, and

price discrimination is not effectively implemented (see Hett and Mourato 2000 or Beltran and Rojas 1996 for examples). Further, many market imperfections are present, such as the monopoly power of institutions and government subsidies, which prevent competitive pricing.

But of specific interest to this paper are the many cultural goods and services that are not traded in the market and that hence do not have a price. This is due to come of the special characteristics of cultural heritage, related to its property rights and type of use, that prevent the existence of the necessary markets for individuals to express their preferences. Using economic terminology, many cultural assets are *nonrival* and *nonexclusive* in consumption; in other words, the fact that one individual enjoys an asset does not prevent others from enjoying it as well, and no one can be excluded from its enjoyment (i.e., open access or common property). Assets with these characteristics are called public goods and are typically provided for collectively by governments and paid for through taxes. A historical town center is a good example of a public good: It is open-access, and large numbers of visitors can enjoy it simultaneously. A similar case occurs when a cultural good has external effects (externalities) that are not captured by the market. For example, conservation works carried out on a historical building may have a positive visual externality for passers-by. This external effect is not captured in any market (pecuniary) transaction.

As noted previously, these situations where the market does not reflect the full welfare provided by the good are called market failures, and they typically occur with assets, such as cultural heritage, that have public-good characteristics. Market failure can result in underpricing and overuse and lead to "free riding" — a situation in which people can enjoy the benefits of the cultural asset without having to pay for them. Going back to the previous example, people may derive utility from viewing the façade of a building without having to pay for it. Market failure provides a justification for government subsidy in support of culture, since commonly, the revenues collected from users are insufficient to cover conservation expenditure. Hence, cultural assets can become overly dependent on (volatile) government subsidy. The inability of the market to reflect the full value of cultural goods also means that many destructive development projects are implemented on the grounds that they appear to generate higher financial benefits.

Evidently, the fact that many public cultural goods are not traded in markets does not mean that they do not have a value. The problem is how to measure that value, given the absence of a market. In the past, taking maintenance costs as a proxy of economic value has too often justified cultural heritage financing and management. But true WTP to prevent damage may be larger, smaller, or equal to maintenance or mitigation costs. This point is best illustrated through an example.

Suppose that a town council is interested in estimating the value of restoring and conserving a decaying ancient historical house, of notable architecture, where a famous musician lived for most of his life. Adopting the maintenance cost approach would mean that the costs of cleaning, repairing, and restoring the fabric of the building would be taken as a proxy for the value of its conservation. But this may seriously miscalculate the true economic value of cultural conservation. On the one hand, restoration and maintenance practices may not prevent damages to the structure of the house from occurring, and some practices may even cause additional injuries. As a result, a part of the total value of the property may be irreversibly lost when the original material is altered or replicated. Furthermore, the "cost" of maintaining the building may seriously underestimate the "benefits" to the public of conserving it, which extend beyond mere users of the building, as the property might be valued by many others for its historical significance and architectural beauty. Hence, existing figures on cultural property costs (say, per user, per area, or per year) should always be accompanied by and compared to similar and commensurable figures on benefits. Decisions should be based on a rigorous assessment of both benefits and costs and not solely on cost considerations.[4]

Valuation Techniques

Recent developments in environmental economic theory and social survey methodology have made it theoretically defensible and practically feasible to value the economic benefits of several types of amenities not traded in markets, such as the benefits from accessing or conserving cultural resources. There is now an extensive literature on the methodologies for measuring the monetary value of changes in nonmarket commodities, which is a major step beyond standard financial analysis that ignores many key values that affect well-being and behavior. The absence of markets is solved by the use of either stated-preference or revealed-preference techniques.[5] The following provides a summary of the available methods applicable to the cultural heritage context.[6]

Revealed-preference methods look at "surrogate markets": They analyze preferences for nonmarket goods as implied by WTP behavior in an associated market. Popular revealed-preference techniques include the hedonic price method, the travel-cost method, and the maintenance-cost method. Although useful and theoretically sound (in the case of hedonic pricing and travel cost), the potential for their use in the estimation of the value attached to cultural sites is limited: revealed-preference methods cannot estimate option and nonuse values and cannot evaluate future marginal changes in cultural assets.

- The hedonic price method is based on the idea that house prices are affected by a house's bundle of characteristics, which may include nonmarket cultural factors, such as historic zone designation (Rosen

1974). Other things being equal, the extra price commanded by a house in a historic area would be a measure of the WTP for historic zone designation. This method is of partial and limited use in the valuation of cultural heritage: It does not measure nonuse or option values and is only applicable to cultural heritage elements that are embodied in property prices. It also relies on the unrealistic assumptions of a freely functioning and efficient property market, where individuals have perfect information and mobility.

• The travel-cost method uses differences in travel costs of individuals making use of a cultural site to infer the value of the site (Clawson and Knetsch 1966). If different individuals incur different costs to visit different places, these "implicit" prices can be used instead of conventional market prices as the basis for estimating the value of cultural sites and changes in their quality. This method also has limited applicability: It can only estimate visitor values for cultural heritage sites and is only useful for sites entailing significant travel. In addition, the valuation of multiattribute cultural sites and the presence of substitute locations present methodological problems.

• As was already mentioned above, the avoided-maintenance-cost approach has often been used to estimate damages to cultural materials (for example, from air pollution). The reason is that cost information is easier to collect than benefit information. The methods consists of calculating the cost savings implied from a reduction in maintenance cycles due to reduced damage rates. However, as noted before, maintenance costs are not the correct measure of the benefits derived by society from reduced damage to cultural resources, and the sole consideration of costs may seriously underestimate true economic values.

In contrast with the group of techniques described above, stated-preference methods use "hypothetical markets," described by means of a survey, to elicit preferences where there may be no surrogate market for a cultural good or service.[7]

The most popular stated-preference method is the contingent valuation (CV) method, which has been widely used in both developed and developing countries, particularly in the last decade, to determine the economic feasibility of public policies for the improvement of environmental quality. By means of an appropriately designed questionnaire, a hypothetical market is described where the good in question can be "traded" (Mitchell and Carson 1989; Bateman et al. 2002). This contingent market defines the good itself, the institutional context in which it would be provided, and the way it would be financed. A random sample of people is then directly asked to express their WTP (or WTA) for a hypothetical change in the level of provision of the good. Respondents are assumed to behave as though they were in a real market. In fact, CV questionnaires bear some resemblance to conventional market research for new or modified products.

As an illustration, in the context of cultural heritage, consider the following contingent scenario used in a CV study designed to estimate the benefits of keeping the Surrey History Centre, a local archive in the United Kingdom, open and running (adapted from Mourato et al. 2001). The CV scenario was preceded by questions about perceptions and attitudes toward recorded heritage conservation, use of the archive, and information about the archive's services and resources. Both direct users and local nonusers of the archive were interviewed.

Please imagine the following situation. Priorities for public spending are changing in the United Kingdom. One of the sectors that will be negatively affected by government budgetary cuts is the libraries and archives sector that contains a great part of our recorded heritage.

Due to this situation, unless additional resources are found, the Surrey History Centre might close down in 2001. As a result, all the resources contained in this archive will be lost as collections and may experience deterioration, or be dispersed (relocated to a number of other institutions) or be sold. Obviously some materials now contained in the Surrey History Centre may also be found elsewhere: but other materials and information are unique and might be therefore lost forever.

Now suppose that the council is considering charging every local household an annual council tax surcharge for an emergency grant to ensure that the Surrey History Centre does not close down, that the services it provides to the community can be maintained at their current levels, and that all scheduled investments will continue to go ahead. It was estimated that this would cost each household in the council £5 per year.

Please think about how much keeping the Surrey History Centre open is worth to you and your household. If it would cost each household only a small amount of money, then you might think that it was a price worth paying. On the other hand, if it was going to be very expensive, then you might not prefer to pay it and to have the archive close down.

Would you agree to pay an extra £5 per year in council taxes to prevent the closure of the Surrey History Centre and to ensure that its services are maintained at their current levels?

In the example above, a dichotomous choice elicitation question was used to uncover WTP. That is, respondents were simply asked whether they would be prepared to pay or not pay a particular amount of money. This amount was varied across subsamples — i.e., different people were asked to pay different amounts. There are many other ways of asking the WTP question, including simply asking respondents what their maximum WTP is (the open-ended format) or asking them to pick their maximum WTP amount from a list of money amounts (the payment card approach).

Theoretically, the CV method is based on welfare economics and assumes that stated WTP amounts are related to respondents' underlying preferences. Furthermore, unlike revealed-preference techniques, CV is able to capture all types of benefits from a nonmarket good or service, including nonuse values. Neglecting the estimation of nonuse values is potentially a serious omission, as many cultural goods arguably generate substantial nonuse benefits, possibly with transnational and intergenerational characteristics. As mentioned in the introduction, much of the impetus for the acceptance of the CV method was the report of the special panel appointed by the U.S. National Oceanic and Atmospheric Administration (NOAA) (Arrow et al. 1993). The NOAA panel concluded that CV studies could produce estimates reliable enough to be used in a judicial process of natural resource damage assessment including nonuse values.

While similarities exist between CV surveys and the type of surveys conducted in other disciplines (Boulier and Goldfarb 1998), CV questionnaires possess some distinguishing features that require special consideration. This is mainly for three reasons:

- CV questionnaires require respondents to consider how a possible change in a good or service that is typically not traded in markets might affect them.
- The type of public and mixed goods and services usually considered can be complex and unfamiliar to respondents.
- Respondents are asked to make a monetary evaluation of the change of interest.

All these aspects introduce a number of questionnaire design issues that do not occur in the case of opinion polls or marketing surveys for private goods. Mitchell and Carson note that "the principal challenge facing the designer of a CV study is to make the scenario sufficiently understandable, plausible, and meaningful to respondents so that they can and will give valid and reliable values despite their lack of experience with one or more of the scenario dimensions" (Mitchell and Carson 1989, 120).

The design of a CV questionnaire comprises three interrelated stages. The first and principal stage consists of identifying the good to be valued, constructing the valuation scenario, and eliciting the monetary values. In the second stage, questions on attitudes and opinions, knowledge, familiarity and use of the good, demographics, and various debriefing questions are added. The third stage consists of piloting the draft questionnaire for content, question wording, question format, and overall structure and layout. For a detailed discussion, see that of Bateman and colleagues (Bateman et al. 2002).

Designing and implementing CV studies may seem to be a trivial task, where all that is required is to put together a number of questions about the subject of interest. But this apparent simplicity lies at the root of many badly designed surveys that elicit biased, inaccurate, and useless information, possibly at a great cost. In fact, even very simple questions require proper wording, format, content, placement, and organization if they are to elicit accurate information. Writing effective questionnaires in which scenarios and questions are uniformly and correctly understood by respondents and which encourage them to answer in a considered and truthful manner is no easy task (Mitchell and Carson 1989). To address these difficulties, a set of guidelines for applying CV to enhance the validity and reliability of estimates for nonuse values in natural resource damage assessment was developed by the NOAA panel (Arrow et al. 1993) and recently updated by Bateman and colleagues for the U.K. government (Bateman et al. 2002). Following these guidelines does not automatically warrant quality — neither does noncompliance necessarily indicate lack of validity. They are, however, a useful reference and the best available set of recommendations for practitioners in all fields.

In the context of the currently available valuation techniques, the CV method and its derivatives can arguably be considered the best available techniques to estimate the total economic value of cultural assets that are not usually traded in the market and where nonuse values are thought to be an important component of value.

Issues and Limitations

But no method is without fault, and CV is no exception. As repeatedly pointed out by critics, a number of factors may systematically bias respondents' answers. Generally, these factors are not specific to CV as such but are common to most survey-based techniques and are predominantly attributable to survey design and implementation problems. Mitchell and Carson and Bateman and colleagues provide an extensive review of possible sources of bias (Mitchell and Carson 1989; Bateman et al. 2002). These include strategic behavior (such as free riding), embedding (where the valuation is insensitive to the scope of the good), anchoring bias (where the valuation depends on the first bid presented in a dichotomous choice context), information bias (when the framing of the question unduly influences the answer), or hypothetical bias (umbrella designation for problems arising from the hypothetical nature of the CV market).

Perhaps the most often quoted criticism of CV studies (and, indeed, of all survey-based research) is "Ask a hypothetical question and you will get a hypothetical answer" (Scott 1965). In addressing this issue, a useful approach is to examine what type of questions are likely to deliver useful information even when they are asked in regards to a hypothetical scenario. Carson, Groves, and Machina show that when respondents feel their response may influence the actions of relevant agencies and when they care about the outcome of the valuation questions, they will answer according to their preferences, so as to maximize their expected well-being (Carson, Groves, and Machina 1999). In order to do so, they will respond to the incentives set out in the survey design: obviously, problems will occur when respondents feel that the survey market provides some incentives to do other than reveal their preferences truthfully. Unfortunately, there are a considerable number of possible situations in which truth telling might not seem the best way to maximize well-being. An example of relevance to cultural heritage studies is the use of charitable donations as a payment vehicle in WTP questions (as opposed to other mechanisms, such as taxes or entry fees). In this case, respondents have an incentive to overstate the WTP amounts in the survey to secure the provision of the good, and then, once the good is provided, they have an incentive to free ride when it comes to actually donating the amounts stated, as payment is voluntary.[8] Hence, one observes stated WTP amounts that are much higher than actual payments, a discrepancy that is not due to the hypothetical nature of the survey market but to the fact that respondents have been given the wrong incentives to reveal their true preferences. This is the issue of "incentive compatibility," and determining whether a given CV study design is incentive compatible is fundamental in order to avoid misrepresentation of values. In the example above, problems could potentially have been avoided by the use of a tax or an entry fee as the payment vehicle in the WTP questions, if at all possible.

Among the types of biases mentioned above, the problem of embedding is arguably the one that raises most concern for cultural valuation. Concerns regarding scope and embedding arise from "the frequent finding that WTP for a good is approximately the same for a more inclusive good" (Fisher 1996, 19). To illustrate, if respondents cannot meaningfully separate out the conservation value of one historic house from the value of all the historic houses in a region, then the validity of their responses has to be questioned. Careful design and pretest of questionnaires is needed to minimize the serious potential for embedding (Bateman et al. 2002). In particular, when scope problems are thought likely to arise (i.e., when one is interested in the benefits of conservation of some parts of a cultural site but not of others, or of some historical buildings in a city but not of others), tests can be built into a survey design in order to see how far responses are sensitive to the scope of the good being valued.

Furthermore, since heritage conservation generates values for the future, a legitimate concern in cultural heritage valuation is that of how future values might be taken into account, since one cannot survey generations yet to come. Of course, generations do overlap to some extent, and part of these future values are taken into account by the bequest motivations of current generations. But problems still arise as cultural heritage conservation sometimes involves very long-term perspectives, and future preferences with respect to art have been found to deviate from the values held by current generations (Frey 2000). It might be that, because of changing tastes, future generations will not want to conserve as much cultural heritage as does the current generation. But, in general, it is arguably more likely that people in the future will value cultural heritage conservation more highly than the living generation. Aside from changing tastes, future generations are expected to be richer than current generations, and hence, they are likely to be wiling to pay more for cultural heritage preservation. Also, it is inevitable that, over time, some cultural heritage will deteriorate or be lost: Given increased scarcity, the value of the heritage will naturally increase. More research is needed on the best way to treat and account for future values. In practical terms, a sensible approach for unique and important cultural resources is to combine economic valuation with a precautionary approach, which means that any decision not to undertake preservation is afforded very careful scrutiny.

Other authors put forward more radical criticisms of CV that question the basis of economic theory, focusing on known psychological anomalies such as the disparity between the value of gains and losses (Frey 2000)— that is, when WTP questions yield different valuations than corresponding WTA questions — or suggesting that respondents may be driven by nonrational/nonmaximizing preferences, acting and behaving as citizens and not as "consumers" when facing choices concerning public goods (Blamey, Common, and Quiggin 1995; Vatn and Bromley 1995). For example, Blamey states, "Respondents often adopt a contribution model when processing scenario information, rather than the purchase model assumed by environmental economists. In contrast to the purchase model, where an individual is assumed to ask herself whether she is prepared to pay the specified amount to obtain the environmental improvement rather than do without it, the contribution model assumes that individuals treat the environmental improvement as a good cause, that warrants supporting.... This has the important implication that individuals may be willing to pay more to a local environmental issue for which there are few contributors than a national issue they value more highly, but for which the costs of the intervention are to be shared by a proportionally larger number of people.... Price fairness is assumed to be one of a number of contingencies influencing behavioral promises in CVM studies" (Blamey 1998, 69).

While psychological anomalies do present a problem in some instances, it is meaningless for economic analysis to try to disentangle the realm of citizens' value and that of consumers' value: The two are intrinsically entangled when the valuation of public policy and public goods is at stake. As citizens, individuals are still influenced by their values and preferences for public goods. What is important to bear in mind is that CV values are contingent to the information provided in the valuation scenario, and preferences are sensitive to the attributes of the contingent market described. This is perfectly rational. As long as the public good and the contingent market are correctly described, credible, and incentive compatible, this should not be an issue.

Finally, in order to avoid easy misunderstanding, it is important to stress that economic valuation methods do not pretend to assess cultural values as such but to assess the economic values associated with cultural heritage — that is, the flow of benefits arising out of a physical stock. Economic values relate to the enhancement of human/individual/social well-being; they are anthropocentric and based on people's preferences (Pearce 1993). They lend themselves to quantification and to the assessment of trade-offs between goals and resources (Robbins 1938). As discussed above, the economic value of cultural heritage is a wide-ranging, complex, and multifaceted concept, as preferences for cultural assets stem from many different motivations, ranging from self-interest to pure altruistic concerns.

Focusing on economic values, as abroad and encompassing as they may be, does not mean that other values are less important. Economists do not claim that all values can be measured in money terms and be captured in actual financial flows: There will be cases where the information is inadequate, the uncertainties too great, or the consequences too profound or too complex to be reduced to a single number (Hanemann 1994). Nor do economists claim that economic values subsume all that is important in cultural heritage conservation policy. Other relevant (nonmonetary) cultural, religious, symbolic, and spiritual values also have a role to play in decision-making processes. The point is that economics, as a social science, can and should provide complementary techniques and investigative tools to disciplines dealing with cultural issues, for a holistic assessment of cultural values.

CV has been extensively applied to the valuation of environmental goods and services (Mitchell and Carson 1989; Carson et al. 1995). However, there have been surprisingly few applications to cultural assets, in spite of the obvious links between questions of the conservation of natural and cultural goods. Cultural policy and management would benefit a great deal from a set of sound, theoretically structured, and operational evaluation tools. The next section discusses the role of economic valuation in cultural heritage and suggests a number of possible areas where these tools might be used successfully.

The Role of Economic Valuation for Cultural Policies and Institutions

It has been argued above that cultural heritage is a mixed good, framed over a multidimensional, multivalue, and multiattribute environment, generating private and public/collective benefits for current, potential, and future users and even for nonusers. How resources are allocated and consequently how institutions and services are managed, organized, and provided affect people's well-being, attitudes, and participation toward cultural heritage. In this context, what are the cultural goals faced by policy makers and managers that economic valuation tools might help to inform? These goals, interrelated in many ways, pertain to three main areas: management, financing, and resource allocation.

Cultural Destinations Management

As far as the management of cultural destinations is concerned, economic valuation may help to inform decisions and policies of the following type:

- assessing what type of changes/attractions/exhibitions/improvements should be introduced in cultural destinations in order to maximize profits/revenues/access
- evaluating pollution, tourism, and development damage done to cultural destinations
- assessing what type and degree of conservation measures should be undertaken (e.g., restoration, replacement, cleaning)
- estimating the demand for a cultural asset and predicting future demand trends.
- assessing nonvisitors' potential demand and investigating the factors that might influence that demand
- estimating price and income elasticities of demand for cultural assets
- designing successful pricing strategies for

cultural destinations: who pays what, when and how

- ranking cultural heritage characteristics, thus assessing priorities for new marginal improvements
- prioritizing among competing projects at the micro/institution level
- assessing visitor preferences both before and after the visit experience an evaluating repeated visitors' experiences
- gathering information on how socioeconomic characteristics (age, sex, membership, income, education, attitudes) explain visitation rates and spending patterns
- identifying groups that might be excluded from enjoying cultural heritage at certain prices and given certain management policies
- evaluating the impacts of congestion-reduction options

Financing Cultural Heritage

As far as the financing of cultural heritage is concerned, the objectives that can be informed by economic valuation may be listed as follows:

- assessing the existence and measuring WTP for access, conservation, and improvements of cultural heritage
- analyzing pricing policies for cultural destinations: uniform pricing, interpersonal price discrimination, voluntary prices, intertemporal price discrimination, etc.
- investigating how the prices that people are prepared to pay vary across different socioeconomic groups (by age, sex, income, education, etc.)
- quantifying the gap between benefits to the community provided by cultural heritage and costs incurred to provide them
- providing information for a multisource funding strategy, based on local and national taxes, private donations, funds, entry fees, and public/private partnerships

designing incentive systems to motivate and finance conservation
- investigation whether subsidies to cultural heritage are justified and informing how much they should be

Resource Allocation

Regarding the macro process of allocation of resources among sites and institutions, pursued by a public evaluator body, economic valuation can be used to help a number of policy decisions:

- allocating funds between cultural heritage and other areas of public spending
- gathering information of strategic policy importance about the level of public support (financial and nonfinancial) for the cultural sector or a specific cultural institution for the process of resource allocation
- allocating cultural budgets within competing institutions/areas
- measuring people's satisfaction for existing cultural services and then ranking institutions with respect to benchmark parameters
- appraising and ranking interventions in the cultural sector — for example, for competitive (grant) allocation
- allocating a budget within one institution/area among competing projects
- deciding whether a given cultural asset is to be conserved and, if so, how and at what level
- assessing which sites, within a city area or a cultural district, are more worthy of investment and for which the impacts are more significant

Management, financing, and resource allocation strategies are evidently entangled, as evidenced above. Economic valuation is of use in all three spheres, for macro and micro cultural policies oriented toward access, conservation, or quality improvement goals.

Of course, economic valuation is just one among other existing economic instruments and tools that can be used in the cultural heritage context: Its main aim is to demonstrate that economic values exist and to measure them. Subsequently, other economic tools can be used to "capture" those estimated values — that is, to transform them into actual cash flows. In particular, economic valuation might precede the use of instruments such as (1) local or national taxes aimed at financing culture, (2) fees aimed at regulating access and raising funds, and (3) voluntary donation mechanisms aimed at raising money without imposing a fee. The focus here is strictly on the argument that cultural economic values exist and that there are ways to measure them validly, rather than on capturing those values (see Pearce and Mourato 1998, and Bailey and Falconer 1998, for a discussion of economic capture instruments).

Despite the potential, existing cultural heritage valuation studies are scarce and limited in scope and content. The next section reviews the current body of evidence and discusses the implications of its findings.

Current Evidence: Lessons and Controversies

This review focuses on the emerging literature on the valuation of cultural benefits by means of stated-preference techniques (mainly CV). As noted above, it is only in recent years that CV methods have started to be applied within the realm of cultural heritage economics, and so far, very few studies have been undertaken. A search of published and unpublished international sources uncovered just over thirty stated-preference studies of cultural goods.[9]

The existing literature is strongly concentrated geographically, with the majority of studies coming from Europe (55 percent) and with the U.K. producing the largest share (29 percent). Some 23 percent of studies were carried out in the United States and Canada.

Early studies on cultural heritage valuation were small-scale surveys, exploratory in nature and mostly confined to finding a price for the good in question using a then-novel methodology in the sector (see, for example, Willis 1994 and Martin 1994). Since then, some progress has been achieved at various levels: sampling, study design, implementation, statistical estimation, testing the validity of the estimates produced, and exploring the nature of people's preferences toward cultural goods. In this respect, however, cultural heritage is still a long way from the level of knowledge already gathered in other areas, such as the environment or health.

Existing studies vary widely, both in terms of the type of good or activity analyzed and the type of benefit evaluated. There are some instances where similar types of goods were evaluated (cathedrals, castles, archaeological sites, groups of historic buildings, recorded heritage). However, the type of benefit estimated is usually different, as is the sample frame used, making it difficult to make meaningful comparisons among studies.

While the conclusions of each study are different, some consistent findings emerge from the studies that have been conducted to date. These are discussed below.

The Significant Value of Heritage Conservation and Use

Generally, the findings suggest that, on average, people attribute a significantly positive value to the conservation or restoration of cultural assets. The implication is that damages to cultural goods are undesirable and that the public would be willing to pay positive amounts to avoid them or to slow the rate at which they occur. Mean values range from less than a dollar (for example, Bulgarians were found to be willing to pay about $0.60–$1 to preserve their famous monasteries [Mourato, Kontoleon, and Danchev 2002]) to over $150 (for example, the conservation of an archaeo-

logical park in Italy was valued at about $216 by local residents [Riganti and Willis 1998]), with the distribution skewed toward lower value ranges. Perhaps a more meaningful measure for comparison purposes is WTP as a proportion of per capita gross national product (GNP): Typical annual household WTP amounts for cultural heritage conservation are calculated to range from 0.01 percent to 0.5 percent of per capita GNP.

The large dispersion of estimated values is due to large differences in the type and scope of the cultural change being evaluated, to taste and income variations in the sampled populations, and to disparities in value elicitation methods. Clearly, these values are only indicative and should be taken cautiously, given the small number of studies on which they are based.

Is It a Minority Benefit?

Several studies show a relatively large proportion of respondents stating a zero WTP (up to 89 percent in the case of the recreational value of defaced aboriginal rock paintings in Canada [Boxall, Englin, and Adomowicz 1998]). Some of these responses can be considered protests against some aspects of the survey instrument (i.e., a dislike of paying taxes or a rejection of the contingent scenario) and thus are not a reflection of people's true preferences. Others, however, are "genuine" zero values arising from budget constraints, from lack of interest in cultural issues, and from the fact that cultural heritage preservation is typically ranked low among competing public issues, as is shown consistently by attitudinal questions. Hence, the welfare of a significant proportion of the population seems to be unaffected by changes in cultural goods/activities. In some instances, the positive estimated values are driven by a minority of the population — typically, the users of the cultural good and the richer and more educated segments of the population (e.g., improving the landscape of Stonehenge in the United Kingdom by tunneling a nearby road generates positive benefits to 35 percent of the U.K. population, a group that was found to be on average wealthier and more educated than the 65 percent who were not willing to pay anything for the improvement [Maddison and Mourato 2002]).

This finding has important implications for the funding of cultural heritage goods. For example, in instances where more than two-thirds of the population express a zero WTP, the imposition of a tax may be infeasible; targeted voluntary donations or entry fees may provide more appropriate means of extracting existing values (although the former invites free-riding behavior); or, if a tax mechanism is used, care must be taken to ensure that the distributional effects are taken into account with offsetting expenditures. In order to reduce distributional conflicts, education and information policies are important and should be targeted at increasing the consumption of culture by affecting tastes or by reducing the costs to disadvantaged groups of consuming culture. There is large potential for cross-fertilization between valuation of preferences for culture and the implementation of cultural educational policy.

The link among income, education, and cultural benefits found in cultural valuation studies also seems to suggest that the value of cultural heritage conservation will grow as incomes and education rise. It lends some support to the proposition that future generations might attribute a larger value to heritage conservation than do present generations, in part because of higher incomes and education levels.

The Importance of Actual Users

Most studies indicate that there can be significant values from recreation and educational visits to cultural destinations (e.g., foreign visitors to the Fes Medina in Morocco valued a visit at $38–$70 [Carson et al. 1997]). Hence, policies aimed at increasing and facil-

itating access to cultural sites can also be expected to enhance economic cultural values.

Nevertheless, it is misleading to assume from these results that charging users optimal entry fees will solve all the financing problems of cultural sites. First, user values alone may not be enough to deliver sustainability for the large proportion of cultural goods and services that are not unique in many respects and where substitute destinations exist, which explains the accumulated deficits and/or degradation experienced by many cultural sites. Second, it may institutionally be difficult to charge optimal prices. For example, entry fees might be regulated, or there might be a membership system in place whereby members can gain free access to certain cultural destinations in exchange for a fixed membership fee. Such a circumstance happens in the United Kingdom with the National Trust, a charity founded in 1895 to preserve places of historic interest or natural beauty permanently, for the benefit of the nation. The National Trust is the largest conservation charity in Europe, with 251 properties opened to the public and 2.5 million members in 1997. Members account for a large proportion of all visits to the Trust's properties, but, as they are entitled to free access via their membership fee, they would therefore not be affected by increases in entry fees.

A number of related issues should also be taken into account when user pricing mechanisms are designed: on the one hand, the effect of higher prices on visitation rates should be carefully considered and addressed, given the current focus on making heritage available to the general public; on the other hand, the possible trade-off between access and conservation (i.e., too many visitors might cause deterioration of a site by overuse) should be analyzed explicitly, and future studies should attempt to measure tourist carrying capacity of a site, as well as calculate any possible congestion costs.

What About Nonusers?

Studies dealing with nonuse values of cultural heritage sites show that these can be important. In cases where the relevant population benefiting from improvement or maintenance of the cultural good is thought to be sizable, possibly crossing national borders, the total aggregated benefit can be very large: Even when individual WTP is very small, when multiplied by a vast number of people, a large value will be obtained. This is the case when unique and charismatic cultural heritage goods are at stake. For example, the estimated value of improving the landscape of Stonehenge for the U.K. population was found to be mainly driven by nonuse values (mainly a desire to protect the site for future generations), with 53 percent of the population never actually having visited the stone circle (Maddison and Mourato 2002).

However, as noted above, there is a trade-off, as the available evidence also suggests that the proportion of those stating zero WTP is largest among nonusers. Drawing from the environmental valuation literature, nonuse values are also thought to decline with the availability of substitute sites and with households' distance from the site ("distance decay"). Future research should pay close attention to the geographical limits of WTP.

The Issue of Embedding

It was already mentioned how the issue of embedding or insensitivity to the scope of the change being valued might affect cultural values. Indeed, in an early cultural valuation study, Navrud, Pedersen, and Strand found that respondents were insensitive to the scope of the air pollution damages to the Nidaros Cathedral in Norway (Navrud, Pedersen, and Strand 1992). This potential problem has been insufficiently addressed by the existing literature.

Evidently, embedding will be less of a problem for flagship cultural goods with no substitutes (e.g., the Pyramids in Egypt). But it may distort results significantly when cultural goods perceived as being nonunique are evaluated (e.g., historical buildings, castles, churches, and cathedrals): For example, the estimated values for a particular cultural good may reflect a desire to preserve all similar goods and thus overstate the value of the good. And, as Navrud, Pedersen, and Strand discussed, this type of bias may also affect the evaluation of the scope and duration of conservation policies for a single site (Navrud, Pedersen, and Strand 1992). More research is needed in this important area.

"Quick and Dirty" Valuation Studies

The lack of financial resources and/or the lack of knowledge about valuation methods has led to several poor valuation studies, in terms of consistency with economic theory, survey design, statistical performance, and sample significance. This is as true for cultural heritage valuation as it is for valuation studies in other areas. In some cases, the lack of sound preliminary investigation — by means of pilot studies, focus groups, and interviews — has led to "quick," and consequently faulty, studies, confirming the golden rule of empirical analysis: The result one gets is dependent on the quality of the data one inputs. Moreover, a good valuation study requires adequate financial and human resources, as it is a time-consuming and complex activity; but, more often than not, sponsoring bodies are unwilling to allocate enough time and resources for practitioners to produce a good study. The recent emphasis on producing best-practice guidelines developed by field practitioners is an attempt to ameliorate this situation (Arrow et al. 1993; Bateman et al. 2000).

Whatever the budget available, good knowledge of the theoretical underpinnings of valuation, of the lessons yielded by previous studies, and of survey implementation guidelines helps in achieving efficiency (measured in quality of output divided by costs). Interdisciplinary teams of economists, other social scientists, cultural managers, and marketing researchers may set up valuable and reliable cost-effective studies, exploiting economies of scale in (1) preparing more than one valuation study/experiment at the same time, and (2) integrating the valuation experiment with broader socioeconomic or marketing investigations.

Should Decisions About Cultural Heritage Conservation Be Left to Experts?

A common criticism of survey-based economic valuation approaches is that decisions about cultural assets should not be left in the hands of the public, thought to be too ignorant about cultural goods to possibly be able to make sensible judgments about them. Is expert judgment an alternative to survey-based (stated- and revealed-) preference analysis? Cultural experts clearly play a leading role in determining the value of cultural heritage. Nonetheless, relying only on experts' judgment may be dangerous, leading to improper allocation of resources, arbitrariness, lobbying pressures for funding, and paternalism.

In fact, cultural valuation studies that have canvassed opinions from both experts and the general public have found consensual views in many areas (Mourato et al. 2001). Moreover, as has been pointed out, most valuation studies have uncovered significant cultural values even for small changes, overcoming the fear that the public does not know enough about the cultural sector to be able to hold sensible values on it.

Top-down experts' perceptions and bottom-up public demands should be brought together and should balance each other within the realm of cultural policy, since cultural heritage is a complex economic good requiring a comprehensive and participatory approach to management that includes all stakeholders. In the context of valuation studies, while expert knowledge should be sought at various stages of the research process, it is probably most useful at the designing stages of the valuation survey, to inform the context and framing of the valuation scenario, enhancing its credibility and the usefulness of the results for formulating policy.

It has been discussed already how demand-led approaches are fundamental to justifying the spending of limited public money on cultural heritage, how resource allocation within the sector is increasingly based on generated "consumer benefits," and how cultural destinations are becoming more consumer oriented — investigating and reaching new markets, encouraging repeat visits by change and renewal, providing integrated experiences, and striving to surpass expectations. The emerging valuation literature supports this modern view: Valuation studies have invariably uncovered large average values among the lay public for cultural assets. Cultural heritage seems to be an important part of people's lives, and accordingly, they are willing to trade off some of their limited income to access it and to protect it. Many more good-quality studies are needed to confirm these early findings and to address the several gaps in knowledge identified above.

A New Framework for the Valuation of Cultural Heritage

In this section, two avenues are proposed for improving the assessment of cultural values in a more integrated and holistic environment. One constitutes an improvement over current economic valuation techniques that comes from within economics; another complements and expands standard economic valuation practices by making use of complementary lines of inquiry from other social disciplines.

New Economic Tools:
Choice Modeling Approaches

Partly as a response to the problems experienced by researchers in CV studies, valuation practitioners are increasingly developing an interest in alternative stated-preference formats such as choice modeling (CM).[10] CM is a family of survey-based methodologies for measuring preferences for nonmarket goods, where goods are described in terms of their attributes and of the levels that these take. Respondents are presented with various alternative descriptions of the good, differentiated by their attributes and levels, and are asked to do one of the following: (1) rank the various alternatives in order of preference, (2) rate each alternative according to a preference scale, or (3) choose their most preferred alternative out of the set. By including price or cost as one of the attributes of the good, WTP can be indirectly recovered from people's ranks, ratings, or choices. As CV, CM can also measure all forms of value, including nonuse values.

CM has one main advantage over standard CV formats: its capability to deal with multidimensional changes. By describing a good or policy in terms of its component attributes, values can be obtained not only for the good/policy as a whole but also for each of its attributes. Furthermore, the method avoids an explicit elicitation of WTP by relying instead on expressed choices or rankings among alternative scenarios from which WTP can be indirectly inferred: This might reduce the incidence of people protesting or refusing to answer the valuation question.

The conceptual microeconomic framework for CM lies in Lancaster's characteristics theory of value, which assumes that the utility that consumers get from a good can be broken down into the utilities of the composing characteristics/attributes of the good (Lancaster 1991). Empirically, variants of CM have been widely used in the market research and transport literatures (e.g., Hensher 1994; Green and Srinivasan 19878; Hensher and Johnson 1974), but the method has only relatively recently been applied to other areas, such as the environment or culture. Louviere, Hensher, and Swait (2000), Bennett and Blamey (2001), and Hanley, Mourato, and Wright (2001) provide recent and extensive overviews of CM techniques and their application to the environmental field.[11]

A typical CM exercise is characterized by a number of key stages.

As an example, consider an area abundant in properties of historic interest, and suppose that the local cultural authorities want to find out which attributes of the properties attract the most visitors and which are valued the most.

Respondents are presented with two imaginary (but realistic) property descriptions (there could be more than two) and then asked to choose which property they would prefer to visit (they are also given the option of not visiting any of the properties described). Each property is defined in terms of five attributes: existence of a garden, architectural style of the house; quality of collections (furniture, porcelain, glass, tapestries, or paintings); visitor facilities (cafeteria/restaurant, shops), and entry fee. Each attribute can take various levels. For example, the garden attribute might have only two levels ("has a garden" or "no garden"), while the entry fee attribute might have four levels ($1, $5, $20, $30). Typically, each respondent would be given a number of these choice sets to answer, each with different property descriptions.

If the 1990s have witnessed the emergence of the CV method within the realm of cultural economics, the first decade of the new century may see the development of CM applications to the cultural heritage valuation arena. This is because the many dimensions, attributes, and values characterizing the supply and demand of cultural goods and services lend themselves to analysis by mechanisms that have the capability of dealing with situations where changes are multidimensional, of analyzing trade-offs among them, and of eliciting separate values for the various functions of interest. In particular, pursuing an attribute-based valuation — by breaking down cultural institutions and policies into a set of functions and services — might serve a number of objectives relevant to cultural policy:

- to measure the total value associated with different cultural property or policy descriptions (i.e., properties/policies described by different attribute levels)
- to measure the contribution to the total value of a cultural site of single attributes, services, or functions (of a public or private nature)
- to determine possible trade-offs among attributes (e.g., such as the intrinsic trade-off between access and conservation)
- to derive an implicit ranking of attributes according to user preferences[12]
- to determine public support of specific cultural property or policy scenarios
- to estimate the market share of a particular site
- to avoid some of the protests arising from direct elicitation of WTP for cultural goods

Being survey based, CM approaches also suffer from the problems associated with survey techniques previously discussed. A further limitation of this approach lies in the cognitive difficulty to respondents associated with complex choices between bundles with many attributes and levels. Previous research in the marketing and environmental literatures by Ben-Akiva, Morikawa, and Shiroishi (1991), Chapman and Staelin (1982), Hausman and Ruud (1987), and Foster and Mourato (2002) found evidence of unreliable and inconsistent choices/ranks. In particular, respondents were found to (1) choose options that are worse than others in all respects (dominated options), (2) make choices that are intransitive (i.e., choose A over B, B over C, and then C over A), and (3) make inconsistent choices across choice sets (i.e., choose A over B in one choice set and B over A in another). The number of il-

logical choices seems to increase with the complexity of the choice/ranking task (i.e., with the number of attributes, levels, choice sets, and scenarios in each task and when choices are made between alternatives that respondents dislike). Possible explanations for the occurrence of these problems include respondent fatigue, learning effects, and the adoption of rules of thumb to facilitate the choice task (like choosing options with reference to one attribute only, ignoring all the others). For these reasons, CM exercises should be as simple as possible, using a limited number of attributes, levels, and choice sets, so as to avoid overburdening respondents with information.

To summarize, CM has explicit advantage over the CV method in the analysis of goods of a multidimensional nature. As far as cultural heritage is concerned, CM brings together a structured economic theoretical framework, a powerful and detailed capacity of evaluation, and a great variety of application possibilities. It is suggested here to add this comprehensive valuation technique to the available box of cultural economic tools to be drawn upon by cultural policy markers and cultural managers as needed. Further research and applications to cultural policy are therefore strongly encouraged.

Integrating Instruments for Socioeconomic Evaluation of Cultural Heritage

Stated-preference techniques were argued above to be capable of producing valid and reliable monetary measures of the benefits associated with cultural heritage access, conservation, and improvements. But the suggestion that these methods produce "theoretically correct" measures of value should not be taken as an argument for their superiority over other evaluation tools. It is one thing to acknowledge that WTP has its theoretical basis in welfare economics (and in that sense is "theoretically correct"), but it is another thing to use that as an argument per se for applying it to cultural values. the rightness of an evaluation approach is to be judged neither from its disciplinary basis (economics) nor from its theoretical foundation (neoclassical welfare economics). Rather, it is to be judged on the basis that its value judgments are compatible to those society holds for cultural values, for which economic valuation is being undertaken.

Furthermore, nonmarket valuation remains controversial. As was discussed above, the techniques are subject to a number of potential flaws — on theoretical, methodological, and empirical grounds — that are all the more serious when studies are conducted without reference to accepted best-practice guidelines (Bateman et al. 2002; Arrow et al. 1993; Mitchell and Carson 1989). Of course, this in itself is hardly surprising, as no method is without problems; but failure to address and resolve these limitations may result in considerable misrepresentation of the impacts of important policies, projects, and regulations, as nonmarket valuation approaches are increasingly used by governments, international organizations, and other public and private bodies.[13]

Hence, as appealing as they may seem to economists, consumer sovereignty and economic valuation should not be the only driving engines as far as cultural policy-making assessment is concerned, and their relative validity should be assessed by comparison with the performance of competing instruments. And herein lies the main problem faced by decision makers and cultural managers interested in applying a scientific approach to assess the value of their policies: While economic valuation critics have been quick to find fault with the technique, they have been very slow to present better and viable alternatives to economic evaluation. Alternative noneconomic approaches at the moment are either incipient or nonexistent. Even if these alternative tools were readily identifiable, the question would still remain of how to interrogate them in a logical, credible, and workable way.

Despite the apparent lack of competing, analytically sound, noneconomic evaluation techniques, it is still worthwhile to try to outline the possible structure of an integrated approach to cultural valuation. Rather than a radical departure from current practice, a possibility is to use existing lines of inquiry from market research, psychology, and other social sciences within an economic valuation study, to complement and enhance its capabilities, using qualitative information to further our understanding of economic values in the context of cultural policy.

The following social science tools might play a useful rule in complementing economic techniques in a new integrated approach to assess cultural values.

Expert Judgment

With careful integration, expert judgments and public valuation may play useful complementary roles toward the assessment of cultural values. As noted previously, valuation practitioners know that the preparation of a well-structured survey needs to receive information from many sources (i.e., experts, people working at cultural institutions, museum managers, users, and nonusers) in order to take into account comprehensively all the relevant aspects of the problem at stake. Integrating expert views in preliminary phases is advisable in this context (see Mourato et al. 2001 for an example).

Taking this practice a step further, alternative approaches to nonmarket valuation, where elicitation of contingent values actually derives from small focus groups of stakeholders (rather than from the general public), have been proposed (Cookson 1998). Although the goal of eliciting people's WTP from well-informed and interested agents is acceptable and useful, to use this technique as the sole method to elicit values seems to be unrealistic and to suffer from many theoretical, statistical, and procedural distortions — namely, departing from a demand-led assessment. Valuation studies should not be influenced by experts' perspective only, which is to be considered among other important views. Hence, in our opinion, the use of experts' perspective only, which is to be considered among other important views. Hence, in our opinion, the use of experts and other key stakeholders has an important role to play, mostly in the design stages of the economic survey instrument and in the ex–post evaluation of results.

Social Assessment

Social assessment methods were developed by the World Bank in order to provide an integrated framework for incorporating participation and social analysis into development projects (World Bank 1994). They involve consultations with stakeholders and directly and indirectly affected groups. These methods offer great potential to complement an economic assessment of cultural policies, as issues such as gender, ethnicity, social impacts, and institutional capacity also need to be taken into account in cultural policy evaluation.

The complementary use of social assessment tools in parallel with an economic valuation methodology will help ensure that the change in the cultural good (e.g., a management change aimed at increasing access) is acceptable to the range of people intended to benefit from it, and that gender and other social differences are reflected in the policy evaluation. It is also essential to identify adverse social impacts of cultural projects and to determine how they can be mitigated (e.g., the local social impacts of increases in entry fees to cultural destinations). Impacts in disadvantaged groups (e.g., the poor, less educated groups, minority groups, and indigenous people) are particularly important to assess and overcome.

Experimental Psychology Tools

Stated-preference methods are designed to uncover values rather than motivations.

Thus, experimental psychologists have argued that there is a need to go deeper into understanding individual motivations for WTP than is common practice among valuation practitioners (Kahneman, Ritov, and Schkade 1999; Tversky and Kahneman 1982; Green and Tunstall 1999; Kahneman and Thaler 1991). In brief, the psychological approach claims that the set of assumptions defining the microeconomic neoclassical environment is too restrictive, too static, and not sufficiently focused on the process of preference formation and on underlying motivations. Several contributions have emerged from this line of psychological/ economic research, with some interesting, although generally ambiguous, results. The abstract idea of *homo economicus* certainly appears in need of being extended and developed, but it does not arise as flawed in its foundations.[14]

It seems that the entangled and complementary realms of individual motivations and economic values should be the joint targets of socioeconomic investigation. In other words, the joint use of economic and behavioral psychology tools is both needed and encouraged. For example, the model developed by Fishbein and Ajzen offers a way to infer behavior by a chain of connections, starting from beliefs and then going to attitudes and intentions and finally to behavior (Fishbein and Ajzen 1975). Along the chain, each step is determinant and explanatory for the following one. Stated-preference methods elicit WTP measures that are "intentions of behavior." Therefore, an interesting way of testing the validity of stated values is to examine closely the relationship between them and the beliefs and attitudes held by respondents toward the cultural good of interest and toward culture in general, via the inclusion of adequate measurement scales in the survey instrument. Since stated-preference studies typically elicit varying amounts of qualitative and nonmonetary information as well as monetary values (both in the focus group stages and in the final questionnaires), it would not be feasible to expand the qualitative component of these surveys. Another avenue already pursued by some authors is to check whether intended behavior, as expressed by WTP, is a satisfactory indicator of real behavior; this checking can be done in a laboratory setting (see Foster, Bateman, and Harley 1997 for a review).

Participatory Rural Appraisal

Participatory rural appraisal (PRA) is an approach for shared learning between local people and outsiders (Chambers 1992). The term is somewhat misleading, as PRA techniques are applicable in urban settings and can be employed to complement economic assessments. In the context of cultural heritage evaluation, these techniques can enable researchers and local people to work together in identifying, planning, and designing the best cultural policy package. There is a wide range of participatory data collection methods that can be used; these include semistructured interviews, focus groups, nonmonetary preference ranking exercises, participant observation, transect walks, mapping exercises, and other visual illustrations.

PRA techniques might constitute a valuable aid in furthering our understanding of people's motivations for cultural use and conservation and in providing insights into their behavior, particularly in what relates to uses of cultural heritage in developing contexts. For example, there may be values that a structured survey will not be able to uncover properly and that only careful observation and group exercises might identify. This might be the case in assessing values that local communities in developing countries hold toward their cultural heritage.

Marketing Research

Marketing studies are highly complementary to economic inquiries. Marketing practitioners have decades of experience in designing surveys, in administration, and in analysis, and these professional are constantly developing new methodological variants and survey interfaces (Malhotra 1999); economic valuation research could advance more rapidly by learning from this related discipline. For example, focus groups are still not used in many CV surveys' developmental stages, although they are standard practice in marketing research. Moreover, the CM framework described above derives from the marketing literature, which was subsequently extended to the economics realm. Marketing investigation and economic studies, although aimed at different goals, share many common objectives within a demand-led approach, and economics of scale can easily be exploited by joint research.

As we can see from the above discussion, there is a great potential for cultural experts (anthropologists, architects, art critics, etc.), psychologists, marketing researchers, and other social scientists to play an important role in the process of economic evaluation of cultural assets. Conversely, the analytic rigor and quantitative precision favored by economic valuation tools can be usefully borrowed by other disciplines.

For this potential to become a reality, economic valuation instruments must break with some misconceptions and be made available for routine use in the cultural field, for the different purposes envisaged in this paper. As Nuti observes, "The real test will come when and if CV will be introduced as a routine method of evaluation in public decisions.... The introduction of criteria and methods as a routine in the control of public expenditure [in Italy] will surely prove to be a lengthy and very frustrating accomplishment — this is not to say that it is not worth pursuing" (Nuti 1998, 96). It will also be necessary for other social scientists to be willing to collaborate with economists in joint research efforts to assess cultural values, and to bring with them to the research forum complementary social research tools as suggested above, both quantitative and qualitative in nature, where cross-fertilization with economics might be feasible and desirable. It would be important, for this aim, to develop investigation and policy using a framework of "tools and targets." After a clear definition of the set of economic and of noneconomic tools and of economic and noneconomic targets, it would be easier and more effective to implement sound strategies and sound multidisciplinary research on cultural issues.

Integrated approaches are what cultural policy needs. Although the development of such approaches has proved to be highly difficult in the past, the authors hope that this paper will contribute to the clarification of misconceptions, to the achievement of reconciliation, and to the mitigation of resistances to the use of economic tools.

Conclusions

This chapter has attempted to highlight what the role of microeconomic evaluation techniques in the cultural sector might be. Despite criticism, economic valuation methods remain among the few analytical instruments capable of producing valid and reliable empirical measures of the benefits of cultural heritage conservation. They are therefore an important tool for ascertaining efficient outcomes of allocating the limited resources available for cultural heritage. While economic valuation does not deny other valuation dimensions, it does have a specific and special role to play in cultural policy toward heritage conservation and development.

More generally, people's preferences should inform and influence the ranking of public priorities, and they should affect the direction of change in policy making in the cultural sector. If individuals would like the government to support the existence and conservation of cultural heritage, consumer sovereignty would be violated if the public authority did not pursue this aim. If people express a positive economic value for future generations, it would be odd if the government and cultural institutions neglected these, however elusive, nonuse values. Similarly, national and local governments should be cautious to invest in cultural infrastructures without having a clear indication of people's preference son public priorities and, specifically, on cultural priorities. In most cases, culture does not rank high in public priorities. Thus, a careful assessment of preferences is a worthwhile exercise for knowing where, at the margin, economic value is highest, across sectors and within the cultural sector. To deny these considerations to be a part of decision making would be to deny the fact that individuals hold strong opinions and values about cultural policy, mankind heritage, and future generations.

As with environmental resources, if the alternative to economic valuation is to put cultural heritage value equal or close to zero, the cultural sector would, as a result, be severely damaged. Ignoring economic preferences can lead to undervaluing and underpricing of cultural assets. This, directly and indirectly, reduces the amount of financial resources available to cultural institutions relative to other public priorities. It also gives an incentive for people to perceive cultural heritage assets as open-access resources without enforced property rights, and not as mixed-collective goods with an attached set of clearly defined values and stakeholders. Open access, if it emerges and affirms itself as the social norm, is disruptive for nonmarket assets.

The aim of the stated preference valuation methods discussed in the paper is not only to justify and influence decisions but also to provide information, as food for decision making in the cultural sector. Three levels of relevancy and use for estimates of economic values were seen to arise in the sector. The first level is concerned with economic-management issues at the level of cultural institutions, and the target is estimating demands schedules, pricing schedules, and price elasticities; prioritizing among projects; ranking potential investments; and evaluating impacts of pollution, tourism, development, and so on. The second level is related to financial aspects and involves analyzing pricing policies, designing incentive systems to encourage conservation, and justifying subsidies. The third level is more politically oriented, and the target is to estimate values for gathering information of strategic policy importance — i.e., allocation of budget to the cultural sector and cultural institutions, reflecting their relative value, and allocation of resources within the sector where the economic value is higher.

For the future, the task is to develop and establish a comprehensive multitool and multidisciplinary framework for the measurement of cultural values, as a response to the complex, multifaceted, and multivalue nature of cultural heritage. The authors have argued that economic instruments should be used as complementary means for socioeconomic analysis, together with a range of other tools from other disciplines. Measuring cultural benefits/values in this context should therefore be the output of a multidisciplinary teamwork that includes not only economists and conservation specialists but also other social scientists.

In what concerns the microeconomic realm, such a framework can be built on a set of economic tools that include revealed- and stated-preference techniques — in particular, CV and CM, which consistently rely on economic theory for estimating economic preferences. In what concerns other disciplines, it was suggested that some existing social research tools could be integrated and used in conjunction with economic valuation methods to provide a fuller assessment of complex cultural values that cannot be fully described and measured by any one discipline or method. This chapter identified a few, by no means exhaustive, complementary lines of inquiry, such as expert judgments, social assessments, psychological measure of attitudes and beliefs, laboratory experiments, participatory appraisal techniques, and marketing research methods. It is likely that many other relevant

measurement approaches exist in other disciplines that could be adapted for the purposes of assessing cultural values, within the proposed multidisciplinary framework.

Hence, by using the largest possible set of theoretically consistent and operational tools, cultural targets will be achieved in a more effective and efficient manner. To make this framework operational, the use and widespread understanding of evaluation technique targets is necessary to close gaps between economics and other social cultural disciplines. A definition in terms of tools and targets is more helpful insofar as it delimits the application environment of each discipline. Building on both economic instruments and other tools developed by social sciences dealing with culture, researches can establish a comprehensive framework of microlevel valuation.

It is hoped that an interdisciplinary discussion might advance and receive stimulus as a result of the ideas developed here.

Notes

1. See, for example, Kenkel, Fabian, and Tolley (1994) for health research examples, Maddison et al. (1996) for transport references, and Cook and Ludwig (2000) for an example of an application to crime reduction.

2. It is also important to note that the concepts of economic value and financial value are distinct, although there are linkages between the two. Financial value, such as the price of an antique manuscript sold in an auction, is part of economic value but does not exhaust it. In many cases, the financial value is not even the most important part of the total economic value of the cultural asset. As mentioned above, economic values embrace also the broader social value of an asset, including option values and a range of nonuse values.

3. Note that the concept of economic value is a reflection of people's preferences and therefore explicitly anthropocentric. An analysis of other types of values is beyond the scope of this paper.

4. In cases where a building or structure has no special cultural significance, the maintenance cost approach may be considered satisfactory, given the cost of conducting original valuation studies and the absence of any significant nonuse values.

5. Other methods used for measuring cultural values include the economic-impact-analysis literature. This analysis is limited to observable effects on indicators such as consumption, employment, income, and public revenue (Vaughan 1984; Greffe 1990; Martin 1994). Economic dimensions such as employment are clearly important; yet, by neglecting nonmarket benefits, potentially powerful additional arguments in favor of cultural heritage conservation are being ignored. Moreover, employment is not a primary goal of cultural policies. There are also some references to the use

of multicriteria analysis in the context of cultural goods, but there are no insights as how actually to estimate nonuse values (Fusco Girard 1990).

6. Detailed reviews of the various techniques can be found in Mitchell and Carson (1989); Freeman (1994); Pearce, Whittington, and Georgiou (1994); Bateman et al. (2002); Garrod and Willis (1999); Bateman and Willis (1999); Hanley, Mourato, and Wright (2001); Louviere, Hensher, and Swait (2000); and Bennett and Blamey (2001).

7. Other stated-preference methods, not addressed here, are political markets (referendum) and the use of laboratory experiments (in place of surveys).

8. Of related interest, Foster et al. (2001) provide a detailed analysis of the extent of free riding in charitable giving in the U.K. and of possible incentives to reduce this behavior.

9. As a comparison, Carson et al. (1995) produced a bibliography of published and unpublished environmental CV studies: Even as early as 1995, their list had over two thousand entries from more than forty countries.

10. A variant of this approach is sometimes known, within the marketing field, as conjoint analysis.

11. In order to reduce the cognitive burden to respondents and to provide more information on specific details of the valuation, some authors have proposed to integrate WTP elicitation within a multiattribute environment structured on a so-called multiattribute analysis (Satterfield, Slovic, and Gregory 2000; Gregory, Lichtenstein, and Slovic 1993). While the valuation tool proposed in this paper is different, it is also framed over a multiattribute environment.

12. The possibility of deriving an implicit ranking of attributes (Hanley, Wright, and Adamowicz 1998) is relevant, as it allows considerations on both monetary and nonmonetary measures of value. Economic appraisal can address choices where all of the costs and benefits can be measured in money terms, but it can also be used as a basis for making decisions and providing information support where elements of costs and benefits cannot be given money values (Creigh-Tyte, Dawe, and Stock 2000). CM is compatible with a broader range of appraisal techniques in which monetary assessments might be complemented by weighting and scoring analysis (multiattribute utility) to assess the importance of benefits that are not measured in monetary terms but that may be quantified. Weighting and scoring allow the construction, for each option, of an index of "suitability," which synthesizes the ratio of quantified benefits and costs. Using the implicit survey rankings as scores/weights reduces the subjectivity of these analyses.

13. Examples of official use of nonmarket valuation techniques in the U.K. government are increasingly frequent: The figures used to estimate the costs of morbidity in the context of transport accidents, air pollution, and violent crime are partly based on CV studies (e.g., Brand and Price 2000); a large-scale CV study was commissioned to assess the external damages caused by quarry activities, in order to inform the level of an aggregates tax (London Economics 1999); and a CV study of the heritage benefits associated with constructing an expensive tunnel for a road near Stonehenge was used as supporting evidence for the social and economic desirability of the project (Maddison and Mourato 2002).

14. See also McFadden (1999) on this core point.

CHAPTER 42

The Economic Impact of Cultural Attractions

Billy Kinsey, Jr.

It has become increasingly important for museums and cultural attractions to be able to demonstrate the many benefits that they provide to surrounding communities and to their region. By analyzing the economic contributions made by their facilities or exhibitions, these sites can gain new information with multiple uses, including the following:

1. to provide a more complete picture of a museum's role in the community
2. to justify the expense of special exhibitions
3. to support a museum's marketing of the full range of benefits it offers
4. to use as supporting evidence when seeking funding from the government or private donors

It is important to understand that an economic approach is not intended to replace the appreciation of the cultural and scholarly aspects of museums. On the contrary, economic insight of a museum and its exhibitions will complement the cultural benefits, giving a much clearer picture of a museum's overall significance.

Economic Contributions

Cultural attractions do not exist for economic reasons. Rather, these attractions are often seen as sources of sources of information about the past; they provide us with an appreciation of other cultures; and they are enjoyable places to spend our time, contemplating the creations of mankind or the beauty of nature. In discussing the importance of museums, the American Association of Museums has pointed out that the value of museums "is in direct proportion to the service they render the emotional and intellectual life of the people."[1] This is not a traditional measure of economic output by an organization. In fact, some administrators and key personnel at museums and other cultural sites are opposed to even considering an economic view of their organization; such individuals "act as though they are above the dirty business of commerce."[2]

Even though cultural attractions are not often thought of as economic entities — and though some individuals might prefer that they never be thought of that way — many of these sites do provide important economic benefits to the area in which the are located, including the following:

Originally published as *The Economic Impact of Museums and Cultural Attractions: Another Benefit to the Community*, 2002, by Virginia Commonwealth University, Richmond. Reprinted with permission of the publisher.

1. **consumers of local goods and services** — Even though some of the items on display at museums, shown in historic homes, or used in the production of plays may not be produced or purchased locally, some likely will be produced in the area. In addition, there are many other types of expenditures that are made in a cultural attraction's hometown. Office supplies, building maintenance and repairs, utilities expenses, furniture, landscaping, consulting services, insurance, and food are just a few of the items that must be purchased for day-to-day operations of sites.

2. an **attraction for tourists** — While in the local area to visit a cultural site, out-of-town tourists will spend money at local restaurants, hotels, stores, and the museum gift shop. The purchases made with local merchants, as well as sales tax revenues for the locality and state, can be significant.

3. **source of jobs** for local residents — Even small attractions require a staff of administrators, custodians, security personnel, and guides. Along with the direct benefit of providing jobs comes the additional advantage that much of the employee wages will be spent locally. Also, employees of the attractions who live in the local area will contribute sales and property taxes to their jurisdiction.

4. **incentive for new businesses or individuals to locate** in the area — While there is strong evidence that museums and other cultural institutions are rarely a determining factor in locational decisions, their presence can still be an important secondary factor.[3] These sites demonstrate a positive quality of life for a region.

Measuring the Economic Impact

In order to measure the impact of cultural attractions, formal economic impact studies are often conducted. These input-output models estimate the way in which money spent within the local area by the site and/or by its out-of-town visitors flows throughout the local economy. Money spent in the area will be received, and ultimately re-spent, by other businesses and individuals. The three components of a total economic impact to the region should be considered — these are the direct, indirect, and induced economic effects.

Direct effects — impacts that come from expenditures by the attraction or by its non-local visitor with businesses in the local area. These expenditures bring "new" money into the local economy that would not have been there otherwise.

Indirect effects — impacts that result from expenditures made by the businesses that received the initial money from visitors or the particular cultural attraction. In order to have sufficient inputs to accommodate the increased demand from the attractions and their visitors, these businesses must purchase more goods from other firms, thereby stimulating the economy.

Induced effects — impacts from changes in household expenditures. As companies receive more business because of the previously mentioned increased purchases, they must hire additional workers or pay existing employees to work longer hours. Employees will then spend more money in the local economy, as their incomes increase.

If an analysis considers the *spending by a cultural attraction*, the site must provide detailed financial information, listing the local purchases of goods and services that they have made for a particular time period. Spending made by the company outside of the local area does not contribute money to that region and should not be considered for the impact analysis.

Similarly, if the focus of the study is *spending by out-of-town visitors*, a survey must be conducted with these individuals, asking how much they spent in the local area on "tourism-related" expenditures such as food, lodging, entertainment, and shopping (both at the museum and elsewhere). Money spent outside of the local area (i.e., the study area) during a visitor's trip is not relevant for the economic impact analysis.

In order to convert spending to an overall economic impact, multipliers must be applied to the spending amounts. The multipliers indicate the total effect as the new money flows throughout the local economy. Multipliers can come from multiple sources, such as the following:

1. **tourism studies conducted elsewhere** — this is convenient and can provide a comparison to studies that have already been conducted; however, the multipliers may not apply for your particular region or for the type of attraction that you're studying
2. **published multiplier lists**, usually from the Federal Government — again, while convenient, these multipliers may not apply for your region or your site
3. **multipliers computed specifically for your site and your local area** — requires analysis using a formal input-output model, that traces the flow of money spent in various sectors as it flows throughout the local economy. A multiplier of 1.6 would mean that for every $100 spent by visitors to the museum (or by the museum, etc.), $160 of economic total impact will be generated for the region. This includes the original $100 spending; i.e., there is $60 of *additional* impact.

"Best Practices" for Impact Studies

1. **Work with the experts**. Economic impact studies can be difficult to conduct and to analyze. Work with individuals who really understand how this type of analysis should be conducted, to make sure that you're getting results that truly reflect your economic impact.

    Who are these experts? The experts can come from in-house staff who know about economic impact studies, private consultants, local or state tourism offices, university and college researchers.
2. Define the geographic **region of study**. The "local" area should be chosen based on the project's area of interest, keeping in mind that the defined region should include any localities that are economically linked to the area in which the museum is located. It is essential to clearly define the area of study before proceeding with the impact.
3. Design **a survey to collect expenditure data** from visitors to the facility or special exhibition
    A. Include questions to determine the following information:
        i. place of residence — local vs. nonlocal. The study is only interested in money spent by individuals who come from outside of the local area. Expenditures made by locals do not add any new money to the area's economy.
        ii. importance of the exhibition or the museum in the respondent's decision to visit area. In order to determine the money brought into the local economy because of the special exhibition or the facility, visitors must be asked whether they came to the local area primarily to see the exhibit or the museum, or if they had other reasons. Spending by visitors for whom another reason was key should *not* be included in the economic impact analysis; their spending is not directly do to the museum.
        iii. money spent locally on "tourism-related" expenditures. The expenditures should only include money spent within the local area, on categories such as food, lodging, entertainment, and shopping (both at the museum and elsewhere). Money spent elsewhere

during a visitor's trip is not relevant.

Questions about demographic characteristics of respondents may also be included in a visitor survey. While not directly relevant for the economic impact estimates, that information will allow for profiles of visitors or visitation behavior.

 B. Determine when the survey will be administered. The survey should represent all of the possible days and times that the museum or special exhibition is open.

 C. Determine a random selection process, so that all potential visitors will be adequately represented in the sample. Using a particular sampling frequency, such as every 10th person who leaves an exhibit area, will prevent bias in the way in which respondents are chosen.

4. Implement the survey on-site, using either in-person interviews or paper-and-pencil questionnaires for the respondent to complete.

5. Isolate the expenditures made by visitors who live outside of the local area and who came to the area *primarily* to the see the exhibition or the museum. These responses are the focus of the research.

6. Estimate the local expenditures made by respondents in the sample, considering only the non-locals who came specifically to see the exhibit.

7. Estimate the local expenditures made by all visitors to the exhibition or facility.

8. Compute or obtain multipliers for these expenditures, to estimate the level at which they are re-spent within the local economy. Pre-defined multipliers for tourism attractions can be applied to the estimate of total local expenditures, to come up with an estimate of the total economic impact. These types of multipliers are easy to use, yet they may not be applicable for all areas and all types of attractions. A second, more technical approach is to use an input-output model to establish multipliers and estimates

specific to this project. This type of model will allow for the estimation of the direct, indirect, and induced effects.

9. Estimated the overall economic impact using multipliers for spending in your region. Keep in mind that the impacts may not be large.

Recent Research

The Virginia Center for Urban Development, at the Virginia Commonwealth University Center for Public Policy, has conducted three economic impact studies for major exhibitions at the Virginia Museum of Fine Arts, in Richmond. These "blockbuster" shows were the *Fabergé in America* and *The Lillian Thomas Pratt Collection of Fabergé* exhibition (1996), *Splendors of Ancient Egypt* (1999), and *Monet, Renoir, and the Impressionist Landscape* (2000). This research analyzed the economic impact of these shows on the **"Richmond metropolitan area,"** comprised of the City of Richmond and the Counties of Chesterfield, Hanover, and Henrico. These jurisdictions have a sufficient economic linkage between them to serve as a useful local region.

These major exhibitions, combined, have brought an estimated $23.9 million to the Richmond metro area (in 2000 dollars). This figure includes the effects of spending within the area by visitors to the exhibitions, as well as the economic impact created when recipients of this money re-spend it within the local economy.

The table on the next page summarizes the samples for each exhibition and also presents the estimated visitor spending and resulting economic impact. All of the economic impact estimates were prepared by economists at the Virginia Center for Urban Development using the Implan Pro model.

Economic Impact Estimates for Three Major Exhibitions
Virginia Museum of Fine Arts — Richmond, Virginia

	Fabergé	*Egypt*	*Monet*
Dates	2½ months	6 months	3 months
Sample Size	1,472	944	1,405
Total Event Attendance	129,543	247,868	100,177
Response Rate	83%	85%	86%
Sampling Error	3%	4%	3%
Est. Total Spending	$4.6 million	$8.0 million	$2.1 million
Est. Total Impact	$9.0 million	$11.7 million	$3.2 million

NOTES

1. Edson, Gary and David Dean. *The Handbook for Museums.* Routledge. 1994. Page 3.

2. Wireman, Peggy. *Partnerships for Prosperity: Museums and Economic Development.* American Association of Museums. 1997. Page 13.

3. Cwi, David and Katharine Lyall. *Economic Impacts of Arts and Cultural Institutions: A Model for Assessment and a Case Study in Baltimore.* Research Division. National Endowment for the Arts. October 1977. Page 1.

CHAPTER 43

Cities, Culture, and the Future

Marcia Trotta and Roger L. Kemp

The case studies presented reveal that cities and towns throughout the country are planning or investing or both in themselves in a number of ways relating to restoring, supporting, and promoting cultural improvements and attractions. The goal is generally twofold: to improve the quality of life in our inner cities and their neighborhoods, and to attract private investment in our aging downtown areas and outlying neighborhoods. Many of these municipal planning and public investment projects go hand-in-hand with private investment. That is, a new downtown library or museum not only improves the quality of life for residents, it may help clean up undesirable areas, attract private investment, and stimulate local commercial activities. Many public improvements bring people back downtown and help jump-start the local economy because people have purchasing power and small businesses and commercial activity will follow. For these reasons, municipal planning efforts and subsequent public investment projects serve a number of different worthwhile economic development purposes. Cultural attractions and amenities create public space in areas where it is sorely needed.

The first step in any revitalization project, or neighborhood improvement program, is self-help. That is, public officials must invest first in their own city or town before seeking investment from the private sector. It also goes without saying that initial municipal planning projects, as well as investment programs, should be target to those improvements that create public space, restore neighborhoods, and bring citizens back to our downtowns and their neighborhoods. In addition to cultural attractions, roadways, walkways, streetscapes, and public transit systems should be in good condition to support the increased level of pedestrian and vehicular traffic that cultural attractions bring to a community. As economic development experts know, many public improvements bring long-term economic returns that far exceed the initial investment of public funds.

The Best Practices

The following information sets forth those planning efforts undertaken, and the type of investments made, by those communities represented in the "best practices" section of this volume. The communities examined in this volume represent all geographic areas of the United States, as well as a variety of types of governance. The municipalities included exhibit many types of planning efforts, and diverse cultural projects in which public funds were invested. The methods used range from investments in upfront planning projects, museums and libraries, to other avenues that facilitated the creation of positive public areas in our nation's downtowns as well as their neighborhoods. Traditionally, municipal government provided financial incentives to the private sector to attract development, people, and business. Nowadays, as demonstrated by this research, a public investment in the right cultural project alone will stimulate private sector investment to help restore our urban centers and neighborhoods.

The various boroughs, cities, communities, and towns examined are presented below using the criteria outlined above. A state, province, or country is listed after the name of each municipality for reference purposes.

- Austin, TX — Use of computer technology for improved public library services.
- Baltimore, MD — Use of public museums to create public space and stimulate economic development.
- Boston, MA — Use of public museums to create public space and stimulate economic development.
- Brooklyn, New York City, NY — Use of computer technology for improved public museum and library services.
- Charles, SC — Use of public branch library to facilitate development in downtown redevelopment area.
- Christchurch, NZ — Use of strategic planning, focusing on public museums and libraries, to stimulate economic development.
- Cincinnati, OH — Use of public museums for inner-city revitalization.
- Denver, CO — Use of public museum to stimulate downtown economic development.
- Des Moines, IA — Use of public libraries to create public space and facilitate development.
- Hartford, CT — Use of improved computer technology at public libraries to improve computer literacy among residents.
- Germantown, TN — Use of alternative funding sources to improve public library services.
- Indianapolis, IN — Use of public main and branch libraries for inner city and neighborhood revitalization.
- Kansas City, MO — Use of strategic planning, focusing on public cultural attractions, to create public space.
- Lanark, IL — Use of public rural libraries to promote community development.
- Little Rock, AR — Use of strategic planning, focusing on public museums and libraries, to promote urban renewal.
- Los Angeles, CA — Use of public branch libraries to revitalize neighborhoods.
- Memphis, TN — Use of public libraries to improve child literacy and school readiness.
- Minneapolis, MN — Use of public museum for inner-city revitalization.
- Miramar, FL — Use of public library, other public facilities, to create public space and facilitate development.
- Pekin, IL — Use of public libraries to enhance and facilitate economic development.
- Phoenix, AZ — Use of public museums, other public facilities, to create public space and to stabilize downtown area.
- Philadelphia, PA — Use of public museums to stimulate mixed-use development and inner city revitalization.
- Portland, OR — Use of public libraries to enhance and facilitate inner city renewal.
- Prince Rupert, BC — Use public libraries to promote "smart communities" and economic development.
- St. Louis, MO — Use of new economic models to determine the financial return of public libraries, as well as to justify public investment in them.
- St. Paul, MN — Use of public libraries, other public facilities, to stimulate mixed-use development and inner city revitalization.
- San Jose, CA — Use "green" public branch library to promote sustainability and reduce operating costs.

- San Jose, CA — Creation of joint public library to improve library services and reduce costs, both capitol and operating.
- Seattle, WA — Use of new public main library to stimulate economic development and inner city revitalization.
- Tacoma, WA — Use of public museums as economic development tool to stimulate private investment in its downtown.
- Tallahassee, FL — Use of new economic models to determine the financial return of public libraries, as well as to justify public investment in them.
- Toronto, ON — Use of public museums, other public cultural facilities, as an economic development tool to stimulate private investment in its downtown.
- Valencia, CA — Use of public museums and libraries to create public space and a sense of community, attracting people back downtown to improve the local economy.
- Wakefield, MA — Use of public libraries as an economic development tool for neighborhood revitalization.

In order to make sense out of the best practices examined in this volume they have been broken down into eight categories for analytical purposes. Further, the number of communities using each best practice is set forth to show the most popular best practices being used today. These groupings include the use of strategic planning practices; the types of investments made in multiple cultural facilities, public museums, main public libraries, and branch public libraries; the development and use of new economic models; improved library services; and the promotion of "smart communities" and "economic development" by public libraries. New economic models include formulas and calculations involved in estimating the financial return of public libraries. Improved library and museum services include the use of new technologies, child literacy, computer literacy, school readiness, and the utilization of alternative funding sources. These eight categories of best prac-

tices, along with those communities using each practice, are set forth below.

- **Use of Strategic Planning Practices —**
  Christchurch, NZ
  Kansas City, MO
  Little Rock, AR
- **Development of New Economic Models —**
  St. Louis, MO
  Tallahassee, FL
- **Investment in Multiple Cultural Facilities —**
  Phoenix, AZ
  Miramar, FL
  St. Paul, MN
  Toronto, ON
  Valencia, CA
- **Investment in Public Museums —**
  Baltimore, MD
  Boston, MA
  Cincinnati, OH
  Denver, CO
  Minneapolis, MN
  Philadelphia, PA
  Tacoma, WA
- **Investment in Public Main Libraries —**
  Des Moines, IA
  Indianapolis, IN
  Pekin, IL
  Portland, OR
  Seattle, WA
  Wakefield, MA
- **Investment in Public Branch Libraries —**
  Charleston, SC
  Indianapolis, IN
  Los Angeles, CA
- **Improved Library and/or Museum Services —**
  Austin, TX
  Brooklyn, NY
  Hartford, CT
  Germantown, TN
  Memphis, TN
  San Jose, CA
- **Promotion of "Smart Communities" and/or "Economic Development"—**

Prince Rupert, BC
San Jose, CA
Lanark, IL

The popularity of these municipal best practice groupings reveals a lot about state of the art initiatives and projects being undertaken by our cities and towns to revitalize our nation's urban center and neighborhoods. These best practice groupings are listed below in hierarchical order, starting with the most popular best practices.

- Investment in Public Museums — Usage: 7
- Investment in Public Main Libraries — Usage: 6
- Improved Library and/or Museum Services — Usage: 6
- Investment in Multiple Cultural Facilities — Usage: 5
- Use of Strategic Planning Practices — Usage: 3
- Investment in Public Branch Libraries — Usage: 3
- Promotion of "Smart Communities" and/or "Economic Development"— Usage: 3
- Development of New Economic Models — Usage: 2

This information reveals that most communities have undertaken investments in public museums to restore their inner city and neighborhood areas. The second most popular category best practices is the investment in public main libraries. The third category involves the investment of public funds to improve municipal library and/or museum services to the public. The fourth category, and the broadest from a public investment standpoint, encompasses the investment of public funds for multiple cultural facilities, such as museums, libraries, art galleries, theaters, concert halls, and similar cultural facilities. Other communities, as reflected in the fifth category, are using modern strategic planning practices, frequently involving inner city and neighborhood stakeholders, to plan for replacement and additional cultural facilities for their re-

spective municipalities. The six most popular practice category involves the investment of funds in public branch libraries, which typically involves neighborhood revitalization. Still other communities, in best practice category seven, are using museums and libraries to promote smart communities and/or economic development. The last best practice category, eight, embraces the development of new economic models to show the financial return of museums and libraries to a community. All of these best practices illustrate that a public investment in cultural amenities has a payoff far greater financial return than the initial investment of tax dollars. In all cases, the economic development benefits far outweigh the initial outlay of public funds for these cultural investments.

Many of the types of public investments being made in a community's cultural amenities depends upon the age of a particular municipality. For older communities, many aging cultural facilities are being replaced, expanded, or modernized. For newer communities, new cultural facilities are being planned knowing the public return from an economic development perspective. In short, the case studies contained in this volume have proven that a public investment in a city or town's cultural attractions is money well spent. A sense of place needs to be created in many of our nation's inner cities and neighborhoods. This is especially true in our suburban areas where urban sprawl has taken place over the past several decades without regard to a sense of public space, or the cultural needs of a community.

As mentioned in the beginning of this volume, the thirty-three communities examined in these case studies represent 22 states in the United States, 2 territories in Canada, and one city in New Zealand. In general, these case studies represent all major geographical areas of our nation. Also, the communities selected for inclusion in these case studies represent various population sizes, different forms and types of municipal government, diverse personal and family income levels, and a variety of different political persuasions. The inclusion of a *Regional Resource Directory* in the appendix of this volume will enable readers to contact any municipality included in the best practices section for additional information about the various cultural initiatives and projects examined in respective communities. The inclusion of the *National Resource Directory* will enable readers to check with other leading national professional membership associations and research organizations for additional information in this rapidly evolving field. Lastly, and possibly most importantly, a bibliography in this field, as well as a listing of acronyms and definitions for cultural organizations, and a cultural policy timeline for our nation, will serve as valuable resources for those readers wishing to pursue additional information about *cities and culture*.

The Future

Lastly, relative to the future of our cities and culture, the editors would like to point out that libraries and museums have been linked together since ancient times. In Egypt, Ptolemy I built the Musaion (from which our modern museum is derived), a temple to the Muses. It was placed where "learned men" would congregate and share their knowledge. His son, Ptolemy II, built the first library dur-

ing his reign in the 3rd century Before the Common Era (b.c.e.) This library became the symbol of knowledge in the ancient world and, along with the museum, drew scholars from all over the world. This first research center at Alexandria accomplished what we have observed current practice attempting — attracting and bringing people into our urban areas.

People will return to city centers if accessibility to cultural amenities and services is made convenient. Museums and libraries are two of the classic cultural institutions that strengthen not only the social, but also the economic stability of a geographic area. Museums and libraries have always had the means to bring people together to create a social life of a community, which is sorely lacking in many modern and suburban communities throughout the world. Satellite development will follow such cultural amenities, including, but certainly not limited to, cafes, restaurants, bookstores, boutiques, and other small shops that encourage people to spend more time, as well as more money, in our urban centers as well as their neighborhoods. Our public officials, and the citizens they represent, including their economic development experts, do not need to "reinvent the wheel" since it was invested three centuries Before the Common Era, or about 23 centuries ago, in a land not far away as the modern jet flies.

Appendices

Containing I. Library Acronyms; II. Museum Acronyms; III. Regional Resource Directory; IV. National Resource Directory; V. Cultural Websites; VI. Facts About Libraries and Museums; VII. Cultural Policy Milestones of the U.S. Federal Government; VIII. State Library Agencies Directory; IX. State Municipal League Directory; X. Council of Regional Museum Associations Directory; XI. Regional Museum Associations Directory; XII. National Museum Directory; XIII. National Art Museum Directory

I. Library Acronyms

Source: American Library Association (ALA), 40 East Huron Street, Chicago, IL 60611

AASL American Association of School Libraries
    A division of ALA serving school library media specialists.
AASLH American Association for State and Local History
ACRL Association of College & Research Libraries
    A division of ALA for academic and research libraries, including large public libraries.
ADA Americans with Disabilities Act
    Federal legislation to protect the rights of citizens with disabilities.
AECT Association for Educational Communications and Technology
    Provides leadership in educational communications and technology by linking professionals holding a common interest in the use of educational technology and its application to the learning process.
ALA American Library Association
    The oldest and largest organization of librarians and libraries in the country, with over 30,000 members. ALA provides leadership for the development, promotion, and improvement of library and information services and the profession of librarianship in order to enhance learning and ensure access to information for all.
ALCTS Association for Library Collections & Technical Services
    A division of ALA.
ALSC Association for Library Service to Children
    A division of ALA.
ALTA Association of Library Trustees and Advocates
    A division of ALA.
ANSI American National Standards Institute
    A private, non-profit organization that administers and coordinates the U.S. voluntary standardization and conformity assessment system.
ANSI/NISO Z39.50
    A protocol that defines a standard method for two computers to communicate for the purpose of information retrieval.
ASCII American Standard Code for Information Interchange
    A standard format for computer language.
ASCLA Association of Specialized and Cooperative Library Agencies
    A division of ALA.
ASIST American Society for Information Science & Technology
    Professional organization for those con-

241

cerned with the design, management and use of information systems and technology.

CE Continuing Education
Advanced training in a profession (not leading to a degree) to learn new skills or keep abreast of developments in the field.

CEU Continuing Education Unit
One CEU is equal to one hour of instruction or contact time. CEUs are required for public school educators, including Library Media Specialists.

CIP Cataloging in Publication
Cataloging information located on the verso of the title page of a book (or other type of material). Provides call number, main entry, subject headings, etc.

CLEC Continuing Library Education Certificate
Awarded for completion of approved continuing education session or workshop.

CLENE Continuing Library Education Networking Exchange
An ALA roundtable.

CNI Coalition for Networked Information
"An organization dedicated to supporting the transformative promise of networked information technology for the advancement of scholarly communication and the enrichment of intellectual productivity."

CORC Cooperative Online Resource Catalog
OCLC product replaced by Cataloging Connexion, an integrated cataloging service.

COSLINE Council of State Library Agencies in the Northeast

DBMS Database Management System

DDC Dewey Decimal Classification
Classification system used by almost all public libraries.

DSL Digital Subscriber Line
A high-speed telecommunications line.

ERP Effective Reference Performance
Advanced training in conducting reference interviews to increase the level of patron satisfaction. Workshop series funded by the State Library.

ESEA Elementary and Secondary Education Act
The Federal act which provides funds for educational purposes, including school library materials.

FAQ Frequently Asked Questions
Many computer sites and discussion lists have FAQs to provide answers to common questions.

FOL Friends of the Library

FOLUSA Friends of Libraries USA
The national organizations for Friends' groups, affiliated with ALA.

FTP File Transfer Protocol (Internet)
A protocol that defines how one computer transfers files to another computer.

GAC Group Access Capability
Allows access to OCLC for interlibrary loan with libraries in New England, New York, New Jersey, Pennsylvania, Delaware, and parts of West Virginia.

GODORT Government Documents Roundtable
An American Library Association Roundtable

GPO Government Printing Office
Prints and sells books, reports and materials produced by government agencies; also makes material available electronically.

GUI Graphical User Interface
Allows computer users to "point and click" with a mouse to navigate on a PC.

HTML Hypertext Mark-up Language
Programming code applied to text and graphics to create a hyperlinked WWW document.

HTTP Hypertext transfer protocol
The portion of a WWW address that signifies that a document was created in HTML.

IFLA International Federation of Library Associations and Institutions
"The leading international body representing the interests of library and information services and their users."

ILL Interlibrary Loan
The process by which a library requests material from, or supplies material to, another library upon the request of a library user.

ILS Integrated Library System

IMLS Institute of Museum and Library Services

Federal grant-making agency that promotes leadership, innovation, and a lifetime of learning by supporting the nation's museums and libraries. It administers LSTA funds.

IP   Internet Protocol

IP Address   A computer's unique numeric Internet address.

IPIG   ILL Protocol Implementers Group
"Formed ... to facilitate use of the international ILL standard (ISO 10160 & 10161) by U.S. vendors and service providers."

ISBN   International Standard Book Number
A unique number assigned to every book published in this country, and many in other countries; recognized internationally. An ISBN has nine or ten digits; the first digit denotes country of publication, the next several the publisher, the remainder identify the item.

ISDN   Integrated Services Digital Network
High-speed digital telecommunications lines that can transmit both voice and data.

ISO   International Organization for Standardization
"A network of national standards institutes from 147 countries working in partnership with international organizations, governments, industry, business and consumer representatives."

ISP   Internet Service Provider

ISSN   International Standard Serial Number
A unique eight-digit number, in two groups of four, assigned to a periodical by the International Serials Data System.

LAMA   Library Administration and Management Association
A division of the American Library Association

LAN   Local Area Network
A network of computers within an institution.

LC   Library of Congress
1. The Library of the U.S. Congress, which also services as our National Library.   2. The classification system used by most larger libraries.

LCCN   Library of Congress Card Number
The number assigned to an item by the Library of Congress, which is also a depository library. Used to order catalog cards from LC and to search the OCLC database.

LITA   Library and Information Technology Association
A division of the American Library Association

LSTA   Library Services and Technology Act
Federal funding for libraries in several areas — technology, interlibrary cooperation, literacy, etc. — and for state library agencies. Replaces LSCA (Library Services and Construction Act).

LT   Library Technician

LTA   Library Technical Assistant

MARC   MAchine Readable Cataloging
MARC records contain data in standardized format and allow conversion to automated cataloging and circulation systems.

MEDLINE   The online database of the National Library of Medicine. Available online and on CD-ROM from several vendors.

MLS   Master's Degree in Library Science
ALA accredits MLS programs in the U.S.

NCIP   NISO Circulation Interchange Protocol
A standard that defines the various transactions needed to support circulation activities among independent library systems.

NCLIS   National Commission on Libraries and Information Service
A federal advisory group composed of representatives from various library groups and distinguished librarians.

NISO   National Information Standards Organization

NLM   National Library of Medicine

NNLM   National Network of Libraries of Medicine

NREN   National Research and Education Network

NUC   National Union Catalog
A national bibliography published by the Library of Congress

OCLC   Online Computer Library Center
A bibliographic utility based in Ohio which provides online cataloging, interlibrary loan, serials control and other services to libraries worldwide.

OPAC   Online Public Access Catalog

A computer workstation for use by the public which is connected to a library's circulation system; can be searched by author, title, etc., and shows an item's status (on-shelf, overdue, etc.).

PAC   Public Access Catalog
May be used interchangeably with the term OPAC. May also mean a catalog of library holdings which is not online.

PC   Personal Computer

PLA   Public Library Association
A division of the American Library Association

PPP   Point to Point Protocol
Enables a computer to connect to the Internet with a modem and a telephone line; allows a user to use a browser such as Netscape or Internet Explorer.

RASD   Reference and Adult Services Division
A division of the American Library Association.

RFC   Request for Comment

RFI   Request for Information

RFP   Request for Proposal

RLIN   Research Libraries Information Network

RUSA   Reference and User Services Association
A division of the American Library Association

SLA   Special Libraries Association
A national association of librarians who work in special libraries. There are two chapters in Connecticut: Fairfield County and Connecticut Valley. Sponsors meetings, workshops, and an annual conference.

SLIP   Serial Line Internet Protocol
Enables a computer to connect to the Internet with a modem and a telephone line; allows a user to use a browser such as Netscape or Internet Explorer.

SUDOC   Superintendent of Documents
SUDOC numbers are assigned by the Government Printing Office to documents and are used to order items from the GPO.

T-1
A digital telephone line connection that can handle 24 voice or data channels; usually used to link computer networks to the Internet.

TCP/IP   Transmission Control Protocol/Internet Protocol

Allows different types of computers to communicate with each other; uses packet-switching to move data among computer networks.

TELNET
A "terminal emulation" protocol or application program that allows users to log in to another computer on the Internet.

URL   Uniform Resource Locator
The address of a WWW site. CLC's URL is *http://www.ctlibrarians.org.*

USF   Universal Service Fund
Provides for discounts of 20–90 percent on a variety of telecommunications services and equipment for schools and libraries.

WAN   Wide Area Network
Electronically links computers at remote locations and allows them to exchange data.

WebPAC
A public access catalog that is Web-accessible.

WWW   World Wide Web

YA   Young Adult
Common term for library users between the ages of 12 and 18.

YALSA   Young Adult Library Services Association
A division of the American Library Association.

II. Museum Acronyms

Source: American Association of Museums (AAM), 1575 Eye Street, NW, Suite 400, Washington, DC 20005

AAA   American Arts Alliance

AAAM   Association of African American Museums

AABGA   American Association of Botanical Gardens and Arboreta

AAM   American Association of Museums

AAMD   Association of Art Museum Directors

AAMV   American Association for Museum Volunteers

AASLH   American Association for State and Local History

ACA   American Council on the Arts

ACUMO   Association of College and University Museum and Galleries

AFA   American Federal of Arts

AIC   American Institute of Conservation

ALHFAM   Association for Living Historical Farms and Agricultural Museums

ALI–ABA   American Law Institute–American Bar Association

ARM   Association of Railway Museums, Inc.

ASC   Association of Systematics Collections

ASMD   Association of Science Museum Directors

ASMHF   Association of Sports Museums and Halls of Fame

ASTC   Association of Science-Technology Centers

AWG   Arts Working Group

AYM   Association of Youth Museums

AZA   Zoo and Aquarium Association

CAA   College Art Association

CAI   Congress of the American Indian

CAJM   Council of American Jewish Museums

CAMM   Council of American Maritime Museums

CARE   Comminee on Audience Research and Evaluation

CMA   Canadian Museum Association

Council for Museum Anthropology

COMPT   Committee on Museum Professional Training

DAM   Development and Membership Committee

FSHC   Federation of State Humanities Councils

HNSA   Historical Naval Ships Association

IAMFA   International Association of Museum Facility Administrators

ICOM   International Council of Museums

IMLS   Institute for Museum & Library Services

IMTAL   International Museum Theater Alliance

IPAM   International Partnerships Among Museums

MAAM   Mid-Atlantic Association of Museums

MAP   Museum Assessment Program

MASC   Museum Association Security Comminee

MAST   Museum Association of States and Territories

MAT   Museum Advocacy Team

MCN   Museum Computer Network

MMC   Midwest Museum Conference or Museum Management Committee

MPMA   Mountain-Plains Museum Association

MSA   Museum Store Association

MTA   Museum Trustee Association

NAGPRA   Native American Graves Protection and Repatriation Act

NALAA   National Association of Local Arts Agencies

NAME   National Association of Museum Exhibition

NARF   Native American Rights Fund

NASAA   National Association of State

NCA   National Cultural Alliance

NEA   National Endowment for the Arts

NEH   National Endowment for the Humanities

NEMA   New England Museum Association

NHA   National Humanities Alliance

NM   National Association of Interpretation

NPS   National Park Service

NSF   National Science Foundation

NSFY   National Science for Youth Foundation

NTHP   National Trust for Historic Preservation

OMD   Official Museum Directory

PIC   Professional Interest Committee Council

- Alliance for Lesbian and Gay Concerns Professional Interest Committee
- Asian Pacific American Professional Interest Committee
- Commercial Member Professional Interest Council
- Historic House Museums Professional Interest Council
- Latino Network Professional Interest Committee
- Museum Theatre Professional Interest Council
- Museum Travel & Tourism Council Professional Interest Committee
- Native American and Museum Collaboration Network
- Packing and Crating Information Network Professional Interest Committee
- Professional Interest Committee on Traveling Exhibitions
- Visitor Services Professional Interest Committee

SAA   Society of American Archivists

SEMC   Southeastern Museums Conference

SPC   Standing Professional Committee

- Committee on Audience Research and Evaluation
- Committee on Museum Professional Training
- Curators' Committee
- Development and Membership Committee
- Education Committee
- Media and Technology Committee
- Museum Association Security Committee
- Museum Management Committee
- National Association of Museum Exhibition
- Public Relations Committee
- Registrars' Committee
- Small Museum Administrators' Committee

TIS   Technical Information Service
USIA   United States Information Agency
WMA   Western Museums Association

III. Regional Resource Directory

Local government organizations, including those boroughs, cities, communities, and towns included in the "best practices" section of this volume, are listed below in alphabetical order.

Austin
(See City of Austin)
Baltimore
(See City of Baltimore)
Boston
(See City of Boston)
Brooklyn
(See Borough of Brooklyn)
Borough of Brooklyn
http://www.brooklyn-usa.org/
Charleston
(See City of Charleston)
Christchurch
(See City of Christchurch)
Cincinnati
(See City of Cincinnati)
City of Austin
http://www.ci.austin.tx.us/
City of Baltimore
http://www.ci.baltimore.md.us/
City of Boston
http://www.cityofboston.gov/
City of Charleston
http://www.charlestoncity.info/

City of Christchurch
http://www.christchurch.org.nz/
City of Cincinnati
http://www.cincinnati-oh.gov/
City of Denver
http://www.denvergov.org/
City of Des Moines
http://www.ci.des-moines.ia.us/
City of Hartford
http://www.hartford.gov/
City of Germantown
http://www.ci.germantown.tn.us/
City of Indianapolis
http://www.indygov.org/
City of Kansas City
http://www.kcmo.org/
City of Lanark
http://www.lanarkil.com/
City of Little Rock
http://www.littlerock.org/
City of Los Angeles
http://www.ci.la.ca.us/
City of Memphis
http://www.cityofmemphis.org/
City of Minneapolis
http://www.ci.minneapolis.mn.us/
City of Miramar
http://www.ci.miramar.fl.us/
City of Pekin
http://www.ci.pekin.il.us/
City of Philadelphia
http://www.phila.gov/
City of Phoenix
http://www.ci.phoenix.az.us/
City of Portland
http://www.portlandonline.com/
City of Prince Rupert
http://www.princerupert.ca/
City of St. Louis
http://stlouis.missouri.org/
City of St. Paul
http://www.stpaul.gov/
City of San Jose
http://www.sanjoseca.gov/
City of Santa Clarita
http://www.santa-clarita.com/
City of Seattle
http://www.seattle.gov/
City of Tacoma
http://www.cityoftacoma.org/
City of Tallahassee
http://www.talgov.com/

City of Toronto
http://www.toronto.ca/
Denver
(See City of Denver)
Des Moines
(See City of Des Moines)
Hartford
(See City of Hartford)
Germantown
(See City of Germantown)
Indianapolis
(See City of Indianapolis)
Kansas City
(See City of Kansas City)
Lanark
(See city of Lanark)
Little Rock
(See City of Little Rock)
Los Angeles
(See City of Los Angeles)
Memphis
(See City of Memphis)
Minneapolis
(See City of Minneapolis)
Philadelphia
(See City of Philadelphia)
Phoenix
(See city of Phoenix)
Portland
(See City of Portland)
Pekin
(See City of Pekin)
Prince Rupert
(See City of Prince Rupert)
Miramar
(See City of Miramar)
St. Louis
(See City of St. Louis)
St. Paul
(See City of St. Paul)
San Jose
(See City of San Jose)
Seattle
(See City of Seattle)
Tacoma
(See City of Tacoma)
Tallahassee
(See City of Tallahassee)
Toronto
(See City of Toronto)
Town of Wakefield
http://www.wakefield.ma.us/

Valencia
(See City of Santa Clarita)
Wakefield
(See Town of Wakefield)

IV. National Resource Directory

Major national professional and research organizations serving public officials, as well as concerned professionals and citizens, are listed below in alphabetical order. Many of these organizations focus on various issues related to cities and culture, and all major programs relating to this topic.

American Association for State and Local History
www.aaslh.org/
American Association of Museums
www.aam-us.org/
American Association of School Libraries
www.ala.aaslhome.org/
American Federation of Arts
www.afaweb.org/
American Institute for Conservation
www.ai.stanford.edu/
American Library Association
www.ala.org/
American Economic Development Council
http://www.aedc.org/
American Planning Association
http://www.planning.org/
American Real Estate and Urban Economics Association
http://www.areuea.org/
Art Libraries Society of America
www.arlisna.org/
Arts and Business Council
http://www.artsandbusiness.org/
Business Committee for the Arts
www.bcainc.org/
Center for Arts and Culture
http://www.culturalpolicy.org/
Committee for Economic Development
http://www.ced.org/
Community Development Society International
http://www.comm-dev.org/
Council on Library and Information Resources
www.clir.org/
Creative Economy Council
www.creativeeconomy.org/

Downtown Development and Research Center
http://www.DowntownDevelopment.com/
Economic Development Administration
www.eda.gov/
Economic Development Directory
www.ecodevdirectory.com/
Economic Research Associates
www.econres.com/
Institute of Museum and Library Services
www.imls.org/
International City/County Management Association
http://www.icma.org/
International Council of Museums
www.icoun.museum.org/
International Downtown Association
http://www.ida-downtown.org/
International Economic Development Council
www.iedconline.org/
International Federation of Library Associations and Institutions
www.ifla.org/
Libraries of the Future
www.lff.org/
Local Government Commission
http://www.lgc.org
National Association of Counties
http://www.naco.org/
National Association of Development Organizations
http://www.nado.org/
National Center for the Revitalization of Central Cities
http://www.uno.edu/-cupa/ncrcc/
National Civic League
http://www.ncl.org/
National Community Development Association
http://www.ncdaonline.org/
National Commission on Libraries and Information Sciences
www.nclis.gov/
National Council for Urban Economic Development
http://www.cued.org/
National Endowment for the Arts
http://www.arts.gov/
National Endowment for the Humanities
http://www.neh.gov/
National Humanities Alliance
http://www.nhalliance.org/

National League of Cities
http://www.nlc.org/
National Main Street Center
http://www.mainst.org/
Public Library Association
www.ala.org/PLA/
Small Museum Association
www.smallmuseum.org/
United States Conference of Mayors
http://www.usmayors.org/
United States Department of Commerce
www.commerce.gov/
United States Department of Education — National Center for Educational Statistics
www.nces.ed.gov/
Urban Institute
www.urban.org/
Urban Land Institute
http://www.uli.org/
Urban Libraries Council
www.urbanlibraties.org/
Volunteer Committees of Art Museums
www.vcam.org/

5. Cultural Websites

Alliance for the Arts
http://www.allianceforarts.org/
American Arts Alliance
http://www.americanartsalliance.org/
American Association of Museums
http://www.aam-us.org/
American Association of School Libraries
http://www.aaslhome.org/
American Federation for the Arts
http://www.afaweb.org/
American Library Association
http://www.ala.org/
Americans for the Arts
http://www.artsusa.org/
Art Libraries Society of America
http://www.arlisna.org/
Association of Science-Technology Centers
http://www.astc.org/
Center for Arts and Culture
http://www.culturalpolicy.org/
Council on Library and Information Resources
http://www.clir.org/
Creative Economy Council
http://www.creativeeconomy.org
International Council of Museums
http://www.icoun.museum.org

International Federation of Library Associations and Institutions
http:/www.ifla.org/

Institute of Museum and Library Services
http://www.imls.gov/

Libraries of the Future
http://www.lff.org/

MuseumLinks Museum of Museums
http://www.museumlink.com/

National Commission on Libraries and Information Sciences
http://www.nclis.org/

National Endowment for the Arts
http://www.arts.gov/

National Endowment for the Humanities
http://www.neh.gov/

National Humanities Alliance
http://www.nhalliance.org/

Public Library Association
http://www.ala.org/PLA/

Small Museum Association
http://www.smallmuseum.org/

Urban Libraries Council
http://www.urbanlibraries.org/

Volunteer Committees of Arts Museums
http://www.vcam.org/

NOTES

1. The field of "cities and culture," and the topics covered in this volume, are relatively knew to the field of literature pertaining to libraries, museums, and other cultural amenities and attractions, and how they are being used for economic development and redevelopment purposes. Many of the publications, including the latest articles and publications in this field, are available from those institutions show above.

2. Other, more general institutions, are shown in the *National Resource Directory*.

VI. Facts About Libraries and Museums

Libraries

The following information has been compiled from a variety of sources about libraries. These sources include the American Library Association; the National Center for Educational Statistics, Institute of Educational Sciences, U. S. Department of Education; and the Institute of Museum and Library Services. The information available from these websites revealed the following information concerning libraries:

- There are over 16,500 public libraries, including both main and branch libraries
- Nearly two-thirds of all American's have active library cards.
- Almost one-half of all citizens use libraries for educational purposes.
- Almost one-half of all citizens use libraries for entertainment purposes.
- Nine out of ten Americans believe that libraries are dynamic places, and that they are an important part of the life of a community.
- Eight out of ten citizens believe that libraries have contributed to the success of their business.
- Four out of ten citizens believe that libraries help attract businesses to their community.
- Nearly one-half of all Americans believe that the presence of libraries help increase property values.

Libraries have also been credited with helping start businesses, assisting people in finding employment, and helping workers to be more productive on their jobs. In fact, a survey in one state revealed that the total direct and indirect financial return for every dollar invested in public libraries returned nearly four and one-half dollars, or almost 350 percent.

For additional information about libraries, please consult the websites of the following organizations:

- American Library Association (http://www.ala.org/)
- National Center for Educational Statistics, Institute of Educational Sciences, U. S. Department of Education (http://nces.edu.gov/)
- Institute of Museum and Library Services (http://www.imls.gov)

Museums

The following information has been compiled from a variety of sources about museums. These sources include the American Association of Museums; the Institute of Museum and Library Services; and MuseumLinks Museum of Museums. The information available from these websites revealed the following information concerning museums:

- There are over 17,000 museums in cities and towns throughout the country.
- American museums average approximately 865 million visits each year.
- The average cost of a museum admission is $6.
- The average cost to operate a museum is $23.35 per visitor.
- Nonprofit arts and cultural organizations generate over $134 billion annually in economic activity.
- According to the American Association of Museums, the median annual attendance for different types of museums is as follows:
  - ➤Arboretums/Botanical Gardens — 119,575
  - ➤Art Museums — 61,312
  - ➤Children's/Youth Museums — 85,088
  - ➤General Museums — 49,983
  - ➤Historic Houses/Sites —16,000
  - ➤History Museums —15,000
  - ➤Natural History/Anthropology Museums — 64,768
  - ➤Nature Centers — 40,500
  - ➤Science/Technology Museums — 183,417
  - ➤Specialty Museums — 32,000
  - ➤Zoos — 520,935

Museums are also consumers of local goods and services. They become attractions for tourists, a source of jobs for people in the community, and an incentive for new business and individuals to locate to those areas where museums are located. From a revenue standpoint, private charitable donations are the largest source of operating income for museums, generating about 35 percent of their total annual revenues. Government funding provides about 25 percent of a museum's annual income. Investment income generated by museums amounts to about 10 percent of their annual income.

For additional information about museums, please consult the websites of the following organizations:

- American Association of Museums (http://www.aam-us.org/)
- Institute of Museum and Library Services (http://www.imls.gov/)
- MuseumLinks Museum of Museums (http://www.museumlink.com/)

VII. Cultural Policy Milestones of the U.S. Federal Government

Source: Canadian Cultural Observatory, 15 Eddy Street, 8th Floor, Gatineau, Quebec KIA OM5, Canada

1780s   1787 — Adoption of the *Constitution of the United States*

1790s   **Access & Equity**

1790 — *Copyright Act of 1790* (major revisions in 1831, 1870, 1909, 1976, 1998/ *Bono Copyright Act*)

Communities and Citizenship

1795 — *First Naturalization Act* establishes the "two-step, five-year" general rule

1798 — *Alien and Sedition Acts* permits deportation, by order of the President, of aliens judged to be dangerous or engaged in treasonous acts

Investment

1791 — *Pierre L'Enfant is commissioned* to provide urban designs for the new capitol city of Washington, D.C.

1798 — Establishment of the *Marine Corps Band* becomes the *first federal support of an artistic discipline*

Law

1791 — *Bill of Rights*, in particular the First and Tenth Amendments

1800s   **Investment**

1800 — *Library of Congress* is established

1804 — *Lewis and Clark Expedition*, first federally funded exploration to collect natural scientific and cultural data

1814 — British forces burn down the Capitol Building which houses the Library of Congress as part of the *burning of Washington* during the War of 1812. The Library is reestablished the following year when the federal government purchases the personal library of Thomas Jefferson.

1817 — First *federal visual arts support* is given with the commission of four *Revolutionary War scenes* by *John Trumbull* for the Capitol Rotunda

1820s **Investment**

1821—*Columbian College* (now at *George Washington University*) created by Congressional Charter

1830s **Access & Equity**

1831— Revision of *Copyright Act.* Copyright protection is extended to 28 years with potential of a 14-year extension

Communities & Citizenship

1830—*Indian Removal Act*

1839 — *Trail of Tears*, 16,000 Cherokee Indians are forcibly relocated from five eastern states to Oklahoma as the final implementation of the *Indian Removal Act* of 1830.

1840s **Investment**

1846 —*Smithsonian Institution established as a trust* (At present includes 16 museums, four research centers, the Smithsonian Institution Libraries, a research library system, the Smithsonian magazine, the Smithsonian Institution Press, a Traveling Exhibition Service and the National Zoo.)

1850s **Law**

1857—*Dred Scott v. Sanford Case*— Supreme Court rules that African-Americans are not citizens of the U.S., forbids congress to legislate against slavery, and nullifies the *Missouri Compromise of 1820*

1860s **Communities & Citizenship**

1861–1865 —*Civil War* erupts between the North and South over the practice of slavery

1862 —*Homestead Act* allows settlers to claim and purchase federally owned land

1863 — Emancipation Proclamation whereby President Lincoln declares slavery illegal

1865 — Constitutional *Amendment XIII* outlaws slavery

1866 — Constitutional *Amendment XIV* addresses citizenship rights and eligibility for election to national public office

Education & the Creative Workforce

1867 —*Department of Education Act* authorizes the first Office of Education

Investment

1862 —*Land-Grant Colleges Act/Morrill Act*— Federal public lands are donated and sold to create endowments, which ultimately leads to the establishment of 102 state colleges and universities

1870s **Access & Equity**

1870— Revision of *Copyright Act.* Copyright administration assumed by the Library of Congress.

1870— Constitutional *Amendment XV* provides voting rights to citizens regardless of race

Preservation

1872 — Yellowstone Park becomes the first National Park

1880s **Communities & Citizenship**

1882 —*Chinese Exclusion Act* prohibits Chinese laborers from emigrating to the U.S. for a period of ten years

1887 —*Dawes Act (General Allotment Act)* allots lands on "reservations" to Native Americans and extends U.S. laws over these lands

1890s **Communities & Citizenship**

1892 —*Ellis Island* Immigration Processing Center established. Over 71 percent of U.S. immigrants (12 million) migrated through this Center before its closing in 1954.

1896 —*Plessy v. Ferguson*— Supreme Court establishes the "separate but equal" verdict on education segregated by race

Education & the Creative Workforce

1890—*Second Morrill Act* gives the *Office of Education responsibility* for the land grant colleges

1900s **Access & Equity**

1909 —*Copyright Act* revision provides protection over all works of authorship and extends terms to 28 years and renewals up to 28 additional years

Investment

1906 —*Antiquities Act becomes* the first law to "establish federal management over cultural and scientific resources"

1910s   Access & Equity

1912 — U.S. ratifies *Berlin Convention* of 1906 (*International Wireless Telegraph Convention*)

1912 —*Act to Regulate Radio Communication* is the first federal legislation pertaining to wireless communications

Communities & Citizenship

1917 — Citizens of *Puerto Rico*, a U.S. territory, are granted U.S. citizenship

Education & the Creative Workforce

1917 —*Smith-Hughes Act* provides federal funding for vocational (agricultural) training

Investment

1910 —*Commission of Fine Arts* established

1917 —*Revenue Act* establishes *deduction for individual charity contributions* but limits amount to 15 percent of annual income

Preservation

1916 —*National Park Service* is created

1920s   Access & Equity

1927 —*Radio Act* creates the *Federal Radio Commission* as a license agency and radio-wave regulator that preceded the *FCC*

Communities & Citizenship

1920— Constitutional *Amendment XIX* awards women the right to vote

1923 —*Equal Rights Amendment* proposed to legislate equal rights for women (*failed in Congress in 1982* and has yet to be ratified)

1924 —*National Origins Act* institutes immigration origin quotas based on the formula of 2 percent of each U.S. resident ethnic demographic in the year 1890

1930s   Investment

1932 —*Gift Tax Act Charitable Deduction* established through the *Revenue Act* of 1932

1933 —*Public Works of Art Project* (PWAP) established as part of the New Deal programs

1934 —*National Archives* and the *National Historical Publications and Records Commission* founded

1935 —*Federal Art Project* established by the *New Deal Works Progress Administration* (WPA) art projects

1935 — Corporations are allowed to claim a charitable tax deduction, as part of the New Deal

1937 —*National Gallery of Art* established from the donation of Andrew Mellon's personal art collection

Law

1934 —*Communications Act of 1934* establishes the Federal Communications Commission (*FCC*) to regulate interstate and international communications

1935 — U.S. becomes party to the *Roerich Pact*, a Pan-American agreement which protects cultural property in times of war

Preservation

1935 —*Historic Sites Act* (amended eight times)

1940s   Education & the Creative Workforce

1944 —*GI Bill* (Servicemen's Readjustment Act) provides educational financial aid for veterans

Cultural Exchanges & Public Diplomacy

1942 —*Voice of America* is established as an international broadcasting service

1946 —*Fulbright Program*, "the flagship international educational program" for international exchange and mutual understanding, is established.

1948 —*U.S. Information and Education Exchange Act* (*Smith-Mundt Act*) prevents the U.S. from disseminating information domestically that has been designed to deliberately influence foreign audiences

Investment

1945 — Founding member of *United National Education, Science and Cultural Organization*

1950s **Communities & Citizenship**

1952 — *Immigration and Nationality Act* (*McCaren-Walter Act*) eliminates racial restrictions but codifies quotas and has been amended

1957 — *Commission on Civil Rights* established as an independent fact-finding agency of the Executive branch

1957 — *Civil Rights Bill* passed

Cultural Exchange & Public Diplomacy

1953 — United States Information Agency (*USIA*) is established

Education & the Creative Workforce

1954 — *Brown v. Board of Education of Topeka* — Supreme Court declares "separate but equal" unconstitutional

1958 — *National Defense Education Act*

Investment

1950 — *National Science Foundation* created

1960s **Access**

1966 — *Freedom of Information Act* (FOIA) allows citizens to request unclassified information about government activities

Citizenship and Immigration

1964 — *Civil Rights Act* protects against discrimination in voting, employment or distribution of public services based on gender, race, religion or national origin

1965 — *Immigration and Nationality Services Act* (*Hart-Celler Act*) eliminates national-origin quotas

Cultural Exchange and Public Diplomacy

1961 — *Mutual Educational and Cultural Exchange Act* (*Fulbright-Hays Act*) establishes the J Visa to support cultural and educational citizen exchanges

1964 — *ART in Embassies Program* is established

1968 — *Woodrow Wilson Center for International Scholars* established

Education & the Creative Workforce

1965 — *Higher Education Act* (*reauthorized* in 1968, 1972, 1976, 1980, 1986, 1992, and 1998)

1965 — Federal *Head Start Program* begins to provide public preschool education as part of the *War on Poverty* Programs

1966 — "*National Defense Education Project* is passed to coordinate the federal role in international education. Later, this project is *incorporated* as *Title VI of the Higher Education Act.*"

1968 — *Title VII Bilingual Education Act* added as a provision of the *Elementary and Secondary Education Act* of 1965 (expired in 2002)

Investment

1965 — *National Foundation on the Arts and Humanities Act* creates the National Endowment for the Arts (*NEA*) and the National Endowment for the Humanities (*NEH*)

1967 — *Public Broadcasting Act* establishes the *Corporation for Public Broadcasting* (CPB) as a private non-profit corporation and it is the largest *single source of funding* for public television and radio programming

1969 — Public Broadcasting Service (*PBS*) is created by the CPB

Law

1966 — U.S. ratifies UNESCO's *Florence Agreement* (1952) concerning the importation of educational, cultural and scientific materials

1967 — U.S. enters into force the 1954 *Beirut Agreement* to facilitate international circulation of visual and auditory materials of an educational, cultural and scientific nature

Preservation

1966 — *National Historic Preservation Act* (NHPA) establishes the *Advisory*

Council on Historic Preservation as an independent federal agency

1968 — *National Historic Preservation Fund* created and administered through the *National Park Service*

1970s   Access & Equity

1972 — *Title 9* is enacted as part of the *Educational Amendments of 1972* to prevent discrimination based on gender

1974 — *Privacy Act* addresses the "collection, maintenance, use, and dissemination of personal information by federal executive branch agencies"

1974 — *Family Education Rights and Privacy Act* protects student records and gives parents some access to their children's records

1976 — *Convention on Political Rights of Women* (1954) ratified by the U.S.

1978 — *American Indian Religious Freedom Act*

Education & the Creative Workforce

1974 — *Bilingual Education Act*, first legislation to address the needs of minority language (non–English) speaking students

1974 — *Women's Educational Equity Act*

1975 — *Education for All Handicapped Children Act*

1979 — *Department of Education* is established

Investment

1970 — *Corporation for Public Broadcasting* creates National Public Radio (*NPR*)

1971 — *John F. Kennedy Center for the Performing Arts* opens its doors in Washington, D.C.

1971 — *NEH initiates State Humanities Program* (*By 1979, there is a citizen-governed humanities council in each of the 50 states, Puerto Rico, and the District of Columbia*)

1972 — NEH's annual *Jefferson Lecture* on the Humanities is established

1974 — *State Arts Agencies* are *operational in all 50 states* (*first was established in Utah in 1899*)

1976 — *Museum Services Act* creates the Institute of Museum Services which is combined in 1996 with the DOE's Library Programs Office (est. 1956) to form the *Institute of Museum and Library Services*

Law

1973 — *Roe v. Wade—Supreme Court* rules that abortion is legal

1976 — Revision of the *Copyright Act* brings U.S. standards in line with international laws and codifies first doctrine and fair use practices. Copyright protection is extended to life of author plus 50 years and includes unpublished works.

Preservation

1972 — The U.S is the *first nation to ratify UNESCO's World Heritage Convention*

1974 — *Archaeological and Historic Preservation Act* (*Moss-Bennett Act*)

1975 — *Arts and Artifacts Indemnity Act* provides support for international museum exhibition exchanges by the federal government's assumption of indemnity

1976 — *Federal Historic Preservation Tax Incentives Program* is initiated under the joint management of the *IRS*, *National Park Service* and State Historic Preservation Offices (*SHPOs*)

1976 — *American Folklife Preservation Act* creates the *American Folklife Center* at the Library of Congress

1979 — *Archaeological Resources Protection Act* (ARPA) (amended four times since)

1980s   Access & Equity

1988 — U.S. signs *Berne Convention* (est. in 1886), which establishes copyright at life of author plus 50 years

Communities

1980 — *Refugee Act* (reauthorized through 2002) provides resettlement of refugees and assists in achieving economic self-sufficiency

1984 — *National Medal of Arts established* and up to twelve are awarded annually henceforth

1986 — *Immigration Reform and Control Act* enacted to address illegal immigration

Investment

1982 — *President's Committee on the Arts & Humanities* established by Executive Order

1985 — *National Capital Arts and Cultural Affairs* program was created under the *NEH* to support arts and cultural initiatives in the capital area. In 1987, responsibility was transferred to the *Commission on Fine Arts*.

1989 — *Culture Wars* begin over *NEA* grant controversy

1989 — PL 1–21 (*Interior Appropriations Bill*) establishes an Independent Commission under the direction of *John Brademas* to review the NEA's grant-making procedures. Their report, *The Independent Commission: A Report to Congress on the National Endowment for the Arts*, September 1990), defends the existence of the NEA and sets standards for publicly funded art.

Law

1986 — *Electronic Communications Privacy Act* protects electronic communications in transit and storage from internet service providers and government surveillance, without a warrant

1986 — *International Telecommunications Convention* of 1982 is ratified

1987 — *Convention on Cultural Property Implementation Act* implements the 1970 *Convention on the Means of Prohibiting and Preventing the Illicit Import, Export and Transfer of Ownership of Cultural Property*, which the U.S. signed in 1983

Preservation

1985 — *National Archives* becomes an independent federal agency

1986 — U.S. begins to observe *Martin Luther King Day*

1990s   Access & Equity

1990 — *Americans with Disabilities Act*

1992 — Copyright renewal becomes automatic

1996 — *Telecom Act* amends the 1934 *Communications Act*

1998 — *Sonny Bono Copyright Term Extension Act* (CTEA) extends protection to life of author plus 70 years

1998 — *Digital Millennium Copyright Act* implements the *WIPO Copyright Treaty* and the *WIPO Performances and Phonograms Treaty*

1998 — *International Religious Freedom Act*

1999 — *Digital Theft Deterrence and Copyright Damages Improvement Act* increases penalties for copyright infringement

Communities & Citizenship

1990 — *Immigration Act* amends the *Immigration and Nationality Act*, provides exceptions to language-testing requirements of the *Naturalization Act of 1906* and creates a lottery.

1992 — *Chinese Student Protection Act*

1996 — *Illegal Immigration Reform and Immigrant Responsibility Act*

Cultural Exchange & Public Diplomacy

1991 — *National Security Education Act* (*Boren Bill*), supports undergraduate study abroad and foreign language and area studies for graduates

1999 — *USIA* is dismantled through the *Foreign Affairs and Restructuring Act* and incorporated into the State Department under the *Bureau of Public Diplomacy and Public Affairs*

Education & the Creative Workforce

1990 — *Individuals with Disabilities Education Act* (IDEA) (reauthorized in *1997* and *2004*)

1994 — *Educate America Act*

Law

1990—*Indian Arts & Crafts Act* provides standards to authenticate and label Native American goods made exclusively by certified tribe artisans

1994 — U.S. ratifies the *International Convention on Elimination of All Forms of Racial Discrimination* of 1965

Preservation

1990—*Native American Graves Protection Repatriation Act* (NAGPRA)

1996 —*Museums and Library Services Act* establishes the *Institute of Museum and Library Services*, which administers the *Library Services and Technology Act* and the *Museum Services Act*. (The *Museum and Library Services Act* was reauthorized in 2003.)

1996 —*National Film Preservation Foundation* created by Congress as an independent non-profit private partnership

1996 —*E.O. 13007* (*Indian Sacred Sites*) dictates that federal land management must accommodate access to and ceremonial use of Indian sacred sites by Indian religious practitioners

1999 —*Save America's Treasures* is founded by Executive Order and administered in partnership with the *National Trust for Historic Preservation* and the *National Park Service*

2000s   Access & Equity

2002 — *Technology Education and Copyright Harmonization Act* clarifies copyright in regards to educational and distance educational purposes

2005 — *Family Entertainment and Copyright Act* includes the *Artist's Rights and Theft Prevention Act* and the *Family Home Movie Act* and institutes criminal penalties for individual who make illegal copies

2006 — *Orphan Works Act* (HR 5439) *introduced* to return works with unknown authorship to the public domain

Communities & Citizenship

2001—*U.S. Patriot Act*, changes surveillance laws and provides additional executive powers to combat terrorism

Cultural Exchange & Public Diplomacy

2002 —*Radio Fardo* and *Radio Sawa* are launched to target the Muslim world

2002 —*Cultural Bridges Act*

2003 —*U.S. Rejoins UNESCO*

2003 — Publication of the *Djerejian Report— Changing Minds, Winnings Peace—A New Strategic Direction for U.S. Public Policy in the Arab and Muslim Worlds*

2003 —*CultureConnect* and the *Cultural Ambassadors Program* are launched

2003 —*Office of Global Communications* is established at the White House

2004 — Inaugural meeting of the *Advisory Committee on Cultural Diplomacy*/PL 107–228 (2002)

2005 —*Cultural Diplomacy—The Linchpin of Public Diplomacy* report synthesizing 30 recent reports on public and cultural diplomacy is released

Education

2001—*No Child Left Behind Act* introduces new standards and accountability in primary and secondary education

Investment

2002 —*Sarbanes-Oxley Act* introduces new auditing standards for corporations, government and foundations

2006 —*National Heritage Areas Act of 2006* reduces royalty for sodium production to provide funds for heritage areas

Law

2000—*Children's Internet Protection Act* restricts access to offensive content on the internet for school and library computers receiving funding from the federal E-Rate program

2003 —*McCreary County v. ACLU— Supreme Court* rules that display of the

Ten Commandments in isolation within federal courthouses is unconstitutional

2003 — *Supreme Court* upholds the *Copyright Term Extension Act* (1998) in *Eldred v. Ashcroft*

2004 — *Supreme Court* rules *against COPA* in *Ashcroft v. ACLU* after previously striking down the *Communications Decency Act in 1997* and the 1996 *Child Pornography Prevention Act in 2002*

2004 — *Satellite Home Viewer Extension and Reauthorization Act*

2005 — *MGM Studios v. Grokster* — Supreme Court rules that enablers of copyright infringement through file sharing can be held liable

2005 — *Family Entertainment and Copyright Act*

Preservation

2000 — *National Recording Preservation Act* establishes the *National Recording Registry* and the *National Recording Preservation Board*

2001 — *Ambassador's Fund for Cultural Preservation*, assists countries with tangible and intangible cultural heritage

2003 — *Preserve America* is initiated by Executive Order, calling on federal agencies to take a lead role in preserving American heritage through upkeep of federal monuments, partnerships and regional cultural tourism

2005 — *National Museum of the American Indian* opens

NOTES

1. This timeline was prepared by The Canadian Cultural Observatory, and reflects a timeline of the cultural policies of the U.S. federal government from 1787 to 2006.

2. The Canadian Cultural Observatory is an information service that is funded by the Canadian Culture Online Strategy, a collaborative initiative of the Department of Canadian Heritage, of the central government of Canada.

3. Additional information on this subject may be obtained from Culturescope.ca (http://www.culturescope.ca/), or by writing The Canadian Cultural Observatory, 15 Eddy Street, 8th Floor, Gatineau, Quebec, Canada.

4. The sources for this timeline, as well as related timelines, are shown below:

American History Timeline, Smithsonian Encyclopedia
Copyright Timeline: A History of Copyright in the United States, Association of Research Libraries
History of the International Visitor Leadership Program, Bureau of Education and Cultural Exchange, U.S. State Department
National Endowment for the Arts Timeline, National Endowment for the Arts
National Endowment for the Humanities Timeline, National Endowment for the Humanities
Timeline of the Civil War, Library of Congress
Timeline of U.S. Immigration, Library of Congress
U.S. History Timeline, Animated Atlas

VIII. State Library Agencies Directory

Source: Institute of Museum and Library Services (IMLS), 1800 "M" Street, NW, 9th Floor, Washington, D.C. 20036.

Alabama
Ms. Rebecca Mitchell
Director
Alabama Public Library Service
6030 Monticello Drive
Montgomery, AL 36130–6000
Phone: 334/213–3902
Fax: 334/213–3993
E-mail: *rmitchell@apls.state.al.us*
http://www.apls.state.al.us

Alaska
Kathryn H. Shelton
Director
Alaska Department of Education, Division of Libraries, Archives & Museums
P.O. Box 110571
Juneau, AK 99811–0571
Phone: 907/465–2912
Fax: 907/465–2151
E-mail: *kay_Shelton@eed.state.ak.us*
http://www.library.state.ak.us

American Samoa
Ms. Cheryl Morales
Territorial Librarian
Feleti Barstow Public Library
P.O. Box 997687
Pago Pago, AS 96799
Phone: 011/684/633–5816
Fax: 011/684/633–5823
E-mail: *feletibarstow@yahoo.com*

Arizona
Ms. GladysAnn Wells
Director and State Librarian

Arizona State Library, Archives and Public Records
1700 West Washington, Room 200
Phoenix, AZ 85007
Phone: 602/542–4035
Fax: 602/542–4972
E-mail: *GAWells@lib.az.us*
http://www.lib.az.us

Arkansas
Ms. Carolyn Ashcraft
State Librarian
Arkansas State Library
One Capital Mall — Fifth Floor
Little Rock, AR 72201–1081
Phone: 501/682–1526
Fax: 501–682–1899
E-mail: *cashcraft@asl.lib.ar.us*
http://www.asl.lib.ar.us

California
Ms. Susan Hildreth
State Librarian of California
California State Library
P.O. Box 942837
Sacramento, CA 94237–0001
Phone: 916/654–0266
Fax: 916/653–7181
E-mail: *shildreth@library.ca.gov*
http://www.library.ca.gov

Commonwealth of the Northern Mariana Islands
Ms. Erlinda Naputi
Acting State Librarian
Joeten-Kiyu Public Library
P.O. Box 501092
Saipan, MP 96950
Phone: 670/235–7324
Fax: 670/235–7550
E-mail: *naputi@saipan.com*

Colorado
Mr. Eugene Hainer
State Librarian
Colorado State Library
201 East Colfax Avenue
Room 309
Denver, CO 80203
Phone: 303/866–6940
Fax: 303/866–6940
E-mail: *hainer_g@cde.state.co.us*
http://www.cde.state.co.us/index_library.htm

Connecticut
Mr. Kendall F. Wiggin
State Librarian
Connecticut State Library
231 Capitol Avenue
Hartford, CT 06106–1537
Phone: 86/757–6510
Fax: 860/757–6503
E-mail: *kwiggin@cslib.org*
http://www.cslib.org

Delaware
Ms. Anne Norman
State Librarian
Delaware Division of Libraries
43 South DuPont Highway
Dover, DE 19901
Phone: 302/739–4748 ext. 126
Fax: 302/739–6787
E-mail: *Norman@lib.de.us*
http:www.state.lib.de.us/index.shtml

District of Columbia
District of Columbia
Ginnie Cooper, Chief Librarian
District of Columbia Public Library
901 G Street, NW; Suite 400
Washington, DC 20001
Phone: 202/727–1101
Fax: 202/727–1129
E-mail: *Ginnie.cooper@dc.gov*
http://dclibrary.org

Federated States of Micronesia
Mr. Nena S. Nena
Secretary
Department of Health, Education and Social Affairs
P.O. Box PS 70
Palikir, Pohnpei, FM 96941
Phone: 011/6691/320–2643
Fax: 011/691/320–5263
E-mail: *nsnena@mail.fm*

Florida
Ms. Judith A. Ring
State Librarian
Division of Library and Information Services
R.A. Gray Building
500 S. Bronough St.
Tallahassee, FL 32399–0250
Phone: 850/245–6604
Fax: 850/488–2746
E-mail: *jring@dos.state.fl.us*
http://dlis.dos.state.fl.us/stlib

Georgia
Dr. Lamar Veatch
State Librarian
Georgia Public Library Services
1800 Century Place
Suite 150
Atlanta, GA 30345–4304
Phone: 404–235–7200
Fax: 404–235–7201
E-mail: *lveatch@state.lib.ga.us*
http://www.georgialibraries.org

Guam
Guam Public Library System
254 Martyr Street
Hagatna, Guam 96910
761/475–4754 or 671/475–4753
Fax: 671/477–9777

Hawaii
Ms. Jo Ann Schindler
State Librarian
Hawaii State Public Library System
44 Merchant Street
Honolulu, HI 96813
Phone: 808/586–3704
Fax: 808/586–3715
E-mail: *joann@librarieshawaii.org*
http://www.librarieshawaii.org

Idaho
Ms. Ann Joslin
Idaho State Librarian
Idaho Commission for Libraries
325 West State Street
Boise, ID 83713
Phone: 208/334–2150
Fax: 208/334–4016
E-mail: *ann.joslin@libraries.idaho.gov*
http://www.lili.org

Illinois
Ms. Anne Craig
Director
Illinois State Library
300 South Second Street
Springfield, IL 62701–1796
Phone: 217/524–4200
Fax: 217/782–6062
E-mail: *acraig@ilsos.net*
http://www.cyberdriveillinois.com/departments/
    library/home/html

Indiana
Ms. Roberta L. Brooker
Interim Director

Phone: 317/232–3693
Fax: 317/232–3713
E-mail: *rbrooker@statelib.lib.in.us*
http://www.statelib.lib.in.us

Iowa
Ms. Mary Wegner
State Librarian
State Library of Iowa
E. 12th & Grand
Des Moines, IA 50319
Phone: 515/281–4105
Fax: 515/281–6191
E-mail: *mary.wegner@lib.state.ia.us*
http://www.silo.lib.ia.us

Kansas
Ms. Christie Pearson Brandau
State Librarian
Kansas State Library
300 SW 10th Avenue
Room 343N
Topeka, KS 66612–1593
Phone: 785/296–3296
Fax: 785/296–6650
E-mail: *christieb@kslib.org*
http://www.skyways.org/KSL

Kentucky
Mr. Wayne Onkst
State Librarian and Commissioner
Kentucky Department for Libraries and Archives
P.O. Box 537, 300 Coffee Tree Road
Frankfort, KY 40602–0537
Phone: 502/564–8300 ext. 312
Fax: 502–564–5773
E-mail: *wayne.onkst@ky.gov*
http://www.kdla.ky.gov

Louisiana
Ms. Rebecca Hamilton
State Librarian
State Library of Louisiana
P.O. Box 131
701 N. Fourth St.
Baton Rouge, LA 70821–0131
Phone: 255/342–4923
Fax: 255/219–4804
E-mail: *rhamilton@crt.state.la.us*
http://www.state.lib.la.us

Maine
Mr. J. Gary Nichols
State Librarian
Maine State Library
LMA Building

64 State House Station
Augusta, ME 04333–0064
Phone: 207/287–5600
Fax: 207/287–5615
E-mail: *gary.nichols@maine.gov*
http://www.state.me.us/msl

Maryland
Ms. Irene Padilla
Assistant State Superintendent for Libraries
Maryland State Department of Education
Division of Library Development & Services
200 W. Baltimore Street
Baltimore, MD 21201
Phone: 410/767–0435
Fax: 410/333–2507
E-mail: *ipadilla@msde.state.md.us*
http://www.sailor.lib.md.us

Massachusetts
Mr. Robert C. Maier
Director
Massachusetts Board of Library Commissioners
648 Beacon Street
Boston, MA 02215
Phone: 617/725–1860 ext. 249
Fax: 617/421/9833
E-mail: *Robert.maier@state.ma.us*
http://mass.gov/mblc

Michigan
Nancy Robertson
Interim State Librarian
Library of Michigan
717 W. Allegan Street
P.O. Box 30007
Lansing, MI 48909–7507
Phone: 517/373–7513
Fax: 517/373–4480
E-mail: *nrobertson@michigan.gov*
http://www.michigan.gov/hal

Minnesota
Ms. Suzanne Miller
State Librarian
Library Development and Services
MN Department of Education
1500 Highway 36 West
Roseville, MN 55113–4266
Phone: 651/582–8722
Fax: 651/582–8897
E-mail: *Suzanne.miller@state.mn.us*
http://www.state.mn.us/libraries/

Mississippi
Ms. Sharman Smith
Executive Director
Mississippi Library Commission
1221 Ellis Avenue
Jackson, MS 39289–0700
Phone: 601/961–4039
Fax: 601/354–6713
E-mail: *sharman@mlc.lib.ms.us*
http://www.mlc.lib.ms.us

Missouri
Margaret Conroy
Director
Missouri State Library
600 West Main
P.O. Box 387
Jefferson City, MO 65102–0387
Phone: 573/751–2751
Fax: 573/751–3612
E-mail: Diana.veryWsos.mo.gov
http://www.sos.mo.gov/library

Montana
Ms. Darlene Staffeldt
State Librarian
Montana State Library
1515 East 6th Avenue
Post Office Box 201800
Helena, MT 59620–1800
Phone: 406/444–3115
Fax: 406/444–0266
E-mail: *dstaffeldt@mt.gov*
http://msl.state.mt.us

Nebraska
Mr. Rodney G. Wagner
Director
Nebraska Library Commission
The Atrium
1200 N Street, Suite 120
Lincoln, NE 68508–2023
Phone: 402/471–2045
Fax: 402/471/2083
E-mail: *rwagner@nlc.state.ne.us*
http://www.nlc.state.ne.us

Nevada
Guy Rocha, Acting Director
Nevada State Library & Archives
100 North Stewart Street
Carson City, NV 89710–4285
Phone: 775/684–3315
Fax: 775/684–3311

E-mail: *glrocha@clan.lib.nv.us*
http://dmla.clan.lib.nv.us

New Hampshire
Mr. Michael York
State Librarian
New Hampshire State Library
20 Park Street
Concord, NH 03301–6314
Phone: 603/271–2397
Fax: 603/271–6826
E-mail: *myork@lib.state.nh.us*
http://www.state.nh.us/nhsl

New Jersey
Ms. Norma E. Blake
State Librarian
New Jersey State Library
P.O. Box 520
Trenton, NJ 08625–0520
Phone: 609/292–6200
Fax: 609/292–2746
E-mail: *nblake@njstatelib.org*
http://www.njstatelib.org

New Mexico
Mr. Richard Akeroyd
State Librarian
New Mexico State Library
1209 Camino Carlos Rey
Santa Fe, NM 87505–6980
Phone:
Fax:
E-mail: *rakeroyd@stlib.state.nm.us*
http://www.stlib.state.nm.us

New York
Mr. Janet M. Welch
State Librarian & Assistant Commissioner for
    Libraries
New York State Library
Cultural Education Center, Room 10C34
Empire State Plaza
Albany, NY 12230
Phone: 518/474–5930
Fax: 518/486–6880
E-mail: jwelch2@mail.nysed.gov
http://www.nysl.nysed.gov

North Carolina
Mary L. Boone
State Librarian
State Library of North Carolina
Administrative Section
4640 Mail Service Center
Raleigh, NC 27699–4640

Phone: 919/807–7410
Fax: 919/733–8748
E-mail: *mboone@library.dcr.nc.us*
http://statelibrary.dcr.state.nc.us

North Dakota
Mr. Doris Ott
State Librarian
North Dakota State Library
604 E. Boulevard Avenue
Dept. 250
Bismarck, ND 58505–0800
Phone: 701/328–2492
Fax: 701/328–2040
E-mail: *dott@state.nd.us*
http://ndsl.lib.state.nd.us

Ohio
Ms. Jo Budler
State Librarian
State Library of Ohio
274 East First Avenue
Columbus, OH 43201
Phone: 614/644–6843
Fax: 614/466–3584
E-mail: *jbudler@sloma.state.oh.us*
http://winslo.state.oh.us

Oklahoma
Ms. Susan McVey
Director
Oklahoma Department of Libraries
200 N.E. 18th Street
Oklahoma City, OK 73105–3298
Phone: 405/52203173
Fax: 405/525–7804
E-mail: *smcvey@oltn.odl.state.ok.us*
http://www.odl.state.ok.us

Oregon
Mr. James B. Scheppke
State Librarian
Oregon State Library
250 Winter Street, N.E.
Salem, OR 97310–0640
Phone: 503/378–4367
Fax: 503/585–8059
E-mail: *jim.b.scheppke@state.or.us*
http://oregon.gov/OSL/

Pennsylvania
Ms. M. Clare Zales
Deputy Secretary of Education & Commissioner
    of Libraries
Pennsylvania Office of Commonwealth Libraries

333 Market Street
Harrisburg, PA 17105
Phone: 717/787–2646
Fax: 717/772–3265
E-mail: *mzales@state.pa.us*
http://www.statelibrary.state.pa.us/libraries

Puerto Rico
Mrs. Aura M. Rodriguez Ramos
Director
Library Services and Information Program
Post Office Box 190759
San Juan, PR 00919–0759
Phone: 787/754–1120
Fax: 787/754–0843
E-mail: *rodrigoezram@de.gobierno.pr*

Republic of Marshall Islands
Mr. Wilbur Allen
Secretary of Internal Affairs
Alele Incorporated
P.O. Box 629
Majuro, MH 96960
Phone: 011/692/625–8240
Fax: 011/692/625–3226
E-mail: *allele@ntamar.net*

Republic of Palau
Mr. Mario Katosang
Minister of Education
Republic of Palau
Box 7080
Koror, PW 96940
Phone: 011/680/488–1464
Fax: 011/680/488–1465
E-mail: *mariok@palaumoe.net*

Rhode Island
Howard Boksenbaum
Office of Library & Information Services
One Capitol Hill
Providence, RI 02908
E-mail: *howardbm@olis.ri.gov*
http://www.olis.ri.gov

South Carolina
David S. Goble
State Librarian/Agency Director
South Carolina State Library
PO Box 11469
Columbia, SC 29211
Phone: 803/734–8656
Fax: 803/734–8676
Email: *dgoble@statelibrary.sc.gov*
http://www.statelibrary.sc.gov

South Dakota
Ms. Dorothy M. Liegl
State Librarian
South Dakota State Library
800 Governors Drive
Pierre, SD 57501–2294
Phone: 605/773–3131
Fax: 605/773–6962
E-mail: *Dorothy.liegl@state.sd.us*
http://www.sdstatelibrary.com

Tennessee
Jeanne D. Sugg
State Librarian/Archivist
Tennessee State Library & Archives
403 7th Avenue North
Nashville, TN 37243–0312
Phone: 615/741–7996
Fax: 615/5342–9293
E-mail: *Jeanne.sugg@state.tn.us*
http://www.tennessee.gov/tsla

Texas
Ms. Peggy Rudd
Director-Librarian
Texas State Library & Archives Commission
P.O. Box 12927
Austin, TX 78711–2927
Phone: 512/463–5460
Fax: 512/463–5436
E-mail: *peggy.rudd@tsl.state.tx.us*
http://www.tsl.state.tx.us

Utah
Ms. Donna Jones Morris
State Librarian/Director
Utah State Library Division
250 North 1950 West
Suite A
Salt Lake City, UT 84116–7901
Phone: 801/715–6770
Fax: 801/715–6767
E-mail: *dmorris@utah.gov*
http://library.ut.gov/index.html

Vermont
Mrs. Sybil Brigham McShane
State Librarian
Vermont Department of Libraries
109 State Street
Montpelier, VT 05609–0601
Phone: 802/828–3265
Fax: 802/828–2199
E-mail: *sybil.mcshane@dol.state.vt.us*
http://dol.state.vt.us

Virgin Islands
Ms. Claudette C. Lewis
Executive Assistant Commissioner
Division of Libraries, Archives & Museums
Cyril E. King Airport Terminal Building
St. Thomas, VI 00802
Phone: 340/774–3320
Fax: 340/775–5706

Virginia
Mr. Nolan T. Yelich
Librarian of Virginia
The Library of Virginia
800 East Broad Street
Richmond, VA 23219–8000
Phone: 804/692–3535
Fax: 804/692–3594
E-mail: *nyelich@lva.lib.va.us*
http://www.lva.lib.va.us

Washington
Ms. Jan Walsh
State Librarian
Washington State Library
P.O. Box 42460
Olympia, WA 98504–2460
Phone: 360/704–5253
Fax: 360/586–7575
E-mail: *jwalsh@secstate.wa.gov*
http://www.secstate.was.gov/library

West Virginia
Mr. J.D. Waggoner
Secretary
West Virginia Library Commission
Cultural Center
1900 Kanawha Blvd., East
Charleston, WV 25305–0620
Phone: 304/558–2041
Fax: 304–558–2044
E-mail: *waggoner@wvlc.lib.wv.us*
http://librarycommision/lib.wv.us

Wisconsin
Mr. Richard Grobschmidt
State Librarian/Assistant Superintendent
Division for Libraries & Community Learning
Department of Public Instruction
125 South Webster Street
P.O. Box 7841
Madison, WI 53707–7841
Phone: 608/266–2205
Fax: 608/267–1052
E-mail: *Richard.grobschmidt@dpi.state.wi.us*
http://www.dpi.state.wi.us/dltcl/pld

Wyoming
Ms. Lesley Boughton
State Librarian
Wyoming State Library
516 South Greeley Highway
Cheyenne, WY 82002
Phone: 307/777/5911
Fax: 307/777–6289
E-mail: *lbough@state.wy.us*
http://www-wsl.state.wy.us

IX. State Municipal League Directory

Source: National League of Cities (NLC), 1301 Pennsylvania Avenue, NW, Suite 550, Washington, D.C. 20004.

Alabama League of Municipalities
Perry Roquemore, Executive Director
P.O. Box 1270 (535 Adams Avenue — 36104)
Montgomery, Alabama 36102
334/262–2566

Alaska Municipal League
Kathie Wasserman, Executive Director
217 Second Street, Suite 200
Juneau, Alaska 99801
907/586–1325

League of Arizona Cities and Towns
Ken Strobeck, Executive Director
1820 West Washington Street
Phoenix, Arizona 85007
602/258–5786

Arkansas Municipal League
Don Zimmerman, Executive Director
P.O. Box 38 (301 W. 2nd Street — 72114)
North Little Rock, Arkansas 72115
501/374–3484

League of California Cities
Christopher McKenzie, Executive Director
1400 K Street, 4th Floor
Sacramento, California 95814
916/658–8200

Colorado Municipal League
Sam Mamet, Executive Director
1144 Sherman Street
Denver, Colorado 80203
303/831–6411

Connecticut Conference of Municipalities
Joel Cogen, Executive Director & General
Counsel

900 Chapel Street, 9th Floor
New Haven, Connecticut 06510–2807
203/498–3000

Delaware League of Local Governments
George C. Wright, Executive Director
P.O. Box 484 (1210 White Oak Road —
19903–0475)
Dover, Delaware 19903–0475
302/678–0991

Florida League of Cities
Michael Sittig, Executive Director
P.O. Box 1757 (301 South Bronough, Suite
300— 32301)
Tallahassee, Florida 32302–1757
850/222–9684

Georgia Municipal Association
Jim Higdon, Executive Director
201 Pryor Street, S.W.
Atlanta, Georgia 30303
404/688–0472

Association of Idaho Cities
Ken Harward, Executive Director
3100 South Vista Ave., Suite 310
Boise, Idaho 83705
208/344–8594

Illinois Municipal League
Ken Alderson, Executive Director
P.O. Box 5180 (500 E. Capitol Avenue — 62701)
Springfield, Illinois 62705–5180
217/525–1220

Indiana Association of Cities and Towns
Mathew C. Greller, Executive Director
200 S. Meridian Street, Suite 340
Indianapolis, Indiana 46225
317/237–6200

Iowa League of Cities
Thomas G. Bredeweg, Executive Director
317 Sixth Avenue, Suite 800
Des Moines, Iowa 50309–4111
515/244–7282

League of Kansas Municipalities
Don Moler, Executive Director
300 S.W. 8th Street
Topeka, Kansas 66603–3912
785/354–9565

Kentucky League of Cities, Inc.
Sylvia L. Lovely, Executive Director
100 East Vine Street, Suite 800
Lexington, Kentucky 40507–3700
859/977–3700

Louisiana Municipal Association
Tom Ed McHugh, Executive Director
P.O. Box 4327 (700 North 10th Street —
70802)
Baton Rouge, Louisiana 70821
225/344–5001

Maine Municipal Association
Christopher G. Lockwood, Executive Director
60 Community Drive
Augusta, Maine 04330
207/623–8428

Maryland Municipal League
Scott A. Hancock, Executive Director
1212 West Street
Annapolis, Maryland 21401
410/268–5514

Massachusetts Municipal Association
Geoffrey Beckwith, Executive Director
One Winthrop Square
Boston, Massachusetts 02110
617/426–7272

Michigan Municipal League
Dan Gilmartin, Executive Director
P.O. Box 1487
(1675 Green Road — 48105–2530)
Ann Arbor, Michigan 48106–1487
734/662–3246

League of Minnesota Cities
James F. Miller, Executive Director
145 University Avenue, West
St. Paul, Minnesota 55103–2044
651/281–1200

Mississippi Municipal League
George Lewis, Executive Director
600 East Amite Street, Suite 104
Jackson, Mississippi 39201
601/353–5854

Missouri Municipal League
Gary Markenson, Executive Director
1727 Southridge Drive
Jefferson City, Missouri 65109
573/635–9134

Montana League of Cities and Towns
Alec Hansen, Executive Director
P.O. Box 1704
(208 North Montana, Suite 201— 59601)
Helena, Montana 59624–1704
406/442–8768

League of Nebraska Municipalities
L. Lynn Rex, Executive Director
1335 L Street
Lincoln, Nebraska 68508
402/476–2829

Nevada League of Cities
David Fraser, Executive Director
310 South Curry Street
Carson City, Nevada 89703
775/882–2121

New Hampshire Local Government Center
John B. Andrews, Executive Director
P.O. Box 617 (25 Triangle Park Drive —
03301)
Concord, New Hampshire 03302–0617
603/224–7447

New Jersey State League of Municipalities
William G. Dressel, Jr., Executive Director
407 West State Street
Trenton, New Jersey 08618
609/695–3481

New Mexico Municipal League
William F. Fulginiti, Executive Director
P.O. Box 846 (1229 Paseo de Peralta — 87501)
Santa Fe, New Mexico 87504–0846
505/982–5573

North Carolina League of Municipalities
Ellis Hankins, Executive Director
P.O. Box 3069 (215 N. Dawson — 27602)
Raleigh, North Carolina 27602–3609
919/715–4000

North Dakota League of Cities
Connie Sprynczynatyk, Executive Director
410 E. Front Ave.
Bismarck, North Dakota 58504–5641
701/223–3518

Ohio Municipal League
Susan J. Cave, Executive Director
175 South Third Street, Suite 510
Columbus, Ohio 43215
614/221–4349

Oklahoma Municipal League
Danny George, Executive Director
201 North East 23rd Street
Oklahoma City, Oklahoma 73105
405/528–7515

League of Oregon Cities
Mike McCauley, Executive Director
P.O. Box 928 (1201 Court Street, N.E., Site
200 — 97301)

Salem, Oregon 97308
503/588–6550

Pennsylvania League of Cities and Municipalities
John A. Garner, Jr., Executive Director
414 North Second Street
Harrisburg, Pennsylvania 17101
717/236–9469

Rhode Island League of Cities and Towns
Daniel Beardsley, Executive Director
1 State Street, Suite 502
Providence, Rhode Island 02908
401/272–3434

Municipal Association of South Carolina
Howard Duvall, Executive Director
P.O. Box 12109 (1411 Gervais Street — 29201)
Columbia, South Carolina 29211
803/799–9574

South Dakota Municipal League
Yvonne Taylor, Executive Director
214 East Capitol
Pierre, South Dakota 57501
605/224–8654

Tennessee Municipal League
Margaret Mahery, Executive Director
226 Capitol Blvd., Room 710
Nashville, Tennessee 37219–1894
615/255–6416

Texas Municipal League
Frank Sturzl, Executive Director
1821 Rutherford Lane, Suite 400
Austin, Texas 78754–5128
512/231–7400

Utah League of Cities and Towns
Kenneth Bullock, Executive Director
50 South 600 East, Suite 150
Salt Lake City, Utah 84102
801/328–1601

Vermont League of Cities and Towns
Steven E. Jeffrey, Executive Director
89 Main Street, Suite 4
Montpelier, Vermont 05602–2948
802/229–9111

Virginia Municipal League
R. Michael Amyx, Executive Director
P.O. Box 12164 (13 East Franklin Street —
23219)
Richmond, Virginia 23241
804/649–8471

Association of Washington Cities
Stan Finkelstein, Executive Director
1076 South Franklin
Olympia, Washington 98501–1346
360/753–4137

West Virginia Municipal League
Lisa Dooley, Executive Director
2020 Kanawha Blvd. East
Charleston, West Virginia 25311
304/342–5564

League of Wisconsin Municipalities
Dan Thompson, Executive Director
202 State Street, Suite 300
Madison, Wisconsin 53703–2215
608/267–2380

Wyoming Association of Municipalities
George Parks, Executive Director
315 West 27th Street
Cheyenne Wyoming 82001
307/632–0398

X. Council of Regional Museum Associations Directory

Source: American Association of Museums (AAM), 1575 Eye Street, NW, Suite 400, Washington, D.C. 20025.

Mountain-Plains Museum Association
Lorne E. Render
Executive Director
Marianna Kistler Beach Art Museum
701 Beach Lane
Manhattan, KS 66506
Phone: 785/532–7718
Fax: 785/532–7498
Email: *lrender@ksu.edu*

Western Museums Association
Greta Brunschwyler
Director
Nevada State Museum
700 Twin Lakes Drive
Las Vegas, NV 89107
Phone: 702/486–5205 ext. 224
Fax: 702/486–5162
Email: *gbrunsch@clan.lib.nv.us*

Association of Midwest Museums
Christopher Reich
Director & CEO

Putnam Museum of History & Natural Science
1717 W. 12th Street
Davenport, IA 52804–9975
Phone: 563/324–1933 ext. 216
Fax: 563/324–6638
Email: *reich@putnam.org*

Mountain Plains Museums Association
Monta Lee Dakin
Executive Director
Mountain-Plains Museums Association
7110 West David Drive
Littleton, CO 80128–5404
Phone: 303/979–9358
Fax: 303/979–3553
Email: *mountplains@aol.com*

Western Museums Association
Melissa Rosengard
Executive Director
Western Museums Association
2960 San Pablo Ave.
Berkeley, CA 94702–2471
Phone: 510/665–0700
Fax: 510/665–9701
Email: *director@westmuse.org*

Association of Midwest Museums
Brian Bray
Executive Director
Association of Midwest Museums
P.O. Box 11940
St. Louis, MO 63112–0040
Phone: 314/746–4557
Fax: 314–746–4569
Email: midwestmuseums@aolcom

Mid-Atlantic Association of Museums
C. Douglass Alves, Jr.
Director & CEO
Calvert Marine Museum
14200 Solomons Island Road
P.O. Box 97
Solomons, MD 20688
Phone: 410/326–2042 ext. 13
Fax: 410/326–6691
Email: *alvescd@co.cal.md.us*

New England Museum Association
Susan Robertson
Executive Director
Gore Place Society
52 Gore Street
Waltham, MA 02453

Phone: 781/894–2798
Fax: 781/894–5745
Email: *susanrobertson@goreplace.org*

Southeastern Museums Conference
Sharon Bennett
Archivist
The Charleston Museum
360 Meeting Street
Charleston, SC 29403
Phone: 843/722–2996
Fax: 843/722–1784
Email: *sharonbennett@charlestonmuseum.org*

New England Museum Association
Katheryn Viens
Executive Director
New England Museum Association
22 Mill Street
Suite 409
Arlington, MA 02476
Phone: 781/641–0013
Fax: 781/641–0053
Email: *nema@tiac.net*

Mid-Atlantic Association of Museums
John T. Suau
Executive Director
Mid-Atlantic Association of Museums
The Carroll Mansion
800 East Lombard Street
Baltimore, MD 21202–4511
Phone: 410/223–1194
Fax: 410/223–2773
Email: *director@midatlanticmuseums.org*

Southeastern Museums Conference
Richard Waterhouse
Executive Director
Southeastern Museums Conference
P.O. Box 9003
Atlanta, GA 31106–1003
Phone: 404/378–3153
Fax: 404/370–1612
Email: *Director@SEMCDirect.net*

Board Liaison
Thomas A. Livesay
Director
Whatcom Museum of History & Art
121 Prospect Street
Bellingham, WA 98225
Phone: 360/676–6981 ext. 210
Fax: 360/738–7409
Email: *tlivesay@cob.org*

AAM Staff Liaison
Kim Igoe
V.P. Policy & Programs
American Association of Museums
1575 Eye Street, NW
Suite 400
Washington, D.C. 20005
Phone: 202/218–7690
Fax: 202/289–6578
Email: *kigoe@aam-us.org*

XI. Regional Museum Associations Directory

Source: American Association of Museums (AAM), 1575 Eye Street, NW, Suite 400, Washington, D.C. 20025.

Mid-Atlantic
Mid-Atlantic Association of Museums
• Delaware Museum Association
• Maryland Association of History Museums
• New Jersey Association of Museums
• New York State's Museums
• Pennsylvania Federation of Museums and Historical Organizations

Midwest
Association of Midwest Museums
• Association of Indiana Museums
• Illinois Association of Museums
• Illinois Heritage Association
• Iowa Museum Association
• Michigan Museums Association
• Minnesota Association of Museums
• Missouri Museums Association
• Ohio Museums Association
• Wisconsin Federation of Museums

Mountain-Plains
Mountain-Plains Museum Association
• Association of South Dakota Museums
• Colorado-Wyoming Association of Museums
• Kansas Museums Association
• Museums Association of Montana
• Museums in North Dakota
• Nebraska Museums Association
• New Mexico Association of Museums
• Oklahoma Museums Association
• Texas Association of Museums

New England
New England Museum Association

- Association of Historical Societies of New Hampshire
- Connecticut League of History Organizations
- Maine Archives & Museums
- Vermont Museum and Gallery Alliance

Southeast
Southeastern Museums Conference

- Alabama Museums Association
- Arkansas Museums Association
- Florida Association of Museums
- Georgia Association of Museums and Galleries
- Kentucky Association of Museums
- Louisiana Association of Museums
- Mississippi Museums Association
- Museums of West Virginia
- North Carolina Museums Council
- South Carolina Federation of Museums
- Tennessee Association of Museums
- Virginia Association of Museums

West
Western Museums Association

- California Association of Museums
- Hawaii Museum Association
- Idaho Association of Museums
- Museum Association of Arizona
- Museums Alaska
- Nevada Museums Association
- Oregon Museums Association
- Utah Museums Association
- Washington Museum Association

XII. National Museum Directory

Source: American Association of Museums (AAM), 1575 Eye Street, NW, Suite 400, Washington, D.C. 20025.

Alabama
Anniston Museum of Natural History, Anniston
Birmingham Civil Rights Institute, Birmingham
Birmingham Museum of Art, Birmingham
Huntsville Museum of Art, Huntsville
Mobile Museum of Art, Mobile
Montgomery Museum of Fine Arts, Montgomery

Alaska
Alaska State Museum & Sheldon Jackson Museum (Sitka), Juneau
Anchorage Museum of History and Art, Anchorage

Pratt Museum, Homer Society of Natural History, Homer
Sheldon Museum and Cultural Center, Haines
University of Alaska Museum of the North, Fairbanks

Arizona
Arizona Historical Society Museum, Southern Arizona Division, Tucson
Arizona State Museum, University of Arizona, Tucson
Arizona–Sonora Desert Museum, Tucson
Boyce Thompson Arboretum, Superior
Desert Botanical Garden, Phoenix
Desert Caballeros Western Museum, Wickenburg
Heard Museum, Phoenix
Phoenix Art Museum, Phoenix
Pueblo Grande Museum, Phoenix
Scottsdale Museum of Contemporary Art, Scottsdale
Sharlot Hall Museum, Prescott Historical Society, Prescott
Tucson Museum of Art and Historic Block, Tucson
University of Arizona Museum of Art, Tucson

Arkansas
Arkansas Arts Center, Little Rock
Arkansas State University Museum, Jonesboro
Arts and Science Center for Southeast Arkansas, Pine Bluff
Historic Arkansas Museum, Little Rock
Museum of Discovery: Arkansas' Museum of Science and History, Little Rock
Old State House Museum, Little Rock
Rogers Historical Museum, Rogers

California
Asian Art Museum of San Francisco, San Francisco
Bakersfield Museum of Art, Bakersfield
Berkeley Art Museum and Pacific Film Archive, University of California, Berkeley
Bowers Museum of Cultural Art, Santa Ana
California Academy of Sciences, San Francisco
California Science Center, Los Angeles
Chula Vista Nature Center, Chula Vista
Crocker Art Museum, Sacramento
De Saisset Gallery and Museum, Santa Clara University, Santa Clara
Descanso Gardens, La Canada Flintridge
Fine Arts Museums of San Francisco: M.H. de Young Memorial Museum and California Palace of the Legion of Honor, San Francisco

Fresno Art Museum, Fresno

Hearst Art Gallery, St. Mary's College, Moraga

Hearst San Simeon State Historical Monument, San Simeon

J. Paul Getty Museum, Los Angeles

Japanese American National Museum, Los Angeles

Judah L. Magnes Museum, Berkeley

Kern County Museum, Bakersfield

Lindsay Wildlife Museum, Walnut Creek

Long Beach Museum of Art, Long Beach

Los Angeles County Museum of Art, Los Angeles

Los Angeles Zoo and Botanical Gardens, Los Angeles

Mingei International Museum, San Diego

Monterey Museum of Art, Monterey

Museum of Contemporary Art Los Angeles, Los Angeles

Museum of Contemporary Art, San Diego, La Jolla

Museum of Photographic Arts, San Diego

Museum of the American West, Autry National Center, Los Angeles

Museums of the San Diego Historical Society, Museum of San Diego History (Casa de Balboa), San Diego

Museums of the San Diego Historical Society, George White and Anna Gunn Marston House, San Diego

Museums of the San Diego Historical Society, Junipero Serra Museum, San Diego

Natural History Museum of Los Angeles County, Los Angeles

Natural History Museum of Los Angeles County, George C. Page Museum of LaBrea Discoveries, Los Angeles

Natural History Museum of Los Angeles county, William S. Hart Museum, Los Angeles

Oakland Museum of California, Oakland

Pacific Grove Museum of Natural History, Pacific Grove

Palm Springs Desert Museum, Palm Springs

Phoebe Apperson Hearst Museum of Anthropology, University of California, Berkeley

Rancho Santa Ana Botanic Garden at Claremont, Claremont

Raymond M. Alf Museum of Paleontology, Claremont

Riverside Metropolitan Museum, Riverside

San Bernardino County Museum and Historic Sites, Redlands

San Diego Aerospace Museum, San Diego

San Diego Model Railroad Museum, San Diego

San Diego Museum of Art, San Diego

San Diego Museum of Man, San Diego

San Diego Natural History Museum, San Diego

San Diego Zoo and Wild Animal Park, Zoological Society of San Diego, San Diego

San Francisco Airport Museums, San Francisco

San Francisco Maritime National Historical Park, National Park Service, San Francisco

San Francisco Museum of Modern Art, San Francisco

San Joaquin County Historical Museum, Lodi

San Jose Museum of Art, San Jose

San Mateo County Historical Museum, Redwood City

Santa Barbara Botanic Garden, Santa Barbara

Santa Barbara Museum of Art, Santa Barbara

Santa Barbara Museum of Natural History, Santa Barbara

Santa Cruz City Museum of Natural History, Santa Cruz

Southwest Museum of the American Indian, Autry National Center, Los Angeles

University Art Museum, University of California, Santa Barbara, Santa Barbara

University Art Museum, California State University, Long Beach

USC Fisher Gallery, Los Angeles

Colorado

Aspen Art Museum, Aspen

Colorado Historical Society, Colorado History Museum, Denver

Colorado Historical Society, Healy House & Dexter Cabin, Denver

Colorado Historical Society, Georgetown Loop Historic Mining & Railroad Park, Denver

Colorado Historical Society, Ft. Garland, Denver

Colorado Historical Society, El Pueblo Museum, Denver

Colorado Historical Society, Byers-Evan House, Denver

Colorado Historical Society, Ute Indian Museum, Denver

Colorado Springs Fine Arts Center, Colorado Springs

Colorado Springs Pioneers Museum, Colorado Springs

Denver Art Museum, Denver

Denver Botanic Gardens, Inc., Denver

Denver Museum of Nature and Science, Denver
Fort Morgan Museum, Fort Morgan
Littleton Historical Museum, Littleton
Loveland Museum and Gallery, Loveland
Museum of Western Colorado, Grand Junction
Sangre de Cristo Arts and Conference Center, Pueblo
University of Colorado Museum, Boulder
Western Museum of Mining and Industry, Colorado Springs

Connecticut

Bruce Museum of Arts and Science, Greenwich
Connecticut River Museum, Essex
Discovery Museum, Bridgeport
Earthplace: The Nature Discovery Center, Westport
Florence Griswold Museum, Lyme Historical Society, Old Lyme
Harriet Beecher Stowe Center, Hartford
Hill-Stead Museum, Farmington
Historic New England, Bowen House, Woodstock
Historical Society of the Town of Greenwich, Cos Cob
Litchfield Historical Society Museum, Litchfield
Lyman Allyn Art Museum, New London
Mark Twain House, Hartford
Mattatuck Museum, Waterbury
Mystic Seaport Museum, Inc., Mystic
New Britain Museum of American Art, New Britain
Noah Webster House: Museum of West Hartford History, West Hartford
Peabody Museum of Natural History, Yale University, New Haven
Wadsworth Atheneum, Hartford
Webb-Deane-Stevens Museum, The National Society of the Colonial Dames of America, Wethersfield
Yale University Art Gallery, New Haven

Delaware

Delaware Art Museum, Wilmington
Hagley Museum and Library, Wilmington
Winterthur Museum & Country Estate, Winterthur

District of Columbia

Corcoran Gallery of Art, Washington
Daughters of the American Revolution Museum, National Society, Daughters of the American Revolution, Washington
Dumbarton House, Washington

Frederick Douglass National Historic Site, National Park Service, Washington
Freer Gallery of Art & Arthur M. Sackler Gallery, Smithsonian Institution, Washington
Hillwood Museum, Washington
National Air and Space Museum, Smithsonian Institution, Washington
National Gallery of Art, Washington
National Museum of African Art, Smithsonian Institution, Washington
National Museum of American History, Smithsonian Institution, Washington
National Museum of Natural History, Smithsonian Institution, Washington
National Portrait Gallery, Smithsonian Institution, Washington
Navy Museum, U.S. Dept. of the Navy, Washington
Octagon, Washington
Phillips Collection, Washington
Smithsonian American Art Museum and Renwick Gallery, Smithsonian Institution, Washington
Textile Museum, Washington
United States Holocaust Memorial Museum, Washington
White House, National Park Service, Washington
Woodrow Wilson House, National Trust for Historic Preservation, Washington

Florida

Bass Museum of Art, Miami Beach
Boca Raton Museum of Art, Boca Raton
Cummer Museum of Art and Gardens, Jacksonville
Fairchild Tropical Botanic Garden, Miami
Florida Holocaust Museum, St. Petersburg
Florida Museum of Natural History, University of Florida, Gainesville
Florida State University Museum of Fine Arts, Tallahassee
Frost Art Museum, Florida International University, Miami
George D. and Harriet W. Cornell Fine Arts Museum, Rollins College, Winter Park
Gulf Coast Museum of Art, Largo
Henry B. Plant Museum, Tampa
Henry Morrison Flagler Museum, Palm Beach
Historic Spanish Point, Gulf Coast Heritage Association, Inc., Osprey

Historical Museum of Southern Florida, Miami

Jewish Museum of Florida, Miami Beach

John and Mable Ringling Museum of Art, Florida State University, Sarasota

Lowe Art Museum, University of Miami, Coral Gables

Marie Selby Botanical Gardens, Sarasota

Mel Fisher Maritime Heritage Society, Key West

Miami Art Museum, Miami

Miami Museum of Science, Inc., Miami

Morikami Museum and Japanese Gardens, Delray Beach

Mote Marine Aquarium, Sarasota

Museum of Art, Fort Lauderdale

Museum of Arts & Sciences, Daytona Beach

Museum of Contemporary Art, North Miami

Museum of Discovery and Science, Fort Lauderdale

Museum of Fine Arts, Saint Petersburg

Museum of Florida History, Tallahassee

Museum of Science & History of Jacksonville, Inc., Jacksonville

Museum of Science & Industry, Tampa

National Museum of Naval Aviation, U.S. Dept. of the Navy, Pensacola

Norton Museum of Art, West Palm Beach

Orange County Regional History Center, Orlando

Orlando Museum of Art, Orlando

Orlando Science Center, Orlando

Pensacola Museum of Art, Pensacola

Polk Museum of Art, Lakeland

Salvador Dali Museum, Inc., St. Petersburg

Samuel P. Garn Museum of Art, University of Florida, Gainesville

Society of the Four Arts, Palm Beach

Tallahassee Museum of History and Natural Science, Tallahassee

Tampa Museum of Art, Tampa

University of South Florida Contemporary Art Museum, Tampa

Vero Beach Museum of Art, Vero Beach

Vizcaya Museum and Gardens, Miami

Wolfsonian–FIU, Florida International University, Miami Beach

Georgia

Albany Museum of Art, Albany

Andersonville National Historic Site, National Park Service, Andersonville

Atlanta History Center, Atlanta Historical Society, Inc., Atlanta

Augusta Museum of History, Augusta

Columbus Museum, Columbus

Fernbank Museum of Natural History, Atlanta

Georgia Museum of Art, University of Georgia, Athens

Georgia Southern University Museum, Statesboro

High Museum of Art, Atlanta

Michael C. Carlos Museum, Emory University, Atlanta

Museum of Arts & Sciences, Macon

Museum of Aviation Flight and Technology Center, United States Air Force, Warner Robins AFB

St. Simons Island Lighthouse Museum, St. Simons Island

Telfair Museum of Art, Savannah

Telfair Museum of Art, Owens-Thomas House, Savannah

Hawaii

Bernice P. Bishop Museum, Honolulu

Honolulu Academy of Arts, Honolulu

Lyman Museum, Hilo

Mission Houses Museum, Honolulu

Idaho

Boise Art Museum, Boise

Herrett Center for Arts and Science, College of Southern Idaho, Twin Falls

Idaho Museum of Natural History, Idaho State University, Pocatello

Idaho State Historical Museum, Boise

Sun Valley Center for the Arts, Sun Valley

Illinois

Adler Planetarium, Chicago

Art Institute of Chicago, Chicago

Chicago Botanic Garden, Glencoe

Chicago History Museum, Chicago

Clarke House Museum, City of Chicago, Chicago

David & Alfred Smart Museum of Art, University of Chicago, Chicago

Early American Museum, Mahomet

Field Museum of Natural History, Chicago

Frank Lloyd Wright Preservation Trust, Oak Park

Glessner House Museum, Chicago

Illinois State Museum, Springfield

Illinois State Museum, Dickson Mounds Museum, Lewiston

Krannert Art Museum, University of Illinois, Champaign

Lake County Discovery Museum, Lake County Forest Preserves, Wauconda

Lakeview Museum of Arts and Sciences, Peoria

McLean County Museum of History, Bloomington

Mexican Fine Arts Center Museum, Chicago

Museum of Contemporary Art, Chicago

Museum of Contemporary Photography, Columbia College, Chicago

Museum of Science and Industry, Chicago

Naper Settlement, Naperville

Peggy Notebaert Nature Museum, Chicago Academy of Sciences, Chicago

Southern Illinois University Museum, Carbondale

Tarble Arts Center, Eastern Illinois University, Charleston

Indiana

Art Museum of Greater Lafayette, Lafayette

Auburn Cord Duesenberg Museum, Auburn

Ball State University Museum of Art, Muncie

Children's Museum of Indianapolis, Indianapolis

Conner Prairie, Earlham College, Fishers

Eiteljorg Museum of American Indians and Western Art, Indianapolis

Evansville Museum of Arts and Science, Evansville

Fort Wayne Museum of Art, Fort Wayne

Indiana State Museum, Indianapolis

Indiana State Museum, Angel Mounds, Evansville

Indiana State Museum, Lanier Mansion, Madison

Indiana State Museum, T.C. Steele Site, Nashville

Indiana University Art Museum, Bloomington

Indianapolis Museum of Art, Indianapolis

Indianapolis Zoo, Indianapolis

Morris-Butler House Museum, Indianapolis

President Benjamin Harrison Home, Indianapolis

Sheldon Swope Art Museum, Inc., Terre Haute

Snite Museum of Art, University of Notre Dame, Notre Dame

South Bend Regional Museum of Art, South Bend

William Hammond Mathers Museum, Indiana University, Bloomington

Iowa

Blanden Memorial Art Museum, Fort Dodge

Cedar Rapids Museum of Art, Cedar Rapids

Charles H. MacNider Museum, Mason City

Dubuque Museum of Art, Dubuque

Family Museum of Arts and Science, Bettendorf

Figge Museum of Art, Davenport

Grout Museum of History and Science, Waterloo

Mississippi River Museum, Dubuque County Historical Society, Dubuque

Muscatine Arts Center, Muscatine

Museum of Art, University of Iowa, Iowa City

Putnam Museum of History and Natural Science, Davenport

Sanford Museum and Planetarium, Cherokee

Science Center of Iowa, Des Moines

Sioux City Art Center, Sioux City

Sioux City Public Museum, Sioux City

University Museums, Iowa State University, Art-on-Campus Program, Ames

University Museums, Iowa State University, Brunnier Art Museum, Ames

University Museums, Iowa State University, Farm House Museum, Ames

University of Northern Iowa Museums & Collections, Cedar Falls

Vesterheim, the Norwegian-American Museum, Decorah

Kansas

Boot Hill Museum, Dodge City

Edwin A. Ulrich Museum of Art, Wichita State University, Wichita

Frontier Army Museum, U.S. Department of the Army, Ft. Leavenworth

Kansas Museum of History, Topeka

Marianna Kistler Beach Museum of Art, Kansas State University, Manhattan

Mulvane Art Museum, Washburn University, Topeka

Old Cowtown Museum, Wichita

Salina Art Center, Salina

Santa Fe Trail Center, Larned

Smoky Hill Museum, Salina

Spencer Museum of Art, University of Kansas, Lawrence

Wichita Art Museum, Wichita

Wichita–Sedgwick County Historical Museum, Wichita

Kentucky

Historic Locust Grove, Louisville

Kentucky Historical Society, Frankfort

Louisville Zoo, Louisville

Speed Art Museum, Louisville
University of Kentucky Art Museum, Lexington

Louisiana
Alexandria Museum of Art, Alexandria
Hermann-Grima & Gallier Historic Houses, New Orleans
Historic New Orleans Collection, New Orleans
Longue Vue House and Gardens, New Orleans
Louisiana Art and Science Museum, Baton Rouge
Louisiana Old State Capitol, Center for Political and Governmental History, Baton Rouge
Louisiana State Museum, New Orleans
Magnolia Mound Plantation, Baton Rouge
Meadows Museum of Art, Centenary College of Louisiana, Shreveport
New Orleans Museum of Art, New Orleans

Maine
Bowdoin College Museum of Art, Brunswick
Brick Store Museum, Kennebunk
Colby College Museum of Art, Waterville
Farnsworth Art Museum, Rockland
Historic New England, Hamilton House, South Berwick
Maine Maritime Museum, Bath
Maine State Museum, Augusta
Owl's Head Transportation Museum, Owl's Head
Peary-MacMillan Arctic Museum, Bowdoin College, Brunswick
Penobscot Marine Museum, Searsport
Portland Museum of Art, Portland

Maryland
Academy Art Museum, Easton
Baltimore Museum of Art, Baltimore
Calvert Marine Museum, Solomons
Chesapeake Bay Maritime Museum, Saint Michaels
Clara Barton National Historic Site, National Park Service, Glen Echo
Havre de Grace Decoy Museum, Havre de Grace
Historic Annapolis Foundation, Annapolis
Historic St. Mary's City, St. Mary's City
Historical Society of Frederick County, Frederick
Jewish Museum of Maryland, The Jewish Historical Society of Maryland, Baltimore
Maryland Historical Society, Baltimore
National Museum of Civil War Medicine, Frederick

St. Mary's County Museum Division, Drayden African-American Schoolhouse, Colton's Point
St. Mary's County Museum Division, St. Clements Island–Potomac River Museum, Colton's Point
St. Mary's County Museum Division, U-1105 Black Panther Historic Shipwreck Preserve, Colton's Point
The Walters Art Museum, Baltimore
Washington County Museum of Fine Arts, Hagerstown

Massachusetts
American Textile History Museum, Lowell
Andover Historical Society Museum, Andover
Boston Children's Museum, Boston
Chesterwood, National Trust for Historic Preservation, Stockbridge
Concord Museum, Concord Antiquarian Society, Concord
Connecticut Valley Historical Museum, Springfield
DeCordova Museum and Sculpture Park, Lincoln
Fitchburg Art Museum, Fitchburg
Fuller Craft Museum, Brockton
Garden in the Woods: Botanical Garden of the New England Wildflower Society, New England Wild Flower society, Framingham
Gore Place, Waltham
Hancock Shaker Village, Inc., Pittsfield
Harvard University Art Museums, Arthur M. Sackler Museum, Cambridge
Harvard University Art Museums, Busch-Reisinger Museum, Cambridge
Harvard University Art Museums, Fogg Art Museum, Cambridge
Heritage Museums and Gardens, Sandwich
Herman Melville's Arrowhead, Berkshire County Historical Society, Pittsfield
Higgins Armory Museum, Worcester
Historic Deerfield, Inc., Deerfield
Historic New England, Boston
Historic New England, Beauport, Gloucester
Historic New England, Codman House, Lincoln
Historic New England, Cogswell's Grant, Essex
Historic New England, Gropius House, Lincoln
Historic New England, Harrison Gray Otis House, Boston
Historic New England, Lyman Estate, Waltham

Historic New England, Spencer-Peirce-Little Farm, Newbury
Institute of Contemporary Art, Boston
Isabella Stewart Gardner Museum, Boston
Jackson Homestead, Newton
Mead Art Museum, Amherst College, Amherst
MIT Museum, Massachusetts Institute of Technology, Cambridge
MIT — List Visual Arts Center, Cambridge
Museum of Fine Arts, Boston
Museum of Science, Boston
National Heritage Museum, Scottish Rite Masonic Museum and Library, Inc., Lexington
New Bedford Whaling Museum, Old Dartmouth Historical Society, New Bedford
New England Aquarium, Boston
Norman Rockwell Museum at Stockbridge, Inc., Stockbridge
Old Sturbridge Village, Sturbridge
Paul Revere House and Hichborn House, Paul Revere Memorial Association, Boston
Peabody Essex Museum, Salem
Peabody Museum of Archaeology and Ethnology, Harvard University, Cambridge
Pilgrim Hall Museum, Plymouth
Sandwich Glass Museum, Sandwich
Smith College Museum of Art, Northampton
Springfield Science Museum, Springfield
Sterling & Francine Clark Art Institute, Williamstown
Tower Hill Botanic Garden, Worcester County Horticultural Society, Boylston
U.S.S. Constitution Museum, Boston
Wenham Museum, Wenham
Williams College Museum of Art, Williamstown
Worcester Art Museum, Worcester

Michigan
Alden B. Dow Museum of Science and Art, Midland
Alfred P. Sloan, Jr. Museum, Flint
Art Center of Battle Creek, Battle Creek
Cranbrook Art Museum, Bloomfield Hills
Cranbrook Institute of Science, Bloomfield Hills
Detroit Institute of Arts, Detroit
Ella Sharp Museum, Jackson
Flint Institute of Arts, Flint
Frankenmuth Historical Association Museum, Frankenmuth
Grand Rapids Art Museum, Grand Rapids
Holland Museum, Holland
Jesse Besser Museum, Inc., Alpena

Kalamazoo Valley Museum, Kalamazoo
Kelsey Museum of Archaeology, University of Michigan, Ann Arbor
Krasl Art Center, St. Joseph
Kresge Art Museum, Michigan State University, East Lansing
Mackinac State Historic Parks, Mackinac Dept. of Natural Resources, Lansing
Michigan Historical Museum System, Lansing
Michigan Historical Museum System, Civilian Conservation Corps Museum, Roscommon
Michigan Historical Museum System, Copper Harbor Lighthouse, Copper Harbor
Michigan Historical Museum System, Father Marquette National Memorial, St. Ignace
Michigan Historical Museum System, Fayette Historic Townsite, Garden
Michigan Historical Museum System, Ft. Wilkins Historic Complex, Copper Harbor
Michigan Historical Museum System, Hartwick Pine Logging Museum, Negaunee
Michigan Historical Museum System, Mann House, Concord
Michigan Historical Museum System, Michigan Historical Museum, Lansing
Michigan Historical Museum System, Michigan Iron Industry Museum
Michigan Historical Museum System, Sanilac Petroglyphs, Lansing
Michigan Historical Museum System, Walker Tavern, Brooklyn
Michigan State University Museum, East Lansing
Muskegon Museum of Art, Muskegon
Public Museum, Van Andel Museum Center, Grand Rapids
Saginaw Art Museum, Saginaw
The Henry Ford, Dearborn
University of Michigan Museum of Art, Ann Arbor

Minnesota
Minneapolis Institute of Arts, Minneapolis
Minnesota History Center, St. Paul
Science Museum of Minnesota, St. Paul
Stearns History Museum, St. Cloud
Walker Arts Center, Minneapolis

Mississippi
Grand Village of the Natchez Indians, Natchez
Lauren Rogers Museum of Art, Laurel
Manship House Museum, Jackson
Mississippi Museum of Natural Science, Jackson
Walter Anderson Museum of Art, Ocean Springs

Missouri

Albrecht-Kemper Museum of Art, St. Joseph

Jefferson National Expansion Memorial (Museum of Westward Expansion, Gateway Arch, St. Louis Old Courthouse), National Park Service, St. Louis

Laumeier Sculpture Park and Museum, St. Louis

Mildred Lane Kemper Art Museum, St. Louis

Missouri Botanical Garden, St. Louis

Missouri History Museum, Missouri Historical Society, St. Louis

Museum of Art and Archaeology, University of Missouri, Columbia

Nelson-Atkins Museum of Art, Kansas City

St. Joseph Museum, St. Joseph

St. Louis Art Museum, St. Louis

St. Louis Science Center, St. Louis

U.S. Army Engineer Museum, U.S. Dept. of the Army, Fort Leonard Wood

Union Station Kansas City, Inc., Kansas City

Montana

Art Museum * Missoula, Missoula

C.M. Russell Museum, Great Falls

Historical Museum at Fort Missoula, Missoula

Montana Historical Society Museum, Helena

Museum of the Rockies, Montana State University, Bozeman

Western Heritage Center, Billings

Nebraska

Joslyn Art Museum, Omaha

Museum of Nebraska History, Nebraska State Historical Society, Lincoln

Sheldon Memorial Art Gallery and Sculpture Garden, University of Nebraska–Lincoln, Lincoln

Stuhr Museum of the Prairie Pioneer, Grand Island

University of Nebraska State Museum, University of Nebraska–Lincoln, Lincoln

Nevada

Museum of the Nevada Historical Society, Reno

Nevada Museum of Art, Reno

Nevada State Museum, Carson City

Nevada State Museum and Historical Society, Las Vegas

New Hampshire

Currier Gallery of Art, Manchester

Historic New England, Governor John Langdon House, Portsmouth

Hood Museum of Art, Dartmouth College, Hanover

Museum of New Hampshire History, New Hampshire Historical Society, Concord

Strawbery Banke, Inc., Portsmouth

New Jersey

Art Museum, Princeton University, Princeton

Mommouth Museum and Cultural Center, Lincroft

Montclair Art Museum, Montclair

Morris, Museum, Morristown

Museum of American Glass, Wheaton Village, Millville

New Jersey State Museum, Trenton

Newark Museum, Newark

Old Barracks Museum, Trenton

Visual Arts Center of New Jersey, Summit

New Mexico

Albuquerque Museum, Albuquerque

Georgia O'Keeffe Museum, Santa Fe

Maxwell Museum of Anthropology, University of New Mexico, Albuquerque

Millicent Rogers Museum, Taos

Museum of Indian Arts & Culture, Museums of New Mexico, Santa Fe

Museum of New Mexico, Museum of Fine Art, Santa Fe

Museum of New Mexico, Museum of Indian Arts & Culture, Santa Fe

Museum of New Mexico, Museum of Int'l Folk Art, Santa Fe

Museum of New Mexico, New Mexico State Monuments, Santa Fe

Museum of New Mexico, Palace of the Governor, Santa Fe

New Mexico Museum of Natural History and Science, Albuquerque

New Mexico Museum of Space History, Alamogordo

Roswell Museum and Art Center, Roswell

Silver City Museum, Silver City

Wheelwright Museum of the American Indian, Santa Fe

New York

Adirondack Museum, Blue Mountain Lake

Albany Institute of History and Art, Albany

Albright-Knox Art Gallery, Buffalo

American Museum of Natural History, New York

American Museum of the Moving Image, Astoria

Arnot Art Museum, Elmira

Brooklyn Children's Museum, Brooklyn

Brooklyn Museum of Art, Brooklyn
Buffalo and Erie County Historical Society Museum, Buffalo
Buffalo Museum of Science, Buffalo
Burchfield-Penney Art Center at Buffalo College, Buffalo State College, Buffalo
Chemung Valley History Museum, Elmira
Cold Spring Harbor Whaling Museum, Cold Spring Harbor
Corning Museum of Glass, Corning
Erie Canal Museum, Syracuse
Everson Museum of Art, Syracuse
Farmers' Museum, New York State Historical Association, Cooperstown
Fenimore Art Museum, New York State Historical Association, Cooperstown
Fort Ticonderoga, Ticonderoga
Frances Lehman Loeb Art Center, Vassar College, Poughkeepsie
Fraunces Tavern Museum, New York
Frederic Remington Art Museum, Ogdensburg
Frick College, New York
George Eastman House, Rochester
Guild Hall Museum, East Hampton
Heckscher Museum of Art, Huntington
Herbert F. Johnson Museum of Art, Cornell University, Ithaca
Historic Cherry Hill, Albany
Hofstra Museum, Hofstra University, Hempstead
Hudson River Museum, Yonkers
Hyde Collection Art Museum, Glens Falls
International Center of Photography, New York
Jewish Museum, New York
Katonah Museum of Art, Katonah
Landmark Society of Western New York, Campbell-Whittlesey House Museum, Rochester
Landmark Society of Western New York, Stone-Tolan House Museum, Rochester
Long Island Museum of American Art, History and Carriages, Stony Brook
Lower East Side Tenement Museum, New York
Memorial Art Gallery, University of Rochester, Rochester
Metropolitan Museum of Art, New York
Morgan Library & Museum, New York
Morris-Jumel Mansion, New York
Mount Vernon Hotel Museum and Garden, New York
Munson-Williams-Proctor Institute Museum of Art, Utica
Museum of Arts and Design, New York

Museum of Modern Art, New York
National Academy of Design Museum, New York
Neuberger Museum of Art, Purchase
New York Botanical Garden, Bronx
Parrish Art Museum, Southampton
Picker Art Gallery, Colgate University, Hamilton
Raynham Hall Museum, Oyster Bay
Rensselaer County Historical Society, Troy
Roberson Museum and Science Center, Binghamton
Rochester Museum and Science Center, Rochester
Rockwell Museum of Western Art, Corning
Rye Historical Society Museum, Rye
Sciencenter, Ithaca
Shaker Museum, Old Chatham
Silas Wright House, St. Lawrence County Historical Association, Canton
Solomon R. Guggenheim Museum of Art, New York
Statue of Liberty National Monument and Ellis Island Immigration Museum, National Park Service, New York
Strong — National Museum of Play, Rochester
Studio Museum in Harlem, New York
Suffolk County Vanderbilt Museum, Centerport
West Point Museum, U.S. Military Academy, U.S. Dept. of the Army, West Point
Whitney Museum of American Art, New York

North Carolina
Ackland Art Museum, The University of North Carolina, Chapel Hill
Asheville Art Museum, Asheville
Cape Fear Museum, Wilmington
Discovery Place, Inc., Charlotte
Gaston County Museum of Art and History, Dallas
Greensboro Historical Museum, Greensboro
Greenville Museum of Art, Inc., Greenville
Health Adventure, Asheville
Hickory Museum of Art, Hickory
Louise Wells Cameron Art Museum, Wilmington
Museum of Early Southern Decorative Arts, Old Salem, Inc., Winston-Salem
Nasher Museum of Art, Durham
Natural Science Center of Greensboro, Greensboro
North Carolina Maritime Museum, Beaufort
North Carolina Museum of Art, Raleigh

North Carolina Museum of History, Raleigh

North Carolina State Museum of Natural Sciences, Raleigh

Old Salem and Museum of Early Southern Decorative Arts, Winston-Salem

Reynolda House Museum of American Art, Winston-Salem

Schiele Museum of Natural History and Planetarium, Gastonia

Southeastern Center for Contemporary Art, Winston-Salem

The Mint Museums, Charlotte

Tryon Palace Historic Sites and Gardens, New Bern

Waterworks Visual Arts Center, Salisbury

Weatherspoon Art Museum, University of North Carolina at Greensboro, Greensboro

North Dakota

North Dakota Heritage Center, State Historical Society of North Dakota, Bismarck

Plains Art Museum, Fargo

Ohio

Akron Art Museum, Akron

Allen County Museum, Lima

Allen Memorial Art Museum, Oberlin College, Oberlin

Arms Family Museum of Local History, Mahoning Valley Historical Society, Youngstown

Boonshoft Museum of Discovery, Dayton

Butler Institute of American Art, Youngstown

Canton Museum of Art, Canton

Cincinnati Art Museum, Cincinnati

Cincinnati Zoo and Botanical Garden, Cincinnati

Cleveland Museum of Art, Cleveland

Cleveland Museum of Natural History, Cleveland

Columbus Museum of Art, Columbus

Dayton Art Institute, Dayton

Holden Arboretum, Kirtland

Johnson-Humrickhouse Museum, Roscoe Village, Coshocton

Massillon Museum, Massillon

Miami University Art Museum, Oxford

National Museum of the United States Air Force, U.S. Air Force, Wright-Patterson AFB

Oberlin Heritage Center, Oberlin

Ohio Historical Center, Ohio Village, Columbus

Rutherford B. Hayes Presidential Center, Fremont

Springfield Museum of Art, Springfield

Stan Hywet Hall and Gardens, Akron

Taft Museum of Art, Cincinnati

Toledo Museum of Art, Toledo

Oklahoma

Fred Jones Jr. Museum of Art, University of Oklahoma, Norman Gilcrease Museum, Tulsa

Museum of the Great Plains, Lawton

National Cowboy and Western Heritage Museum, Oklahoma City

Oklahoma City Museum of Art, Oklahoma City

Oklahoma City National Memorial Museum, Oklahoma City

Oklahoma City Zoological Park and Botanical Garden, Oklahoma City

Omniplex, Oklahoma City

Philbrook Museum of Art, Tulsa

Sam Noble Oklahoma Museum of Natural History, University of Oklahoma, Norman

Tulsa Zoo & Living Museum, Tulsa

Oregon

Columbia Gorge Discovery Center and Museum, The Dalles

Columbia River Maritime Museum, Astoria

High Desert Museum, Bend

Jordan Schnitzer Museum of Art, University of Oregon, Eugene

Oregon Historical Society, Portland

Portland Art Museum, Portland

Pennsylvania

Academy of Natural Sciences of Philadelphia, Philadelphia

Allentown Art Museum, Allentown

Bowman's Hill Wildflower Preserve, Pennsylvania Historical 7 Museum Commission, New Hope

Brandywine River Museum, Chadds Ford

Bucks County Historical Society, Fonthill Museum, Doylestown

Bucks County Historical Society, Mercer Museum, Doylestown

Carnegie Museum of Art, Carnegie Institute, Pittsburgh

Carnegie Science Center, Carnegie Institute, Pittsburgh

Drake Well Museum, Pennsylvania Historical and Museum Commission, Titusville

Ephrata Cloister, Pennsylvania Historical and Museum Commission, Ephrata

Franklin Institute, Philadelphia

Hershey Museum and Gardens, Hershey

Independence National Historical Park, National Park Service, Philadelphia

Independence Seaport Museum, Philadelphia

James A. Michener Art Museum, Doylestown

Kemerer Museum of Decorative Arts, Historic Bethlehem Partnership, Inc., Bethlehem

Morris Arboretum, University of Pennsylvania, Philadelphia

Museum of the Pennsylvania Academy of Fine Arts, Philadelphia

National Canal Museum, Hugh Moore Historical Park and Museums, Inc., Easton

North Museum of Natural History & Science, Lancaster

Pennsbury Manor, Pennsylvania Historic and Museum Commission, Morrisville

Philadelphia Museum of Art, Philadelphia

Philip and Muriel Berman Museum of Art at Ursinus College, Collegeville

Please Touch Museum, Philadelphia

Reading Public Museum, Reading

Scott Arboretum, Swarthmore College, Swarthmore

Southern Alleghenies Museum of Art, Loretto

State Museum of Pennsylvania, Pennsylvania Historical and Museum Commission, Harrisburg

Thomas T. Taber Museum of the Lycoming County Historical Society, Williamsport

University of Pennsylvania Museum of Archaeology and Anthropology, Philadelphia

Westmoreland Museum of American Art, Greensburg

Woodmere Art Museum, Inc., Philadelphia

Puerto Rico

Museo de Arte de Ponce, Ponce

Rhode Island

Museum of Art, Rhode Island School of Design, Providence

Museum of Rhode Island History at Aldrich House, Rhode Island Historical Society, Providence

Museum of Rhode Island History at Aldrich House, Rhode Island Historical Society, John Brown House, Providence

Newport Art Museum and Art Association, Newport

Preservation Society of Newport County, Newport

Preservation Society of Newport County, The Breakers, Newport

Preservation Society of Newport County, Chateau-sur-Mer, Newport

Preservation Society of Newport County, Chepstow, Newport

Preservation Society of Newport County, The Elms, Newport

Preservation Society of Newport County, Green Animals Topiary Garden, Newport

Preservation Society of Newport County, Hunter House, Newport

Preservation Society of Newport County, Isaac Bell House, Newport

Preservation Society of Newport County, Kingscote, Newport

Preservation Society of Newport County, Marble House, Newport

Preservation Society of Newport County, Rosecliff, Newport

Slater Mill Historic Site, Pawtucket

South Carolina

Brookgreen Gardens, Pawleys Island

Charleston Museum, Charleston

Columbia Museum of Art, Columbia

Drayton Hall, National Trust for Historic Preservation, Charleston

Fort Sumter National Monument, National Park Service, Sullivan's Island

Gibbs Museum of Art, Charleston

Greenville County Museum of Art, Greenville

Historic Columbia Foundation, Hampton-Preston Mansion, Columbia

Historic Columbia Foundation, Robert Mills Historic House, Columbia

Historic Columbia Foundation, Woodrow Wilson Boyhood Home, Columbia

McKissick Museum, University of South Carolina, Columbia

South Carolina Confederate Relic Room and Museum, Columbia

South Carolina State Museum, Columbia

York County Culture & Heritage Museums, Rock Hill

South Dakota

National Music Museum (America's Shrine to Music Museum), Vermillion

South Dakota Art Museum, South Dakota State University, Brookings

Tennessee

Carroll Reece Museum, East Tennessee State University, Johnson City

Cheekwood Museum of Art, Nashville

Country Music Hall of Fame and Museum, Nashville

Dixon Gallery and Gardens, Memphis

Frank H. McClung Museum, University of Tennessee, Knoxville

Hunter Museum of American Art, Chattanooga

Knoxville Museum of Art, Knoxville

Memphis Brooks Museum of Art, Memphis

Memphis Pink Palace Family of Museums, Lichterman Nature Center, Memphis

Memphis Pink Palace Family of Museums, Memphis Pink Palace Museum and Planetarium, Memphis

Memphis Pink Palace Family of Museums, Magevney House, Memphis

Memphis Pink Palace Family of Museums, Mallory-Neely House, Memphis

National Civil Rights Museum, Memphis

Rocky Mount Museum, Piney Flats

Tennessee State Museum, Nashville

Texas

Amarillo Museum of Art, Amarillo

American Airpower Heritage Museum, Midland

Amon Carter Museum, Fort Worth

Art Center of Waco, Waco

Blanton Museum of Art, Austin

Contemporary Arts Museum Houston, Houston

Corpus Christi Museum of Science and History, Corpus Christi

Dallas Heritage Village, Dallas County Heritage Society, Dallas

Dallas Museum of Art, Dallas

Dallas Museum of Natural History, Doing Business as: Museum of Science and Nature, Dallas

El Paso Museum of Art, El Paso

Ellen Noel Art Museum of the Permian Basin, Odessa

Fort Bend Museum Association, Richmond

Fort Worth Museum of Science and History, Fort Worth

Heritage Farmstead Museum, Plano

Heritage Society, Houston

Historic Waco Foundation Museums: East Terrace, McCulloch House, Earle-Napier-Kinnard House, Fort House, Waco

Houston Museum of Natural Science, Houston

International Museum of Art and Science, McAllen

McFaddin-Ward House, Beaumont

McNay Art Museum, San Antonio

Modern Art Museum of Fort Worth, Fort Worth

Museum of Fine Arts, Houston, Houston

Museum of Texas Tech University, Lubbock

Museum of the Southwest, Midland

Old Jail Art Center, Albany

Panhandle-Plains Historical Museum, Canyon

Sam Houston Memorial Museum, Sam Houston State University, Huntsville

San Angelo Museum of Fine Arts, San Angelo

San Antonio Museum of Art, San Antonio

Scurry County Museum, Snyder

Sixth Floor Museum at Dealey Plaza, Dallas

Star of the Republic Museum, Washington

Texarkana Museums System, Texarkana

Texas Maritime Museum, Rockport

The Grace Museum, Abilene

The Science Place, Doing Business as: Museum of Science and Nature, Dallas

Tyler Museum of Art, Tyler

U.S. Army Medical Department Museum, U.S. Dept. of the Army, Fort Sam Houston

Witte Museum, San Antonio

Utah

College of Eastern Utah Prehistoric Museum, Price

Monte L. Bean Life Science Museum, Brigham Young University, Provo

Nora Eccles Harrison Museum of Art, Utah State University, Logan

Utah Museum of Fine Arts, University of Utah, Salt Lake City

Utah Museum of Natural History, University of Utah, Salt Lake City

Vermont

American Museum of Fly Fishing, Manchester

Bennington Museum, Bennington

Fairbanks Museum and Planetarium, St. Johnsbury

Middlebury College Museum of Art, Middlebury

Robert Hull Fleming Museum, University of Vermont, Burlington

Virginia

Art Museum of Western Virginia, Roanoke

Carlyle House Historic Park, Northern Virginia Regional Park Authority, Alexandria

Chrysler Museum of Art, Norfolk

Colonial Williamsburg, Williamsburg

Colonial Williamsburg, Abby Aldrich Rockefeller Folk Art Center, Williamsburg

Colonial Williamsburg, Basset Hall, Williamsburg

Colonial Williamsburg, Colonial Williamsburg Historic District, Williamsburg

Colonial Williamsburg, DeWitt Wallace Decorative Arts Gallery, Williamsburg

Fairfax County Park Authority, Resource Management Division, Colvin Run Mill, Fairfax

Fairfax County Park Authority, Resource Management Division, Green Springs Garden Park, Fairfax

Fairfax County Park Authority, Resource Management Division, Sully Historic Site, Fairfax

Fort Ward Museum, Office of Historic Alexandria, Alexandria

Fredericksburg Area Museum and Cultural Center, Inc., Fredericksburg

Frontier Culture Museum, Staunton

Gadsby's Tavern Museum, Alexandria

Gari Melchers Home and Studio, University of Mary Washington, Fredericksburg

Gunston Hall Plantation, Mason Neck

Jamestown-Yorktown Foundation Museum, Williamsburg

Manassas National Battlefield Park, National Park Service, Manassas Mariners' Museum, Newport News

Muscarelle Museum of Art, The College of William & Mary, Williamsburg

Peninsula Fine Arts Center, Newport News

Piedmont Arts Association, Martinsville

Science Museum of Virginia including the Virginia Aviation Museum, Richmond

Science Museum of Western Virginia, Roanoke

The Lyceum, Office of Historic Alexandria, Alexandria

U.S. Army Quartermaster Museum, U.S. Department of the Army, Fort Lee

University of Virginia Art Museum, University of Virginia, Charlottesville

Valentine Richmond History Center, Richmond

Virginia Historical Society Museum, Richmond

Virginia Living Museum, Newport News

Virginia Military Institute Museum Operations, New Market Battlefield State Historic Park/Hall of Valor Museum, New Market

Virginia Military Institute Museum Operations, VMI Museum, Lexington

Virginia Museum of Fine Arts, Richmond

Virginia War Museum, Newport News

Virginia War Museum, Endview Plantation, Newport News

Virginia War Museum, Lee Hall Mansion, Newport News

William King Regional Arts Center, Abingdon

Wilton House Museum, The National Society of The Colonial Dames of America, Richmond

Woodrow Wilson Presidential Library (formerly: WW Birthplace), Staunton

Washington

Burke Museum of Natural History and Culture, University of Washington, Seattle

Frye Art Museum, Seattle

Henry Art Gallery, University of Washington, Seattle

Maryhill Museum of Art, Goldendale

Museum of Flight, Seattle

Museum of History and Industry, Seattle

Naval Undersea Museum, U.S. Dept. of the Navy, Keyport

Northwest Museum of Arts and Culture, Spokane

Seattle Art Museum, Seattle

Tacoma Art Museum, Tacoma

Washington State Historical Society, Washington State Capitol Museum and Heritage Resource Center, Olympia

Washington State Historical Society, Washington State History Museum, Tacoma

Washington State Historical Society, WSHS Research Center, Tacoma

Whatcom Museum of History and Art, Bellingham

Yakima Valley Museum, Yakima

West Virginia

Clay Center for the Arts and Sciences of West Virginia, Charleston

Harpers Ferry National Historical Park, National Park Service, Harpers Ferry

Huntington Museum of Art, Huntington

Museums of Oglebay Institute, Wheeling

Wisconsin

Bergstrom-Mahler Museum, Neenah

Charles A. Wustum Museum of Fine Arts, Racine

Chazen Museum of Art (formerly Elvehjem Museum of Art), University of Wisconsin at Madison, Madison

Chippewa Valley Museum, Eau Claire

EAA AirVenture Museum, Oshkosh

Kenosha Public Museum, Kenosha

Leigh Yawkey Woodson Art Museum, Wausau

Logan Museum of Anthropology, Beloit College, Beloit

Madison Museum of Contemporary Art, Madison

Milwaukee Art Museum, Milwaukee

Milwaukee Public Museum, Milwaukee

Neville Public Museum of Brown County, Green Bay

Oshkosh Public Museum, Oshkosh

Paine Art Center and Gardens, Oshkosh

Rahr-West Art Museum, Manitowoc

Wisconsin Maritime Museum, Manitowoc

Wisconsin Veterans Museum, Madison

Wyoming

Buffalo Bill Historical Center, Cody

Jim Gatchell Memorial Museum, Buffalo

National Museum of Wildlife Art, Jackson

University of Wyoming Art Museum, Laramie

Wyoming State Museum, Cheyenne

XIII. National Art Museum Directory

Source: Association of Art Museum Directors (AAMD), 120 East 56th Street, Suite 520, New York, NY 10022.

Ackland Museum
Emily Kass
University of North Carolina at Chapel Hill
Campus Box 3400
Chapel Hill, NC 27599–3400

Addison Gallery of American Art
Brian Allen, Director
180 Main Street
Andover, MA 01810

Akron Art Museum
Mitchell Kahan, Director
70 E. Market Street
Akron, OH 44308

AlbrightKnox Art Gallery
Louis Grachos, Director
1285 Elmwood Avenue
Buffalo, NY 14222

Allen Memorial Art Museum
Stephanie Wiles, Director
87 North Main Street
Oberlin, OH 44074

Allentown Art Museum
David Brigham, Director
Fifth and Court Streets
Allentown, PA 18105

The Andy Warhol Museum
Thomas Sokolowski, Director
117 Sandusky Street
Pittsburgh, PA 15212

Arkansas Arts Center
Ellen Plummer, Director
P.O. Box 2137
Little Rock, AR 72203

Art Gallery of Ontario
Matthew Teitelbaum, Director
317 Dundas Street West
Toronto, ON M5T1G4
Canada

Art Institute of Chicago
James Cuno, Director
111 South Michigan Avenue
Chicago, IL 60603

Asia Society Museum
Melissa Chiu, Director
725 Park Avenue
New York, NY 10021

Asian Art Museum of San Francisco
Emily Sano, Director
200 Larkin Street
San Francisco, CA 94102

Austin Museum of Art
Dana Friis-Hansen, Director
823 Congress Avenue
Austin, TX 78701

Baltimore Museum of Art
Doreen Bolger, Director
Art Museum Drive
Baltimore, MD 21218

Bass Museum of Art
Diane Camber, Director
212 Park Avenue
Miami Beach, FL 33139

Berkeley Art Museum
Kevin Consey, Director
University of California
2625 Durant Avenue
Berkeley, CA 94720

Birmingham Museum of Art
Gail Andrews, Director
2000 8th Avenue North
Birmingham, AL 35203

Brandywine River Museum
James Duff, Director
P.O. Box 141
Chadds Ford, PA 19317

Brigham Young University Museum of Art
Campbell Gray, Director
North Campus Drive
Provo, Utah 84602

Brooklyn Museum of Art
Arnold L. Lehman, Director
200 Eastern Parkway
Brooklyn, NY 11238

Butler Institute of American Art
Louis A. Zona, Director
524 Wick Avenue
Youngstown, OH 44502

Canadian Center for Architecture
Mirko Zardini, Director
1920 Baile Street
Montreal, QC H3H 2S6
Canada

Cantor Arts Center
Thomas K. Seligman, Director
Stanford University
Lomita Drive and Museum Way
Stanford, CA 94305

Carnegie Museum of Art
Richard Armstrong, Director
4400 Forbes Avenue
Pittsburgh, PA 15213

Chazen Museum of Art
Russell Panczenko, Director
800 University Avenue
Madison, WI 53706

Chrysler Museum
William J. Hennessey, Director
Onley Roach and Mowbray Arch
Norfolk, VA 23510

Cleveland Museum of Art
Timothy Rub, Director
11150 East Boulevard
Cleveland, OH 44106

Colonial Williamsburg Foundation
Ronald L. Hurst, Director
DeWitt Wallace Gallery
P.O. Box 1776
Williamsburg, VA 23187

Columbia Museum of Art
Karen Brosius, Director
P.O. Box 2068
Columbia, SC 29202

Columbus Museum
Charles T. Butler, Director

1251 Wynnton Road
Columbus, GA 31906

Columbus Museum of Art
Nannette Maciejunes, Director
480 East Broad Street
Columbus, OH 43215

Contemporary Arts Museum Houston
Marti Mayo, Director
5216 Montrose Boulevard
Houston, TX 77006

The Contemporary Museum
Georgianna M. Lagoria, Director
2411 Makiki Heights Drive
Honolulu, HI 96822

Cooper-Hewitt National Design Museum
Paul Warwick Thompson, Director
Smithsonian Institution
2 East 91st Street
New York, NY 10128

Crocker Art Museum
Lial A. Jones, Director
216 O Street
Sacramento, CA 95814

Cummer Museum of Art & Gardens
Maaren van de Guchte, Director
829 Riverside Avenue
Jacksonville, FL 32204

Currier Museum of Art
Susan E. Strickler, Director
201 Myrtle Way
Manchester, NH 03104

Dallas Museum of Art
John R. Lane, Director
1717 North Harwood
Dallas, TX 75201

David and Alfred Smart Museum of Art
Anthony Hirschel, Director
University of Chicago
5550 South Greenwood
Chicago, IL 60637

DeCordova Museum and Sculpture Park
Paul Master-Karnik, Director
Sandy Pond Road
Lincoln, MA 01773

Delaware Art Museum
Danielle Rice, Director
2301 Kentmere Parkway
Wilmington, DE 19806

Denver Art Museum
Lewis I. Sharp, Director
100 West 14th Avenue Parkway
Denver, CO 80204

Des Moines Art Center
Jeff Fleming, Director
4700 Grand Avenue
Des Moines, IA 50312

Detroit Institute of Arts
Graham W.J. Beal, Director
5200 Woodward Avenue
Detroit, MI 48202

Dixon Gallery and Gardens
James J. Kamm, Director
4339 Park Avenue
Memphis, TN 38117

El Museo del Barrio
Julian Zufazagoitia, Director
1230 Fifth Avenue
New York, NY 10029

Farnsworth Art Museum
Lora S. Urbanelli, Director
16 Museum Street
Rockland, ME 04841

Fine Arts Museums of San Francisco
John Buchanan, Jr., Director
Golden Gate Park
50 Hagiwara Tea Garden Drive
San Francisco, CA 94118

Flint Institute of Arts
John B. Henry III, Director
1120 East Kearsley Street
Flint, MI 48503

Frederick R. Weisman Art Museum
Lyndel King, Director
333 East River Road
Minneapolis, MN 55455

Freer Gallery of Art & Sackler Gallery
Julian Raby, Director
P.O. Box 37012, MRC 707
Washington, DC 20013

Frick Art and Historical Center
William B. Bodine, Jr., Director
7227 Reynolds Street
Pittsburgh, PA 15208

Frick Collection
Anne Poulet, Director
1 East 70th Street
New York, NY 10021

George Eastman House
Anthony Bannon, Director
900 East Avenue
Rochester, NY 14607

Georgia Museum of Art
William E. Eiland, Director
The University of Georgia
90 Carlton Street
Athens, GA 30602

Georgia O'Keeffe Museum
George G. King, Director
217 Johnson Street
Santa Fe, NM 87501

Grand Rapids Art Museum
Celeste Adams, Director
155 North Division Street
Grand Rapids, MI 49502

Hammer Museum
Ann Philbin, Director
10899 Wilshire Boulevard
Los Angeles, CA 90024

Harvard University Art Museum
Thomas W. Lentz, Director
32 Quincy Street
Cambridge, MA 02138

Henry Art Gallery
Richard Andrews, Director
University of Washington
P.O. Box 351410
Seattle, WA 98195

Herbert F. Johnson Museum of Art
Franklin W. Robinson, Director
Cornell University
Ithaca, NY 14853

High Museum of Art
Michael E. Shapiro, Director
1280 Peachtree Street, N.E.
Atlanta, GA 30309

Hirshhorn Museum and Sculpture Garden
Olga Viso, Director
P.O. Box 37012
MRC 350, Independence Ave. at 7th St. SW
Washington, DC 20013

Honolulu Academy of Arts
Stephen Little, Director
900 South Beretania Street
Honolulu, HI 96814

Hudson River Museum
Michael Botwinick, Director

511 Warburton Ave.
Yonkers, NY 10701

Hunter Museum of America Art
Robert A. Kret
10 Bluff View
Chattanooga, TN 37403

Huntington Library and Art Collections
John Murdoch, Director
1151 Oxford Road
San Marino, CA 91108

Indiana University Art Museum
Adelheid M. Gealt, Director
Bloomington, IN 47405

Indianapolis Museum of Art
Maxwell L. Anderson, Director
4000 Michigan Road
Indianapolis, IN 46208

Institute of Contemporary Art, Boston
Jill Medvedow, Director
955 Boylston Street
Boston, MA 02115

Institute of Contemporary Art, Philadelphia
Claudia Gould, Director
University of Pennsylvania
188 S. 36th Street
Philadelphia, PA 19104

International Center of Photography
Willis Harshorn, Director
1114 Avenue of the Americas
New York, NY 10036

Isabella Stewart Gardner Museum
Anne Hawley, Director
Two Palace Road
Boston, MA 02115

J. Paul Getty Museum
Michael Brand, Director
1200 Getty Center Drive
Los Angeles, CA 90049

Jack S. Blanton Museum of Art
Jessie Otto Hite, Director
University of Texas at Austin
23rd and San Jacinto Streets
Austin, TX 78712

Jane Voorhees Zimmerli Art Museum
Gregory J. Perry, Director
71 Hamilton Street
New Brunswick, NJ 08901

Jewish Museum
Joan H. Rosenbaum, Director

1109 Fifth Avenue
New York, NY 10128

John and Mable Ringling Museum of Art
John Wetenhall, Director
5401 Bay Shore Road
Sarasota, FL 34243

Joslyn Art Museum
J. Brooks Joyner, Director
2200 Dodge Street
Omaha, NE 68102

Kalamazoo Institute of Arts
James Bridenstine, Director
314 S. Park Street
Kalamazoo, MI 49007

Kimbell Art Museum
Timothy Potts, Director
3333 Camp Bowie Boulevard
Fort Worth, TX 76107

Los Angeles County Museum of Art
Michael Govan, Director
5905 Wilshire Boulevard
Los Angeles, CA 90036

Lowe Art Museum
Brian A. Dursum, Director
1301 Stanford Drive
Coral Gables, FL 33124

McNay Art Museum
William J. Chiego, Director
P.O. Box 6069
San Antonio, TX 78209

Memorial Art Gallery of Rochester
Grant Holcomb, Director
University of Rochester
500 University Avenue
Rochester, NY 14607

Memphis Brooks Museum of Art
Kaywin Feldman, Director
1934 Poplar Avenue
Memphis, TN 38104

The Menil Collection
Joseph Helfenstein, Director
1511 Branard Street
Houston, TX 77006

Metropolitan Museum of Art
Philippe de Montebello, Director
1000 Fifth Avenue
New York, NY 10028

Michael C. Carlos Museum
Bonnie Speed, Director

Emory University
571 Kilgo Circle
Atlanta, GA 30322

Milwaukee Art Museum
David Gordon, Director
750 North Art Museum Drive
Milwaukee, WI 53202

Modern Art Museum of Forth Worth
Marla Price, Director
3200 Darnell
Fort Worth, TX 76107

Montclair Art Museum
Patterson Sims, Director
3 South Mountain Avenue
Montclair, NJ 07042

Montgomery Museum of Fine Arts
Mark Johnson, Director
One Museum Drive
Montgomery, AL 36117

The Morgan Library and Museum
Charles E. Pierce, Jr., Director
225 Madison Avenue
New York, NY 10016

Munson-Williams-Proctor Arts Institute
Paul D. Schweizer, Director
310 Genesee Street
Utica, NY 13502

Musee d'art contemporain de Montreal
Marc Mayer, Director
185 Sainte-Catherine Ouest
Montreal, QB H2X 3X5
Canada

Museo de Arte de Ponce
Agustin Arteaga, Director
P.O. Box 9027
Ponce, Puerto Rico 00732

Museo de Arte Moderno
Luis-Martin Lozano, Director
Paseo de la Reforma
Bosque de Chapultepec
Mexico City, D.F. 11560
Mexico

Museo del Palacio de Bellas Artes
Mercedes Iturbe, Director
Av. Juarez, Num 1
5 Piso, Col. Centro
Mexico City, D.F. 06050
Mexico

Museo Dolores Olmedo Patino
Carlos Phillips Olmedo, Director
Av. Mexico 5843
La Noria Xochimilco
Mexico City, D.F. 16030
Mexico

Museo Franz Mayer
Hector Rivero Borrell, Director
Ave Hidalgo No. 45
Mexico City, D.F. 06300
Mexico

Museo Nacional de Arte
Roxana Velasquez, Director
Tacuba 8
Centro Historico
Mexico City, D.F. 06000
Mexico

Museo Nacional del Virreinato
Miguel Fernandez Felix, Director
Palza Cirenial 99
Tepotzotlan, Estado 54600
Mexico

Museo Tamayo Arte Contemporeano
Ramiro Martinez Estrada, Director
Paseo del la Reforma
Bosque de Chapultepec
Mexico City, D.F. 11580
Mexico

Museo Universitario de Ciencias y Arte
Graciela de la Torre, Director
Ciudad Universitaria C.P.
Mexico City, D.F. 04510
Mexico

Museum for African Art
Elsie Crum McCabe, Director
36–01 43rd Avenue
Long Island City, NY 11101

Museum of Art, Fort Lauderdale
Lirvin Lippman, Director
1 East las Olas Boulevard
Ft. Lauderdale, FL 33301

Museum of Contemporary Art, Chicago
Robert Fitzpatrick, Director
220 East Chicago Avenue
Chicago, IL 60611

Museum of Contemporary Art, Los Angeles
Jeremy Strick, Director
250 S. Grand Avenue
Los Angeles, CA 90012

Museum of Contemporary Art, San Diego
Hugh M. Davies, Director
700 Prospect Street
La Jolla, CA 92037

Museum of Fine Arts, Boston
Malcolm Rogers, Director
465 Huntington Ave. of the Arts
Boston, MA 02115

Museum of Fine Arts, Houston
Peter C. Marzio, Director
1001 Bissonnet
Houston, TX 77005

Museum of Glass
John Timothy Close, Director
1801 Dock Street
Tacoma, WA 98402

Museum of Modern Art
Glenn Lowry, Director
11 West 53rd Street
New York, NY 10019

Nasher Museum of Art at Duke University
Kimerly Rorschah, Director
Box 90732
Durham, NC 27708

Nasher Sculpture Center
Steven Nash, Director
2001 Flora Street
Dallas, TX 75201

National Academy of Design
Annette Blaugrund, Director
1083 Fifth Avenue
New York, NY 10128

National Gallery of Art
Earl A. Powell, III, Director
6th and Constitution Avenue, NW
Washington, DC 20565

National Gallery of Canada
Pierre Theberge, Director
380 Sussex Drive, P.O. Box 427
Ottawa, Ontario K1N 9N4
Canada

National Museum of African Art
Sharon F. Patton, Director
P.O. Box 37012
Washington, DC 20013

National Portrait Gallery
Marc Pachter, Director
Victor Building, Suite 8300, MRC 973
Washington, DC 20013

Nelson-Atkins Museum of Art
Marc F. Wilson, Director
4525 Oak Street
Kansas City, MO 64111

Neuberger Museum of Art
Thom Collins, Director
Purchase College
735 Anderson Hill Road
Purchase, NY 10019

New Museum of Contemporary Art
Lisa Phillips, Director
210 11th Avenue, 2nd Floor
New York, NY 10001

New Orleans Museum of Art
E. John Bullard, Director
P.O. Box 19123
New Orleans, LA 70179

Newark Museum
Mary Sue Sweeney Price, Director
49 Washington Street
Newark, NJ 07102

The Noguchi Museum
Jenny Dixon, Director
32–37 Vernon Boulevard
Long Island City, NY 11106

Norman Rockwell Museum
Laurie Norton Moffatt, Director
P.O. Box 308
Stockbridge, MA 01262

North Carolina Museum of Art
Lawrence Wheeler, Director
2110 Blue Ridge Road
Raleigh, NC 27607

Norton Museum of Art
Christina Orr-Cahall, Director
1451 South Olive Avenue
West Palm Beach, FL 33401

Oakland Museum of California
Philip E. Linhares, Director
1000 Oak Street
Oakland, CA 34607

Orange County Museum of Art
Dennis Szakacs, Director
850 San Clemente Drive
Newport Beach, CA 92660

Orlando Museum of Art
Marena Grant Morrisey, Director
2415 North Mills Avenue
Orlando, FL 32803

Palm Springs Desert Museum
Janice Lyle, Director
101 Museum Drive
Palm Springs, CA 92263

Palmer Museum of Art
Jan Keene Muhlert, Director
Pennsylvania State University
University Park, PA 16802

Parrish Art Museum
Trudy C. Kramer, Director
25 Job's lane
Southampton, NY 11968

Peabody Essex Museum
Dan Monroe, Director
East India Square
Salem, MA 01970

Philadelphia Museum of Art
Anne d'Harnoncourt, Director
P.O. Box 7646
Philadelphia, PA 19101

The Phillips Collection
Jay Gates, Director
1600 21st Street, N.W.
Washington, DC 20009

Phoenix Art Museum
James K. Ballinger, Director
1625 North Central Avenue
Phoenix, AZ 85004

Portland (Maine) Museum of Art
Daniel E. O'Leary, Director
7 Congress Square
Portland, ME 04101

Portland (Oregon) Art Museum
Brian J. Ferriso
1219 SW Park Avenue
Portland, OR 97205

Princeton University Art Museum
Susan M. Taylor, Director
Princeton University
Princeton, NJ 08544

Queens Museum
Tom Finkelpearl, Director
Flushing Meadow Corona Park
Queens, NY 11368

Saint Louis Art Museum
Brent R. Benjamin, Director
1 Fine Arts Drive
St. Louis, MO 63110

St. Petersburg Museum of Fine Arts
John Scholder, Director
255 Beach Drive North East
St. Petersburg, FL 33701

Samuel P. Harn Museum of Art
Rebecca Nagy, Director
University of Florida
P.O. Box 112700
Gainesville, FL 32611

San Antonio Museum of Art
Marion Oettinger, Jr., Director
200 West Jones Avenue
San Antonio, TX 78215

San Diego Museum of Art
Derrick Cartwright, Director
P.O. Box 122107
San Diego, CA 32611

San Francisco Museum of Modern Art
Neal Benezra, Director
151 Third Street
San Francisco, CA 94103

Santa Barbara Museum of Art
Phillip Johnston, Director
1120 State Street
Santa Barbara, CA 93101

Seattle Art Museum
Mimi Gates, Director
P.O. Box 22000
Seattle, WA 98122

Sheldon Memorial Art Gallery
Janice Driesbach, Director
University of Nebraska–Lincoln
12th and R Streets
Lincoln, NE 68588

Smith College Museum of Art
Jessica F. Nicoll, Director
Brown Fine Art Center — Tryon Hall
Elm Street at Bedford Terrace
Northampton, MA 01063

Smithsonian American Art Museum
Elizabeth Broun, Director
P.O. Box 37012
Victor Building, Suite 9550, MRC-970
Washington, DC 20013

Snite Museum of Art
Charles R. Loving, Director
University of Notre Dame
P.O. Box 368
Notre Dame, Indiana 46556

Solomon R. Guggenheim Museum
Lisa Dennison, Director
1071 Fifth Avenue
New York, NY 10128

Speed Art Museum
Peter Morrin, Director
2035 South Third Street
Louisville, KY 40208

Spencer Museum of Art
Saralyn Reece Hardy, Director
University of Kansas
1201 Mississippi Street
Lawrence, KS 66045

Sterling & Francine Clark Art Institute
Michael Conforti, Director
225 South Street
P.O. Box 8
Williamstown, MA 01267

Studio Museum Harlem
Thelma Golden, Director
144 W. 125th Street
New York, NY 10027

Tacoma Art Museum
Stephanie Stebich
1701 Pacific Avenue
Tacoma, WA 98402

Taft Museum
Philip C. Long, Director
316 Pike Street
Cincinnati, OH 45202

Telfair Museum of Art
Steven S. High, Director
P.O. Box 10081
Savannah, GA 31412

Toledo Museum of Art
Don Bacigalupi, Director
P.O. Box 1013
Toledo, OH 43697

University of Iowa Museum of Art
Howard Collinson, Director
150 N. Riverside Drive
Iowa City, IA 52242

University of Michigan Museum of Art
James C. Steward, Director
525 South State Street
Ann Arbor, MI 48109

Utah Museum of Fine Arts
David Dee, Director
The University of Utah

410 Campus Center Drive
Salt Lake City, UT 84112

Vancouver Arts Gallery
Kathleen Bartels, Director
750 Hornby Street
Vancouver, B.C. V6Z 2H7
Canada

Vero Beach Museum of Art
Lucinda Gedeon, Director
3001 Riverside Park Drive
Vero Beach, FL 32963

Virginia Museum of Fine Arts
Alexander Lee Nyerges, Director
200 North Boulevard
Richmond, VA 23220

Wadsworth Atheneum
Willard Holmes, Director
600 Main Street
Hartford, CT 06103

Walker Art Center
Kathey Halbreich, Director
Vineland Place
Minneapolis, MN 55403

The Walters Art Museum
Gary Vikan, Director
600 North Charles Street
Baltimore, MD 21201

Wexner Center for the Arts, O.S.U.
Sherri Geldin, Director
1871 North High Street
Columbus, OH 43210

Whitney Museum of American Art
Adam Weinberg, Director
945 Madison Avenue
New York, NY 10021

Wichita Art Museum
Charles K. Steiner, Director
619 Stackman Drive
Wichita, KS 67203

Williams College Museum of Art
Lisa G. Corrin
15 Lawrence Hall Drive
Suite 2
Williamstown, MA 01267

Winterthur Museum, Garden and Library
Leslie Greene Bowman, Director
Route 52, Kennett Pike
Winterthur, DE 19735

The Wolfsonian
Cathy Leff, Director
Florida International University
1001 Washington Avenue
Miami Beach, FL 33139

Worcester Art Museum
James A. Welu, Director
55 Salisbury Street
Worcester, MA 01609

Yale Center for British Art
Amy Meyers, Director
1080 Chapel Street
P.O. Box 208280
New Haven, CT 06520

Yale University Art Gallery
Jock Reynolds, Director
Box 208271
New Haven, CT 06520

About the Editors and Contributors

Editors (and Contributors)

Roger L. Kemp, PhD, has been a Chief Executive Officer of cities on both coasts of the Unites States for more than two decades. Roger lectures, writes, and speaks from his accumulated experience in local government operations. He received his B.S. and M.P.A. degrees from San Diego State University, a Ph.D. from Golden Gate University, and is a graduate of the Program for Senior Executives in State and Local Government at the John F. Kennedy School of Government, Harvard University. Dr. Kemp is presently the Chief Executive Officer of the Town of Berlin, CT, which was incorporated in 1785, and is one of the oldest communities in New England. Roger is also past-president of the Connecticut City and Town Management Association, is past-president of the Connecticut Chapter of the American Society for Public Administration, and presently serves as a Professorial Lecturer and Visiting Scholar at Golden Gate University, San Francisco, CA, and Capella University, Minneapolis, MN.

Marcia Trotta, MLS, served as the Director of Library Services for the City of Meriden, CT, for a number of years, and now serves as a Library Director at The Berlin Free Library, located in the Town of Berlin, CT. The Berlin Free Library was founded in 1893, and is one of the oldest public libraries in the nation. Marcia lectures, writes, and speaks from her accumulated experience in municipal library services, which extends for nearly three decades. She received her Bachelor's Degree from Albertus Magnus College and received an M.L.S. degree from Southern Connecticut State University. Marcia is also the past-president of the Connecticut Library Association, and has been twice honored as their Outstanding Librarian of the Year. Presently, Ms. Trotta serves as an Adjunct Professor at the School of Library Science and Information Technology at Southern Connecticut State University and Albertus Magnus College, both located in New Haven, CT.

Contributors

Affiliations are as of the times the articles were written.

Cheryl Bartholow, Director of Programs, Brooklyn Children's Museum, New York, NY.

Richard Bertman, Partner; CBT/Childs, Bertman, and Tseckares, Inc.; Boston, MA.

Raymond L. Buse III, Public Relations Director, Cincinnati USA Regional Chamber of Commerce, Cincinnati, OH.

Susan Breitkopf, Freelance Writer, Washington, DC.

Brandy H. M. Brooks, Marketing Director, Loheed Design Partnership, Somerville, MA.

Robert A. Brown, Partner; CBT/Childs, Bertman, and Tseckares, Inc.; Boston, MA.

Jane Christophersen, Associate Editor, *Western City*, League of California, Sacramento, CA.

Gregory Dale, Principal; McBride, Dale, and Clarion; Cincinnati, OH.

Christopher Duerksen, Managing Director, Clarion Associates, Denver, CO.

Nancy Egan, Consultant and Manager, New Voodou, New York, NY.

John M. Eger, Executive Director, International Center for Communications, San Diego State University, San Diego, CA.

Donald Elliot, Professor and Chair, Economics Department, Southern Illinois University, Edwardsville, IL.

William Fulton, Member, Ventura Library Advisory Commission, Ventura, CA.

Robert J. Gorman, Consultant and Vice President, MRA International, Philadelphia, PA; and President, Gorman Design, Columbia, MD.

John J. Gruidl, Associate Professor, Illinois Institute for Rural Affairs, Western Illinois University, Macomb, IL.

Glen E. Holt, Director, Youth Services and Family Literacy, St. Louis Public Library, St. Louis, MO.

Glenda E. Hood, Secretary of State, Department of State, State of Florida, Tallahassee, FL.

Trina A. Innes, Section Head, Education and Outreach, Environmental Partnerships and Education Branch, Alberta Environment, Edmonton, Alberta, Canada.

Chris Jackson, Freelance Writer, Ventura, CA.

Anne Jordan, Managing Editor, *Governing*, Congressional Quarterly Inc., Washington, DC.

Cynthia L. Kemper, Principal, Marketekture, Denver, CO.

Billy Kinsey, Jr., Economist and Sr. Research Associate, Virginia Center for Urban Development, Center for Public Policy, Virginia Commonwealth University, Richmond, VA.

Howard Kozloff, M.S. Degree Candidate (Real Estate); School of Architecture, Planning and Preservation; Columbia University, New York, NY.

Patrick Lawton, City Manager, Germantown, TN.

Thomas L. Lee, Chair and Chief Executive Officer, Newhall Land and Farming Co., Valencia, CA.

Charles Lockwood, Freelance Writer, Topanga, CA.

Phillip N. Loheed, Principal, Loheed Design Partnership, Somerville, MA.

Guillermo Lopez, Vice President, Development Design Group, Baltimore, MD.

Massimiliano Mazzanti, Professor, Department of Economic Institutions and Territory, University of Ferrara, Ferra, Italy.

Amonia Moore, Research Associate, St. Louis Public Library, St. Louis, MO.

Nancy Moses, Cultural Development Consultant, Philadelphia, PA.

Susan Mourato, Senior Lecturer; T. H. Huxley School of Environmental, Earth Sciences, and Engineering; Imperial College of Science, Technology, and Medicine; London, United Kingdom.

Lorraine Oback, Marketing Communications Director, San Jose Public Library, San Jose, CA.

Ellen Perlman, Staff Writer, *Governing*, Congressional Quarterly Inc., Washington, DC.

Karen Scott, Library Development Consultant, Alliance Library System, East Peoria, IL.

Mike Sheridan, Financial Journalist, Houston, TX.

Kathleen Sylvester, Vice President of Domestic Policy, Progressive Policy Institute, Washington, DC.

Urban Libraries Council, a membership organization of North America's premier public library systems, Chicago, IL.

Bernard Vavrek, Professor of Library Science, Center for the Study of Rural Librarianship, Clarion University, Clarion, PA.

Norman Waizer, Director, Illinois Institute of Rural Affairs, Western Illinois University, Macomb, IL.

Jonathan Walters, Staff Correspondent, *Governing*, Congressional Quarterly Inc., Washington, DC.

Albert Warson, Freelance Writer, Toronto, Ontario, Canada.

Anne Watts, Head, Special Projects Office, St. Louis Public Library, St. Louis, MO.

Wendy Wheeler, Communications Manager, Keewaydin Real Estate Advisors, Minneapolis, MN.

Juli Wilkerson, Director; Department of Community, Trade, and Economic Development; State of Washington, Seattle, WA.

Alfred Wojciechowski, Partner; CBT/Childs, Bertman, and Tseckares, Inc.; Boston, MA.

J. Lindsey Wolf, Public Affairs Manager, Environmental Services Department, City of San Jose, CA.

Index